THE

REPUBLIC

A DIALOGUE

CONCERNING

JUSTICE

With an introduction, copious notes, and an
Apology for the Fables of Homer by Proclus,
introducing the 2nd and 3rd Books of the Republic.

Stephanus numbers included.

FROM

THE WORKS OF PLATO:
His Fifty-Five Dialogues and Twelve Epistles, 1804

BY THOMAS TAYLOR

FIRST PUBLISHED, 1804.
RE-PRINTED WITH NEW FORMATTING, 2016.

www.kshetrabooks.com

"The Republic,"
from *The Works of Plato,*
viz. His Fifty-Five Dialogues, and Twelve Epistles
First Edition, 1804

Re-print from 1st Edition
(with new formatting)

ISBN: 978-1533351616

Contents

Foreword

The present volume is a reproduction of Thomas Taylor's translation of the Republic, drawn from his five-volume set of the complete *Works of Plato*, originally published in 1804. There is a specific order to the dialogues that Taylor chose to follow, which he explains in his *General Introduction to the Philosophy and Writings of Plato*. The first dialogue presented by Taylor is the First Alcibiades, a dialogue that acts as a sort of *preface* to the works of Plato. In it, the fundamental issue of two-fold ignorance is addressed, *i.e.* the condition or disease of the multitude wherein we are not only ignorant, but ignorant of our own ignorance!

If one has studied, understood and incorporated the teachings of the First Alcibiades, one shall have advanced from the condition of two-fold ignorance to the state of simple ignorance, wherein one is ignorant but has acknowledged one's ignorance. It is this state that is a requisite for the beginning of all true philosophic inquiry.

Following the First Alcibiades, Taylor proceeds to what is perhaps Plato's most widely known and widely studied dialogue, the Republic. The topic of discussion, throughout all ten of its books, is Justice—justice in the polity of the city-state, and justice as a virtue of our soul. The key feature of this dialogue, the thread the binds it together from beginning to end, is the correspondence between these two.

> "The design of Plato, says Proclus, in this dialogue, is both concerning a polity and true justice, not as two distinct things, but as the same with each other. For what justice is in one soul, that such a polity as is delineated by Plato is in a well inhabited city." (Taylor)

v

The First Alcibiades gave us our initial look at ourselves, urging us to break through the thick veil of two-fold ignorance. Coming then to the Republic, in a state of simple ignorance, we are given our first look at the nature and constitution of Man and the nature of his primary virtue.

The Republic opens with an exploration of what is best or most beneficial for man: to be just or to be unjust. While on the surface this may seem, morally at least, to be a simple question with a simple answer, strong arguments are made for the benefits of acting unjustly, especially if one is able to simultaneously act unjustly and gain the reputation of a just man: for in such a case, one will procure all that can be gained from unjust actions (increased wealth, position, power, etc.) while facing none or very few of the common disadvantages of being unjust (punishments, low public opinion, etc.). It is argued, one might say quite fairly based on common experience, that justice is rarely pursued for the sake of justice itself, but rather for the perceived benefit to the individual, *i.e.* the common man only seeks justice if they find there to be some personal advantage in doing so. Socrates addresses these fundamental questions and the several arguments levelled against justice in the opening book of the Republic, and demonstrates, with clear and detailed reasonings, several of the glaring deficiencies in these arguments.

The question of whether justice is truly better than injustice is not left to such initial reasonings, however, as Socrates's companions urge him into the greater depths of the subject. This naturally opens the dialogue to a fuller exploration of the nature of justice: what it is, what relation is has to our soul, to our city, and so on.

The dialogue thus treads through much territory, centering initially around an ideal construction of a just city, while using the knowledge gained through its analysis to shed light on the role of justice in each individual. It passes on to a definition and unveiling of the nature of a true philosopher, and their proper role in such a just city, and from there to an exploration of the forms of polity and their correspondence with types of men (*i.e.* Timocratic, Oligarchic, Democratic, Tyrannic), relating the conditions and attitudes of each polity to the same conditions and attitudes within the corresponding man. Book 9 provides what may be viewed as a conclusion on what is better: justice or injustice, covering three major points of argument. The close of the dialogue (Book 10) presents us with something a little different: a view of the immortality of the soul and a vision of death and rebirth, complete with postmortem judgment and necessity, corresponding with the common "eastern" notions of karma and reincarnation. Here we see justice and injustice dealt with in direct relation to the immortal soul, beyond the realm of worldly utilitarianism.

Throughout this range of subjects, along with many seeming digressions, the keynote of Justice is ever held as the spoke of the wheel, acting as the "thread-soul" we might say, of the dialogue. The eager student will find (with the aid of Taylor's notes and several key quotations from the writings of Proclus provided therein) a gradual unfolding of the Platonic division of the Soul and its accompanying Virtues. The extensive quotation from the exposition of the more difficult questions in the Republic by Proclus given in the Additional Notes to Book IV is of particular value in clarifying the division of the soul into its three parts and the relation of each part to each of the four virtues. The sincere student who is able to work through the many details, digressions, allegories and reasonings of the Republic whilst ever keeping in mind the overarching question of Justice may thus take their initial steps from simple ignorance to the first stages of knowledge.

In closing this brief foreword, it may be helpful to provide the general schema of the Republic developed through the efforts of scholars and philosophers such as Cornford, Hildebrandt, and Voegelin. The serious student ought to refer to Eric Voegelin's *Plato* (1957), p. 46 etc. for a detailed analysis of the contents of the Republic.

Organization of the Republic

Prologue

(1)	I.1	327a–328b	Descent to the Piraeus
(2)	I.2–I.5	328b–331d	Cephalus. Justice of the Older Generation
(3)	I.6–1.9	331e–336a	Polemarchus. Justice of the Middle Generation
(4)	I.10–I.24	336b–354c	Thrasymachus. Justice of the Sophist

In the present edition, the formatting of the original has been changed in order to render the text more easily readable. The copious footnotes found in the original have been collected and placed in order at the end of the book, allowing for a more easily readable layout throughout, and Taylor's "Additional Notes" have been moved to the end of each corresponding dialogue.

In the outer margins we have added the pagination of the original edition, so that all references made to the original over the intervening centuries may be easily traced in the present volume, despite its altered pagination. We have also added the standard Stephanus numbering throughout the dialogue, shown also in the outer margins.

Besides these changes, and minor changes in formatting style, the text has not been altered, except in cases where certain Greek characters were in need of modernization, and a very few cases where the English was similarly in need of modernization (for example, the past tense of the verb "to be" which appears as "was" instead of "were" in certain cases: *i.e.* "you was" has been updated to "you were" solely for the ease of the modern English reader).

THE
REPUBLIC

General Introduction

The design of Plato, says Proclus, in this dialogue, is both concerning a polity and true justice, not as two distinct things, but as the same with each other. For what justice is in one soul, that such a polity as is delineated by Plato is in a well inhabited city. Indeed, the three genera from which a polity consists are analogous to the three parts of the soul: the *guardian*, as that which consults, to reason; the *auxiliary*, as engaging in war, to anger; and the *mercenary*, as supplying the wants of nature, to the desiderative part of the soul. For, according to Plato, it is one and the same habit, which adorns a city, a house, and an individual. But if what the people are in a city, that the desiderative part is in an individual, and that which consults in the former is analogous to reason in the latter, as Plato asserts in his Laws, justice according to him will be the polity of the soul, and the best polity of a city will be justice. If these things then are true, he who teaches concerning justice, if he does not teach it imperfectly, will, from perceiving justice every where, teach concerning a polity: and he who speaks concerning an upright polity, if he surveys every, and not some particular, polity, will also speak concerning justice, which both subsists in one polity, and arranges the people in the soul, through our auxiliary part, according to the decision of our guardian reason.

That this was the opinion of Plato respecting these particulars will be evident from considering that, in passing from the investigation concerning justice to the discourse concerning a polity, he says the transition is to be made, not as from one thing to another naturally different, but as from small letters to such as are large and clear, and

100 which manifest the same things. The matter therefore of justice and a polity is different, in the same manner as that of small and large letters, but the form is the same. Hence the transition is from polity to polity;—from that which is beheld in one individual, to that which is beheld in many: and from justice to justice;—from that which is contracted to that which is more apparent. Nor ought we to wonder that Plato does not express the thing discussed in this dialogue by the name of justice, but by that of a polity, in the same manner as he signifies another subject of discussion by the appellation of laws. For it is requisite that inscriptions should be made from things more known; but the name of a polity or republic is more known, as Plato also says, than that of justice.

With respect to the form of the dialogue, it will be requisite to recollect that Plato himself in this treatise says that there are only three forms of diction, *viz.* the dramatic and imitative, such as that of comedy and tragedy; the narrative and unimitative, such as is employed by those who write dithyrambics, and the histories of past transactions, without prosopopœia; and a third species which is mixed from both the preceding, such as the poetry of Homer; diversifying some parts of the poem by the narration of things, and others by the imitations of person. Such being the division of the forms of diction according to Plato, it is necessary to refer the present treatise to the mixed form of diction, which relates same things as transactions, and others as discourses, and alone preserves an accurate narration of persons and things; such as are—descending to the Piræum, praying to the goddess, beholding the festival, and the like. But in the several discourses it makes the most accurate imitation; same things being spoken in the character of old men, others fabulously, and others sophistically; and attributes a knowledge and life adapted to the different speakers. For to preserve the becoming in these particulars is the province of the highest imitation.

With respect to justice, the subject of this dialogue, such according to Plato is its universality and importance, that, if it had no subsistence, injustice itself would be sluggish and in vain. Thus, for instance, if a city were full of injustice, it would neither be able to effect any thing with respect to another city, nor with respect to itself,
101 through the dissension arising from those that injure and are injured.

In a similar manner too in an army, if it abounded with every kind of injustice, it would be in sedition with itself; and being in sedition with itself, it must be subverted, and become inefficacious as to the purposes of war. Thus too, a house in which there is no vestige of justice, as it must necessarily be full of dissension, will be incapable of effecting any thing, through the want of concord in its inhabitants. But that which is the most wonderful of all is this, that injustice, when inherent in one person only, must necessarily fill him with sedition towards himself, and through this sedition must render him more imbecil with respect to various endurance, and incapable of pleasing himself. Of necessity, therefore, every one who acts unjustly, if he is able to effect any thing whatever, must possess some vestige of justice; so inseparable is the union between power and justice.

From what has been said, the following syllogism arises. All injustice separate from justice is imbecil. Every thing separate from justice, being imbecil, requires justice to its possession of power. All injustice therefore requires justice in order to its possession of power. —Again, we have the following syllogism. All injustice requires justice, to be able to effect any thing. Every thing which requires justice to be able to effect any thing, is more imbecil than justice. All injustice, therefore, is more imbecil than justice. And this was the thing proposed to be shown. Hence it follows that, even in the worst habit of the soul, in which reason is blinded and appetite perverted, such habit is indeed inefficacious, in consequence of justice being most obscure in such a soul, so as to appear to have no subsistence whatever; yet such a habit has a being in a certain respect, so far as it is impossible that common conceptions can entirely desert the soul, and especially in its desire of good. So far therefore as it is impelled towards good, it participates of justice. And if it were possible that the soul could be perfectly, that is in every respect, unjust, it would perhaps perish: for this is the case with the body when perfectly diseased. But that in such a habit there is a vestige of justice is evident. For it is unwilling to injure itself, and to destroy things pertaining to itself. As it therefore preserves that which is just towards itself, it is not alone unjust; but not knowing how it should preserve itself, it is unjust, attempting to preserve itself through such things as are not proper.

From hence we may also collect the following porism, or corollary, which was first perceived by Amelius the fellow disciple with Porphyry of Plotinus, that from a greater injustice lesser evils are frequently produced, but from a lesser injustice greater evils. For, when injustice perfectly subdues the soul, life is inefficacious; but, when justice is associated with injustice, a certain action is the result. Nor let any one think that this assertion is false because greater evils are produced from intemperance than incontinence: for intemperance is a vice, but incontinence is not yet a complete vice; because, in the incontinent man, reason in a certain respect opposes passion; so that on this account a lesser evil arises from incontinence, because it is mingled from vice and that which is not vice.

I shall only add further at present, that the republic of Plato pre-subsists, or is contained causally, in an intelligible nature,—subsists openly in the heavens,—and is, in the last place, to be found in human lives. As it therefore harmonizes in every respect with each of these, it is a polity perfect in all its parts; and may be considered as one of the greatest and most beneficial efforts of human intellect that has appeared, or ever will appear, in any of the infinite periods of time.

THE REPUBLIC

BOOK I.

SPEAKERS:

SOCRATES,	GLAUCO,[1]
CEPHALUS,	ADIMANTUS,
POLEMARCHUS,	THRASYMACHUS,

THE WHOLE IS A RECITAL BY SOCRATES.

The SCENE is in the House of CEPHALUS, at the Piræum

SOCRATES: I went down yesterday to the Piræum,[2] with Glauco, the son of Aristo, to pay my devotion to the Goddess; and desirous, at the same time, to observe in what manner they would celebrate the festival,[3] as they were now to do it for the first time:. The procession of our own countrymen seemed to me to be indeed beautiful; yet that of the Thracians appeared no less proper. After we had paid our devotion, and seen the solemnity, we were returning to the city; when Polemarchus, the son of Cephalus, observing us at a distance hurrying home, ordered his boy to run and desire us to wait for him: and the boy, taking hold of my robe behind, "Polemarchus," says he, "desires you to wait." I turned about, and asked where he was. "He is coming

up," said he, "after you; but do you wait for him." "We will wait," said
327c Glauco; and soon afterwards came Polemarchus, and Adimantus the
brother of Glauco, and Niceratus the son of Nicias, and same others as
from the procession. Then said Polemarchus, "Socrates! you seem to
me to be hurrying to the city." "You conjecture," said I, "not amiss."
"Do you not see, then," said he, "how many there are of us?"
"Undoubtedly I do." "Therefore, now, you must either be stronger
than these, or you must stay here." "Is there not," said I, "one way still
remaining? May we not persuade you that you must let us go?" "Can
you be able to persuade such as will not hear?" "By no means," said
Glauco. "Then, as if we are not to hear, determine accordingly." "But
328a do you not know," said Adimantus, "that there is to be an
illumination in the evening, on horseback, to the goddess?" "On
horseback?" said I. "That is new. Are they to have torches, and give
them to one another, contending together with their horses? or how
105 do you mean?" "Just so," replied Polemarchus. "And besides, they will
perform a nocturnal solemnity[4] worth seeing. For we shall rise after
supper, and see the nocturnal solemnity, and shall be there with many
328b of the youth, and converse together: But do you stay, and do not do
otherwise." "It seems proper, then," said Glauco, "that we should
stay." "Nay, if it seem so," said I, "we ought to do it."

We went home therefore to Polemarchus's house; and there we
found both Lysias and Euthydemus, brothers of Polemarchus;
likewise Thrasymachus the Chalcedonian, and Charmantides the
Pæoncian, and Clitipho the son of Aristonimus; Cephalus the father
of Polemarchus was likewise in the house; he seemed to me to be far
328c advanced in years, for I had not seen him for a long time. He was
sitting crowned, on a certain couch and seat; for he had been offering
sacrifice in the hall. So we sat down by him; for some seats were placed
there in a circle. Immediately, then, when Cephalus saw me, he
saluted me, and said, "Socrates, you do not often come down to us to
the Piræum, nevertheless you ought to do it; for, were I still able easily
328d to go up to the city, you should not need to come hither, but we
would be with you. But now you should come hither more frequently:
106 for I assure you that, with relation to myself, as the pleasures
respecting the body languish, the desire and pleasure of conversation
increase. Do not fail, then to make a party often with these youths,

and come hither to us, as to your friends and intimate acquaintance."
"And, truly," said I, "Cephalus, I take pleasure in conversing with
those who are very far advanced in years; for it appears to me proper,   328e
that we learn from them, as from persons who have gone before us,
what the road is which it is likely we have to travel; whether rough
and difficult, or plain and easy. And I would gladly learn from you, as
you are now arrived at that time of life which the poets call the
threshold of old-age, what your opinion of it is; whether you consider
it to be a grievous part of life, or what you announce it to be?" "And I
will tell you, Socrates," said he, "what is really my opinion; for we   329a
frequently meet together in one place, several of us who are of the
same age, observing the old proverb. Most of us, therefore, when
assembled, lament their state, when they feel a want of the pleasures
of youth, and call to their remembrance the delights of love, of
drinking, and feasting, and some others akin to these: and they
express indignation, as if they were bereaved of some mighty things.
In those days, they say, they lived well, but now they do not live at all:
some of them, too, bemoan the contempt which old-age meets with   329b
from their acquaintance: and on this account also they lament old-
age, which is to them the cause of so many ills. But these men,
Socrates, seem not to me to blame the real cause; for, if this were the
cause, I likewise should have suffered the same things on account of
old-age; and all others, even as many as have arrived at these years:
whereas I have met with several who are not thus affected; and
particularly was once with Sophocles the poet, when he was asked by
some one, 'How,' said he, 'Sophocles, are you affected towards the   329c
pleasures of love? are you still able to enjoy them?' 'Softly, friend,'
replied he, 'most gladly, indeed, have I escaped from these pleasures, as
from some furious and savage master.' He seemed to me to speak well
at that time, and no less so now: for, certainly, there is in old-age
abundance of peace and freedom from such things; for, when the
appetites cease to be vehement, and are become easy, what Sophocles
said certainly happens; we are delivered from very many, and those   329d
too insane masters. But with relation to these things, and those
likewise respecting our acquaintance, there is one and the same cause;   107
which is not old age, Socrates, but manners: for, if indeed they are
discreet and moderate, even old-age is but moderately burdensome: if

not, both old age, Socrates, and youth are grievous to such." Being
delighted to hear him say these things, and wishing him to discourse
329e further, I urged him, and said, "I think, Cephalus, the multitude will
not agree with you in those things; but will imagine that you bear
old-age easily, not from manners, but from possessing much wealth;
for the rich say they, have many consolations." "You say true," replied
he, "they do not agree with me; and there is something in what they
say; but, however, not so much as they imagine. But the saying of
Themistocles was just; who, when the Seriphian reviled him, and said
330a that he was honoured, not on his own account, but on that of his
country, replied That neither would himself have been renowned had
he been a Seriphian, nor would he, had he been an Athenian. The
same saying is justly applicable to those who are not rich, and who
bear old-age with uneasiness, That neither would the worthy man,
were he poor, bear old-age quite easily; nor would he who is
unworthy, though enriched, ever be agreeable to himself." "But,
whether, Cephalus," said I, "was the greater part of what you possess,
left you; or have you acquired it?" "Somewhat, Socrates," replied he,
330b "I have acquired: as to money-getting, I am in a medium between my
grand father and my father: for my grandfather, of the same name
with me, who was left almost as much substance as I possess at present,
made it many times as much again; but my father Lysanias made it
yet less than it is now: I am satisfied if I leave my sons here, no less,
but some little more than I received." "I asked you," said I, "for this
330c reason, because you seem to me to love riches moderately; and those
generally do so who have not acquired them: but those who have
acquired them are doubly fond of them: for, as poets love their own
poems, and as parents love their children, in the same manner, those
who have enriched themselves value their riches as a work of their
own, as well as for the utilities they afford, for which riches are valued
330d by others." "You say true," replied he. "It is entirely so," said I. "But
further, tell me this: What do you think is the greatest good derived
from the possession of much substance?" "That, probably," said he,
"of which I shall not persuade the multitude. For be assured,
108 Socrates," continued he, "that after a man begins to think he is soon
to die, he feels a fear and concern about things which before gave him
no uneasiness: for those stories concerning a future state, which

represent that the man who has done injustice here must there be punished, though formerly ridiculed, do then trouble his soul with *330e* apprehensions that they may be true; and the man, either through the infirmity of old-age, or as being now more near those things, views them more attentively: he becomes therefore full of suspicion and dread; and considers, and reviews, whether he has, in any thing, injured any one. He then who finds in his life much of iniquity, and is wakened from sleep, as children by repeated calls, is afraid, and lives in miserable hope. But the man who is not conscious of any iniquity,

> Still pleasing hope, sweet nourisher of age!   *331a*
> Attends—

as Pindar says. This, Socrates, he has beautifully expressed; that, whoever lives a life of justice and holiness,

> Sweet hope, the nourisher of age, his heart
> Delighting, with him lives; which most of all
> Governs the many veering thoughts of man.

So that he says well, and very admirably; wherefore, for this purpose, I deem the possession of riches to be chiefly valuable; not to every man, *331b* but to the man of worth: for the possession of riches contributes considerably to free us from being tempted to cheat or deceive; and from being obliged to depart thither in a terror, when either indebted in sacrifices to God, or in money to man. It has many other advantages besides; but, for my part, Socrates, I deem riches to be most advantageous to a man of understanding, chiefly in this respect." "You speak most handsomely, Cephalus," replied I. "But *331c* with respect to this very thing, justice: Whether shall we call it truth, simply, and the restoring of what one man has received from another? or shall we say that the very same things may sometimes be done justly, and sometimes unjustly? My meaning is this: Every one would somehow own, that if a man should receive arms from his friend who was of a sound mind, it would not be proper to restore such things if he should demand them when mad; nor would the restorer be just: nor again would he be just, who, to a man in such a condition, should *109* willingly tell all the truth." "You say right," replied he. "This, then, to *331d* speak the truth, and restore what one hath received, is not the definition of justice?" "It is not, Socrates," replied Polemarchus, "if at least we may give any credit to Simonides." "However that be, I give up," said Cephalus, "this conversation to you; for I must now go to take care of the sacred rites." "Is not Polemarchus," said I, "your heir?" "Certainly," replied he smiling, and at the same time departed to the sacred rites.

331e   "Tell me, then," said I, "you who are heir in the conversation, what is it which, according to you, Simonides says so well concerning justice?" "That to give every one his due, is just," replied he; "in saying this, he seems to me to say well." "It is, indeed," said I, "not easy to disbelieve Simonides, for he is a wise and divine man; but what his meaning may be in this, you, Polemarchus, probably know it, but I do not; for it is plain he does not mean what we were saying just now; that, when one deposits with another any thing, it is to be given back to him when he asks for it again in his madness: yet what has been

332a deposited is in some respect, at least, due; is it not?" "It is." "But yet, it is not at all, by any means, then, to be restored, when any one asks for it in his madness." "It is not," replied he. "Simonides then, as it should seem, says something different from this, that to deliver up what is due, is just?" "Some thing different, truly," replied he: "for he thinks that friends ought to do their friends some good, but no ill."

332b "I understand," said I. "He who restores gold deposited with him, if to restore and receive it be hurtful, and the restorer and receiver be friends, does not give what is due. Is not this what you allege Simonides says?" "Surely." "But what? are we to give our enemies too, what may chance to be due to them?" "By all means," replied he, "what is due to them; and from an enemy, to an enemy, there is due, I imagine, what is fitting, that is, some evil." "Simonides, then, as it should seem," replied I, "expressed what is just, enigmatically, and

332c after the manner of the poets; for he well understood, as it appears, that this was just, to give every one what was fitting for him, and this he called his due." "But, what," said he, is your opinion?" "Truly," replied I, "if any one should ask him thus: Simonides, what is the art, which, dispensing to certain persons something fitting and due, is called medicine? what would he answer us, do you think?" "That art,

110   surely," replied he, "which dispenses drugs, and prescribes regimen of meats and drinks to bodies." "And what is the art, which, dispensing to certain things something fitting and due, is called cookery?" "The

art which gives seasonings to victuals." "Be it so." "What then is that 332d art, which, dispensing to certain persons something fitting and due, may be called justice?" "If we ought to be any way directed, Socrates, by what is said above, it is the art which dispenses good offices to friends, and injuries to enemies." "To do good, then, to friends, and ill to enemies, he calls justice?" "It seems so." "Who, then, is most able to do good, to his friends, when they are diseased, and ill to his enemies, with respect to sickness and health?" "The physician." "And 332e who, when they sail, with respect to the danger of the sea?" "The pilot." "But as to the just man, in what business, and with respect to what action, is he most able to serve his friends, and to hurt his enemies?" "It seems to me, in fighting in alliance with the one, and against the other." "Be it so." "But, surely, the physician is useless, Polemarchus, to those, at least, who are not sick?" "It is true." "And the pilot, to those who do not sail?" "He is." "And is the just man, in like manner, useless to those who are not at war?" "I can by no means think that he is." "Justice, then, is useful likewise in time of peace." "It is." "And so is agriculture, is it not?" "It is." "Towards the 333a possession of grain?" "Certainly." "And is not shoemaking likewise useful?" "It is." "Towards the possession of shoes, you will say, I imagine." "Certainly."

"But what, now? For the use, or possession of what, would you say that justice were useful in time of peace?" "For co-partnerships, Socrates." "You call co-partnerships, joint companies, or what else?" "Joint companies, certainly." "Whether, then, is the just man, or the 333b dice-player, a good and useful co-partner, for playing at dice?" "The dice-player." "But, in the laying of tiles or stones, is the just man a more useful and a better partner than the mason?" "By no means." "In what joint company, now, is the just man a better co-partner thin the harper, as the harper is better than the just man for touching the strings of a harp?" "In a joint company about money, as I imagine." "And yet it is likely, Polemarchus, that with regard to the making use of money, when it is necessary jointly to buy or sell a horse, the 333c jockey, as I imagine, is then the better co-partner. Is he not?" "He would appear so." "And with respect to a ship, the ship-wright, or ship-master?" "It would seem so." "When then is it, with respect to the joint application of money, that the just man is more useful than others?" "When it is to be deposited, and be safe, Socrates." "Do you not mean, when there is no need to use it, but to let it lie?" "Certainly." "When money then is useless, justice is useful with regard 333d to it?" "It seems so." "And when a pruning-hook is to be kept, justice is useful, both for a community, and for a particular person: but when it is to be used, the art of vine-dressing is useful." "It appears so." "And you will say that, when a buckler, or a harp, is to be kept, and not to be used, then justice is useful; but when they are to be used, then the military, and the musical art?" "Of necessity." "And with reference to all other things, when they are to be used, justice is useless; but when 333e they are not to be used, it is useful?" "It seems so." "Justice, then, my friend! can be no very important matter, if it is useful only in respect of things, which are not to be used. But let us consider this matter: Is not he who is the most dexterous at striking, whether in battle or in boxing, the same likewise in defending himself?" "Certainly." "And is not he who is dexterous in warding off and shunning a distemper, most dexterous too in bringing it on?" "So I imagine." "And he too 334a the best guardian of a camp, who can steal the counsels, and the other operations of the enemy?" "Certainly." "Of whatever, then, any one is a good guardian, of that likewise he is a dexterous thief." "It seems so." "If therefore the just man be dexterous in guarding money, he is dexterous likewise in stealing?" "So it would appear," said he, "from this reasoning."

"The just man, then, has appeared to be a sort of thief; and you 334b seem to have learned this from Homer; for he admires Autolycus, the grandfather of Ulysses by his mother, and says that he was distinguished beyond all men for thefts and oaths. It seems, then, according to you, and according to Homer and Simonides, that justice is a sort of thieving, for the profit indeed of friends, and for the hurt of enemies. Did not you say so?" "No, by no means; nor indeed do I know any longer what I said; yet I still think that justice profits 334c friends, and hurts enemies." "But, whether do you pronounce such to be friends, as seem to be honest? or, such as are so, though they do not seem; and in the same way as to enemies?" It is reasonable," said he, "to love those whom a man deems to be honest; and to hate those whom he deems to be wicked." "But do not men mistake in this; so as that many who are not honest appear so to them, and many

contrariwise?" "They do mistake." "To such, then, the good are ₁₁₂
enemies, and the bad are friends?" "Certainly." "But, however, it is
then just for them to profit the bad; and to hurt the good." "It appears 334d
so." "But the good are likewise just, and such as do no ill." "True."
"But, according to your speech, it is just to do ill to those who do no
ill." "By no means, Socrates," replied he; "for the speech seems to be
wicked."

"It is just, then," said I, "to hurt the unjust, and to profit the just."
"This speech appears more handsome than the other." "Then, it will
happen, Polemarchus, to many,—to as many indeed of mankind as
have misjudged, that it shall be just to hurt their friends, who are 334e
really bad; and to profit their enemies, who are really good; and so we
shall say the very reverse of what we affirmed Simonides said?" "It
does, indeed," said he, "happen so. But let us define again; for we seem
not to have rightly defined a friend and an enemy."

"How were they defined, Polemarchus?" "That he who seems
honest is a friend." "But how shall we now define, said I?" "That he
who seems," replied he, "and likewise is honest, is a friend; but he
who seems honest, yet is not, seems, yet is not a friend. And we must 335a
admit the distinction about an enemy to be the very same." "The
good man, according to this speech, will, as it seems, be the friend;
and the wicked man, the enemy." "Yes." "Do you now require us to
describe what is just, as we did before, when we said it was just to do
good to a friend, and ill to an enemy? Or shall we add to the
definition, and now say, that it is just to do good to a friend, when he
is good; and ill to an enemy, when he is bad?" "This last," said he, 335b
"seems to me to be perfectly well expressed." "Is it, then," said I, "the
part of a just man to hurt any man?" "By all means," said he, "he
ought to hurt the wicked, and his enemies." "But, do horses, when
they are hurt, become better or worse?" "Worse." "Whether in the
virtue of dogs, or of horses?" "In that of horses." "And, do not dogs,
when they are hurt, become worse in the virtue of dogs, and not of
horses?" "Of necessity." "And shall we not in like manner, my friend, 335c
say that men, when they are hurt, become worse in the virtue of a
man?" "Certainly." "But is not justice the virtue of a man?" "Of
necessity this likewise." "Of necessity then, friend, those men who are
hurt must become more unjust." "It seems so." "But can musicians, by

music, make men unmusical?" "It is impossible." "Or horsemen, by
335d horsemanship, make men unskilled in horsemanship?" "It cannot
113 be." "Or can the just, by justice, make men unjust? Or in general, can
the good, by virtue, make men wicked?" "It is impossible." "For, it is
not, as I imagine, the effect of heat, to make cold, but of its
contrary." "Yes." "Nor is it the effect of drought, to make moist; but
its contrary." "Certainly." "Neither is it the part of a good man, to
hurt; but of his contrary." "It appears so." "But, the just is good."
"Certainly." "Neither, then, is it the part of a just man, Polemarchus,
to hurt either friend, or any other, but the part of his contrary, the
unjust man."

"In all respects," said he, "you seem to me, Socrates, to say true."
335e "If, then, any one says that it is just to give every one his due, and
thinks this with himself, that hurt is due to enemies from a just man,
and profit to his friend; he was not wise who said so, for he spoke not
the truth. For it has no where appeared to us, that any just man hurts
any one." "I agree," said he. "Let us jointly contend, then," said I, "if
any one shall say that a Simonides, a Bias, a Pittacus, said so; or any
other of those wise and happy men." "I am ready," said he, "to join in
336a the fight." "But do you know," said I, "whose saying I fancy it is, That
it is just to profit friends, and hurt enemies?" "Whose?" said he. "I
fancy it is the saying of Periander, or Perdiccas, or Xerxes, or Ismenius
the Theban; or some other rich man, who thought himself able to
accomplish great things." "You say most true," said he. "Be it so," said
I. "But as this has not appeared to be justice, nor the just, what else
may one assert it to be?"

336b Thrasymachus frequently, during our reasoning, rushed in the
midst, to lay hold of the discourse; but was hindered by those who sat
near him, and who wanted to hear the conversation to an end. But,
when we paused, and I had said these things, he was no longer quiet;
but, collecting himself as a wild beast, he came upon us as if he would
have torn us in pieces. Both Polemarchus and I, being frightened,
were thrown into the utmost consternation: but he, roaring out in
336c the midst: "What trifling," said he, "Socrates, is this which long ago
possesses you; and why do you thus play the fool together, yielding
mutually to one another? But, if you truly want to know what is just:,
ask not questions only, nor value yourself in confuting, when any one

answers you any thing; (knowing this, that it is easier to ask than to answer;) but answer yourself, and tell what it is you call just. And you 336d are not to tell me that it is what is fit; nor what is due, nor what is profitable, nor what is gainful, nor what is advantageous; but, what 114 you mean tell plainly and accurately; for I will not allow it, if you speak such trifles as these." When I heard this, I was astonished, and, looking at him, was frightened; and I should have become speechless, I imagine, if I had not perceived him before he perceived me. But I had observed him first, when he began to grow fierce at our reasoning; so that I was now able to answer him, and said, trembling: 336e "Thrasymachus! be not hard on us; for, if we mistake in our inquiries, Polemarchus and I, be well assured that we mistake unwittingly: for think not that in searching for gold, we would never willingly yield to one another in the search, and mar the finding it; but that, searching for justice, an affair far more valuable than a great deal of gold, we should yet foolishly yield to each other, and not labour, friend, with the utmost ardour, that we may discover what it really is. But I am afraid we are not able to discover it. It is more reasonable, then, that we be pitied, than be used hardly by you who are men of 337a ability." Having heard this, he laughed aloud in a very coarse manner, and said "By Hercules! this is Socrates's wonted irony. This I both knew and foretold to these, here, that you never incline to answer if any one ask you any thing." "You are a wise man, therefore, Thrasymachus," said I. "For you knew well, that if you asked any one, 'How many is twelve?' and, when you ask, should previously tell him, 337b 'You are not, friend, to tell me that twelve is twice six; nor that it is three times four; nor that it is four times three; for I will not admit it, if you trifle in such a manner';—I fancy it is plain to you that no man would answer one asking in such a way. But if he should say to you, 'Wonderful Thrasymachus! how do you mean? May I answer in none of those ways you have told me; not even though the real and true answer happen to be one of them, but I am to say something else than the truth? Or, how is it you mean?' What would you say to him in 337c answer to these things?" "If they were alike, I should give an answer; but how are they alike?" "Nothing hinders it," said I; "but, though they were not alike, but should appear so to him who was asked, would he the less readily answer what appeared to him; whether we

forbade him or not?" "And will you do so now?" said he. "Will you say
in answer some of these things which I forbid you to say?" "I should

115   not wonder I did," said I, "if it should appear so to me on inquiry."
337d   "What then," said he, "if I shall show you another and a better
answer, besides all these about justice; what will you deserve to suffer?"
"What else," said I, "but what is proper for the ignorant to suffer?
And it is proper for them to learn somewhere from a wise man. I shall
therefore deserve to suffer this." "You are pleasant now," said he, "but
together with the learning, do you pay money likewise." "Shall it not
be after I have got it?" said I. "But it is here," said Glauco; "so as to
money, Thrasymachus, say on; for all of us will advance for Socrates."
337e   "I truly imagine so," said he, "that Socrates may go on in his wonted
manner; not answer himself, but, when another answers, he may take
up the discourse, and confute." "How," said I, "most excellent
Thrasymachus, can a man answer? In the first place, when he neither
knows, nor says he knows; and, then, if he have any opinion about
these matters, he is forbid by no mean man to advance any of his
338a   opinions. But it is more reasonable that you speak, as you say you
know, and can tell us: Do not decline then, but oblige me in
answering, and do not grudge to instruct Glauco here, and the rest of
the company."

When I had said this, both Glauco and the rest of the company
entreated him not to decline it. And Thrasymachus appeared plainly
desirous to speak, in order to gain applause; reckoning he had a very
fine answer to make; yet pretended to be earnest that I should be the
answerer, but at last he agreed.

338b   And then, "This," said he, "is the wisdom of Socrates: Unwilling
himself to teach, he goes about learning from others, and gives no
thanks for it." "That, indeed, I learn from others," said I,
"Thrasymachus, is true; but in saying that I do not give thanks for it,
you are mistaken. I pay as much as I am able; and I am only able to
commend them; for money I have not: and how readily I do this,
when any one appears to me to speak well, you shall perfectly know
338c   this moment, when you make an answer; for I imagine you are to
speak well." "Hear then," said he; "for I say, that what is just, is
nothing else but the advantage of the more powerful. But why do not
you commend? You are unwilling." "Let me learn first," said I, "what

you say; for as yet I do not understand it. The advantage of the more powerful, you say, is what is just. What is this which you now say, Thrasymachus? For you certainly do not mean such a thing as this: If *116* Polydamus, the wrestler, be more powerful than we; and if beef be beneficial for his body, that this food is likewise both just and *338d* advantageous for us, who are weaker than he." "You are most impudent, Socrates, and lay hold of my speech on that side where you may do it the greatest hurt." "By no means, most excellent Thrasymachus," said I, "but tell more plainly what is your meaning." "Do not you then know," said he, "that, with reference to states, some are tyrannical; others democratical; and others aristocratical?" "Why are they not?" "And is not the governing pact in each state the more powerful?" "Certainly." "And every government makes laws for *338e* its own advantage; a democracy, democratic laws; a tyranny, tyrannic; and others the same way. And when they have made them, they show that to be just for the governed, which is advantageous for themselves and they punish the transgressor of this as one acting contrary both to law and justice. This, then, most excellent Socrates, is what I say, that, in all states, what is just, and what is advantageous for the established *339a* government, are the same; it hath the power. So that it appears to him who reasons rightly, that, in all cases, what is the advantage of the more powerful, the same is just."

"Now I have learned," said I, "what you say. But whether it be true, or not, I shall endeavour to learn. What is advantageous, then, Thrasymachus, you yourself have affirmed to be likewise just; though you forbid me to give this answer; but, indeed, you have added to it *339b* that of the more powerful." "Probably," said he, "but a small addition." "It is not yet manifest, whether it is small or great; but it is manifest that this is to be considered, whether you speak the truth; since I too acknowledge that what is just is somewhat that is advantageous: but you add to it and say that it is that of the more powerful. This I do not know, but it is to be considered." "Consider then," said he.

"That," said I, "shall be done. And tell me do not you say that it is just to obey governors?" "I say so." "Whether are the governors in the *339c* several states infallible? or are they capable of erring?" "Certainly," said he, "they are liable to err." "Do they not, then, when they attempt to make laws, make some of them right, and some of them not right?" "I imagine so." "To make them right, is it not to make them advantageous for themselves; and to make them not right, disadvantageous? Or what is it you mean?" "Entirely so." "And what they enact is to be observed by the governed, and this is what is just?" "Why not?" "It is, then, according to your reasoning, not only just to do what is advantageous for the more powerful; but also to do the contrary, what is not advantageous." "What do you say?" replied he. "The same, I imagine, that you say yourself. But let us consider better: have we not acknowledged that governors, in enjoining the governed to do certain things, may sometimes mistake what is best for themselves; and that what the governors enjoin is just for the governed to do? Have not these things been acknowledged?" "I think so," said he. "Think, also, then," said I, "that you have acknowledged that it is just to do what is disadvantageous to governors, and the more powerful; since governors unwillingly enjoin what is ill for themselves; and you say that it is just for the others to do what these enjoin. Must it not then, most wise Thrasymachus, necessarily happen, that, by this means, it may be just to do the contrary of what you say? For that which is the disadvantage of the more powerful, is sometimes enjoined the inferiors to do?" "Yes, indeed, Socrates," said Polemarchus, "these things are most manifest." "Yes, if you bear him witness," said Clitipho. "What need," said I, "of a witness? For Thrasymachus himself acknowledges that governors do indeed sometimes enjoin what is ill for themselves; but that it is just for the governed to do these things. For it has, Polemarchus, been established by Thrasymachus, to be just to do what is enjoined by the governors; and he has likewise, Clitipho, established that to be just, which is the advantage of the more powerful; and, having established both these things, he has acknowledged likewise, that the more powerful sometimes enjoin the inferiors and governed to do what is disadvantageous for themselves; and, from these concessions, the advantage of the more powerful can no more be just than the disadvantage." "But," said Clitipho, "he said the advantage of the more powerful; that is, what the more powerful judged to be advantageous to himself; that this was to be done by the inferior, and this he established as just." "But," said Polemarchus, "it was not said so." "There is no difference, Polemarchus," said I. "But, if Thrasymachus says so now, we $_{118}$ shall allow him to do it. And tell me, Thrasymachus, was this what you meant to say was just? The advantage of the more powerful, such as appeared so to the more powerful, whether it is advantageous, or is not. Shall we say that you spoke thus?"

"By no means," said he. "For, do you imagine I call him the more powerful who misjudges, at the time he misjudges?" "I thought," said I, "you said this, when you acknowledged that governors were not infallible; but that in some things they even erred." "You are a $_{340d}$ sycophant," said he, "in reasoning, Socrates. For, do you now call him who mistakes about the management of the sick, a physician; as to that very thing in which he mistakes? or, him, who mistakes in reasoning, a reasoner, when he errs, and with reference to that very error? But, I imagine, we say, in common language, that the physician erred; that the reasoner erred, and the grammarian: Thus, however, I imagine, that each of these, as far as he is what we call him, errs not at $_{340e}$ any time: So that, according to accurate discourse (since you discourse accurately), none of the artists errs: for he who errs, errs by departing from science; and, in this, he is an artist. So that no artist, or wise man, or governor errs; in so far as he is a governor. Yet any one may say the physician erred; the governor erred: Imagine then, it was in this way I now answered you. But the most accurate answer is this: That the governor, in as far as he is governor, errs not; and, as he does $_{341a}$ not err, he enacts that which is best for himself; and this is to be observed by the governed: So that what I said from the beginning, I maintain, is just. To do what is the advantage of the more powerful."

"Be it so," said I, "Thrasymachus! Do I appear to you to as the sycophant?" "Certainly, indeed," said he. "For you imagine that I spoke as I did, insidiously, and to abuse you." "I know it well," said he, "but you shall gain nothing by it; for, whether you abuse me in a concealed manner, or otherwise, you shall not be able to over come $_{341b}$ me by your reasoning." "I shall not attempt it," said I, "happy Thrasymachus! But, that nothing of this kind may happen to us again, define, whether you speak of a governor, and the more powerful, according to common, or according to accurate discourse, as you now said, whose advantage, as he is the more powerful, it shall be just for the inferior to observe." "I speak of him," said he, "who, in $_{119}$

the most accurate discourse, is governor. For this, now, abuse me, and
341c all the sycophant, if you are able. I do not shun you; but you cannot do
it." "Do you imagine me," said I, "to be so mad as to attempt to shave
a lion, and act the sycophant with Thrasymachus?" "You have now,"
said he, "attempted it, but with no effect." "Enough," said I, "of this.
But tell me, with reference to him, who, accurately speaking, is a
physician, whom you now mentioned, whether is he a gainer of
money, or one who takes care of the sick? and speak of him who is
really a physician." "He is one who takes care," said he, "of the sick."
"But what of the pilot, who is a pilot, truly? Whether is he the
341d governor of the sailors, or a sailor?" "The governor of the sailors."
"That, I think, is not to be considered, that he sails in the ship; nor
that he is called a sailor; for it is not for his sailing that he is called
pilot, but for his art, and his governing the sailors." "True," said he.
"Is there not then something advantageous to each of these?"
"Certainly." "And does not art," said I, "naturally tend to this, to seek
out and afford to every thing its advantage?" "It tends to this," said
he. "Is there, now, any thing else advantageous to each of the arts but
to be the most perfect possible?"

341e   "How ask you this?" "As, if you asked me," said I, "whether it
sufficed the body to be body, or if it stood in need of any thing,—I
would say, that it stood in need of something else. For this reason is
the medicinal art invented, because the body is infirm, and is not
sufficient for itself in such a state; in order therefore to afford it
things for its advantage, for this purpose, art has been provided. Do I
seem to you," said I, "to say right, or not, in speaking in this
342a manner?" "Right," said he. "But what now? This medicinal art itself,
or any other, is it imperfect, so long as it is wanting in a certain
virtue? As the eyes, when they want seeing; and the ears, hearing; and,
for these reasons have they need of a certain art, to perceive, and
afford them what is advantageous for these purposes? And is there,
still, in art itself, some imperfection; and does every art stand in need
of another art, to perceive what is advantageous to it, and this stand in
need of another, in like manner, and so on, to infinity? Or shall each
342b art perceive what is advantageous to itself; and stand in need neither
of itself, nor of another, to perceive what is for its advantage, with
120 reference to its own imperfection? For there is no imperfection, nor

error, in any art. Nor does it belong to it to seek what is advantageous to any thing, but to that of which it is the art. But it is, itself, infallible, and pure, being in the right. So long as each art is an accurate whole, whatever it is. And consider now, according to that accurate discourse, whether it be thus, or otherwise." "Thus," said he, "it appears." "The medicinal art, then," said I, "does not consider 342c what is advantageous to the medicinal art, but to the body." "Yes," said he. "Nor the art of managing horses, what is advantageous for that art; but what is advantageous for horses. Nor does any other art consider what is advantageous for itself, (for it hath no need,) but what is advantageous for that of which it is the art!" "So," replied he, it appears." "But, Thrasymachus, the arts rule and govern that of which they are the arts." He yielded this, but with great difficulty. "No science, then, considers the advantage of the more powerful, nor enjoins it; but that of the inferior, and of what is governed." He 342d consented to these things at last, though he attempted to contend about them, but afterwards he consented.

"Why, then, said I, no physician, so far as he is a physician, considers what is advantageous for the physician, nor enjoins it; but what it advantageous for the sick; for it has been agreed, that the accurate physician is one who takes care of sick bodies, and not an amasser of wealth. Has it not been agreed?" He assented. "And likewise that the accurate pilot is the governor of the sailors, and not 342e a sailor?" "It has been agreed." "Such a pilot, then, and governor will not consider and enjoin what is the advantage of the pilot, but what is advantageous to the sailor, and the governed." He consented, with difficulty. "Nor, yet, Thrasymachus," said I, "does any other, in any government, as far as he is a governor, consider or enjoin his own advantage, but that of the governed, and of those to whom he ministers; and, with an eye to this, and to what is advantageous and suitable to this, he both says what he says, and does what he does."

When we were at this part of the discourse, and it was evident to all 343a that the definition of what was just, stood now on the contrary side, Thrasymachus, instead of replying, "Tell me," said he, "Socrates, have you a nurse?" "What," said I, "ought you not rather to answer, than ask such things?" "Because," said he, "she neglects you when your nose is stuffed, and does not wipe it when it needs it, you who understand

neither what is meant by sheep, nor by shepherd." "For what now is
343b all this?" said I. "Because you think that shepherds, and neatherds,
ought to consider the good of the sheep, or oxen, to fatten them, and
to minister to them, having in their eye, something besides their
master's good and their own. And you fancy that those who govern in
cities, those who govern truly, are somehow otherwise affected
towards the governed than one is towards sheep; and that they are
343c attentive, day and night, to somewhat else than tis, how they shall be
gainers themselves; and so far are you from the notion of the just and
of justice, and of the unjust and injustice, that you do not know that
both justice and the just are, in reality, a foreign good, the advantage
of the more powerful, and of the governor; but properly, the hurt of
the subject, and the inferior; a injustice is the contrary. And justice
governs such as are truly simple and just; and the governed do what is
for the governor's advantage, he being more powerful, and
343d ministering to him, promote his happiness, but by no means their
own. You must thus consider it, most simple Socrates! that, on all
occasions, the just man gets less than the unjust. First, in co-
partnerships with one another, where the one joins in company with
the other, you never can find, on the dissolving of the company, that
the just man gets more than the unjust, but less. Then, in civil affairs,
where there are taxes to be paid from equal substance; the just man
pays more, the other less. But when there is any thing to be gained,
343e the one gains nothing, but the gain of the other is great. For, when
each of them governs in any public magistracy, this, if no other loss,
befalls the just man, that his domestic affairs, at least, are in a worse
situation through his neglect; and that he gains nothing from the
public, because he is just. Add to this, that he comes to be hated by his
domestics and acquaintance, when at no time he will serve them
beyond what is just. But all these things are quite otherwise with the
344a unjust; such an one, I mean, as I now mentioned; one who has it
greatly in his power to become rich. Consider him, then, if you would
judge how much more it is for his private advantage to be unjust than
just, and you will most easily understand it if you come to the most
finished in justice; such as renders the unjust man most happy, but the
122 injured, and those who are unwilling to do injustice, most wretched;
and that is tyranny, which takes away the goods of others, both by

secret fraud, and by open violence; both things sacred and holy, both private and public, and these not by degrees, but all at once. In all 344b particular cases of such crimes, when one, committing injustice, is not concealed, he is punished, and suffers the greatest ignominy. For according to the several kinds of the wickedness they commit, they are called sacrilegious, robbers, house-breakers, pilferers, thieves. But when any one, besides these thefts of the substance of his citizens, shall steal and enslave the citizens themselves; instead of those disgraceful names, he is called happy and blessed; not by his citizens alone, but likewise by others, as many as are informed that he has 344c committed the most consummate wickedness. For such as revile wickedness, revile it not because they are afraid of doing, but because they are afraid of suffering, unjust things. And thus, Socrates, injustice, when in sufficient measure, is both more powerful, more free, and hath more absolute command than justice: and, (as I said at the beginning,) the advantage of the more powerful, is justice; but injustice is the profit and advantage of oneself."

Thrasymachus having said these things, inclined to go away; like a 344d bath-keeper after he had poured into our ears this rapid and long discourse. These, however, who were present, would not suffer him, but forced him to stay, and give an account of what he had said. I too myself earnestly entreated him, and said, "divine Thrasymachus! after throwing in upon us so strange a discourse, do you intend to go away before you teach us sufficiently, or learn yourself, whether the case be as you say, or otherwise? Do you imagine you attempt to determine a small matter, and not the guide of life, by which, each of us being 344e conducted, may lead the most happy life." "But I imagine," said Thrasymachus, "that this is otherwise." "You seem truly," said I, "to care nothing for us; nor to be any way concerned, whether we shall live well or ill, whilst we are ignorant of what you say you know: But, good Thrasymachus, be readily disposed to show it also to us, nor will 345a the favour be ill placed, whatever you shall bestow on so many of us as are now present. And I, for my own part, tell you, that I am not persuaded, nor do I think that injustice is more profitable than justice; not although it should be permitted to exert itself, and be no 123 way hindered from doing whatever it should incline. But, good Thrasymachus, let him be unjust, let him be able to do unjustly, either

in secret, or by force, yet will you not persuade me at least that
345b injustice is more profitable than justice, and probably some other of us
here is of the same mind, and I am not single. Convince us then,
blessed Thrasymachus! that we imagine wrong, when we value justice
more than injustice."

"But how," said he, "shall I convince you? For, if I have not
convinced you by what I have said already, what shall I further do for
you? Shall I enter into your soul, and put my reasoning within you?"
"God forbid," said I, "you shall not do that. But, first of all, whatever
you have said, abide by it: or, if you do change, change openly; and do
345c not deceive us. For now you see, Thrasymachus, (for let us still
consider what is said above,) that when you first defined the true
physician, you did not afterwards think it needful that the true
shepherd should, strictly, upon the like principles, keep his flock; but
you fancy that, as a shepherd, he may feed his flock, not regarding
what is best for the sheep, but as some glutton, who is going to feast
345d on them at some entertainment; or yet to dispose of them as a
merchant; and not a shepherd. But the shepherd-art hath certainly no
other care, but of that for which it is ordained, to afford it what is
best: for its own affairs are already sufficiently provided for; so as to be
in the very best state while it needs nothing of the shepherd-art. In
the same manner, I at least imagined, there was a necessity for
agreeing with us in this, that every government, in as far as it is
government, considers what is best for nothing else but for the
345e governed, and those under its charge; both in political and private
government. But do you imagine that governors in cities, such as are
truly governors, govern willingly?" "Truly," said he, "as for that, I not
only imagine it, but am quite certain."

"Why now," said I, "Thrasymachus, do you not perceive, as to all
other governments, that no one undertakes them willingly, but they
ask a reward; as the profit arising from governing is not to be to
346a themselves, but to the governed? Or, tell me this now? do not we say
that every particular art is in this distinct, in having a distinct power?
And now, blessed Thrasymachus, answer not differently from your
sentiments, that we may make some progress." "In this," said he, "it is
124 distinct." "And does not each of them afford us a certain distinct
advantage, and not a common one? As the medicinal affords health,

the pilot art, preservation in sailing; and the others in like manner." "Certainly." "And does not the mercenary art afford a reward, for this is its power? Or, do you call both the medicinal art, and the pilot art, 346b one and the same? Or, rather, if you will define them accurately, as you proposed; though one in piloting recover his health, because sailing agrees with him, you will not the more on this account call it the medicinal art?" "No, indeed," said he. "Nor will you, I imagine, call the mercenary art the medicinal, though one in gaining a reward, recover his health." "No, indeed." "What now? Will you call the 346c medicinal, the mercenary art, if one in performing a cure gain a reward?" "No," said he. "Have we not acknowledged, then, that there is a distinct advantage of every art?" "Be it so," said he. "What is that advantage, then, with which all artists in common are advantaged? It is plain it must be in using something common to all that they are advantaged by it." "It seems so," said he. "Yet we say that artists are profited in receiving a reward arising to them from the increase of a lucrative art." He agreed with difficulty. "Has not, then, every one this advantage in his art, the receiving a reward. Yet, if we are to 346d consider accurately, the medicinal art produces health, and the mercenary art a reward; masonry, a house, and, the mercenary art accompanying it, a reward. And all the others, in like manner, every one produces its own work, and benefits that for which it was ordained; but, if it meet not with a reward, what is the artist advantaged by his art?" "It does not appear," said he. "But does he then no service when he works without reward?" "I think he does." 346e "Is not this, then, now evident, Thrasymachus, that no art, nor government, provides what is advantageous for itself; but, as I said long ago, provides and enjoins what is advantageous for the governed; having in view the profit of the inferior, and not that of the more powerful. And, for these reasons, friend Thrasymachus, I likewise said now, that no one is willing to govern, and to undertake to rectify the ills of others, but asks a reward for it; because, whoever will perform 347a the art handsomely, never asks what is best for himself, in ruling according to art, but what is best for the governed; and on this account, it seems, a reward must be given to those who shall be willing to govern; either money, or honour; or punishment, if they 125 will not govern."

"How say you, Socrates," said Glauco; "two of the rewards I understand; but this punishment you speak of, and here you mention it in place of a reward, I know not." "You know not, then," said I, 347b "the reward of the best of men, on account of which the most worthy govern, when they consent to govern. Or, do you not know, that to be ambitious and covetous, is both deemed a reproach, and really is so?" "I know," said he. "For those reasons, then," said I, "good men are not willing to govern, neither for money, nor for honour; for they are neither willing to be called mercenary, in openly receiving a reward for governing, nor to be called thieves, in taking clandestinely from those under their government; as little are they willing to 347c govern for honour, for they are not ambitious.—Of necessity then, there must be laid on them a fine, that they may consent to govern. And hence, it seems, it hath been accounted dishonourable to enter on government willingly, and not by constraint. And the greatest part of the punishment is to be governed by a base person, if one himself is not willing to govern: and the good seem to me to govern from a fear of this, when they do govern: and then, they enter on the government, not as on any thing good, or as what they are to reap advantage by, but as on a necessary task, and finding none better than 347d themselves, nor like them to entrust with the government: since it would appear that, if there was a city of good men, the contest would be, not to be in the government, as at present it is, to govern: And hence it would be manifest, that he who is indeed the true governor, does not aim at his own advantage, but at that of the governed; so that every understanding man would rather choose to be served, than 347e to have trouble in serving another. This, therefore, I, for my part, will never yield to Thrasymachus; that justice is the advantage of the more powerful; but this we shall consider afterwards. What Thrasymachus says now, seems to me of much more importance, when he says that the life of the unjust man is better than that of the just. You, then, Glauco," said I, "which side do you choose; and which seems to you moat agreeable to truth?"

"The life of the just," said he, "I, for my part, deem to be the more 348a profitable." "Have you heard," said I, "how many good things Thrasymachus just now enumerated in the life of the unjust?" "I heard," said he, "but am not persuaded." "Are you willing, then, that we should persuade him, (if we be able any how to find arguments), 126 that there is no truth in what he says?" "Why not," said he. "If then," said I, "pulling on the other side, we advance argument for argument, how many good things there are in being just, and then again, he on the other side, we shall need a third person to compute and estimate what each shall have said on either side; and we shall likewise need 348b some judges to determine the matter. But, if, as now, assenting to one another, we consider these things; we shall be both judges and pleaders ourselves." "Certainly," said he. "Which way, then," said I, "do you choose?" "This way," said he.

"Come then," said I, Thrasymachus, answer us from the beginning. Do you say that complete injustice is more profitable than complete justice?" "Yes, indeed, I say so," replied he, "and the reasons for it I 348c have enumerated." "Come now, do you ever affirm any thing of this kind concerning them? Do you call one of them, virtue; and the other, vice?" "Why not?" "Is not then, justice, virtue; and injustice, vice?" "Very likely," said he, "most pleasant Socrates! after I say that injustice is profitable; but justice is not." "What then?" "The contrary," said he. "Is it justice you call vice?" "No, but I call it, altogether genuine simplicity." "Do you, then, call injustice, cunning?" "No," said he, "but I call it sagacity." Do the unjust seem to 348d you, Thrasymachus, to be both prudent and good?" "Such, at least," said he, "as are able to do injustice in perfection; such as are able to subject to themselves states and nations; but you probably imagine I speak of those who cut purses: Even such things as these," he said, "are profitable if concealed; but such only as I now mentioned are of any 348e worth." "I understand," said I, "what you want to say: But this I have wondered at, that you should deem injustice to be a part of virtue and of wisdom and justice among their contraries." "But I do deem it altogether so." "Your meaning," said I, "is now more determined, friend, and it is no longer easy for one to find what to say against it: for, if when you had set forth injustice as profitable, you had still allowed it to be vice or ugly, as some others do, we should have had something to say, speaking according to the received opinions: But now, it is plain, you will call it beautiful and powerful; and all those other things you will attribute to it which we attribute to the just 349a man, since you have dared to class it with virtue and wisdom." "You conjecture," said he, "most true." "But, however, I must not grudge," said I, "to pursue our inquiry so long as I conceive you speak as you think; for to me you plainly seem now, Thrasymachus, not to lie in irony, but to speak what you think concerning the truth." "What is the difference to you," said he, "whether I think so or not, if you do not confute my reasoning;" "None at all," said I. "But endeavour, further, to answer me this likewise—Does a just man seem to you desirous to have more than another just man?" "By no means," said he; "for otherwise he would not be courteous and simple, as we now supposed him." "But what, will he not desire it in a just action?" "Not even in a just action," said he. "But, whether would he deem it proper to exceed the unjust man and count it just? or would be not?" "He would, said he, both count it just and deem it proper but would not be able to effect it." "That," said I, "I do not ask. But, whether a just man would neither deem it proper, nor incline to exceed a just man, but would deem it proper to exceed the unjust?" "This last," said he, "is what he would incline to do." "But what would the unjust man do? Would he deem it proper to exceed the just man even in a just action?" "Why not," said he, "he who deems it proper to exceed all others." "Will not then the unjust man desire to exceed the unjust man likewise, and in an unjust action; and contend that he himself receive more than all others?" "Certainly." "Thus, we say, then," said I, "the just man does not desire to exceed one like himself, but one unlike. But the unjust man desires to exceed both one like, and one unlike himself." "You have spoken," said he, "perfectly well." "But," said I, "the unjust man is both wise and good; but the just man is neither." "This, too," said he, "is well said." "Is not, then," said I, "the unjust man like the wise and the good, and the just man unlike?" "Must he not," said he, "be like them, being such an one as we have supposed; and he who is otherwise, be unlike them?" "Excellently. Each of them is indeed such as those he resembles." "What else?" said he.

"Be it so, Thrasymachus, "Call you one man musical and another unmusical?" "I do." "Which of the two call you wise and which unwise?" "I call the musical, wise, and the unmusical, unwise." "Is he not good in as much as he is wise, and ill in as much as he is unwise?" "Yes." "And what as to the physician? Is not the case the same?" "The same." "Do you imagine, then, most excellent Thrasymachus, that any musician, in tuning a harp, wants to exceed, or deems it proper to have more skill than a man who is a musician, with reference to the intention or remission of the strings?" "I am not of that opinion." "But what say you of exceeding a man who is no musician?" "Of *128* necessity," said he, "he will deem it proper to exceed him." "And what as to the physician? In presenting a regimen of meats or drink does he *350a* want to exceed another physician in medical cases?" "No indeed." But to exceed one who is no physician?" "Yes." "And as to all science and ignorance does any one appear to you intelligent who wants to grasp at or do or say more than another intelligent in the art; and not to do the same things, in the same affair, which one equally intelligent with himself doth?" "Probably there is a necessity," said he, "it be so." "But what, as to him who is ignorant; will not he want to exceed the *350b* intelligent and the ignorant both alike?" "Probably." "But the intelligent is wise?" "I say so." "And the wise is good?" "I say so." "But the good and the wise will not want to exceed one like himself; but the unlike and contrary?" "It seems so," said he. "But the evil and the ignorant wants to exceed both one like himself and his opposite?" "It appears so." "Why, then, Thrasymachus," said I, "the unjust desires to exceed both one unlike and one like himself. Do not you say so?" "I do," said he. "But the just man will not desire to exceed one like *350c* himself, but one unlike?" "Yes." "The just man, then," said I, "resembles the wise and the good; and the unjust resembles the evil and the ignorant." "It appears so." "But we acknowledged that each of them was such as that which they resembled." "We acknowledged so, indeed." "The just man, then, has appeared to us to be good and wise; and the unjust to be ignorant and depraved."

Thrasymachus now confessed all these things not easily, as I now *350d* narrate them, but dragged and with difficulty and prodigious sweat, it being now the summer season. And I then saw, but never before, Thrasymachus blush. After we had acknowledged that justice was virtue and wisdom, and injustice was vice and ignorance, "well," said I, "let this remain so. But we said likewise that injustice was powerful. Do not you remember, Thrasymachus?" "I remember," said he. "But what you now say does not please me; and I have somewhat to say concerning it which I well know you would call declaiming if I *350e* should advance it; either, then, suffer me to say what I incline, or if you incline to ask, do it; and I shall answer you "be it so," as to old women telling stories; and small ascent and dissent." "By no means," said I, "contrary to your own opinion." "Just to please you," said he; "since you will not allow me to speak. But do you want anything further?" "Nothing, truly," said I: "but if you are to do thus, do; I shall ask." "Ask then." "This, then, I ask, which I did just now; (that we may in an orderly way see through our discourse,) of what kind is justice, compared with injustice; for it was surely said that injustice was more powerful and stronger than justice." "It was so said just now," replied he. "But, if justice be both virtue and wisdom, it will easily, I imagine, appear to be likewise more powerful than injustice; since injustice is ignorance; of this now none can be ignorant. But I am willing, for my own part, Thrasymachus, to consider it not simply in this manner, but some how thus. Might you not say that a state was unjust, and attempted to enslave other states unjustly, and did enslave them; and had many states in slavery under itself?" "Why not," said he: "and the best state will chiefly do this, and such as is most completely unjust." "I understand," said I, "that this was your speech; but I consider this in it; Whether this state, which becomes more powerful than the other state, shall hold this power without justice, or must it of necessity be with justice?" "With justice," said he, "if indeed, as you now said, justice be wisdom; but, if as I said, with injustice." "I am much delighted," said I, "Thrasymachus, that you do not merely assent and dissent, but that you answer so handsomely." "I do," it said he, "to gratify you."

"That is obliging in you. But gratify me in this likewise, and tell me; do you imagine that a city, or camp, or robbers, or thieves, or any other community, such as jointly undertakes to do any thing unjustly, is able to effectuate any thing if they injure one another?" "No indeed," said he. "But what, if they do not injure one another; will they not do better?" "Certainly." "For injustice, some how, Thrasymachus, brings seditions, and hatreds, and fightings among them; but justice affords harmony and friendship. Does it not?" "Be it so," said he, "that I may not differ from you." "You are very obliging, most excellent Thrasymachus! But tell me this. If this be the work of injustice, wherever it is, to create hatred, will it not then, when happening among free men and slaves, make them hate one another,

129
351a

351b

351c

351d

and grow seditious, and become impotent to do any thing together in company?" "Certainly." "But what, in the case of injustice between any two men, will they not differ, and hate, and become enemies to one another, and to just men?" "They will become so," said he. "If now, wonderful Thrasymachus, injustice be in one, whether does it lose its power, or will it no less retain it?" "Let it," said he, "no less retain it." "Does it not then appear to have such a power as this—That wherever it is, whether in a city, or tribe, or camp, or wherever else, in the first place, it renders it unable for action in itself, through seditions and differences; and, besides, makes it an enemy to itself, and to every opponent, and to the just? Is it not thus?" "Certainly." "And, when injustice is in one man, it will have, I imagine, all these effects, which it is natural for it to produce. In the first place, it will render him unable for action whilst he is in sedition and disagreement with himself; and next as he is an enemy both to himself, and to the just. Is it not so?" "Yes." "But the Gods, friend, are likewise just." "Let them be so," said he. "The unjust man then, Thrasymachus, shall be an enemy also to the Gods; and the just man, a friend." "Feast yourself," said he, "with the reasoning boldly; for I will not oppose you, that I may not render myself odious to these Gods." "Come then," said I, "and complete to me this feast; answering as you were doing just now: for the just already appear to be wiser, and better, and more powerful to all; but the unjust are not able to act any thing with one another: and what we said with reference to those who are unjust,—that they are ever at any time able strenuously to act jointly together; this we spoke not altogether true, for they would not spare one another; being thoroughly unjust; but it is plain that there was in them justice, which made them refrain from injuring one another, and those of their party; and by this justice they performed what they did. And they rushed on unjust actions, through injustice; being half wicked; since those who are completely wicked, and perfectly unjust, are likewise perfectly unable to act. This then I understand is the case with reference to these matters, and not as you were establishing at first. But whether the just live better than the unjust, and are more happy (which we proposed to consider afterwards), is now to be considered; and they appear to do so even at present, as I imagine, at least, from what has been said. Let us,

351e

130

352a

352b

352c

352d

however, consider it further. For the discourse is not about an accidental thing, but about this, in what manner we ought to live."

352e "Consider then," said he. "I am considering," said I, "and tell me;
131 does there any thing seem to you to be the work of a horse?" "Yes." "Would you not call that the work of a horse, or of any one else, which one does with him only, or in the best manner?" "I do not understand," said he. "Thus then: Do you see with any thing else but the eyes?" "No indeed." "What now, could you hear with any thing but the ears?" "By no means." "Do we not justly then call these things
353a the works of these?" "Certainly." "But what, could not you with a sword, a knife, and many other things, cut off a branch of a vine?" "Why not?" "But with nothing, at least I imagine, so handsomely, as with a pruning hook, which is made for that purpose: shall we not then settle this to be its work?" "We shall then settle it." "I imagine, then, you may now understand better what I was asking when I inquired whether the work of each thing were not that which it alone performs, or performs in the best manner." "I understand you," said
353b he; and this does seem to me to be the work of each thing." "Be it so," said I. "And is there not likewise a virtue belonging to every thing to which there is a certain work assigned? But let us go over again the same things: We say there is a work belonging to the eyes?" "There is." "And is there not a virtue also belonging to the eyes?" "A virtue also." "Well then, was there any work of the ears?" "Yes." "Is there not then a virtue also?" "A virtue also." "And what as to all other things? Is it not thus?" "It is." "But come, could the eyes ever handsomely
353c perform their work, not having their own proper virtue; but, instead of virtue, having vice?" "How could they," said he, "for you probably mean their having blindness instead of sight." "Whatever," said I, "be their virtue, for I do not ask this; but, whether it be with their own proper virtue that they handsomely perform their own proper work, whatever things are performed, and by their vice, unhandsomely?" "In this at least," said he, "you say true." "And will not the ears likewise, when deprived of their virtue, perform their work ill?"
353d "Certainly." "And do we settle all other things according to the same reasoning?" "So I imagine." "Come, then, after these things, consider this. Is there belonging to the soul a certain work, which, with no one other being whatever, you can perform; such as this, to care for, to

govern, to consult, and all such things; is there any other than the soul, to whom we may justly ascribe them, and say they properly belong to it?" "No other." "But what of this? To live; shall we say it is the work of the soul?" "Most especially," said he. "Do not we say, then, that there is some virtue of the soul, likewise?" "We say so." "And shall, then, the soul, ever at all, Thrasymachus, perform her works handsomely, whilst deprived of her proper virtue? or, is this impossible?" "It is impossible." "Of necessity, then, a depraved soul must in a bad manner govern, and take care of things; and a good soul perform all these things well." "Of necessity." "But did not we agree that justice was the virtue of the soul; and injustice its vice?" "We did agree." "Why, then, the just soul, and the just man, shall live well; and the unjust, ill." "It appears so," said he, "according to your reasoning." "But, surely, he who lives well is both blessed and happy, and he who does not is the opposite." "Why not?" "The just, then, is happy; and the unjust, miserable." "Let them be so," said he. "But it is not advantageous to be miserable, but to be happy." "Certainly." "At no time, then, blessed Thrasymachus, is injustice more advantageous than justice." "Thus, now, Socrates," said he, "have you been feasted in Diana's festival." "By you, truly, I have, Thrasymachus," said I; "since you are grown meek; and have ceased to be troublesome: I have not feasted handsomely, owing to myself, and not to you: But as voracious guests, snatching still what is bringing before them, taste of it before they have sufficiently enjoyed what went before; so I, as I imagine, before I have found what we first inquired into,—what justice is,—have left this, hurrying to inquire concerning it, whether it be vice and ignorance, or wisdom and virtue. And, a discourse afterwards falling in, that injustice was more profitable than justice, I could not refrain from coming to this from the other: So that, from the dialogue, I have now come to know nothing; for whilst I do not know what justice is, I shall hardly know whether it be some virtue or not, and whether he who possesses it be unhappy or happy."

THE END OF THE FIRST BOOK.

132

353e

354a

354b

354c

INTRODUCTION

TO THE

SECOND AND THIRD BOOKS
OF THE REPUBLIC

CONTAINING

AN APOLOGY FOR
THE FABLES OF HOMER.

As a very considerable part both of the second and third books of The Republic consists in examining and reprobating the assertions of the poets and particularly the fables of Homer, concerning divine natures, it appeared to me that I could not more essentially benefit the reader than by presenting him with the following defence of Homer and divine fables in general, from the exposition of the more difficult questions in this dialogue, by that coryphæus of all true philosophers Proclus. For in this apology Homer and Plato are so admirably reconciled, that the poetry of the one and the philosophy of the other are in the highest degree honoured by the expulsion of the former from the polity of the latter. In short, it will be found, however paradoxical it may appear, that the most divine of poets ought beyond all others to be banished from a republic planned by the prince of philosophers. Such readers, too, as may fortunately possess a genius adapted for these speculations, will find that the fables of Homer are replete with a theory no less grand than scientific, no less accurate than sublime; that they are truly the progeny of divine fury; are worthy to be ascribed to the Muses as their origin; are capable of exciting in those that understand them the most exalted conceptions, and of raising the imagination in conjunction with intellect, and thus purifying and illuminating its figured eye.

Though I availed myself in this translation of the epitome made by Gesner of this apology, who seems to have consulted a more perfect manuscript than that from which the Basil edition was printed, yet I frequently found it necessary to correct the Greek text from my own conjecture, as the learned reader will readily perceive. Some of these emendations I have noted in the course of the translation; but as they are numerous many are omitted.

I. CONCERNING THE MODE OF THE APPARATUS OF DIVINE FABLES WITH THEOLOGISTS.—THE CAUSES OF SUCH FABLES ASSIGNED; AND A SOLUTION OF THE OBJECTIONS AGAINST THEM.

Since Socrates accuses the mode of fables according to which Homer and Hesiod have delivered doctrines concerning the Gods, and prior to these Orpheus, and any other poets, who with a divine mouth, ειθεω στοματι, have interpreted things which have a perpetual sameness of subsistence, it is necessary that we should in the first place show that the disposition of the Homeric fables is adapted to the things which it indicates. For it may be said, How can things which are remote from the good and the beautiful, and which deviate from order,—how can base and illegal names, ever be adapted to those natures whose essence is characterized by the good; and is consubsistent with the beautiful, in whom there is the first order, and from whom all things are unfolded into light, in conjunction with beauty and undefiled power? How then can things which are full of tragical portents and phantasms which subsist with material natures, and are deprived of the whole of justice and the whole of divinity, be adapted to such natures as these? For is it not unlawful to ascribe to the nature of the Gods, who are exempt from all things through transcendent excellence, adulteries, and thefts, precipitations from heaven, injurious conduct towards parents, bonds, and castrations,

134

and such other particulars as are celebrated by Horner and other
ancient poets? But, as the Gods are separated from other things, are
united with *the good*, or the ineffable principle of things, and have
nothing of the imperfection of inferior natures belonging to them,
but are unmingled and undefiled with respect to all things,
presubsisting uniformly according to one bound and order,—in like
manner it is requisite to employ the most excellent language in
speaking of them, and such appellations as are full of intellect, and
which are able to assimilate us, according to their proper order, to
their ineffable transcendency. It is also necessary to purify the notions
of the soul from material phantasms, in the mystic intellectual
conceptions of a divine nature; and, rejecting every thing foreign and
all false opinions, to conceive every thing as small with respect to the
undefiled transcendency of the Gods, and believe in right opinion
alone, and the more excellent spectacles of intellect in the truth
concerning the first of essences.

Let no one therefore say to us that such things harmonize with the
Gods as are adapted to men, nor endeavour to introduce the passions
of material irrationality to natures expanded above intellect, and an
intellectual essence and life: for these symbols do not appear similar to
the hyparxes[1] of the Gods. It is therefore requisite that fables, if they
do not entirely wander from the truth inherent in things, should be
in a certain respects assimilated to the particulars, the occult theory of
which they endeavour to conceal by apparent veils. Indeed, as Plato
himself often mystically teaches us divine concerns through certain
images, and neither any thing base, nor any representation of
disorder, nor material and turbulent phantasm, is inserted in his
fables,—but the intellectual conceptions concerning the Gods are
concealed with purity, before which the fables are placed like
conspicuous statues, and most similar representations of the inward
arcane theory,—in like manner it is requisite that poets, and Homer
himself, if they devise fables adapted to the Gods, should reject these
multiform compositions, and which are at the same time replete with
names most contrary to things, but employing such as regard the
beautiful and the good, should, through these, exclude the multitude
from a know ledge concerning the Gods, which does not pertain to
them, and at the same time employ in a pious manner fabulous

devices reflecting divine natures.

These are the things which, as it appears to me, Socrates objects to the fables of Homer, and for which perhaps some one besides may accuse other poets, in consequence of not admitting the apparently monstrous signification of names. In answer then to these objections, we reply that fables fabricate all that apparatus pertaining to them, which first presents itself to our view, instead of the truth which is established in the arcana, and employ apparent veils of conceptions invisible and unknown to the multitude. This indeed is their distinguishing excellence, that they narrate nothing belonging to natures truly good to the profane, but only extend certain vestiges of the whole mystic discipline to such as are naturally adapted to be led from these to a theory inaccessible to the vulgar. For these, instead of investigating the truth which they contain, use only the pretext of fabulous devices; and, instead of the purification of intellect, follow phantastic and figured conceptions. Is it not therefore absurd in these men to accuse fables of their own illegitimate conduct, and not themselves for the erroneous manner in which they consider in them?

In the next place, do we not see that the multitude are injured by such things as are remarkably venerable and honourable, from among all other things, and which are established in and produced by the Gods themselves? For who will not acknowledge that the mysteries and perfective rites lead souls upwards from a material and mortal life, and conjoin them with the Gods, and that they suppress all that tumult which insinuates itself from the irrational part into intellectual illuminations, and expel whatever is indefinite and dark from those that are initiated, through the light proceeding from the Gods? Yet at the same time nothing can refrain the multitude from sustaining from these all-various distortions, and, in consequence of using the good, and the powers proceeding from these, according to their perverted habit, departing from the Gods, and truly sacred ceremonies, and falling into a passive and irrational life. Those indeed that accuse the mysteries for producing these effects in the multitude, may also accuse the fabrication of the universe, the order of wholes, and the providence of all things, because those that receive the gifts of these, use them badly; but neither is such an accusation holy, nor is it fit that fables should be calumniated on account of the perverted conceptions of the multitude. For the virtue and vice of things are not to be determined from those that use them perversely; but it is fit that every thing should be estimated from its own proper nature, and the *135* rectitude which it contains. Hence the Athenian guest, in the Laws of Plato, is of opinion that even intoxication ought not to be expelled from a well-instituted city, on account of the views of the multitude and its corrupt use; for he says it greatly contributes to education, if it is properly and prudently employed. And yet it may be said that intoxication corrupts both the bodies and souls of those that are subject to it; but the legislator does not on this account detract from its proper worth, and the aid it affords to virtue.

But if any one accuses fables on account of their apparent depravity, and the base names which they employ,—since things of this kind are by no means similar to the divine exemplars of which fables are the images,—we reply in the first place, that there are two kinds of fables, those adapted to the education of youth, and those full of a divine fury, and which rather regard the universe itself than the habit of those that hear them. In the next place we must distinguish the lives of those that use fables; and we must consider that some are juvenile, and conversant with simple habits; but that others are able to be excited to intellect, to the whole genera of the Gods, to their progressions through all things, their series, and their terminations, which hasten to be extended as far as to the last of things. This being premised, we must say that the fables of Homer and Hesiod are not adapted to the education of youth, but that they follow the nature of wholes, and the order of things, and conjoin with true beings such as are capable of being led to the elevated survey of divine concerns. For the fathers of fables—perceiving that nature, fabricating images of immaterial and intelligible forms, and diversifying the sensible world with the imitations of these, adumbrated things impartible partibly, but expressed things eternal through such as proceed according to time, things intelligible through sensibles, that which is immaterial materially, that which is without interval with interval, and through mutation that which is firmly established, conformably to the nature and the progression of the phænomena,—they also, devising the resemblances and images of things divine in their verses, imitated the transcendent power of exemplars by contrary and most remote

adumbrations. Hence they indicated that which is supernatural in
things divine by things contrary to nature, that which is more divine
than all reason, by that which is contrary to reason, and that which is
expanded above all partial beauty, by things apparently base. And thus
by an assimilative method they recalled to our memory the exempt
supremacy of divine natures.

Besides this, according to every order of the Gods, which beginning
from on high gradually proceeds as far as to the last of things, and
penetrates through all the genera of beings, we may perceive the
terminations of their series exhibiting such idioms as fables attribute
to the Gods themselves, and that they give subsistence to, and are
connective of, such things as those through which fables conceal the
arcane theory of first essences. For the last of the dæmoniacal genera,
and which revolve about matter, preside over the perversion of natural
powers, the baseness of material natures, the lapse into vice, and a
disorderly and confused motion. For it is necessary that these things
should take place in the universe, and should contribute to fill the
variety of the whole order of things, and that the cause of their
shadowy subsistence and of their duration, should be comprehended
in perpetual genera. The leaders of sacred rites, perceiving these
things, ordered that laughter and lamentations should be consecrated
to such-like genera in certain definite periods of time, and that they
should be allotted a convenient portion of the whole of the sacred
ceremonies pertaining to a divine nature. As therefore the art of
sacred rites, distributing in a becoming manner the whole of piety to
the Gods and the attendants of the Gods, that no part of worship
might be omitted adapted to such attendants, conciliated the
divinities by the most holy mysteries and mystic symbols, but called
down the gifts of dæmons by apparent passions, through a certain
arcane sympathy,—in like manner the fathers of these fables,
looking, as I may say, to all the progressions of divine natures, and
hastening to refer fables to the whole series proceeding from each,
established the imagery in their fables, and which first presents itself
to the view, analogous to the last genera, and to those that preside
over ultimate and material passions; but to the contemplators of true
being they delivered the concealed meaning, and which is unknown
to the multitude, as declarative of the exempt and inaccessible essence

of the Gods. Thus, very fable is dæmoniacal according to that which is apparent in it, but is divine according to its recondite theory. If these things then are rightly asserted, neither is it proper to deprive the fables of Homer of an alliance to things which have a true subsistence, because they are not serviceable to the education of youth; for the end of such fables is not juvenile tuition, nor did the authors of fables devise them looking to this, nor are those written by Plato to be referred to the same idea with those of a more divinely inspired nature, but each is to be considered separately; and the latter are to be established as more philosophic, but the former as adapted to sacred ceremonies and institutions. The latter likewise are fit to be heard by youth, but the former by those who have been properly conducted through all the other parts of learning.

Socrates, indeed, sufficiently indicates this to those who are able to perceive his meaning, and also that he only blames the fables of Homer so far as they are neither adapted to education, nor accord with the restless and simple manners of youth. He likewise signifies that the recondite and occult good of fables requires a certain mystic and entheastic (*i.e.* divinely inspired) intelligence. But the multitude, not perceiving the meaning of the Socratic assertions, and widely deviating from the conceptions of the philosopher, accuse every such-like kind of fables. But it is worth while to hear the words of Socrates, and through what cause he rejects such a mythology:

> "The young person," says he "is not able to judge what is allegory, and what is not; but whatever opinions he receives at such an age are with difficulty washed away, and are generally immoveable. On these accounts, care should be taken, above all things, that what they are first to hear be composed in the most handsome manner for exciting them to virtue."

With great propriety, therefore, do we say that the Homeric fables do not well imitate a divine nature; for they are not useful to legislators for the purposes of virtue and education, nor for the proper tuition of youth, but in this respect indeed they do not appear at all similar to things themselves, nor adapted to those that preside over the politic science; but, after another manner, they harmonize with the Gods, and lead those who possess a naturally good disposition to the contemplation of divine natures; and the good which they contain is not disciplinative, but mystic, nor does it regard a juvenile, but an aged habit of soul. This also Socrates himself testifies, when he says that:

140 "such fables should be heard in secrecy, by as few as possible, after they had sacrificed not a hog, but some great and wonderful sacrifice."

Socrates therefore is very far from despising this kind of fables, according to the opinion of the multitude; for he evinces that the hearing of them is coordinated with the most holy initiations, and the most subtle mysteries.[2] For to assert that such fables ought to be used in secret with a sacrifice the *greatest* and *most perfect*, manifests that the contemplation of them is mystic, and that they elevate the souls of the hearers to sublime speculations. Whoever therefore has divested himself of every puerile and juvenile habit of the soul, and of the indefinite impulses of the phantasy, and who has established intellect as the leader of his life, such a one will most opportunely participate of the spectacles concealed in suchlike fables; but he who still requires instruction and symmetry of manners, cannot with safety engage in their speculation.

It follows therefore, according to Socrates himself, that there is a two-fold species of fables, one of which is adapted to the instruction of youth, but the other is mystic; one is preparatory to moral virtue, but the other imparts a conjunction with a divine nature; one is capable of benefiting the many, the other is adapted to the few; the one is common and known to most men, but the other is recondite and unadapted to those who do not hasten to become perfectly established in a divine nature; and the one is co-ordinate with juvenile habits but the other scarcely unfolds itself with sacrifices and mystic tradition. If therefore Socrates teaches us these things, must we not say that he harmonizes with Homer respecting fables? But he only rejects and reprobates them so far as they appear unadapted to the hypothesis of his discourse, and the narration of the education of youth.

But if it be requisite that legislators should in one way he conversant with mythical fictions, and those who endeavour to cultivate more imperfect habits, but in another way those who indicate by the divinely inspired intuitive perceptions of intellect the ineffable essence of the Gods to those who are able to follow the most elevated contemplations, we shall not hesitate to refer the precipitations of Vulcan to the irreprehensible science concerning the Gods, nor the Saturnian bonds, nor the castrations of Heaven, which Socrates says are unadapted to the ears of youth, and by no means harmonize with those habits which require juvenile tuition. For, in short, the mystic knowledge of divine natures can never subsist in foreign receptacles. To those therefore that are capable of such sublime speculations we must say, that the precipitation of Vulcan indicates the progression of a divine nature from on high, as far as to the last fabrication in sensibles, and this so as to be moved and perfected and directed by the demiurgus and father of all things. But the Saturnian bonds manifest the union of the whole fabrication of the universe,[3] with the intellectual and paternal supremacy of Saturn. The castrations of Heaven obscurely signify the separation of the Titanic[4] series from the connective[5] order. By thus speaking we shall perhaps assert things that are known, and refer that which is tragical and fictitious in fables to the intellectual theory of the divine genera. For whatever among us appears to be of a worse condition, and to belong to the inferior coordination of things, fables assume according to a better nature and power. Thus, for instance, a bond with us impedes and restrains energy, but there it is a contact and ineffable union with causes. A precipitation here is a violent motion from another; but with the Gods it indicates prolific progression, and an unrestrained and free presence to all things, without departing from its proper principle, but in an orderly manner proceeding from it through all things. And castrations in things partial and material cause a diminution of power, but in primary causes they obscurely signify the progression of secondary natures into a subject order, from their proper causes; things first at the same time remaining established in themselves undiminished, neither moved from themselves through the progression of these, nor mutilated by their separation, nor divided by their distribution in things subordinate. These things, which Socrates justly says are not fit to be heard by youth, are not on that account to be entirely rejected. For the same

141

142 thing takes place with respect to these fables, which Plato somewhere says happens to divine and all-holy dogmas: For these are ridiculous to the multitude, but to the few who are excited to intellectual energy they unfold their sympathy with things, and through sacred operations themselves procure credibility of their possessing a power connate with all that is divine. For the Gods, hearing these symbols, rejoice, and readily obey those that invoke them, and proclaim the characteristic of their natures through these, as signs domestic and especially known to them. The mysteries likewise and the greatest and most perfect of sacrifices (τελεται) possess their efficacy in these, and enable the mystics to perceive through these, entire, stable and simple visions, which a youth by his age, and much more his manners, is incapable of receiving. We must not therefore say that such-like fables do not instruct in virtue, but those that object to them should show that they do not in the highest degree accord with the laws pertaining to sacred rites. Nor must it be said that they dissimilarly imitate divine natures, through obscure symbols, but it must be shown that they do not prepare for us an ineffable sympathy towards the participation of the Gods. For fables which are composed with a view to juvenile discipline should possess much of the probable, and much of that which is decorous in the fabulous, in their apparent forms, but should be entirely pure from contrary appellations, and be conjoined with divine natures through a similitude of symbols. But those fables which regard a more divinely inspired habit, which co harmonize things last with such as are first through analogy alone, and which are composed with a view to the sympathy in the universe between effects and their generative causes,—such fables, despising the multitude, employ names in an all-various manner, for the purpose of indicating divine concerns. Since also, with respect to harmony, we say that one kind is poetic, and which through melodies exciting to virtue cultivates the souls of youth; but another divine, which moves the hearers, and produces a divine mania, and which we denominate better than temperance: and we admit the former as completing the whole of education, but we reject the latter as not adapted to political administration. Or does not Socrates expel the Phrygian harmony from his Republic as producing ecstasy in the soul, and on this account separate it from other harmonies which are

subservient to education?

As, therefore, harmony is two-fold, and one kind is adapted to   *143*
erudition, but the other is foreign from it; in a similar manner,
likewise, is mythology divided; into that which contributes to the
proper tuition of youth, and into that which is subservient to the
sacred and symbolic invocation of a divine nature. And the one, *viz.*
the method through images, is adapted to those that philosophize in
a genuine manner; but the other, which indicates a divine essence
through recondite signs, to the leaders of a more mystically-perfective
operation; from which Plato himself also renders many of his peculiar
dogmas more credible and clear. Thus, in the Phædo, he venerates
with a becoming silence that recondite assertion, that we are confined
in body as in a prison secured by a guard, and testifies, according to
the mysteries, the different allotments of the soul, when in a pure or
impure condition, on its departure to Hades; and again, its habitudes,
and the triple paths arising from its essence, and this according to
paternal sacred institutions; all which are full of a symbolic theory,
and of the ascent and descent of souls celebrated by poets, of
Dionysiacal signs, and what are called Titanic errors, the triviæ, and
wandering in Hades, and everything else of this kind. So that Plato
does not entirely despise this mode of mythologizing, but considers it
as foreign from juvenile tuition, and, on this account, delivers types of
theology commensurate with the manners of those that are
instructed.

It likewise appears to me, that whatever is tragical, monstrous, and
unnatural, in poetical fictions, excites the hearers, in an all-various
manner, to the investigation of the truth, attracts us to recondite
knowledge and does not suffer us through apparent probability to rest
satisfied with superficial conceptions, but compels us to penetrate into
the interior parts of fables, to explore the obscure intention of their
authors, and survey what natures and powers they intended to signify
to posterity by such mystical symbols.[6]

Since therefore fables of this kind excite those of a naturally more
excellent disposition to a desire of the concealed theory which they
contain, and to an investigation of the truth established in the adyta[7]   *144*
through their apparent absurdity, but prevent the profane from
busying themselves about things which it is not lawful for them to

touch, are they not eminently adapted to the Gods themselves, of whose nature they are the interpreters? For many genera are hurled forth before the Gods,[8] some of a dæmoniacal, and others of an angelic order, who terrify those that are excited to a participation of divinity, who are exercised for the reception of divine light, and are sublimely elevated to the union of the Gods. But we may especially perceive the alliance of these fables with the tribe of dæmons, whose energies manifest many things symbolically, as those know who have met with dæmons when awake,[9] or have enjoyed their inspiration in dreams, unfolding many past or future events. For, in all such phantasies, after the manner of the authors of fables, some things are indicated by others. Nor, of the things which take place through this, are some images, but others paradigms; but some are symbols, and others sympathize with these from analogy. If, therefore, this mode of composing fables is dæmoniacal, must we not say that it is exempt from every other variety of fables, as well that which regards nature, and interprets natural powers, as that which presides over the instruction of the forms of the soul?

145   II. WHAT THE DIFFERENT MODES OF THEOMACHY, OR, THE BATTLES OF THE GODS, ARE, AMONG THEOLOGISTS, AND AN INTERPRETATION OF THE OCCULT TRUTH WHICH THEY CONTAIN.

And thus much concerning those forms of fables according to which other poets and Homer have delivered mystic conceptions respecting the Gods, and which are unapparent to the vulgar. After this, it follows I think that we should distinctly consider the several fables in the order in which they are mentioned by Socrates, and contemplate according to what conceptions of the soul Homer represents the Gods fighting, or doing or suffering any thing else, in his poems. And in the first place let us consider this *theomachy* as it is called, or battles of the Gods, which Homer devises, but Socrates thinks worthy of animadversion, as by no means adapted to the education of youth. For, that there is neither sedition, nor dissension and division, as with mortals, among the Gods, but peace and an inoffensive life, the poet himself testifies when he somewhere says concerning Olympus, that it is a substratum to the Gods, who possess every possible joy, and spectacles of immense beauty:

The blessed Gods in joy unceasing live.

What discord and war then can find any entrance among those who are allotted eternal delight, who are perpetually propitious, and rejoicing in the goods which they possess? But if it be proper that discourses concerning the Gods should regard as well their providence as the nature of the beings for whom they provide, I think we may interpret as follows their opposition to each other:

In the first place, the divided progressions of all things, and their separations according to essence, supernally originate from that division of first operating causes[10] which is unknown to all things; and subsisting according to those principles which are expanded above wholes, they dissent from each other; some being suspended from the unifying monad *bound*, and about this determining their subsistence, but others receiving in themselves a never-failing power from that infinity which is generative of wholes, and is a cause productive of multitude and progression, and about this establishing their proper hyparxis. After the same manner, therefore, in which the first principles of things are separated from each other, all the divine genera and true beings have a progression orderly divided from each other; and some of them are the leaders of *union* to secondary natures, but others impart the power of *separation;* some are the causes of *conversion,* convolving the multitude of progressions to their proper principles; but others *bound the progressions*, and the subordinate *generation* from the principles. Again, some supply a *generative abundance* to inferior natures, but others impart an *immutable* and *undefiled purity;* some bind to themselves the cause of *separate* goods, but others, of those goods that are *consubsistent* with the beings by whom they are received. And thus in all the orders of being is such a contrariety of genera diversified. Hence *permanency,* which establishes things in themselves, is opposed to *efficacious powers*, and which are full of *life* and *motion*. Hence the kindred communion of *sameness* receives a division according to species, opposite to the separations of *difference;* but the genus of *similitude* is allotted an order contrary to *dissimilitude,* and that of *equality* to *inequality,* according to the same analogy. And the divisions of all these are

146

supernally defined from that duad which subsists as a principle, according to which all beings are distinguished by their proper boundaries, proceed with an opposite division to each other from their generative causes, and from their connection with each other generate all the variety of secondary natures. Is it therefore any longer wonderful, if the authors of fables, perceiving such contrariety in the Gods themselves and the first of beings, obscurely signified this to their pupils, through battles? the divine genera indeed being perpetually united to each other, but at the same time containing in themselves the causes of the union and separation of all things.

We may also, I think, adduce another mode of solution: that the Gods themselves are impartibly connascent with each other, and subsist uniformly in each other, but that their progressions into the universe and their communications are separated in their participants, become divisible, and are thus filled with contrariety; the objects of their providential exertions not being able to receive in an unmingled manner the powers proceeding from thence, and without confusion their multiform illuminations. We may likewise say, that the last orders which are suspended from divine natures, as being generated remote from first causes, and as being proximate to the subjects of their government, which are involved in matter, participate themselves of all-various contrariety and separation, and partibly preside over material natures, minutely dividing those powers which presubsist uniformly and impartibly in their first operating causes. Such then and so many being the modes according to which the mystic rumours of theologists are wont to refer war to the Gods themselves, other poets, and those who in explaining divine concerns have been agitated with divine fury, have ascribed wars and battles to the Gods, according to the first of those modes we related, in which the divine genera are divided conformably to the first principles of wholes. For those powers which *elevate to causes* are after a manner opposed to those that are the *sources of generation*, and the *connective* to the *separating;* those that *unite*, to those that *multiply* the progression of things; *total* genera, to such as fabricate *partibly;* and those which are *expanded above*, to those that *preside over* partial natures: and hence fables concealing the truth assert that such powers fight and war with each other. On this account, as it appears to me,

147

they assert that the Titans were the antagonists of Bacchus, and the Giants of Jupiter; for union, indivisible operation, and a wholeness prior[II] to parts, are adapted to those artificers that have a subsistence prior to the world; but the Titans and Giants produce the demiurgic powers into multitude, divisibly administer the affairs of the universe, and are the proximate fathers of material concerns.

We may also conceive that the Homeric fables after another manner have devised the battles of the Gods. For, in the first place, Homer exempts the demiurgic monad from all the multitude of the Gods, and neither represents him proceeding to the contrariety of generation, nor in any respect opposing it; but, while this is firmly established in itself, the number of the Gods proceeds from it, which number both abides and proceeds into the universe, and on this account is said to be divided about the providence of the natures *148* which it governs. In the next place, of these Gods which are distributed from their father, some abide in him, and have an unproceeding subsistence in their proper monad, which the poetry of Homer says are established in the abode of Jupiter, and together with their father providentially preside in an exempt manner over wholes. That these war against, or oppose each other, the fable does not even according to the apparent description admit. But it represents those Gods as warring against each other, who proceeding from the demiurgic monad, subside into multiform orders, become more partial, and more proximate to the objects of their government, and give completion to the angelic or dæmoniacal armies, through their abundant sympathy with subordinate natures and partial allotment of providential energy. For to these I think the passions of the subjects of their providential care are more allied, such as wounds, blows, and repercussions; and, in short, the contrariety of generation is not very remote from the administration of these Gods. That which is partial likewise in the fabrication of things secondary, and a minute distribution of providence, are adapted to such like powers, but not to those which rank as principles, and are exempt from all the objects of their providential energy, and subsist as separate causes.

Moreover, since the angelic orders are suspended from the government of the more excellent genera of Gods, and preserve the characteristics of their leaders though in a partial and multiplied

manner, they are called by their names; and as they subsist
analogously to the first Gods, they appear in their progressions to be
the same with their more total causes. And this not only the fables of
the Greeks have occultly devised,—I mean that leading Gods and
their attendants should be called by the same names,—but this is also
delivered in the initiatory rites of the Barbarians. For they say that
angels suspended from the Gods, when invoked, particularly rejoice to
be called by the appellations, and to be invested with the vehicles, of
the leaders of their series, and exhibit themselves to theurgists in the
place of these leading deities. If therefore we refer Minerva, Juno, and
Vulcan when engaged in war below about generation, and likewise
Latona, Diana, and the river Xanthus, to other secondary orders, and
149   which are proximate to divisible and material things, we ought not to
wonder on account of the communion of names. For each series bears
the appellation of its monad, and partial spirits love to receive the
same denomination with wholes. Hence there are many and all-
various Apollos, Neptunes, and Vulcans; and some of them are
separate from the universe, others have an allotment about the
heavens, others preside over the whole elements, and to others the
government of individuals belongs. It is not therefore wonderful if a
more partial Vulcan, and who is allotted a dæmoniacal order, possesses
a providential dominion over material fire, and which subsists about
the earth, or that he should be the inspective guardian of a certain art
which operates in brass. For, if the providence of the Gods has a
subjection according to an ultimate division, being allotted a well-
ordered progression supernally from total and united causes, this
Vulcanian dæmon also will rejoice in the safety of that which he is
allotted, and will be hostile to those causes which are corruptive of its
constitution. War therefore in such like genera, a division of all-
various powers, mutual familiarity and discord, a divisible sympathy
with the objects of their government, verbal contentions, revenge
through mockery, and other things of this kind, are very properly
conceived to take place about the terminations of the divine orders.
Hence fables, in representing such like powers discordant with and
opposing each other on account of the subjects over which they
providentially preside, do not appear to be very remote from the
truth. For the passions of the things governed are proximately

referred to these.

In short, since we may perceive two conceptions of battles celebrated by poets inspired by Phœbus, one of these considers the well-ordered division of the divine genera about those two principles of wholes which *the one*, the exempt cause of all things, produced, and according to the opposition of these principles represents the Gods also as acting contrary to each other. For, whether it be proper to call those first natures bound and infinity, or monad and indefinite duad, they will entirely appear to be oppositely divided with respect to each other, according to which the orders of the Gods are also separated from each other. But the other conception arises from considering the contrariety and variety about the last of things, and referring a discord of this kind to the powers that proximately preside over it, and thus feigning that the Gods, proceeding into a material nature, and distributed about this, war with each other. Homer, to those who consider his poems with attention, will appear to speak about the former mode of divine contention when he says,

> When Saturn was by Jove all-seeing thrust
> Beneath the earth:

And in another place[12] respecting Typhon,

> Earth groan'd beneath them; as when angry Jove
> Hurls down the forky lightning from above,
> On Arime when he the thunder throws,
> And fires Typhæus with redoubled blows,
> Where Typhon, prest beneath the burning load,
> Still feels the fury of th' avenging God.

For in these verses he obscurely signifies a Titanic war against Jupiter, and what the Orphic writers call precipitations into Tartarus (καταταρταρωσεις). But he particularly introduces the Gods warring with each other, and dissenting about human affairs, according to the second conception of divine battles, in which the divine and intellectual disposition of the figments adopted by the poet is worthy of the greatest admiration. For, in describing their battles (who though they are allotted a subsistence at the extremities of the divine progressions, yet are suspended from the Gods, and are proximate to the subjects of their government, and are allied to their leaders), he indicates their sympathy with inferior natures, referring a divided life, battle, and opposition from things in subjection to the powers by which they are governed; just as Orpheus conjoins with Bacchic images compositions, divisions and lamentations, referring all these to them from presiding causes. But Homer represents the alliance of these divisible spirits with the series from which they proceed, by the same names through which he celebrates the powers exempt from material natures, and employs numbers and figures adapted to their whole orders. For those who engage in battle are eleven in number, imitating the army of the Gods and dæmons following Jupiter, and distributed into eleven[13] parts. Of these, those that preside over the better coordination are contained in the pentad; for the odd number, the spheric,[14] and the power of leading all secondary natures according to justice, and of extending from the middle to every number, are adapted to those who desire to govern more intellectual and perfect natures, and such as are more allied to *the one.* But those of an inferior destiny, and who are the guardians of material natures, proceed according to the hexad, possessing indeed a perfective power over the subjects of their providential care through a proper[15] number; but in consequence of this number being even, and coordinate with a worse nature, they are subordinate to the other powers. Nor is it wonderful if same one should call these genera Gods, through their alliance to their leaders, and should represent them as warring through their proximate care of material natures. The opposition therefore of Neptune and Apollo signifies that these powers preside over the apparent contrariety of all sublunary wholes: and hence these Gods do not fight with each other. For parts are preserved by their containing wholes, as long as they subsist. But the opposition of Juno and Diana referents the opposite division of souls in the universe, whether rational or irrational, separate or inseparable, supernatural or natural; the former of these powers presiding over the more excellent order of souls, but the latter bringing forth and producing into light those of all inferior condition. Again, the discord of Minerva and Mars represents the division of the whole of the war in generation into providence subsisting according to intellect, and that which is perfected through necessity; the former power intellectually presiding over contraries, and the latter corroborating their natural powers, and exciting their mutual opposition. But the battle between Hermes and Latona insinuates the all-various differences of souls according to their gnostic and vital motions; Hermes giving perfection to their knowledge, and Latona to their lives; which two often differ from and are contrary to each other. Lastly, the battle between Vulcan and the river Xanthus adorns in a becoming manner the contrary principles of the whole corporeal system; the former assisting the powers of heat and dryness, and the latter of cold and moisture, from which the whole of generation receives its completion. But since it is requisite that all contrarieties should end in mutual concord, Venus is present, producing friendship[16] in the adverse parties, but at the same time assisting those powers that belong to the worse coordination; because these are especially adorned, when they possess symmetry and familiarity with the better order of contrary natures. And thus much concerning the divine battles of Homer.

III. IN WHAT MANNER AN APOLOGY IS TO BE MADE FOR THOSE DIVINE FABLES WHICH APPEAR TO MAKE THE GODS THE CAUSES OF EVIL.

In the next place let us consider how, since the Gods in the summit of their essence are particularly characterized by goodness, poetry makes them to be the authors of both evil and good, though it is proper to refer to them the principal cause of what is good alone. For this, Socrates, demonstrating that divinity gives subsistence to good alone, but to nothing evil, thinks worthy of animadversion in the poems of Homer. And it seems that he reprobates the battles of the Gods, as subverting divine union, but condemns what we now propose to investigate, as diminishing the goodness of the Gods. For,

> Two vessels on Jove's threshold ever stand,
> The source of evil one, and one of good.[17]

To this objection, we answer that there are two coordinations of things in the world, which, as we have before observed, supernally proceed from the Gods themselves. For all things are divided by the biformed principles[18] of things, *viz.* the orders of the Gods, the natures of beings, the genera of soul, physical powers, the circulations of the heavens, and the diversities of material things; and lastly human affairs, and allotments according to justice, thence receive a two-fold generation. For, of these, some are of a better, and others of an inferior condition. I mean, for instance, that the natural habits of bodies, *viz.* beauty, strength, health, and also such things as, independent of the corporeal constitution, pertain to souls, *viz.* power, and honour, and riches, belong to allotments of a better condition; but those habits and circumstances which are opposite to these, belong to those of an inferior condition. These things then being necessarily divided after the above-mentioned manner, those which belong to the better portion it was usual with the ancients immediately to denominate good, but those of the contrary portion they denominated evil; yet not in the same signification as when we call an unjust and intemperate habit of the soul evil; but as impediments of energies, as darkening our natural dispositions, and disturbing the providence of the soul in its tranquil management of human affairs, they admitted them to be evil, and to be so denominated, but after a different manner from what are called the evils of the soul. Thus also they were accustomed to call disease, imbecility, and a privation of the necessaries of life, evils. And why is it necessary to adduce all poetry as a witness of the use of this name? For the Pythagoreans also, in establishing two-fold coordinations[19] of things in all orders, did not refuse to call one of these good, and the other evil. Though, how can any one admit that the even, the oblong, and motion, are to be enumerated among those evils which we define as privations of good? How can we say that the feminine, the genus of difference and of dissimilitude, are contrary to nature? But I think this entirely evident, that, according to every progression of things, they called the subordinate series of things opposite, evil, as deserting the other series, and being neither primarily beneficent, nor distant by the same interval from the one cause of every thing beautiful and good, It is requisite therefore to suspend these two-fold coordinations of good and evil in the universe from the demiurgic monad. For the divisions of the Gods, and of the genera posterior to the Gods, depend on that first principle. The cause likewise of the good and evil which happen from fate, and which are allotted to souls about generation, according to justice, must be referred to the dispensator of the universe, who also sends souls into the region of mortality. For the effects of fate are suspended from demiurgic providence, about which the series of justice also subsists, and the boundaries of which it follows, being, as the Athenian guest in Plato observes, the avenger of the divine law. Lastly, the gifts of fortune, and the distribution of all things according to justice, are determined according to the will of the father. The demiurgus and father therefore of the universe has pre-established in himself the cause of every thing good and evil, of more excellent and subordinate gifts, of prosperous events, and of such as are impediments to the energies of the soul in externals; and he governs all things according to intellect, distributing to every being such things as are fit, and referring all things to his own paternal administration. For he distributes to souls, with a view to good, both things of the better and of the inferior coordination; looking in his distribution to the perfection of the recipients.

If these things then are rightly asserted we must admit the Homeric arrangement, which places in the demiurgic intellect of Jupiter twofold primary causes of the goods and the ills which he imparts to souls. For, of all the intellectual kings, the duad especially belongs to the demiurgus of the universe: since, according to the Oracle, "the duad is seated with him; and, by his governing all things, and disposing every thing in its proper place, he shows virtue to be victorious, and vice to be vanquished in the universe." For what difference is there between asserting these things, and comparing the demiurgus to one playing at chess, and sending souls in to lives adapted to their respective natures? These two fountains therefore of a better and worse condition of things, by which the demiurgus conducts souls according to justice, the poet mythologizing denominates *tubs;*[20] whether indicating that divinity assigns to every thing its proper boundary through intellectual *persuasion* (for intellect, says Timæus, is the principle of necessity, persuading it to lead all things to that which is best), or the capaciousness of these principles, and their comprehending all-various effects. For the demiurgus and father of the universe contains unitedly in himself the dispersed multitude of all that he distributes to souls. So that, according to this reasoning, Plato and the Homeric poetry accord with each other. For the former says that it is not proper to make God the cause of any evil; but the other perpetually produces every thing

good from thence: yet, since goods are two-fold, and each kind
benefits those by whom it is received, hence the Homeric poetry
distributes them into twofold coordinations, and, indicating their
difference with respect to each other, denominates the one as
absolutely good, but places the other separate, as contrary to good. But
that what is called evil by Homer is not such as that which Plato
denies to be given by the Gods, the poet himself declares in the
following verses,[21]

> The Gods on Peleus from his birth bestow'd
> illustrious gifts . . . .
> With these God also evil join'd . . . .

What this evil is he immediately tells us:

> No race succeeding to imperial sway;
> An only son, and he (alas!) ordain'd
> To fall untimely in a foreign land.
> See him in Troy the pious care decline
> Of his weak age, to live the curse of thine!

In these verses, it appears that Homer does not make divinity the
cause of real evils, since he calls the loss of a son, and the being
deprived of his attendance in old age, evils. But in what manner these
are evils, we have above explained, *viz.* so far as they cause difficulty in
the present life, and sorrow in the soul. For, though it is not lawful for
those who philosophize in a genuine manner to call these evils, yet
they appear to be impediments of a life according to virtue, to those
who make choice of a practical life.. Hence the Athenian guest also
contends that all such things are, in a certain respect, evil to good
men, but good to such as are depraved; though he makes God to be
the cause, both of these, and of every thing imparted from the
universe. So that not only Homer, and Achilles in Horner assert these
things, but Plato himself, and the legislator according to Plato.

IV. HOW THE POETRY Of HOMER SEEMS TO REFER A VIOIATION OF
OATHS TO THE GODS:—THE TRUTH RESPECTing THIS U NFOLDED.

In the net place let us consider how leagues and oaths, according to
the poetry of Homer, are violated with the will of he mighty Jupiter,

and of Minerva acting in subserviency to the will of her father: for this also Socrates reprobates, a referring the principle of evils to the first. of the Gods.

And here indeed it is worth while especially to doubt, how he who makes divinity to be the cause of these things, does not make him to be the cause of the greatest and real evils. For Homer cannot here be defended by saying, that he represents poverty, disease, and things of this kind, as proceeding from the Gods, but he ascribes to divinity the cause of these things which are acknowledged by all men to be evils. Timæus, indeed, in Plato, represents the demiurgus as entirely prescribing laws to souls prior to their descent into generation, that he may not be accused as the cause of their consequent evils; but these verses of Homer admit that the principle of the greatest evils is imparted to them from divinity, when they have descended, and are conversant with generation. How then shall we reply to these animadversions, so as to harmonize the doctrine of Homer with the nature of things, and the narration of Plato? We may reply as follows: That fables of this kind are not adapted to the habit of youth, as has been asserted by us before, and we shall now, and in all that follows repeat the assertion. For it is not possible for youth to distinguish the nature of things, nor to refer the apparent signs of truth to an unapparent theory, nor to see how every thing in the universe is accomplished according to the will of divinity, through other intervening causes. But we shall show that these things are agreeable to the philosophy of Plato.

The Athenian guest then, in the Laws, says, that "God is the beginning, the middle, and end of all things, and that justice follows him, taking vengeance on those that desert the divine law: but these, as he informs us, are such as through youth and folly have their soul inflamed with insolence, and for a certain time appear to themselves to govern, but afterwards suffer the proper punishment of their conduct from justice, and entirely subvert themselves, their city, and their family." These things are asserted by the Athenian guest politically; but Homer,[22] relating them in a divinely inspired manner (ενθεαστικω), says that those who have often sinned, and committed the greatest crimes, are punished for their offences according to the single will of Jupiter, and are deprived of life together with their wives

157

and children. He further informs us, that Jupiter first of all accomplishes this punishment, and in a manner exempt and unapparent to all; but Minerva in the second place, being subservient to and cooperating with the paternal providence of Jupiter; for, as Orpheus says, "she is the powerful queen of the intellect of Saturnian Jove."[23] The same poet likewise adds, that "his brain who violates leagues and oaths shows on the ground like wine." In consequence, therefore, of this violation, such men subject themselves to justice, and render themselves adapted to punishment. Hence the violation of leagues and oaths is especially perpetrated by those who, prior to this, have deserved the vengeance of the Gods, who justly govern mortal affairs and thus punish former crimes. But such are said to be moved, and led forth into energy by the Gods themselves: not that the Gods render men who are to be punished impious and unjust, but as calling into energy those that are adapted to the perpetration of such-like actions, that by once energizing according to their inward habit and producing into light the progeny of depraved actions with which they are pregnant, they may become worthy of punishment. For we should rather say, according to Plato, that vengeance, the attendant of justice, is perfected in such, than divine justice itself; since the just and justice are beautiful things. But both he on whom vengeance is inflicted, and he on whom it is not, are miserable. Men therefore, who have committed many and the greatest crimes, and who have a depraved habit which is parturient with greater and more weighty evil, in the first place sustain vengeance, which appears indeed to crush those that suffer it, leading them to the violation of oaths, but in reality brings them to suffer the punishment of their crimes, effecting that which is similar to the opening of ulcers by the surgeon's instrument, which produces an increase of pain at the time, but, by discharging the putridity and the latent humour, becomes the cause of future health. But the poetry of Homer says that this punishment, beginning supernally from Jupiter (for justice, as we have before observed, follows him, taking vengeance on those that desert the divine law), is perfected through Minerva as the medium. For the Trojans, seeing into what an evil they had brought themselves, and that their life was obnoxious to deserved punishment, rendered this inevitable to themselves, by the violation of oaths and leagues.

Again then, it must be in the first place said that the Gods were not the causes of this confused and disorderly conduct to the Trojans, but that they through their own depravity rendered themselves worthy of an energy of this kind, and among these Pandarus in an eminent degree, as being a man ambitious, avaricious, and leading an atheistical life. Hence Minerva, proceeding according to the intellect of her father, does not excite any one casually to this action, but is said to seek Pandarus,[24] as particularly adapted to an avenging energy.

She ev'ry where the godlike Pandarus explor'd.[25]

For a man who is capable of doing and suffering any thing, and who also opposes himself to divinity, through a certain gigantic and audacious habit of soul, is rare, and truly difficult to be found. As therefore physicians are not the causes of cuttings and burnings, but the diseases of those that are cured, so neither are the Gods the causes of the impiety respecting oaths and leagues, but the habits of those by whom it is committed.

In the second place, this also must be considered, that Minerva is not said to prepare Pandarus for the deed, but only to try if he gave himself up to this energy. For divinity does not destroy the freedom of the will, not even in such as are consummately wicked:

Lycaon's warlike son, what I suggest,
Wilt thou obey?

But Pandarus, incited by an immoderate desire of riches and power, leaps to unjust energies, the poet all but exclaiming in the very words of Socrates in the Republic,[26] that "many things are extended to souls from the universe, which astonish the stupid, and cause them to err respecting the elections of lives." As therefore the prophet extends a tyrannic life, and he who first chooses this is said to be stupid, although he by whom it was extended was entirely a divine nature; so here, when Minerva offers to the choice of Pandarus a more powerful and rich condition with impiety, or one entirely contrary to this, he makes choice of the worse. And in this case Minerva is not the cause of the election, but the improbity of him by whom the election is made. For neither is the prophet in Plato the cause of a tyrannic life, but the intemperance of him that chose it. Hence Pandarus, in obeying Minerva, is said to suffer this through his stupidity. For

159

indeed (to speak accurately) he did not obey Minerva, but the avaricious and stupid habit of his soul. Though, is it not wonderful that Minerva, in this instance, is not the cause of wisdom, but of folly? But, says, Plotinus, "Craft is produced from a defluxion of intellect; an illumination of temperance becomes intemperance; and audacity is the gift of fortitude." For such as are the forms of life, such also from necessity must be the participations from more excellent natures. Hence some participate of intelligibles intellectually, others according to opinion, and others phantastically. Others again participate of passions impassively, others with mediocrity of passion, and others with perfect passivity. But all things are moved by the Gods, according to their respective aptitudes. So that the violation of oaths did not proceed from Jupiter and Minerva, but from Pandarus and the Trojans. This action however is suspended from the Gods, as being the forerunner of justice, and as preparing those by whom it was perpetrated for the perfect punishment of their guilt.

Nor is a divine nature the cause of true evil to souls, but the depraved habits of these are the sources to them of their depraved energies. But every energy, though it proceeds with depravity into the universe, is under the direction of presiding Gods, and of a more total or partial providence. For it becomes, says Plotinus, an unjust action to him who does it, so far as pertains to the doing it, but just to him who suffers for it, so far as he suffers. And so far as an action of this kind is atheistical, it originates from a partial cause, which gives perfection to an action full of passion; but so far as it is good, it obtains from presiding powers its proper end. For it is necessary that the authors of the greatest crimes should some time or other be called to punishment; but this would never take place, unless their depravity received its completion. Many habits therefore, remaining unenergetic, render those by whom they are possessed incapable of obtaining their proper cure. Hence, on the Gods consulting concerning bringing the war to an end, and saving the Trojans, the goddess who presides over justice prevents any energy of this kind, that the Trojans may more swiftly suffer the punishment of their crimes; and Minerva, who cooperates with this divinity, excites to the violation of the oath, that, energizing according to the whole of their depravity, they may receive the punishment of the whole of it. For neither was it good for them to remain without a cure, nor that their latent depravity should be healed prior to their second offences. All their unjust life therefore being unfolded, punishment follows, correcting the whole of their impious conduct.

V. THE WHOLE THEORY OF THE FABLE UNFOLDED, IN WHICH
JUPITER, THROUGH THEMIS, EXCITES THE GODS TO CONTENTION.

In the next place, since Socrates mentions the judgment of the Gods in Homer, and the strife to which Jupiter excites the multitude of the Gods, through Themis elevating all of them to himself, let us also speak concerning these things. That Jupiter then is a monad separated from the universe, and the multitude of mundane Gods, and that he is able to produce all things from, and again convert them to himself, has often been said. But since his energy proceeding to the multitude of Gods is two-fold, one of which converts and the other moves the Gods to the providence of inferior natures, poetry also describes two-fold speeches[27] of Jupiter to the Gods. According to the first of these, the one and whole demiurgus of the universe is represented as communicating an unmingled purity to the multitude of the Gods, and imparting to them powers separate from all division about the world. Hence he orders all the Gods to desist from the war and the contrariety of mundane affairs. But, according to the second of these speeches, he excites them to the providence of subordinate natures, and permits their divided progressions into the universe, that they may not only be contained in one demiurgic intellect, which, as the poet says,

None can escape, or soaring run beyond—

but may energize in the subjects of their providential care, according to their own characteristics. Hence Jupiter says to them,

Each, as your minds incline, to either host
Your succour lend.[28]

But as the progressions of the Gods are not divulsed from the demiurgic monad, Themis first converts them to this monad.

But Jove to Themis gives command, to call
The Gods to council—

that, acting providentially according to the will of their father, they may also energize according to the judgment of Themis. And the poet indeed delivers to us separate speeches of the one demiurgus of the universe to the junior Gods; but Timæus represents him in one speech converting the multitude of these Gods to himself, and exciting them to the providence of mortal affairs, that they may govern all *162* secondary natures according to justice. But these things in no respect differ from exciting them to war, and through Themis converting them to himself. For those who preside over generation govern the war in matter; and those who energize according to justice are suspended from the whole of Themis, of whom justice is the daughter, and imitate the one demiurgic intellect to whom it is not lawful to do any thing but what is most beautiful, as Timæus himself asserts.

VI. WHAT THE JUDGMENT OF THE GODS IS IN THE FABLFS OF THE POET, AND WHAT DIFFERENCES OF LIVES IT OBSCURELY SIGNIFIES.

Again, it is not proper to think that the celebrated judgment of the Gods, which fables say was accomplished by Paris, was in reality a strife of the Gods with each other, under the judgment of a barbarian; but we ought to consider the elections of lives, which Plato delivers in many places, as subsisting under the Gods who are the inspection guardians of souls. And this indeed Plato clearly teaches us in the Phædrus, when he says that a royal life is the gift of Juno, a philosophic life of Jupiter, and an amatory life of Venus. Since therefore souls, from among a multitude of lives proposed to them from the universe, embrace some according to their own judgment and reject others, hence fables, transferring to the Gods themselves the peculiarities of lives, assert that not the diversities of living, but the Gods that preside over these diversities, are judged by those that choose them. According to this reasoning, Paris also is said to have been appointed a judge of Minerva, Juno and Venus; and that of three lives which were proposed to him, he chose the amatory life: and this not with prudence, but recurring to apparent beauty, and pursuing the image of that beauty which is intelligible. For he who is truly amatory, taking intellect and prudence for his guides, and with these contemplating both true and apparent beauty, is no less the votary of

Minerva than of Venus. But he who alone pursues the amatory form of life by itself, and this accompanied with passion, deserts true beauty, but through folly and luxury leaps to the image of beauty, lies about it in a fallen condition, and does not attain to a perfection adapted to an amatory character. For he who is truly amatory and studious of Venus, is led to divine beauty, and despises all that is beautiful in the regions of sense. Since however there are certain dæmons with the characteristics of Venus, who preside over apparent beauty, and which subsists in matter, hence he who embraces the image of beauty, is said to have Venus cooperating with him in all his undertakings.

VII. WHAT THE MUTATIONS OF THE GODS ARE, WHICH ARE INTRODUCED IN FABLES, AND IN HOW MANY WAYS, AND THROUGH WHAT CAUSES, THEY ARE DEVISED.

Since a divine nature is not only beneficent, but likewise immutable, without form, simple, and always subsisting according to the same, and after the same manner, Socrates very properly considers the following verses of Homer worthy of animadversion,

> The Gods at times, resembling foreign guests,
> Wander o'er cities in all-various forms.[29]

And again those respecting Proteus and Thetis, in which they are represented as changing their forms, and variously appearing. Indeed, that fables of this kind ought not to be heard by those who genuinely receive a political education, is perfectly evident; since it is requisite that the paradigm of a polity which is to be stable, should be immutable, and not obnoxious to all-various mutations. But here also it is requisite to collect by reasoning the divine dianoëtic conceptions of Homer, though I am not ignorant that the above verses are ascribed to one of the suitors, and that on this account the poet is free from blame. For neither should we think it right to take the opinion of Plato from what is said by Callicles or Thrasymachus, or any other sophists that are introduced in his writings; but when Parmenides or Socrates, or Timæus, or any other of such divine men speaks, then we think that we hear the dogmas of Plato. In like manner we should form at judgment of the conceptions of Homer, not from what is said by the suitors, or any other depraved character in his poems, but from what the poet himself, or Nestor, or Ulysses, appears to say.

If any one however is willing to ascribe this dogma concerning the mutation of the Gods to Homer himself, he will not be destitute of arguments which accord with all sacred concerns, with the greatest sacrifices and mysteries, and with those appearances of the Gods which both in dreams and true visions, the rumour of mankind has supernally received. For in all these the Gods extend many forms of themselves, and appear passing into many figures. And sometimes an unfigured light of them presents itself to the view; at other times this light is fashioned in a human form, and at others again assumes a different shape. These things also the discipline of divine origin pertaining to sacred concerns delivers. For thus the Oracles[30] speak:

> "A similar fire extending itself by leaps through the waves of the air; or an unfigured fire whence a voice runs before; or a light beheld near, every way splendid, resounding and convolved. But also to behold a horse full of refulgent light; or a boy carried on the swift back of a horse,—a boy fiery, or clothed with gold, or, on the contrary, naked; or shooting an arrow, and standing on the back of the horse."

And such things as the oracles add after these, not at any time attributing either internal change, or variety, or any mutation to a divine nature, but indicating its various participations. For that which is simple in the Gods appears various to those by whom it is seen, they neither being changed, nor wishing to deceive; but nature herself giving a determination to the characteristics of the Gods, according to the measures of the participants. For that which is participated, being one, is variously participated by intellect, the rational soul, the phantasy, and sense. For the first of these participates it impartibly, the second in an expanded manner, the third accompanied with figure, and the fourth with passivity. Hence that which is participated is uniform according to the summit of its subsistence, but multiform according to participation. It is also essentially immutable and firmly established, but at different times appearing various to its participants through the imbecility of their nature. And not only these things follow, but that which is without weight appears heavy to those that are filled with it: "The miserable heart by whom I am received cannot bear[31] me," says some one of the Gods. Whence Homer also perceiving the truth of these things through divine inspiration says concerning Minerva:

> Loud crash'd the beechen axle with the weight,
> For strong and dreadful was the power it bore.[32]

Though here it may be said, how can that which is without weight be the cause of weight? But such as is the participant, such necessarily must that which is participated appear.[33] Whether, therefore, some of the Gods have appeared similar to guests, or have been seen in some other form, it is not proper to attribute the apparent mutation to them, but we should say that the phantasy is varied in the different recipients. And this is one way in which the poetry of Homer delivers multiform mutations of immutable natures.

But there is another way, when a divine nature itself, which is all powerful and full of all-various forms, extends various spectacles to those that behold it. For then, according to the variety of powers which it possesses, it is said to be changed into many forms, at different times extending different powers; always indeed energizing according to all its powers, but perpetually appearing various to the transitive intellections of souls, through the multitude which it comprehends. According to this mode, Proteus also is said to change his proper form to those that behold it, perpetually exhibiting a different appearance. For though he is subordinate to the first Gods, and immortal indeed, but not a God; the minister of Neptune, but not allotted a leading dignity; yet he is a certain angelic intellect belonging to the series of Neptune, possessing and comprehending in himself all the forms of generated natures. Idothea has the first arrangement under him; the being a certain dæmoniacal soul conjoined to Proteus as to her proper divine intellect, and connecting her intellections with his intelligible forms. Another number of rational and perpetual souls follows, which the fable denominates Phocæ. Hence Proteus is represented as *numbering* these, poetry indicating by this the perpetuity of their nature. For the multitude of things which are generated and perish is *indefinite*. Partial souls therefore beholding Proteus, who is an intellect possessing many powers and full of forms, whilst at different times they convert

166

themselves to the different forms which he contains, fancy that the transition of their own intellections is a mutation of the intelligible objects. Hence to those that retain him he appears to become all things—

> Water, and fire divine, and all that creeps
> On earth.

For such forms as he possesses and comprehends, or rather such as he perpetually is, such does he appear to become when these forms are considered separately, through the divisible conception of those that behold them.

In the third place, therefore, we say that the Gods appear to be changed, when the same divinity proceeds according to different orders, and subsides as far as to the last of things, multiplying himself according to number, and descending into subject distinctions; for then again fables say, that the divinity, which supernally proceeds into this form, is changed to that into which it makes its progression. Thus they say that Minerva was assimilated to Mentor, Mercury to the bird called the sea-gull, and Apollo to a hawk; indicating by this their more dæmoniacal orders, into which they proceed from those of a superior rank, Hence when they describe the *divine* advents of the Gods, they endeavour to preserve them formless and unfigured. Thus, when Minerva appears to Achilles,[34] and becomes visible to him alone, the whole camp being present, there Homer does not even fabulously ascribe any form and figure to the goddess, but only says that she was present, without expressing the manner in which she was present. But when they intend to signify angelic appearances, they introduce the Gods under various forms, but these such as are total; as for instance, a human form, or one common to man or woman indefinitely. For thus, again, Neptune and Minerva were present with Achilles:

> Neptune and Pallas haste to his relief,
> And thus in *human form* address the chief.[35]

Lastly, when they relate dæmoniacal advents, then they do not think it improper to describe their mutations into individuals and partial natures; whether into particular men, or other animals. For the last of those genera that are the perpetual attendants of the Gods are manifested by these figures. And here you may see how particulars of this kind are devised according to the order of things. For that which is simple is adapted to a divine nature, that which is universal to an angelic, and the rational nature to both these; and that which is partial and irrational accords with a dæmoniacal nature for a life of this kind is connected with the dæmoniacal order. And thus much concerning the modes according to which the Homeric fables devise mutations of things immutable, and introduce various forms to uniform natures.

VIII. CONCERNING THE DREAM SENT TO AGAMEMNON, WHICH APPEARS TO ACCUSE THE GODS OF FALSEHOOD, AND HOW IT MAY BE SHOWN THAT A DIVINE NATURE IS VOID OF FALSEHOOD.

It now remains that we speak concerning the dream sent by Jupiter to Agamemnon; for Socrates, at the end of his theological types, reprobates this, because the whole of a divine and dæmoniacal nature is without falsehood, as he collects by demonstrative arguments. But Homer says that Agamemnon was deceived through this dream. Though, is it not absurd, if this dream is from Jupiter, according to the assertion of the poet, that this alone nearly, of all the particulars which are mentioned as deriving their origin from Jupiter, should be attended with fraud? *168*

In answer to this objection, we may say what is usually asserted by most of the interpreters, that the fallacy had its subsistence in the phantasy of Agamemnon. For Jupiter in his speech to the dream, and the dream again in its address to Agamemnon, evidently indicate that it would be requisite to call together *all* the army, and to attack the enemy with *all* his forces; for this is the meaning of the word πανσυδίη in, which is used in both the speeches. But Agamemnon, not understanding the mandate, neglected the greatest part of his army, and, engaging in battle without the aid of Achilles, was frustrated in his expectations through his unskillfulness in judging of divine visions. So that Jupiter is not the cause of the deception, but he who did not properly understand the mandates of Jupiter.

We shall also add the solution given by our preceptor Syrianus, which both accedes to the meaning of Homer and the truth of things. For, if Jupiter is represented as providing for the honour of the hero

Achilles, and consulting how he may destroy the greatest number of
the Greeks, is it not necessary that he must previously comprehend in
himself the cause of the deception? For, if Achilles had been associated
with the army, the Greeks would not have been destroyed, nor would
they have been punished for their unjust conduct towards him. It is
better therefore to say that the deception was from divinity for the
good of the deceived. For good is better than truth. And among the
Gods, indeed, they are conjoined with each other: for neither is
intellect without divinity, nor divinity without an intellectual
essence. But in their participants they are often separated; and good is
produced through falsehood, and truth is frustrated of good. Whence
also Socrates himself, when he is framing laws for the guardians of his
republic, orders falsehood to be employed, through the opinion of the
stupid, who are not otherwise able to obtain the good which is
adapted to their condition. If therefore it be said that divinity benefits
some through truth, and others through falsehood, and at the same
time leads all of them to good, it is by no means wonderful. For, of
generated natures, some subsist without matter, but others with
matter, in which fallacy is inherent; or, rather, matter is true fallacy
itself. So that, in the providence of souls, if they are, as we have said,
variously benefited by divinity, some immaterially through truth, but
others materially through falsehood, such providential energy will be
adapted to the nature of the Gods.

But, if it be requisite, this also may be asserted, that deception and
falsehood are generated in the participant, and that this takes place
according to the will of divinity, that he who has acted erroneously
may through the deception become more worthy: just as that which is
material is generated in these lower regions, but subsists according to
demiurgic providence, that there may be generation and corruption
in order to the completion of the universe. Divinity therefore does
not deceive, but he who is deceived is deceived by himself; and this
takes place, according to the will of divinity for the good of him who
sustains the deception. For, God making immaterially, that which is
generated is generated materially; and he energizing impartibly, that
which proceeds from this energy, receives its completion partibly; and
he signifying intellectually, falsehood obtains a shadowy subsistence
in the being that receives what is signified. But the divine poet himself

169

manifests, that, truth dwelling with the Gods, deception is generated from the opinion of the recipients, when he makes Jupiter commanding the dream say—

All that I order tell with *perfect* truth.

How then is there falsehood in divinity, according to Homer? And how is divinity the cause of deception? Unless it should be said he is the cause in such a manner, as that neither is the shadowy subsistence of deception in these lower regions contrary to his will. But the habit of youth is incapable of distinguishing and contemplating, how, wholes remaining void of evil, in the natures which receive them divisibly evil appears; how, natures more excellent than ours not deceiving, we are often deceived; and how, when deceived, we suffer this according to the will of providence. Hence Socrates is not willing   *170* that young men should hear things of this kind, as being incapable of forming properly distinct opinions of things.

IX. A COMMON APOLOGY BOTH FOR THE HOMERIC AND PLATONIC FABLES, IN WHICH THEY SPEAK OF THE JUDGMENTS IN HADES, OF SOULS, AND THE DIFFERENT ALLOTMENTS WHICH THEY RECEIVE ON DEPARTING FROM THEIR BODIES, ACCORDING TO THE IDIOMS OF THE LIFE IN THE BODY.

Having then discussed these things, let us examine what is written in the third book of the Republic, and, prior to other things, what the poet either himself asserts, or introduces another asserting, mythologically concerning Hades; and let us consider whether they contain anything of truth, and accord with the narrations of Plato. What then are we to understand, when the poet represents Achilles as preferring servitude in the present life to the possession of every thing in Hades? What is the meaning of those dreadful habitations, which are odious to the Gods, of the image and the soul, of shades wandering without intellect, of lives compared to shadows, of the lamentations of souls passing thither, of their being assimilated to bats, of smoke, a crashing noise, and such like particulars, which the poems of Homer contain? What likewise are the rivers in Hades, and those appellations, which are the most tragical? For these Socrates reprobates, but at the same time adds, what is common to all fables, "that they contribute to something else; but we," says he, "are afraid for our guardians, lest from these terrible relations, they should think death to be dreadful."

However, that Socrates himself in many places uses names and ænigmas of this kind, is obvious to every one. For, that I may omit the rivers mentioned in the Phædo, the wanderings of souls, their anxieties, the three roads, the punishments, the being carried in rivers, the lamentations and exclamations there, and the supplications of injurers to the injured, of all which Plato says Hades is full;— though these things should be omitted, yet does not what we find written at the end of the Republic accord with the intention of the Homeric poetry, *viz.* the bellowing mouth, Tartarus, fiery dæmous, the tearing off the flesh of the tyrant Aridæus, and souls full of dust and filth? For, what is there in these which falls short of the tragical in the extreme? So that for the same reason these also are to be rejected, or the Homeric doctrine is not to be reprehended. In defence of both therefore, whether some Epicurean or any other endeavours to accuse such-like fables, we say, that the habits of souls liberated from the body are different, and the places of the universe are multiform, into which they are introduced. Of these also some are so separated from mortal instruments, as neither to have any habitude to things of a worse condition, nor to be filled with the tumult which they contain, and material inanity. The vehicles of such are necessarily pure and luciform, not disturbed by material vapours, nor thickened by a terrestrial nature. But others who are not yet perfectly purified by philosophy, but are drawn down to an affection towards the testaceous body, and pursue a life conjoined with this,—these exhibit such like vehicles suspended from their essence to those who are capable of beholding them, *viz.* shadowy, material, drawing downwards by their weight, and attracting much of a mortal condition. Hence Socrates, in the Phædo, says that such souls, rolling about sepulchres, exhibit shadowy phantasms; and the poet relates that they are impelled along similar to shadows.

Further still, of those souls which yet embrace a corporeal life there are many differences. For some live a more practic life, and not yet deserting a life of this kind, embrace an organ adapted to practical energies, from which when they are separated they are indignant; as was the case with the soul of Patroclus,

> Which leaving youth and manhood wail'd its fate.

And when in Hades, they still desire an association with this organ, as did the soul of Achilles,[36] because he preferred a life on earth to a separate life, according to which he was not able to energize, but very much excelled in an active life. Others again, through the infelicity of their condition, eagerly embrace the testaceous body, and think that the life conjoined with it differs in no respect from the proper life of the soul. Such as these the divine poetry of Homer assimilates to bats, as looking to that which is dark in the universe, and its very extremity, and which may be denominated a stupendous cavern; and as having the winged nature of the soul gross and terrestrial. Is it therefore wonderful that Achilles, who possessed practical virtue, should desire a life in conjunction with body, and which was capable of being subservient to his actions? For Hercules, being purified through the telestic science, and partaking of undefiled fruits, obtained a perfect restoration among the Gods; whence the poet says of him,

172

> He with th' immoital Gods delighted lives,
> And beauteous Hebe crowns his joys.———

But Achilles, since he embraces rectitude in practical affairs, and the present life, pursues also and desires an instrument adapted to this life. Plato himself, therefore, also says that souls according to the manners to which they have been accustomed, make choice of secondary lives. Is not this likewise worthy of admiration in the divine tradition of Homer—I mean the separation of the soul from its image, and intellect from the soul? Also that the soul is said to use the image,[37] but that intellect is more divine than both these? And again, that the image and the soul may in a certain respect be known while yet detained in the body; and that the soul takes care of and providentially attends to the testaceous body, and, when this is not effected, desires its accomplishment; but that intellect is incomprehensible by our phantastic and figured motions? Hence Achilles, on beholding Patroclus speaking concerning the burial of his body, was led to believe that the soul and its image were in Hades, but that intellect was not there, nor prudence, by which these are used. For the energies of the irrational life hastened to adopt this position, but could not credit the reception of the intellectual soul in Hades from the visions of dreams.

Does it not also most perfectly accord with things themselves to say, that the multitude of souls depart from their bodies lamenting, and are divulsed from them with difficulty, through the alluring life and manifold pleasures which they enjoy in them? For every corporeal pleasure, as Socrates says in the Phædo, as if armed with a nail, fastens the soul to the body.

173 And such souls after deserting their bodies use shadowy vehicles, which are disturbed by the ponderous and terrene vapours[38] of the Sirens, and utter an uncertain voice, and a material sound, which the Homeric poetry denominates a crashing noise. For, as the instruments of ascending souls emit a harmonious sound, and appear to possess an elegant and well-measured motion, so the found of more irrational souls descending under the earth is similar to a crashing noise, bearing an image of an appetitive and phantastic life alone. Nor must we think that the places in Hades, and the tribunals under the earth, and the rivers which both Homer and Plato teach us are there, are merely fabulous, prodigies: but, as many and all-various places are assigned to souls ascending to the heavens, according to the allotments which are there; in like manner it is proper to believe that places under the earth are prepared for those souls that still require punishment and purification. These places, as they contain the various defluxions of the elements on the earth, are called by poets rivers and streams. They likewise contain different orders of presiding dæmons; some of whom are of an avenging, others of a punishing, others of a purifying, and, lastly, others of a judicial characteristic. But if the Homeric poetry calls these places

Horrid and dark, and odious to the Gods,

neither is it proper to condemn it for this. For souls are terrified through the variety and phantasy of the presiding dæmons which are there. The infernal region likewise is extended according to all-various allotments, adapted to the different habits of those that descend thither.[39] It is also most remote from the Gods, as being the extremity of the universe, and as possessing much of material disorder, and never enjoying the splendor of the solar rays. And thus much concerning those verses which Socrates thinks should be obliterated, and should by no means be heard by those whom he educates: for through these, says he, the love of the soul for the body will be increased, and a separation from it will appear to be of all things most dreadful.

X. WHAT THE CAUSES ARE THROUGH WHICH THE POETRY OF HOMER ASCRIBES LAMENTATIONS BOTH TO HEROES AND GODS; AND LIKEWISE TO THE BEST OF HEROES AND THE GREATEST OF THE GODS.

It now follows that we should consider how the poetry of Homer does not represent one of us weeping and lamenting, when he also ascribes these effects of sorrow to his heroes, but makes the Gods themselves to weep, for the death of mortals whom they loved; though, according to Plato, Socrates neither wept, nor suffered any perturbation of mind, when his familiars wept on account of his approaching death; but Apollodorus, who wept abundantly, and any other who was similarly affected, were reproved by their master. But the divine poet represents his heroes immoderately lamenting the loss of their familiars. And, though some one should say that such things as the following became Priam who was a barbarian, and more irrational in his conduct:

> Roll'd in the dust he suppliant call'd on all,
> And nam'd them one by one:[40]

yet is it not absurd that Achilles, the son of a goddess, should at one time lie supine, at another prone, and, at another on his side, and, defiling his head with dust, weep in a very puerile manner? And even if such passions were proper in men who are allotted a mortal nature, yet they ought not to be ascribed to the Gods themselves. Why then is it requisite that Thetis should say weeping:

> Ah wretched me! unfortunately brave
> A son I bore.[41]

For a divine nature is established very remote from pleasure and pain. But though some one should dare to introduce the Gods affected in this manner,[42] yet it is not fit that the greatest of the Gods should lament and mourn both for Hector when pursued by Achilles, and for his son Sarpedon, and exclaim respecting both, "Ah me!" For such an imitation does not appear to be in any respect adapted to its paradigms, since it ascribes tears to things without tears, pain to things void of pain, and in short passion to things free from passion. These things Socrates reprobates in Homer, and expels from the education of youth, fearful lest some impediment should arise, through such-like assertions, to a right discipline according to virtue. For education is particularly conversant with pleasure and pain; which being increased, the legislator must necessarily be frustrated of his proper end.

To these objections we reply, that since the poet introduces heroes engaged in practical affairs, and living a life adapted to these, he very properly represents them as affected with particular events, and living conformably to such affections. For to philosophers, and those who energize cathartically, pleasures and pains, and the mixtures of these, are by no means adapted; since they are separated from these, lay aside all the trifling of mortality, and hasten to be divested of the forms of life with which they are surrounded from the elements, rapidly withdrawing themselves from material passions the offspring of generation. But pleasures, pains, sympathies, and a scene of all-various passions, are coordinated to those engaged in war, and who energize according to the passive part of the soul. And how could the vehement about actions take place, without the impulse of the appetites? Priam, therefore, and Achilles, neither being philosophers, nor willing to separate themselves from generation, nor living after the manner of the guardians of Plato's republic,—if they lament and commiserate their familiars, it is by no means wonderful. For the loss of friends, the being destitute of children, and the subversions of cities, appear to warriors to impart a great portion of misery. The accomplishment of mighty deeds, therefore, is adapted to these, as being allotted an heroic nature; and in conjunction with this the pathetic, from their being conversant with particulars.

With respect to the Gods, however, when they are said to weep for or lament those that are most dear to them, another mode of interpretation is to be adopted, and which was formerly admitted by the authors of fables, who indicated by tears the providence of the

Gods about mortal, generated, and perishable natures. For this object of providential energy naturally calling for tears afforded a pretext to the inventors of fables; and through these they obscurely signified providence itself. Hence some one, in a hymn to the Sun, says,

> Phœbus, the much-enduring race of men
> Thy tears excite.[43]———

And on this account, in the mysteries also, we mystically assume sacred lamentations, as symbols of the providence pertaining to us from more excellent natures. Thetis therefore, and Jupiter, are said to lament those most dear to them, when in extreme danger—not that they are passively disposed after the manner of men, but because a certain separate providence proceeds from them, and gifts to particulars. And when the order of the universe concurs with this divisible providence, the preserving energy of that which provides is unimpeded; but when this order opposes, and that which is the object of a particular providence, as being a part of the universe, and allotted generation, sustains that corruption which is adapted to its nature, then fables, adducing the idiom or peculiarity of the providence which this object received according to its order, say that the powers who exert this providential energy lament, but not with exclamation: so that grief with them is a sign of the energy of a particular providence about individuals. After this manner, then, we attribute lamentations to the first Gods; since the greatest and most perfect[44] of mystical sacrifices (τελεται) deliver in the arcana certain sacred lamentations of Proserpine and Ceres, and of the greatest[45] goddess herself.

But it is by no means wonderful if the λαοτ of the genera which are the perpetual attendants of the Gods, and which proximately attend to the affairs of mortals, in consequence of employing appetites and passions, and having their life in these, should rejoice in the safety of the objects of their providence, but be afflicted and indignant when they are corrupted, and should suffer a mutation according to passions: *177*

> The Nymphs lament when trees are leafless found;
> But when the trees through fertilizing rain
> In leaves abound, the Nymphs rejoice again—

says a certain poet. For all things subsist divinely in the Gods, but divisibly and dæmoniacally in the divided guardians of our nature. And thus much may suffice concerning the lamentations of the Gods.

XI. WHAT THE CAUSE IS OF THE LAUGHTER ASCRIBED TO THE GODS IN FABLES, AND WHY THE POETRY OF HOMER MAKES THE GODS TO LAUGH IMMODERATELY AT VULCAN.

Let us in the next place consider whether fables properly attribute to the Gods a passion contrary to that which we have just now discussed, *viz.* immoderate laughter, and which is thought worthy of reprehension by Socrates.

> Vulcan ministrant when the Gods beheld,
> Amidst them laughter unextinguish'd rose.[46]

What then is the laughter of the Gods? and why do they laugh in consequence of Vulcan moving and energizing? Theologists, therefore, say that Vulcan, as we have elsewhere observed, is the demiurgus and maker of every thing apparent.[47] Hence he is said to have constructed habitations for the Gods:

> Then to their proper domes the Gods depart,
> Form'd by lame Vulcan with transcendent art.

And this, in consequence of preparing for them mundane receptacles. He is also said to be lame in both his feet, because his fabrication is without legs. For that which is moved with a motion about intellect and prudence does not, says Timæus, require feet. He is likewise said to preside over the brazier's art, and he himself energizes working in brass. Hence, in the poetry of Homer, heaven is often celebrated as brazen; and many other particulars confirm this opinion. But since every providential energy about a *sensible nature*, according to which the Gods assist the fabrication of Vulcan, is said to be the *sport* of divinity, hence Timæus also appears to me to call the mundane Gods *junior*, as presiding over things which are perpetually in generation, or becoming to be, and which may be considered as ludicrous. The authors of fables are accustomed to call this peculiarity of the providence of the Gods energizing about the world, *laughter*. And when the poet says that the Gods, being delighted with the motion of Vulcan, laughed with inextinguishable laughter, nothing else is indicated than that they are cooperating artificers; that they jointly give perfection to the art of Vulcan, and supernally impart joy to the universe. For Vulcan suspends all their mundane receptacles, and extends to the providence of the Gods whole physical powers. But the Gods, energizing with a facility adapted to their nature, and not departing[48] from their proper hilarity, confer on these powers also their characteristic gifts, and move wholes by their perfective providence. In short, we must define the laughter of the Gods to be their exuberant energy in the universe, and the cause of the gladness of all mundane natures. But, as such a providence is incomprehensible, and the communication of all goods from the Gods is never-failing, we must allow that the poet very properly calls their laughter unextinguished. And here you may again see how what we have said is conformable to the nature of things. For fables do not assert that the Gods always weep, but that they laugh without ceasing. For tears are symbols of their providence in mortal and frail concerns, and which now rise into existence, and then perish; but laughter is a sign of their energy in wholes, and those perfect natures in the universe which are perpetually moved with undeviating sameness. On which account I think, when we divide demiurgic productions into Gods and men, we attribute laughter to the generation of the Gods, but tears to the formation of men and animals; whence the poet whom we have before mentioned, in his hymn to the Sun, says,

179

> Mankind's laborious race thy tears excite,
> But the Gods, laughing, blossom'd into light.

But when we make a division into things celestial and sublunary, again after the same manner we must assign laughter to the former, and tears to the latter; and when we reason concerning the generations and corruptions of sublunary natures themselves, we must refer the former to the laughter, and the latter to the tears, of the Gods. Hence, in the mysteries also, those who preside over sacred institutions order both these to be celebrated at stated times. And we have elsewhere observed, that the stupid are neither able to understand things employed by theurgists in secrecy, nor fictions of this kind. For the hearing of both these, when unaccompanied with science, produces dire and absurd confusion in the lives of the multitude, with respect to the reverence pertaining to divinity.

XII. AN APOLOGY FOR THOSE PARTS IN THE POETRY OF HOMER,
  WHICH APPEAR IN ALL-VARIOUS WAYS TO EXCITE THE HEARERS TO
  A CONTEMPT OF TEMPERANCE.

It now follows that we should consider whether the poems of
Homer are inimical to the acquisition of temperance. The greatest
species therefore of temperance, says Socrates, is reverence towards
governors; the next to this is a command over the pleasures and
desires of the soul; and there is a third consequent to these, which we
shall shortly after contemplate. Achilles appears to have erred
according to the first of these, when he freely says to the commander
of all the Grecian forces,

> Drunkard, dog-eyed, with heart of deer![49]

But Ulysses according to the third of these, when, defining the most
beautiful life, he says that he particularly approves that polity of men
in which there are

> The heav'n-taught poet, and enchanting strain;
> The well-fill'd palace, the perpetual feast,
> A land rejoicing, and a people blest!
> The plenteous board high-heap'd with cates divine,
> And o'er the foaming bowl the laughing wine![50]

For in these verses he places the end of life in nothing else than variety
of pleasure, and the gratification of desire. Such then being the
objections made by Socrates to the verses of Homer, in answer to the
first we say, that those guardians which he places over his city, and
who are allotted such a transcendency, on account of their erudition
and virtue, over those whom they govern, demand the most abundant
and the greatest honour, both from their associates and all others; as
they are truly the saviours and benefactors of the whole polity over
which they preside: nor is it to be supposed that the governed will ever
suffer any thing unholy or unjust from them, governing as they do
according to intellect and justice. But the poet neither admits that
Agamemnon excels all those that are subject to him, in virtue, nor in
benefiting others; but he ranks him among those that are benefited

by others, and particularly by the military science of Achilles. Very properly, therefore, does he represent him as reviled by those more excellent than himself, and consider the general good of the governed, against which Agamemnon sinned, as of more consequence than gratifying the passions of the chief. The poet therefore introduces the best of the Greeks freely speaking to Agamemnon, without regarding the multitude of soldiers that followed him, or his naval power. For virtue is every where honourable, but not the instruments of virtue. We must not therefore say, that he who employs such disgraceful epithets sins against the rulers and saviours of the whole army, when they are only superior by the multitude of those that are subject to their command, but are far inferior in virtue. For even the commander himself of so great an army, and so difficult to be numbered, acknowledges, a little after, how much Achilles excels him in virtue, laments his own infelicity, *181* and says,

> For I have err'd, nor this win I deny.

And,

> That happy man whom Jove still honours most,
> Is more than armies, and himself an host.

With respect to the word of Ulysses, we may say in their defence, that every thing of thing, kind is interpreted more symbolically by those who transfer to other conceptions his wanderings, and who think it proper to rank both the Phæacians and their felicity[51] higher than human nature. For with them the festival, the dainties, and the enchanting strain, have a different signification from that which is obvious to the multitude. It may also be said, that even those who do not depart from the apparent meaning of the poet, may nevertheless reply to such objections, and show, in the first place, that Ulysses, the wisest of the Greeks, does not think it fit that pleasure should have dominion in well-instituted polities, but worthy joy (ευφροσυνη). And how much these differ from each other, we may learn from Plato himself. In the second place, Ulysses approves of the whole city becoming harmonized and unanimous with itself through music, being an auditor of such melodies as lead to virtue. For it is of great consequence to the whole polity, and to true erudition and virtue, that he who exercises music among the vulgar should not be any casual person, but one who derives his knowledge of it supernally through divine inspiration, from its presiding deity. In the third place, such harmony, to those that partake of it, adds an abundance of things necessary, which the multitude in cities very much require. For Ulysses does not remarkably praise a life filled with things of this kind, but that life which is in want of nothing necessary to mortal existence. The wisest of the Greeks, therefore, appears to speak conformably to our dogmas, and to unperverted preconceptions respecting divine felicity. But if Ulysses thought that he deserves approbation w ho takes away worthy delight, and the discipline subsisting through divine music, alone regarding feasting, and immoderate enjoyments, destitute of the Muse, and directs his attention to pleasure, Socrates with great propriety says that things of this kind are remote from his polity. For it is by no mean fit that immoderate pleasure, and a life adapted to gluttony, should have dominion in a city consisting of the happy.

XIII. WHAT THE CONNECTION OF JUPITER WITH JUNO OBSCURELY SIGNIFIES; WHAT THE ORNAMENT OF JUNO IS; AND WHAT THE PLACE IN WHICH THEY WERE CONNECTED. WHAT THE LOVE OF JUPITER SIGNIFIES; WHAT THE DIVINE SLEEP IS; AND, IN SHORT, THE WHOLE INTERPRETATION OF THAT FABLE.

To such objections therefore of Socrates it is not difficult to reply; but a doubt yet remains to be solved by us, greater and more difficult, respecting the connection of Jupiter with Juno; for this Socrates reprehends, as by no means fit to be heard by youth. For, does it not appear to be perfectly impious, to suspect of the greatest of the Gods, that through his love to Juno he should be forgetful of all his former decrees, should have connection with the goddess on the ground, not waiting to enter into her bedchamber, and should condescend to speak in the language of human lovers? For these in the first place prefer before all things a conjunction with the objects of their love; and in the next place say, that they experience the power of love more than in any former time. For Jupiter is made to speak in this manner in the following verses;

Ne'er did my soul so strong a passion prove,
Or for an earthly, or a heavenly love.[52]

And also that he loved her more

Than when, ascending to the nuptial couch,
In love they mingled, from their parents hid.

Our preceptor[53] in a most divinely inspired manner has unfolded the occult theory of this fable; from whose writings extracting as much as is sufficient to the present purpose, we shall briefly explain the several parts of the fable, and show that Homer is free from all blasphemy in the preceding verses.

All the divine orders, therefore, proceeding from the one principle of wholes, which Plato usually calls *the good*, and from those biformed causes proximately appearing after this principle, which Socrates in the Philebus denominates *bound* and *infinity*, but other wife men have venerated by other names; these orders likewise being divided and separated from each other, in a manner adapted to the Gods, through those second biformed principles,—the interpreters of the truth concerning the Gods usually oppose in their divisions the male to the female, the even to the odd, and the paternal to the maternal genera. But these divine orders again hastening to union and a connate communion, through the first cause, which is the leader of united goods to all beings, hence I think the authors of fables took occasion in their symbolical theory to ascribe marriage to the Gods, connections, and a progeny from these, and also celebrated the connections and conjunctions of their progeny, till they had perfectly contemplated the whole extent of a divine nature, diversified by such like progressions and conjunctions supernally, as far as to mundane natures. As therefore, among the Gods prior to the fabrication of the world, they celebrate the connections of Saturn and Rhea, of Heaven and Earth, and their cogenerations, in the same manner also, among the fabricators of the universe, they inform us that the first conjunction is that of Jupiter and Juno; Jupiter being allotted a paternal dignity, but Juno being the mother of every thing of which Jupiter is the father. The former likewise produces all things in the rank of a monad, but the latter in conjunction with him gives subsistence to secondary natures, according to the prolific duad: and the former is assimilated to intelligible bound, but the latter to intelligible infinity. For, according to every order of Gods, it is requisite that there should be primary causes subsisting analogously to those two principles. But, to the union of these greatest divinities, it is necessary that there should previously subsist a oneness of transcendency of the monadic and demiurgic God, and a perfect conversion to him of the generative and dyadic cause. For the connate communion of more excellent natures is after this manner effected, more elevated causes being established in themselves, and in natures more divine than themselves, but such as are subordinate giving themselves up to those that are superior. Through these causes, as it appears to me, Juno hastening to a connection with Jupiter, perfects her whole essence, and prepares it with all-various powers, the undefiled, the generative, the intellectual, and the unific; but Jupiter excites the divine love in himself, according to which he also fills his proximate participants with good, and extends to them a cause collective of multitude, and an energy convertive of secondary natures to himself. But the union and indissoluble conjunction of both these divinities is effected separate from the universe, and exempt from the mundane receptacles. For Jupiter elevates to this communion, Juno extending to him that which is subordinate and mundane; the Gods indeed being always united, but fables separating them from each other; and referring a connection separate[54] from the universe to the will of Jupiter, but the common cooperation of these divinities proceeding into the world, to the providence of Juno. The reason of this is, that every where the paternal cause is the leader of exempt and more uniform good, but the maternal of that good which is proximate to its participants, and is multiplied according to all-various progressions. With great propriety, therefore, are sleep and wakefulness usurped separately in the symbols of fables; wakefulness manifesting the providence of the Gods about the world, but sleep a life separate from all subordinate natures; though the Gods at the same time both providentially energize about the universe, and are established in themselves. But as Timæus represents the demiurgus of wholes, at one time energizing, and giving subsistence to the earth, the heavens, the planets, the fixed stars, the circles of the soul, and the mundane intellect, but at another time abiding in himself, after his accustomed manner, and exempt from all those powers that energize in the universe; so, long before Timæus, fables represent the father of all mundane natures, at one time awake, and at another asleep, for the purpose of indicating his two-fold life and energy. "For he contains intelligibles in his intellect, but introduces sense to the worlds,"[55] says one of the Gods. According to the former energy, therefore, he may be said to be awake; for wakefulness with us is an energy of sense; but according to the latter to sleep, as separated from sensibles, and exhibiting a life defined according to a perfect intellect. It may also be said, that he consults about human affairs when awake; for according to this life he provides for all mundane concerns; but that when asleep, and led together with Juno to a separate union, he is not forgetful of the other energy, but, possessing and energizing according to it, at the same time contains both. For he does not, like nature, produce secondary things without intelligence, nor through intelligence is his providence in subordinate natures diminished, but at the same time he both governs the objects of his providence according to justice, and ascends, to his intelligible watch-tower. The fable, therefore, indicates this exempt transcendency, when it says that his connection with Juno was on mount Ida; for there Juno arriving gave herself to the embraces of the mighty Jupiter. What else, then, shall we say mount *Ida* obscurely signifies, but the region of *ideas* and an intelligible nature, to which Jupiter ascends, and elevates Juno through love;—not converting himself to the participant, but through excess of goodness imparting this second union with himself, and with that which is intelligible? For such are the loves of more excellent natures,—they are convertive of things subordinate to things first, give completion to the good which they contain, and are perfective of subject natures. The fable, therefore, does not diminish the dignity of the mighty Jupiter, by representing him as having connection on the ground with Juno, and refusing to enter into her bed-chamber; for by this it insinuates that the connection was supermundane, and not mundane. The chamber, therefore, constructed by Vulcan indicates the orderly composition of the universe, and the sensible region; for Vulcan, as we have said before, is the artificer of the universe.

If you are also willing to consider the dress of Juno, through which

she conjoined herself to the greatest of the Gods, and called forth the
paternal providence of Jupiter to a communion with her own prolific
powers, you will, I think, in a still greater degree behold the excess of
the separate union of the Gods, celebrated in this fable. For she
assimilates herself all-variously to the mother of the Gods, from
whom she also proceeds, and is adorned with the more partial powers
of those natures which presubsist in her totally, and, becoming all but
another Rhea, proceeds to the demiurgus of the universe, who had
then ascended to his proper intelligible. For she who is about to be
conjoined with him who imitates his father, through a life separate
from mundane natures, assimilates also her own perfection to the
mother of all the divine orders, and thus enters into a connate
communion with him. The hairs therefore of the goddess, and her
ringlets widely spreading, which she again binds, are evidently
analogous to the hairs of the mother of the Gods: "for her hairs
appear similar to rays of light ending in a sharp point," says some one
of the Gods. And the poet calls the hairs of Juno *shining*. But her
zone, with the fringes depending on and not cut off from it,
resembles the whole and all-perfect girdle of Rhea. For Juno also is a
vivific goddess, and is generative of all the multitude of souls, which
the number of the depending fringes symbolically indicates. Her
earrings and her sandals represent the first and the last of the partial[56]
powers which flow from thence, some of which subsist about the
highest powers of the goddess, and thence depend, but others are
situated about her lowest progressions. The ambrosia and the oil are
signs of the undefiled powers of the goddess; for the inflexible[57] order
of Gods subsists about her. What therefore that untamed genus of
Gods and cause of purity is to Juno, that is here signified through
these symbols. For ambrosia represents a power superior to all
impurity and all defilement, and oil, as it produces strength, and is
adapted to gymnastic exercises, properly belongs to Curetic deity. For
the first Curetes are in other respects ascribed to the order of Minerva,
and are said by Orpheus to be crowned with a branch of olive.

The Goddess, therefore, being perfectly furnished with such like
symbols, and becoming as it were a partial Rhea, proceeds to the
demiurgus of the universe, that the may be conjoined with him
according to that life by which he particularly imitates Saturn; not

186

187

proceeding into the universe, but being separate from mundane natures; nor consulting about things which are here, according to the sleepless providence of wholes, but exempt from sensibles, according to divine sleep; and in this respect emulating his father, who is represented as sleeping the first of the Gods.

> When Saturn tasted the deceitful food,
> Loud snoring lay the God.

Since therefore Jupiter thus imitates his father Saturn, with great propriety does the dress of Juno regard the whole of Rhea; and hence Jupiter, through his similitude to Saturn, prefers a connection on mount Ida to that which proceeds into the universe.

The girdle also, and the assistance of Venus, assimilate Juno still more to Rhea. For there also was the presubsisting monad of this goddess, proceeding supernally from the connective divinity of Heaven, through Saturn as a medium, and illuminating the whole of an intellectual life with the light of beauty. Venus is said to carry this girdle in her bosom, as possessing its powers conspicuously extended; but Juno after a manner conceals it in her bosom, as being allotted a different idiom of hyparxis, but as possessing the girdle also, so far as the likewise is filled with the whole of Venus. For she does not externally derive the power which conjoins her with the demiurgus, but comprehends it also in herself. But the general opinion of mankind evinces the comm union of these Goddesses: for they honour Juno as Nuptial and Pronuba, as beginning such like energies from herself. For she conjoins herself with the demiurgus through the girdle in herself; and hence the likewise imparts to all others a legitimate communion with each other.

But how are Jupiter and Juno said to have been at first connected with each other, concealed from their parents, but that now they are connected in a greater degree, through the excess of love with which Jupiter then loved Juno? Shall we say that the peculiarities of other goods are also two-fold; and that, of union, one kind is connate to those that are united, but that the other supernally proceeds to them from more perfect causes? According to the former of these, *188* therefore, they are said to be concealed from their parents, in consequence of being allotted this union as peculiar to themselves; but according to the other they are elevated to their causes, and hence this is said to be a greater and more perfect union than the former. But both these unions eternally subsisting together, with the Gods, fables separate them, in the same manner as sleep and wakefulness, progression and conversion, a communication of proper goods to things secondary, and a participation of primary causes; for these the authors of fables, concealing the truth, separate, though they are consubsistent with each other. Every thing, therefore, is asserted by Homer respecting the connection of the great Jupiter and Juno after a theological manner; which is also testified by Socrates in the Cratylus, who derives the etymology of Juno from nothing else than *love*, as being, says he, lovely to Jupiter. According to an occult theory, there fore, we must not accuse Homer for writing such things concerning these mighty divinities. But if it should be objected, that things of this kind are not fit to be heard by youth, according to their apparent signification, poets the authors of such fables will say, Our fables are not for youth, nor did we write such things with a view to juvenile discipline, but with an insane mouth; for these are the productions of the mania of the Muses, of which whoever being deprived arrives at the poetic gates, will be both as to himself and his poetry imperfect. And thus much may suffice for these particulars.

XIV. WHAT THE MYTHOLOGY OF HOMER OBSCURELY SIGNIFIES CONCERNING VENUS AND MARS, AND THE BONDS OF VULCAN, WITH WHICH BOTH ARE SAID TO BE BOUND.

Let us now consider the connection between Mars and Venus, and the bonds of Vulcan. For Socrates says that neither must these be admitted, nor must such fables be delivered to youth. Let us, therefore, concisely relate what the poetry of Homer obscurely signifies by these things. Both these divinities then, I mean Vulcan and Mars, energize about the whole world, the latter separating the contrarieties of the universe, which he also perpetually excites, and immutably preserves, that the world may be perfect, and filled with forms of every kind; but the former artificially fabricating the whole sensible order, and filling it with physical reasons and powers. He also fashions twenty tripods about the heavens, that he may adorn them with the most perfect of many-sided[58] figures and fabricates various and many-formed sublunary species,

> Clasps, winding bracelets, necklaces, and chains.[59]

Both these divinities require the assistance of Venus to their energies; the one, that he may insert order and harmony in contraries; and the other, that he may introduce beauty and splendour as much as possible, into sensible fabrications, and render this world the most beautiful of things visible. But, as Venus is every where, Vulcan always enjoys her according to the superior, but Mars according to the inferior, orders of things. Thus, for instance, if Vulcan is supermundane, Mars is mundane; and if the former is celestial, the latter is sublunary. Hence the one is said to have married Venus according to the will of Jupiter, but the other is fabled to have committed adultery with her. For a communion with the cause of beauty and conciliation is *natural* to the demiurgus of sensibles; but is in a certain respect foreign to the power which presides over division, and imparts the contrariety of mundane natures; for the separating are opposed to the collective genera of Gods. Fables therefore denominate this conspiring union of dissimilar causes adultery. But a communion of this kind is necessary to the universe, that contraries may be co-harmonized, and the mundane war terminate in peace. Since, however, on high among celestial natures, beauty shines forth, together with forms, elegance, and the fabrications of Vulcan, but beneath, in the realms of generation, the opposition and war of the elements, contrariety of powers, and in short the gifts of Mars, are conspicuous, on this account the sun from on high beholds the connection of Mars and Venus, and discloses it to Vulcan, in consequence of cooperating with the whole productions, productions *190* of this divinity. But Vulcan is said to throw over them all various bonds, unapparent to the other Gods, as adorning the mundane genera with artificial reasons, and producing one system from martial contrarieties, and the co-harmonizing goods of Venus. For both are necessary to generation. Since too, of bonds, some are celestial, but others sublunary (for some are indissoluble, as Timæus says, but others dissoluble); on this account, Vulcan again dissolves the bonds with which he had bound Mars and Venus, and this he particularly accomplishes in compliance with the request of Neptune; who being willing that the perpetuity of generation should be preserved, and the circle of mutation revolve into itself, thinks it proper that generated natures should be corrupted, and things corrupted be sent back again to generation. What wonder is it, then, if Homer says that Mars and Venus were bound by the bonds of Vulcan, since Timæus also denominates those demiurgic reasons bonds, by which the celestial Gods give subsistence to generated natures? And does not Homer speak conformably to the nature of things when he says the bonds were dissolved, since these are the bonds of generation? Indeed the demiurgus of wholes, by composing the world from contrary elements, and causing it through analogy to be in friendship with itself, appears to have collected into union the energies of Vulcan, Mars and Venus. In producing the contrarieties of the elements, too, he may be said to have generated them according to the Mars which he contains in himself; but, in devising friendship, to have energized according to the power of Venus. And in binding together the productions of Venus with those of Mars, he appears to have previously comprehended in himself, paradigmatically, the art of Vulcan. He is therefore all things, and energizes in conjunction with all the Gods. The junior artificers also, imitating their father, fabricate mortal animals, and again receive them when they are corrupted, generating, in conjunction with Vulcan, sublunary bonds and previously containing in themselves the causes of their solution. For every where, he who comprehends in himself a bond, knows also the necessity of its solution.

XV. WHAT MUST BE SAID TO THE ANIMADVERSIONS OF SOCRATES, RESPECTING THE AVARICE ASCRIBED BY HOME R TO HIS HEROES.

Let us now consider those places in the poems of Homer, which, according to Socrates, increase the love of riches in our souls. For why does Phœnix advise Achilles to receive gifts when he lays aside his anger, but otherwise not to lay it aside? Why also does Achilles receive gifts from Agamemnon for his insolence, and refuse to restore the dead body of Hector, unless it was redeemed with money? For he who becomes an auditor of things of this kind is in danger of falling into a dire and insatiable avarice. To these objections we shall briefly say, that Phœnix advises Achilles to lay aside his anger on receiving the gifts, and Achilles, on receiving them, did lay it aside, both of them considering the gifts as an argument of the repentance of the giver; but not that they might satisfy the avaricious disposition of their soul, nor considering an increase of riches as the boundary of felicity. For they did not from the first demand these presents, but received them when they were spontaneously offered. But if Achilles restored the dead body of Hector to Priam, on its being redeemed by money, perhaps we may say that it was at that time customary to receive a ransom for the bodies of enemies. This also must be considered, that it belongs to the art of commanding an army, to cut off the riches of the enemy, but to increase the property of those who are compelled to oppose the enemy in a foreign country. But all these and such-like particulars may be defended as the transactions of those heroes who energized according to circumstances, and whose actions are to be estimated according to other manners than those of common men: they are, however, entirely unfit to be heard by those educated under the legislator of Socrates, whose geniuses are philosophic, whose erudition regards a philosophic life, and who are entirely deprived of possessions and property.

If you are willing, we may also add to what has been said respecting Achilles, that he himself accuses Agamemnon of avarice, and reprobates this passion as disgraceful.

> Atrides, who in glory art the first,
> And no less avaricious than renown'd![60]

Besides, he indicates to us his contempt of wealth, when he says to Agamemnon, *192*

> Thine in each contest is the wealthy prey,
> Though mine the sweat and danger of the day.
> Some trivial present to my ships I bear,
> Or barren praises pay the wounds of war.[61]

Further still, neither would he accept the gifts at first, when they were offered by Agamemnon, because he did not think it was then fit to be reconciled to him. So that it was not the promise of riches which made him more mild to Agamemnon, by whom he had been treated with insolence; but, when he thought it was proper to lay aside his anger, he prepared himself for battle that he might revenge his friend and when Agamemnon sent him the gifts, he neither looked at them, nor thought that any accession would thence be made to his own goods. Besides, his contempt of these things is evident from the multitude of rewards proposed by him in the funeral games: for he honoured the several champions with proper gifts; and magnificently bellowed upon Nestor, who through his age was unable to engage in the games, a golden bowl. How therefore, according to Homer, could he be avaricious, who used riches in a proper manner, who when they were present despised them, when absent did not anxiously desire them, and could endure to receive less of them than others? To which we may add, that he reprobated, in the midst of the Greeks, that passion of the soul as a disease, which aspires after immoderate wealth. How likewise can it be said that Phœnix was the teacher of avarice, who exhorts Achilles to imitate the ancient custom of the Greeks? For he says,

> Thus ancient heroes, when with rage inflam'd,
> By words were soften'd, and by gifts appeas'd.[62]

But these things, which are adapted to heroic times, and to the customs which then subsisted among heroes, were considered by Homer as deserving the highest imitation; though they are by no means adapted to the youth educated by Socrates, who are assigned no other employment by the legislator, than discipline and the study of virtue. But an attention to riches, and such things as are necessary to the preservation of the life of mortals, is assigned to others who are necessary to the perfection of an inferior republic.

XVI. IN WHAT MANNER IT IS REQUISITE TO APOLOGIZE FOR THE NEGLIGENCE OF HEROES RESPECTING A DIVINE NATURE, WHICH APPEARS TO TAKE PLACE IN THE POETRY OF HOMER.

It now follows that we should consider how we are to answer Socrates, when he accuses Achilles of negligence respecting a divine nature. For how can he be pious and a worshipper of the Gods, who dares to say to Apollo,

Me thou hast injur'd most pernicious God?[63]

who also opposes the river Xanthus though a God, and presents his locks to the dead body of Patroclus, though he had promised them to the river Sperchius? That Achilles therefore, according to Homer, was remarkably cautious respecting a divine nature, is evident from his advising the Greeks to reverence Apollo, to send a sacrifice to him, and to appease Chryses the priest of Apollo. This also follows from his readily obeying the commands of Minerva, when she appeared to him, though contrary to the impulse of his wrath. He likewise asserts that a subserviency to the Gods, and a compliance with the will of more excellent natures, is of all things the most useful; and offers a libation and prays to Jupiter, with science adapted to the Gods. For his first purifying the bowl, and in an especial manner consecrating it to Jupiter alone, and standing in the middle of the enclosure, invoking the power that pervades every where from the middle of the universe, afford a sufficiently conspicuous argument of his piety to a divine nature, and of his knowledge of the signs adapted to the objects of worship.

But if he appears to have spoken to Apollo more boldly than is fit, it is requisite to know that the Apolloniacal orders pervade from on high, as far as to the last of things; and some of them are divine, others angelic, and others dæmoniacal, and these multiformly divided. It must be considered, therefore, that these words were not addressed to a God, but to a dæmoniacal Apollo, and this not the first in rank, and coordinated with those that have a total dominion, but one who proximately presides over individuals; and, in short, (for why should I not speak clearly?) the guardian of Hector himself. For the poet perspicuously says,

194

Apollo now before Achilles stood,
In all things like Agenor————

This Apollo, therefore, Achilles calls most pernicious, so far as he was a hindrance to his actions, by preserving his enemy uninjured. Nor does he by thus speaking sin against a God, but against a power who ranks amongst the most partial of the Apolloniacal series. For it is not proper to refer either all the speeches or energies to that first Apollo, but we should also attend to his second and third progressions. Thus, for instance, we should consider who the Apollo is that fits with Jupiter and the Olympian Gods; who, that convolves the solar sphere; who the aerial Apollo is; who the terrestrial; who, that presides over Troy; and who, that is the peculiar guardian of Hector, concerning whom the poet also says,

> He fled to Hades by Apollo left.

For, by looking to all these orders, we shall be able to refer the speeches of Achilles to same such partial power, who was willing to preserve the object of his care, and impede Achilles in his strenuous exertions. For the words "thou hast injured me" are very properly addressed to a dæmon of this kind, who deprives him of the end of his present labours; and the epithet "most pernicious" clearly evinces that this power is more adverse to him than any other God or dæmon. For he who preserves uninjured a principal enemy, becomes more than any one noxious to the person injured, by impeding his avenging the injury. But, as such language even to such an inferior power is not unattended with punishment, it is said that Achilles shortly after was slain by a certain power of the Apolloniacal order, which Hector when he was dying thus predicts to him:

> Paris and Phœbus shall avenge my fate,
> And stretch thee here before this Scæan gate.

195 Does not therefore the poetry of Homer by these things make us more modest respecting a divine nature, since we learn from it that even the most subordinate powers cannot be offended with impunity? Though I am not ignorant that those who are skilled in mystic sacrifices dare many things of this kind respecting dæmons; but perhaps they are defended by more divine natures from sustaining any such injury from subordinate powers. In the mean time justice follows other men, correcting the improbity of their speech.

It is also not difficult to reply to what is said in objection to the contest of Achilles with the river Xanthus. For he was not disobedient to the God himself, but he either contended with the apparent water which hindered his impulse against the enemy, or with some one of the indigenous powers, the associate of the Gods in battle: for Minerva and Neptune were present with him, and afforded him assistance. And it appears to me, indeed, that the poetry of Homer devises contests according to all possible diversities; sometimes relating the battles of men with men, and sometimes of the more excellent genera with each other, as in what is called *theomachy*, or the battles of the Gods; and sometimes, as in the instance before us, the oppositions of heroes to certain dæmoniacal natures; indicating to those that are able to understand things of this kind, that the first of last natures are after a manner equal to the last of such as are first, and particularly when they are guarded and moved by the Gods. Hence, not only Achilles is said to have contended with Xanthus, but Hercules also with the river Achelous, of whose life Achilles being emulous, he did not avoid similar contests.

Lastly, we may solve the third of the proposed inquiries by saying that the first and principal design of Achilles was, on returning to his country, to offer to the river Sperchius his locks, as he had promised; but when he despaired of his return, in consequence of hearing from his mother,

Soon after Hector shall thy death succeed,

was it not then necessary that he should cut off his hair in honour of his friend? For Socrates in Plato received the crowns which Alcibiades was to have offered to a God, and was crowned with them; nor did he think that he sinned by so doing, or injured the young man. I omit to say that the hairs of Achilles were not yet sacred to the river: for he who had promised to consecrate them on his return, when deprived of this, was also deprived of the consecration of his hairs. *196*

XVII. AN APOLOGY FOR THE UNWORTHY TREATMENT OF THE DEAD BODY OF HECTOR, AND FOR THE TWELVE TROJANS SLAIN AND BURNT ON THE FUNERAL PILE OF PATROCLUS, SINCE THESE THINGS EVIDENTLY APPEAR TO BE CRUEL, ABSURD, AND UNBECOMING THE CHARACTER OF HEROES.

It now remains that we consider the conduct of Achilles to Hector, his dragging him round the tomb of Patroclus, and his sacrificing twelve Trojan youths on his pile; for these things, says Socrates, can not be truly ascribed to Achilles, who was the son of a goddess, and of the most temperate Peleus descended from Jupiter, and who was educated by the wife Chiron. In the first place, then, it is said by the ancients that this was the custom of the Thessalians, as the Cyrenæan poet also testifies, when he informs us, that "it is an ancient Thessalian custom, to drag round the tomb of the slain the body of the slaughterer."

Achilles therefore thus acted conformably to the custom of his country, that all due honours might be paid to the funeral of Patroclus. But if Hector dragged Patroclus when a dead body, threatened to cut off his head, and cast his corpse to the Trojan dogs, which is also told to Achilles by Iris—

> A prey to dogs he dooms the corse to lie,
> And marks the place to fix his head on high.[64]
> Rise and prevent (if yet you think of fame)
> Thy friend's disgrace, thy own eternal shame!

does not Achilles, therefore, insist a proper punishment on Hector, in dragging him round the tomb of Patroclus? For thus he both revenges the cruelty of Hector, and openly testifies his benevolence to his friend. He does not, however, accomplish what he intended; for he restores the dead body of Hector to his friends, and suffers him to be buried. He therefore who introduces such measures to his actions energizes according to the whole of justice, and the providence of the Gods. Hence the poet also says, that, by complying with the will of more excellent natures, he was rendered so mild with respect to Hector, that with his own hands he placed him on the bier.

> Two splendid mantles, and a carpet spread,
> They leave, to cover and inwrap the dead;
> Then call the handmaids with assistant toil
> To wash the body, and anoint with oil.
> This done, the garments o'er the corse they spread;
> Achilles lifts it to the funeral bed.[65]

Achilles, therefore, performed every thing pertaining to the dead in a manner adapted to his character. For he illustriously honoured his friend by the vengeance which he inflicted on his enemy, and, afterwards becoming more mild, behaved with great philanthropy to Priam, and paid him the utmost attention and respect.

With respect to the Trojan youths that were slaughtered at the funeral pile of Patroclus, it may be said, that by this action, according to appearance, Achilles perfectly honoured his friend, and that he did nothing more to these Trojans than he was accustomed to do to other enemies, *viz.* slaying those whom he happened to meet. For what difference is there between dying at a funeral pyre, or in a river? Does he not indeed act better by these, whose bodies were totally destroyed by fire, than by those whose bodies were torn in pieces by savage beasts, and who suffer the same things with Lycaon? to whom Achilles says,

> Lie there, Lycaon! let the fifth surround.
> Thy bloated corse, and suck thy gory wound.[66]

But if it be requisite to recall to our memory the more occult speculations of our preceptor respecting these particulars, we must say that the whole transaction of Achilles concerning the pyre imitates the immortalizing of the soul (της ψυχης αποθανατισμος) by theurgists, and pertains to the separate soul of Patroclus. Hence, before the pyre was enkindled, he is said to have invoked the winds, the north and the west, that the apparent vehicle of Patroclus, through their visible motion, might obtain a convenient culture, and that the vehicle, which is more divine than this, might be invisibly purified, and restored to its proper allotment, "being drawn upwards by aërial, lunar and solar splendours," as one of the Gods somewhere asserts. It is also related of him, that he made a libation all night on the pyre:

198

> All night Achilles hails Patroclus' soul
> With large libations from the golden bowl.[67]

The poet all but proclaiming to us, in these verses, that Achilles was busily employed about the soul of his friend, and not about his visible body only, and that all things are symbolically usurped by him. For the libation from a golden bowl signifies the defluxion of souls from their fountain; which defluxion imparts a more excellent life to a partial soul, and is able through undefiled purity to lead it from bodies to an invisible and divine condition of being. And, in short, many arguments in confirmation of this opinion may be derived from the writings of our preceptor.

Since then it appears that Achilles celebrated the funeral of Patroclus mystically, it may be not improperly said, that these twelve

Trojans that were slaughtered at the pyre were coordinated as attendants with the soul of Patroclus, the ruling nature of which was both known and reverenced by Achilles. Hence, he chose this number as most adapted to attendants, and as sacred to the all-perfect progressions of the Gods.[68] By no means, therefore, did Achilles slay these Trojans from a certain dire and savage cruelty of soul, but performed the whole of this transaction in conformity with certain sacred laws pertaining to the souls of those that die in battle. Nor ought he to be accused of a proud contempt of Gods and men; nor ought we to deny that he was the son of a goddess and Peleus, and the disciple of Chiron, for acting in this manner. For some of his actions he performed as regarding universal justice, others as a warrior, and others as employing sacred methods. But in all these the poet has perfectly preserved the measures of imitation. And such is the answer to all that Socrates objects to in Homer, as deserving reprehension.

But if any one should say that the fable is not to be admitted, which says that Theseus and Pirithoüs ravished Helen, and descended into Hades, perhaps these things also, which are asserted more mythologically, may be properly solved by saying that these heroes, being lovers both of unapparent and visible beauty, are fabled to have ravished Helen, and to have descended into the invisible regions; and that, when there, one of them (Pirithoüs), through the elevation, of his intellect was led back by Hercules, but that the other in a certain respect remained in Hades, from not being able to raise himself to the arduous altitude of contemplation. And though some one should contend that this is not the true meaning of the fable, it does not affect the poetry of Homer, which every where attributes, according to imitation, that which is adapted to the Gods, to the genera more excellent than human nature, and to heroic lives; indicating some things more occultly, teaching us other particulars about these things, with intellect and science, and leaving no genus of beings uninvestigated, but delivering each as energizing with respect to itself and other things, according to its own order.

BOOK II.

When I had said these things I imagined that the debate was at an end; but this it seems was only the introduction: for Glauco, as he is on all occasions most courageous, so truly at that time did not approve of Thrasymachus in giving up the debate; but said, "Socrates, do you with to seem to have persuaded us, or to have persuaded us in reality, that in every respect it is better to be just than unjust?" "I would choose," said I, "to do it in reality, if it depended on me." "You do not then," said he, "do what you desire. For, tell me, does there appear to you any good of this kind, such as we would choose to have; not regarding the consequences, but embracing it for its own sake? as joy, and such pleasures as are harmless; though nothing else arises afterwards from these pleasures, than that the possession gives us delight." "There seems to me," said I, "to be something of this kind." "But what? is there something too, which we both love for its own sake, and also for what arises from it? as wisdom, sight, and health; for we somehow embrace these things on both accounts." "Yes," said I. "But do you perceive," said he, "a third species of good, among which is bodily labour, to be healed when sick, to practise physic, or other lucrative employment? for we say, those things are troublesome, but that they profit us; and we should not choose these things for their own sake, but on account of the rewards and those other advantages which arise from them." "There is then, indeed," said I, "likewise this third kind." "But what now? in which of these," said he, "do you place justice?" "I imagine," said I, "in the most handsome;

which, both on its own account, and for the sake of what arises from it, is desired by the man who is in pursuit of happiness." "It does not, however," said he, "seem so to them any, but to be of the troublesome kind, which is pursued for the sake of glory, and on account of rewards and honours; but on its own account is to be shunned, as being difficult." "I know," said I, "that it seems so, and it was in this view that Thrasymachus sometimes since despised it, and commended injustice; but it seems I am one of those who are dull in learning." "Come then," said he, "hear me likewise, if this be agreeable to you; for Thrasymachus seems to me to have been charmed by you, like an adder, sooner than was proper; but, with respect to myself, the proof has not yet been made to my satisfaction, in reference to either of the two; for I desire to hear what each is, and what power it has by itself, when in the soul-bidding farewell to the rewards, and the consequences arising from them. I will proceed, therefore, in this manner, if it seem proper to you: I will renew the speech of Thrasymachus; and, first of all, I will tell you what they say justice is, and whence it arises; and, secondly, that all those who pursue it pursue it unwillingly, as necessary, but not as good; thirdly, that they do this reasonably; for, as they say, the life of an unjust man is much better than that of the just. Although, for my own part, to me, Socrates, it does not yet appear so; I am, however, in doubt, having my ears stunned in hearing Thrasymachus and innumerable others. But I have never, hitherto, heard from any one such a discourse as I wish to hear concerning justice, as being better than in justice: I wish then to hear it commended, as it is in itself, and I most especially imagine I shall hear this from you: wherefore, pulling oppositely, I shall speak in commendation of an unjust life; and, in speaking, shall show you in what manner I want to hear you condemn injustice, and commend justice. But see if what I say be agreeable to you." "Extremely so," said I; "for what would any man of intellect delight more to speak, and to hear of frequently?"

"You speak most handsomely," said he. "And hear what I said I was first to speak of; what justice is, and whence it arises; for they say that, according to nature, to do injustice is good; but to suffer injustice is bad; but that the evil which arises from suffering injustice is greater than the good which arises from doing it: so that, after men had done

one another injustice, and likewise suffered it, and had experienced both, it seemed proper to those who were not able to shun the one, and choose the other, to agree among themselves, neither to do injustice, nor to be injured: and that hence laws began to be established, and their compacts; and that which was enjoined by law they denominated lawful and just; and that this is the origin and essence of justice: being in the middle between what is best, when he who does injustice is not punished, and of what is worst, when the injured person is unable to punish; and that justice, being thus in the middle of both these, is desired, not as good, but is held in honour from an imbecility in doing injustice: for the man who had ability to do so would never if really a man, agree with any one either to injure, or to be injured; for otherwise he were mad. This then, Socrates, and of such a kind as this, is the nature of justice; and this, as they say, is its origin. And we shall best perceive that these who pursue it, pursue it unwillingly, and from an impotence to injure if we imagine in our mind such a case as this: Let us give liberty to each of them, both to the just and to the unjust, to do whatever they incline; and then let us follow them, observing how their inclination will lead each of them. We should then find the just man, with full inclination, going the same way with the unjust, through a desire of having more than others. This, every nature is made to pursue as good, but by law is forcibly led to an equality.

"And the liberty which I speak of may be chiefly of this kind; if they happened to have such a power, as they say happened once to Gyges, the progenitor of Lydus: for they say that he was the hired shepherd of the then governor of Lydia; and that a prodigious rain and earth quake happening, part of the earth was rent, and an opening made in the place where he pastured her flocks; that when he beheld, and wondered, he descended, and saw many other wonders, which are mythologically transmitted to us, and a brazen horse likewise, hollow and with doors; and, on looking in, he saw within, a dead body larger in appearance than that of a man, which had nothing else upon it but a gold ring on its hand; which ring he took off, and came up again. That when there was a convention of the shepherds, as usual, for reporting to the king what related to their flocks, he also came, having the ring: and whilst he sat with the

359a

202

359b

359c

359d

359e

others, he happened to turn the stone of the ring to the inner part of
360a his hand; and when this was done he became invisible to those who
sat by, and they talked of him as absent: that he wondered, and, again
handling his ring, turned the stone outward, and on this became
203 visible; and that, having observed this, he made trial of the ring
whether it had this power: and that it happened, that on turning the
stone inward he be came invisible, and on turning it outward he
became visible. That, perceiving this, he instantly managed so as to be
360b made one of the embassy to the king, and that on his arrival he
debauched his wife; and, with her, assaulting the king,[1] killed him,
and possessed the kingdom. If now, there were two such rings, and the
just man had the one and the unjust the other, none, it seems, would
be so adamantine as to persevere in justice, and dare to refrain from
the things of others, and not to touch them, whilst it was in his power
360c to take, even from the Forum, without fear, whatever he pleased; to
enter into houses, and embrace any one he pleased; to kill, and to
loose from chains, whom he pleased; and to do all other things with
the same power as a God among men:—acting in this manner, he is
in no respect different from the other; but both of them go the same
road. This now, one may say, is a strong proof that no one is just from
choice, but by constraint; as it is not a good merely in itself, since
360d every one does injustice wherever he imagines he is able to do it; for
every man thinks that injustice is, to the particular person, more
profitable than justice; and he thinks justly, according to this way of
reasoning: since, if any one with such a liberty would never do any
injustice, nor touch the things of others, he would be deemed by men
of sense to be most wretched, and most void of understanding; yet
would they commend him before one another, imposing on each
other from a fear of being injured. Thus much, then, concerning
these things.

360e "But, with reference to the difference of their lives whom we speak
of, we shall be able to discern aright, if we set apart by themselves the
most just man, and the most unjust, and not otherwise; and now,
what is this separation? Let us take from the unjust man nothing of
injustice, nor of justice from the just man; but let us make each of
them perfect in his own profession. And first, as to the unjust man, let
him act as the able artists; as a complete pilot, or physician, he

comprehends the possible and the impossible in the art; the one he 361a attempts, and the other he relinquishes; and, if he fail in anything, he is able to rectify it: so, in like manner, the unjust man attempting 204 pieces of injustice in a dexterous manner, let him be concealed, if he intend to be exceedingly unjust; but, if he be caught, let him be deemed worthless: for the most complete injustice is, to seem just, not being so. We must give then to the completely unjust the most complete injustice; and not take from him, but allow him, whist doing the greatest injustice, to procure to himself the highest reputation for justice; and, if in any thing he fail, let him be able to 361b rectify it: and let him be able to speak so as to persuade if any thing of his injustice be spread abroad: let him be able to do by force, what requires force, through his courage and strength, and by means of his friends and his wealth: and having supposed him to be such an one as this, let us place the just man beside him, in our reasoning, a simple and ingenuous man, desiring, according to Æschylus, not the appearance but the reality of goodness: let us take from him the appearance of goodness; for, if he shall appear to be just, he shall have 361c honours and rewards; and thus it may be uncertain whether he be such for the sake of justice, or on account of the rewards and honours: let him be stripped of every thing but justice, and be made completely contrary to the other; whilst he does no injustice, let him have the reputation of doing the greatest; that he may be tortured for justice, not yielding to reproach, and such things as arise from it, but may be immoveable till death; appearing indeed to be unjust through life, yet 361d being really just; that so both of them arriving at the utmost pitch, the one of justice, and the other of injustice, we may judge which of them is the happier."

"Strange!" said I, "friend Glauco, how strenuously you purify each of the men, as a statue which is to be judged of!" "As much," said he, "as I am able: whilst then they continue to be such, there will not, as I imagine, be any further difficulty to observe what kind of life remains to each of them. It must therefore be told. And if possibly it should be 361e told with greater rusticity, imagine not, Socrates, that it is I who tell it, but those who commend injustice preferably to justice; and they will say these things: That the just man, being of this disposition, will be scourged, tormented, fettered, have his eye burnt, and lastly, 362a having suffered all manner of evils, will be crucified; and he shall know, that he should not desire the reality but the appearance of justice: and that it is much more proper to pronounce that saying of Æschylus, concerning the unjust man: for they will in reality say that the unjust man, as being in pursuit of what is real, and living not according to the opinion of men, wants not to have the appearance but the reality of injustice:

205

> Reaping the hollow furrow of his mind,
> Whence all his glorious councils blossom forth.

362b

In the first place, he holds the magistracy in the state, being thought to be just; next, he marries wherever he inclines, and matches his children with whom he pleases; he joins in partnership and company with whom he inclines; and, besides all this, he will succeed in all his projects for gain; as he does not scruple to do injustice: when then he engages in competitions, he will both in private and in public surpass and exceed his adversaries; and by this means he will be rich, and serve his friends, and hurt his enemies: and he will amply and magnificently render sacrifices and offerings to the Gods, and will honour the Gods, and such men as he chooses, much better than the just man. From whence they reckon, that it is likely he will be more beloved of the Gods than the just man. Thus, they say, Socrates, that both with Gods and men there is a better life prepared for the unjust man than for the just."

362c

When Glauco had said these things, I had a design to say something in reply. But his brother Adimantus said—"Socrates, you do not imagine there is yet enough said on the argument." "What further then?" said I. "That has not yet been spoken," said he, "which ought most especially to have been mentioned." "Why then," said I, "the proverb is, 'A brother is help at hand.' So do you assist, if he has failed in any thing. Though what has been said by him is sufficient to throw me down, and make me unable to succour justice."

362d

362e

"You say nothing," replied he. "But hear this further. For we must go through all the arguments opposite to what he has said, which commend justice and condemn injustice, that what Glauco seems to me to intend may be more manifest. Now, parents surely tell and exhort their sons, as do all those who have the care of any, that it is

363a

necessary to be just; not commending justice in itself, but the honours arising from it; that whilst a man is reputed to be just, he may obtain *206* by this reputation magistracies and marriages, and whatever Glauco just now enumerated as the consequence of being reputed just: but these men carry this matter of reputation somewhat further; for, throwing in the approbation of the Gods, they have unspeakable blessings to enumerate to holy persons; which, they say, the Gods bestow. As the generous Hesiod and Homer say, the one, that the *363b* Gods cause the oaks to produce to just men

> Acorns at top, and in the middle bees;
> Their woolly sheep are laden with their fleece;[2]

and a great many other good things of the same nature. In like manner, the other,

> The blameless king, who holds a godlike name,
> Finds his black mould both wheat and barley bear; *363c*
> With fruit his trees are laden, and his flocks
> Bring forth with ease; the sea affords him fish.[3]

But Musæus and his son tell us that the Gods give just men more splendid blessings than these; for, carrying them in his poem into Hades, and placing them in company with holy men at a feast prepared for them, they crown them, and make them pass the whole *363d* of their time in drinking, deeming eternal inebriation[4] the finest reward of virtue. But some carry the rewards from the Gods still further; for they say that the offspring of the holy, and the faithful, and their children's children, still remain. With these things, and such as these, they commend justice. But the unholy and unjust they bury in Hades, in a kind of mud,[5] and compel them to carry water in a sieve; and make them, even whist alive, to live in infamy. Whatever *363e* punishments were assigned by Glauco to the just, whilst they were reputed unjust, these they assign to the unjust, but mention no others. This now is the way in which they commend and discommend them severally: but besides this, Socrates, consider another kind of *207* reasoning concerning justice and injustice, mentioned both privately *364a* and by the poets: for all of them with one mouth celebrate temperance and justice as indeed excellent, but yet difficult and laborious; and intemperance and injustice as indeed pleasant and easy to attain; but, by opinion only, and by law, abominable: and they say that for the most part unjust actions are more profitable than just. And they are gladly willing, both in public and private, to pay honour to wicked rich men, and such as have power of any kind, and to

364b pronounce them happy, but to contemn and overlook those who are any how weak and poor, even whilst they acknowledge them to be better than the others. But, of all these speeches, the most marvellous are those concerning the Gods and virtue: as if even the Gods gave to many good men misfortunes and an evil life, and to contrary persons a contrary fate: and mountebanks and prophets, frequenting the gates of the rich, persuade them that they have a power granted them by the Gods, of expiating by sacrifices and songs, with pleasures and with

364c feastings, if any injustice has been committed by any one, or his forefathers: and if he wishes to blast any enemy at a small expense, he shall injure the just in the same manner as the unjust; by certain blandishments and bonds, as they say, persuading the Gods to succour them: and to all these discourses they bring the poets as witnesses; who, mentioning the proneness to vice, say,

> How vice at once, and easily is gain'd;
364d > The way is smooth, and very nigh it dwells;
> Sweat before virtue stands, so Heav'n ordain'd[6]—

and a certain long and steep way. Others make Homer witness how the Gods are prevailed upon by men, because he says,

> . . . . The Gods themselves are turn'd
> With sacrifices and appealing vows;
364e > Fat off'rings and libation them persuade;
> And for transgressions suppliant pray'r atones.[7]

They show likewise many books of Musæus and Orpheus, the offspring, as they say, of the Moon, and of the Muses; according to

208 which they perform their sacred rites, persuading not only private persons, but states likewise, that there are absolutions and purgations

365a from iniquities by means of sacrifices, sports and pleasures; and this, for the benefit both of the living and of the dead: these they call the mysteries[8] which absolve us from evils there; but they assert that dreadful things await those who do not offer sacrifice. All these, and so many things of the kind, friend Socrates, being said of virtue and vice, and their reward both with men and Gods; what do we imagine the souls of our youth do, when they hear them; such of them as are well born, and able as it were to rush into all these things which are said, and from all to deliberate, in what sort of character and in what 365b sort of road one may best pass through life? It is likely he might say to himself, according to that of Pindar,

> Whether shall I the lofty wall
> Of justice try to scale;
> Or, hedg'd within the guileful maze
> Of vice, encircled dwell?

For according to what is said, though I be just, if I be not reputed so, there shall be no profit, but manifest troubles and punishments. But the unjust man, who procures to himself the character of justice, is said to have a divine life. Since then the appearance surpasses the 365c reality, as wise men demonstrate to me, and is the primary part of happiness, ought I not to turn wholly to it; and to draw round myself as a covering, and picture, the image of virtue; but to draw after me the cunning and versatile fox of the most wise Archilochus? But perhaps some one will say, It is not easy, being wicked, always to be concealed. Neither is any thing else easy (will we say) which is great. 365d But, however, if we would be happy, thither let us go where the vestiges of the reasonings lead us. For, in order to be concealed, we will make conjurations and associations together; and there are masters of persuasion, who teach a popular and political wisdom; by which means, whilst partly by persuasion and partly by force we seize 209 more than our due, we shall not be punished. But, surely, to be concealed from the Gods, or to overpower them, is impossible.

"If then they are not, or care not about human affairs, we need not 365e have any concern about being concealed: but if they really are, and care for us, we neither know nor have heard of them otherwise than from traditions, and from the poets who write their genealogies; and these very persons tell us, that they are to be moved and persuaded by sacrifices, and appeasing vows, and offerings; both of which we are to believe, or neither. If then we are to believe both, we may do injustice, and of the fruits of our injustice offer sacrifice. If we be just, we shall 366a indeed be unpunished by the Gods; but then we shall not have the

gains of injustice. But if we be unjust, we shall make gain; and after we have transgressed and offended, we shall appease them by offerings, and be liberated from punishment. But we shall be punished in the other world for our unjust doings here; either we ourselves, or our children's children. But, friend, will the reasoner say, the mysteries
366b can do much; the Gods are exorable, as say the mightiest states, and the children of the Gods, the poets; who are also their prophets, and who declare that these things are so.

"For what reason, then, should we still prefer justice before the greatest injustice; which if we shall attain to with any deceiving appearance, we shall fare according to our mind, both with reference to Gods and men, both living and dying, according to the speech now mentioned of many and excellent men? From all that has been said,
366c by what means, O Socrates, shall he incline to honour justice, who has any ability of fortune or of wealth, of body or of birth, and not laugh when he hears it commended? So that, though a man were able even to show what we have said to be false, and fully understood that justice is better, he will, however, abundantly pardon and not be angry with the unjust; for he knows, that unless one from a divine nature abhor
366d to do injustice, or from acquired knowledge abstain from it, no one of others is willingly just; but either through cowardice, old age, or same other weakness, condemns the doing injustice when unable to do it. That it is so is plain. For the first of these who arrives at power is the first to do injustice, as far as he is able. And the reason of all this is
210 no other than that from whence all this discourse proceeded, Socrates,
366e because, O wonderful man! among all those of you that call yourselves the commenders of justice, beginning from those ancient heroes of whom any accounts are left to the men of the present time, no one hath at any time condemned injustice, nor commended justice, otherwise than regarding the reputations, honours and rewards arising from them: but no one has hitherto sufficiently examined, neither in poetry nor in prose discourse, either of them in itself, and subsisting by its own power, in the soul of him who possesses it, and concealed from both Gods and men: how that the one is the greatest of all the evils which the soul hath within it, and justice the greatest
367a good: for, if it had thus from the beginning been spoken of by you all, and you had so persuaded us from our youth, we should not need to

watch over our neighbour lest he should do us injustice, but every man would have been the best guardian over himself, afraid lest in doing injustice he should dwell with the greatest evil. These things now, Socrates, and probably much more than these, Thrasymachus or some other might say of justice and injustice, inverting their power, disagreeably as I imagine for my own part. But I (for I want to conceal 367b nothing from you) being desirous to hear you on the opposite side, speak the best I am able, pulling the contrary way. Do not, therefore, only show us in your reasoning that justice is better than injustice; but in what manner each of them by itself, affecting the mind, is, the one evil, and the other good. And take away all opinions, as Glauco likewise enjoined: for, if you do not take away the false opinions on both sides, and add the true ones, we will say you do not commend justice, but the appearance; nor condemn being unjust, but the 367c appearance; that you advise the unjust man to conceal himself; and that you assent to Thrasymachus that justice is a foreign good; the profit of the more powerful; and that injustice is the profit and advantage of oneself, but unprofitable to the inferior. Wherefore, now, after you have acknowledged that justice is among the greatest goods, and such as are worthy to be possessed for what arises from them, and much more in themselves, and for their own sake; such as sight, hearing, wisdom, health, and such other goods as are real in 367d their own nature, and not merely in opinion; in the same manner commend justice; how, in itself, it profits the owner, and injustice hurts him. And leave to others to commend the rewards and 211 opinions; for I could bear with others in this way, commending justice, and condemning injustice, celebrating and reviling their opinions and rewards; but not with you (unless you desire me), because you have passed the whole of life considering nothing else but this. 367e Show us, then, in your discourse, not only that justice is better than injustice; but in what manner each of them by itself affecting the owner, whether he be concealed or not concealed from Gods and men, is, the one good, and the other evil."

On hearing these things, as I always indeed was pleased with the disposition of Glauco and Adimantus, so at that time I was perfectly delighted, and replied: "It was not ill said concerning you, sons of that 368a worthy man, by the lover of Glauco, who wrote the beginning of the

Elegies, when, celebrating your behaviour at the battle of Megara, he
sang,

> Aristo's sons! of an illustrious man,
> The race divine.

"This, friend, seems to be well said; for you are truly affected in a
divine manner, if you are not persuaded that injustice is better than
368b justice, and yet are able to speak thus in its defence: and to me you
seem, truly, not to be persuaded; and reason from the whole of your
other behaviour, since, according to your present speeches at least, I
should distrust you. But the more I can trust you, the more I am in
doubt what argument I shall use. For I can neither think of any
assistance I have to give (for I seem to be unable, and my mark is, that
you do not accept of what I said to Thrasymachus when I imagined I
showed that justice was better than injustice), nor yet can I think of
368c giving no assistance; for I am afraid lest it be an unholy thing to
desert justice when I am present, and see it accused, and not assist it
whilst I breathe and am able to speak. It is best then to succour it in
such a manner as I can."

Hereupon Glauco and the rest entreated me, by all means, to assist,
and not relinquish the discourse; but to search thoroughly what each
of them is, and which way the truth lies, as to their respective
advantage. I then said what appeared to me: That the inquiry we were
368d attempting was not contemptible, but was that of one who was sharp-
sighted, as I imagined. "Since then," said I, "we are not very expert, it
212 seems proper to make the inquiry concerning this matter, in such a
manner as if it were ordered those who are not very sharp-sighted, to
read small letters at a distance; and one should afterwards understand,
that the same letters are greater somewhere else, and in a larger field:
it would appear eligible, I imagine, first to read these, and thus come
to consider the lesser, if they happen to be the same." "Perfectly
368e right," said Adimantus. "But what of this kind, Socrates, do you
perceive in the inquiry concerning justice?" "I shall tell you," said I.
"Do not we say there is justice in one man, and there is likewise justice
in a whole state?" "It is certainly so," replied he. "Is not a state a
greater object than one man?" "Greater," said he. "It is likely, then,
that justice should be greater in what is greater, and be more easy to

be understood: we shall first, then, if you incline, inquire what it is in   369a
states; and then, after the same manner, we shall consider it in each
individual, contemplating the similitude of the greater in the idea of
the lesser." "You seem to me," said he, "to say right." "If then," said I,
"we contemplate, in our discourse, a state existing, shall we not
perceive its justice and injustice existing?" "Perhaps," said he. "And is
there not ground to hope, if this exists, that we shall more easily find
what we seek for?" "Most certainly." "It seems, then, we ought to   369b
attempt to succeed, for I imagine this to be a work of no small
importance. Consider then." "We are considering," said Adimantus,
"and do you no otherwise."

   "A city, then," said I, "as I imagine, takes its rise from this, that
none of us happens to be self-sufficient, but are indigent of many
things; or, do you imagine there is any other origin of building a
city?" "None other," said he. "Thus, then, one taking in one person   369c
for one indigence, and another for another; as they stand in need of
many things, they assemble into one habitation many companions
and assistants; and to this joint-habitation we give the name city, do
we not?" "Certainly." "And they mutually exchange with one
another, each judging that, if he either gives or takes in exchange, it
will be for his advantage." "Certainly." "Come, then," said I, "let us,
in our discourse, make a city from the beginning. And, it seems, our
indigence has made it." "Why not?" "But the first and the greatest of   369d
wants is the preparation of food, in order to subsist and live." "By all
means." "The second is of lodging. The third of clothing; and such
like." "It is so." "But, come," said I, "how shall the city be able to
make so great a provision? Shall not one be a husbandman, another a
mason, some other a weaver? or, shall we add to them a shoemaker, or   213
some other of those who minister to the necessaries of the body?"
"Certainly." "So that the most indigent city might consist of four or
five men?" "It seems so." "But, what now? Must each of those do his   369e
work for them all in common? As, the husbandman, being one, shall
he prepare food for four? and consume quadruple time, and labour, in
preparing food, and sharing it with others? or, neglecting them, shall
he for himself alone make the fourth part of this food, in the fourth   370a
part of the time? and, of the other three parts of time, shall he employ
one in the preparation of a house, the other in that of clothing, the

other of shoes, and not give himself trouble in sharing with others, but do his own affairs by himself?"

Adimantus said:—"And probably, Socrates, this way [the former] is more easy than the other." "No, certainly," said I; "it would be absurd. For, whilst you are speaking, I consider that we are born not 370b perfectly resembling one another, but differing in disposition; one being fitted for doing one thing, and another for doing another: does it not seem so to you?" "It does." "But, what now? Whether will a man do better, if, being one, he works in many arts, or in one?" "When in one," said he. "But this, I imagine, is also plain; that if one miss the season of any work, it is ruined." "That is plain." "For, I imagine, the work will not wait upon the leisure of the workman; but of necessity 370c the workman must attend close upon the work, and not in the way of a by-job." "Of necessity." "And hence it appears, that more will be done, and better, and with greater ease, when every one does but one thing, according to their genius, and in proper season, and freed from other things." "Most certainly," said he. "But we need certainly, Adimantus, more citizens than four, for those provisions we mentioned: for the husbandman, it would seem, will not make a 370d plough for himself, if it is to be handsome; nor yet a spade, nor other instruments of agriculture: as little will the mason; for he, likewise, needs many things: and in the same way, the weaver and the shoemaker also. Is it not so?" "True." "Joiners, then, and smiths, and other such workmen, being admitted into our little city, make it throng." "Certainly." "But it would be no very great matter, neither, if we did not give them neatherds likewise, and shepherds, and those 370e other herdsmen; in order that both the husbandmen may have oxen 214 for ploughing, and that the masons, with the help of the husband men, may use the cattle for their carriages; and that the weavers likewise, and the shoemakers, may have hides and wool." "Nor yet," said he, "would it be a very small city, having all these." "But," said I, it is almost impossible to set down such a city in any such place as that it shall need no importations." "It is impossible." "It will then certainly want others still, who may import from another state what it needs." "It will want them." "And surely this service would be 371a empty, if it carry out nothing which these want, from whom they import what they need themselves. It goes out empty in such a case, does it not?" "To me it seems so." "But the city ought not only to make what is sufficient for itself; but such things, and so much also, as may answer for those things which they need." "It ought." "Our city, then, certainly wants a great many more husbandmen and other workmen?" "A great many more." "And other servants betides, to import and export the several things; and these are merchants, are they not?" "Yes." "We shall then want merchants likewise?" "Yes, indeed." "And if the merchandise is by sea, it will want many others; such as are skilful in sea affairs." "Many others, truly." "But what as to the city within itself? How will they exchange with one another the things which they have each of them worked; and for the sake of which, making a community, they have built a city?" "It is plain," said he, "in selling and buying." "Hence we must have a forum, and money, as a symbol, for the sake of exchange." "Certainly." 371b

371c

"If now the husbandman, or any other workman, bring any of his work to the forum, but come not at the same time with those who want to make exchange with him, must he not, desisting from his work, sit idly in the forum?" "By no means," said he. "But there are some who, observing this, set themselves to this service; and, in well-regulated cities, they are mostly such as are weakest in their body, and unfit to do any other work. There they are to attend about the forum, to give money in exchange for such things as any may want to sell; and things in exchange for money to such as want to buy." "This indigence," said I, "procures our city a race of shopkeepers; for, do not we call shopkeepers, those who, fixed in the forum, serve both in selling and buying? but such as travel to other cities we call merchants." "Certainly." 371d

215

"There are still, as I imagine, certain other ministers, who, though unfit to serve the public in things which require understanding, have yet strength of body sufficient for labour, who selling the use of their strength, and calling the reward of it hire, are called, as I imagine, hirelings: are they not?" "Yes, indeed." "Hirelings then are, it seems, the complement of the city?" "It seems so." "Has our city now, Adimantus, already so increased upon us as to be complete?" "Perhaps." "Where now, at all, should justice and injustice be in it; and, in which of the things that we have considered does it appear to exist?" "I do not know," said he, "Socrates, if it be not in a certain use, 371e

372a

The Republic

somehow, of these things with one another." "Perhaps," said I, "you say right. But we must consider it, and not be weary. First, then, let us consider after what manner those who are thus procured shall be supported. Is it any other way than by making bread and wine, and clothes, and shoes, and building houses? In summer, indeed, they will work for the most part without clothes and shoes; and, in winter, they 372b will be sufficiently furnished with clothes and shoes; they will be nourished, partly with barley, making meal of it, and partly with wheat, making loaves, boiling part and toasting part, putting fine loaves and cakes over a fire of stubble, or over dried leaves; and resting themselves on couches, strawed with smilax and myrtle leaves, they and their children will feast; drinking wine, and crowned, and singing to the Gods, they will pleasantly live together, begetting 372c children, not beyond their substance, guarding against poverty or war."

Glauco replying says, "You make the men to feast, as it appears, without meats." "You say true," said I; "for I forget that they shall have meats likewise. They shall have salt, and olives, and cheese; and they shall boil bulbous roots, and herbs of the field; and we set before 372d them desserts of figs, and vetches, and beans; and they will toast at the fire myrtle berries, and the berries of the beech-tree; drinking in moderation, and thus passing their life in peace and health; and dying, as is likely, in old age, they will leave to their children another such life." "If you had been making, Socrates," said he, "a city of 216 hogs, what else would you have fed them with but with these things?" "But how should we do, Glauco?" said I. "What is usually done," said he. "They must, as I imagine, have their beds, and tables, and meats, 372e and deserts, as we now have, if they are not to be miserable." "Be it so," said I; "I understand you." "We consider, it seems, not only how a city may exist, but how a luxurious city: and perhaps it is not amiss; for, in considering such an one, we may probably see how justice and injustice have their origin in cities. But the true city seems to me to be such an one as we have described; like one who is healthy; but if you incline that we likewise consider a city that is corpulent, nothing 373a hinders it. For these things will not, it seems, please some; nor this sort of life satisfy them; but there shall be beds, and tables, and all other furniture; seasonings, ointments, and perfumes; mistresses, and confections, and various kinds of all these. And we must no longer consider as alone necessary what we mentioned at the first; houses, and clothes, and shoes; but painting too, and all the curious arts must be set a-going, and carving, and gold, and ivory; and all these things must be procured, must they not?" "Yes," said he. "Must not the city, 373b then, be larger? For that healthy one is no longer sufficient, but is already full of luxury; and of a crowd of such as are no way necessary to cities; such as all kinds of sportsmen, and the imitative artists, many of them imitating in figures and colours, and others in music: poets too, and their ministers, rhapsodists, actors, dancers, undertakers, workmen of all forts of instruments; and what has 373c reference to female ornaments, as well as other things. We shall need likewise many more servants. Do not you think they will require pedagogues, and nurses, and tutors, hair-dressers, barbers, victuallers too, and cooks? And further still, we shall want swine-herds likewise: of these there were none in the other city, (for there needed not) but in this we shall want these, and many other sorts of herds likewise, if any eat the several animals, shall we not?" "Why not?" "Shall we not 373d then, in this manner of life, be much more in need of physicians than formerly?" "Much more." "And the country, which was then sufficient to support the inhabitants, will, instead of being sufficient, become too little; or how shall we say?" "In this way," said he. "Must we not then encroach upon the neighbouring country, if we want to 217 have sufficient for plough and pasture, and they, in like manner, on us, if they likewise suffer themselves to accumulate wealth to infinity; going beyond the boundary of necessaries?" "There is great necessity 373e for it, Socrates." "Shall we afterwards fight, Glauco or how shall we do?" "We shall certainly," said he. "But we say nothing," said I, "whether war does any evil, or any good; but thus much only, that we have found the origin of war: from whence, most especially, arise the greatest mischiefs to states, both private and public." "Yes, indeed." "We shall need then, friend, still a larger city; not for a small, but for 374a a large army, who, in going out, may fight with those who assault them, for their whole substance, and every thing we have now mentioned." "What," said he, "are not these sufficient to fight?" "No; if you, at least," said I, "and all of us, have rightly agreed, when we formed our city: and we agreed, if you remember, that it was

impossible for one to perform many arts handsomely." "You say
374b true," said he. "What, then," said I, "as to that contest of war; does it
not appear to require art?" "Very much," said he. "Ought we then to
take more care of the art of shoe-making than of the art of making
war?" "By no means." "But we charged the shoe-maker neither to
undertake at the same time to be a husbandman, nor a weaver, nor a
mason, but a shoe-maker; that the work of that art may be done for
us handsomely: and, in like manner, we allotted to every one of the
rest one thing, to which the genius of each led him, and what each
took care of, freed from other things, to do it well, applying to it the
374c whole of his life, and not neglecting the seasons of working. And
now, as to the affairs of war, whether is it of the greatest importance,
that they be well performed? Or, is this so easy a thing, that one may
be a husbandman, and likewise a soldier, and shoe-maker; or be
employed in any other art? But not even at chess, or dice, can one ever
play skilfully, unless he study this very thing from his childhood, and
374d not make it a by-work. Or, shall one, taking a spear, or any other of
the warlike arms and instruments, become instantly an expert
combatant, in an encounter in arms, or in any other relating to war?
And, shall the taking up of no other instrument make a workman, or
a wrestler, nor be useful to him who has neither the knowledge of
218 that particular thing, nor has bestowed the study sufficient for its
attainment?" "Such instruments," said he, "would truly be very
valuable."

"By how much then," said I, "this work of guards is one of the
374e greatest importance, by so much it should require the greatest leisure
from other things, and likewise the greatest art and study." "I
imagine so," replied he. "And shall it not likewise require a
competent genius for this profession?" "Why not?" "It should surely
be our business, as it seems, if we be able, to choose who and what
kind of geniuses are competent for the guardianship of the city."
"Ours, indeed." "We have truly," said I, "undertaken no mean
375a business; but, however, we are not to despair, so long at least as we
have any ability." "No indeed," said he. "Do you think then," said I,
"that the genius of a generous whelp differs any thing for
guardianship, from that of a generous youth?" "What is it you say?"
"It is this. Must not each of them be acute in the perception, swift to

pursue what they perceive, and strong likewise if there is need to conquer what they shall catch?" "There is need," said he, "of all these." "And surely he must be brave likewise, if he fight well." "Why not?" "But will he be brave who is not spirited, whether it is a horse, a dog, or any other animal? Or, have you not observed, that the spirit is 375b somewhat insurmountable and invincible; by the presence of which every soul is, in respect of all things whatever, unterrified and unconquerable?" "I have observed it." "It is plain then what sort of a guard we ought to have, with reference to his body." "Yes." "And with reference to his soul, that he should be spirited." "This likewise is plain." "How then," said I, "Glauco, will they not be savage towards one another and the other citizens, being of such a temper?" "No truly," said he, "not easily." "But yet it is necessary that towards their 375c friends they be meek, and fierce towards their enemies; for otherwise they will not wait till others destroy them; but they will prevent them, doing it themselves." "True," said he. "What then," said I, "shall we do? Where shall we find, at once, the mild and the magnanimous temper? For the mild disposition is somehow opposite to the spirited." "It appears so." "But, however, if he be deprived of either of these, he cannot be a good guardian; for it seems to he impossible; and thus it appears, that a good guardian is an impossible 375d thing." "It seems so," said he.

After hesitating and considering what had passed: "Justly," said I, 219 "friend, are we in doubt; for we have departed from that image which we first established." "How say you?" "Have we not observed, that there are truly such tempers as we were not imagining, who have these opposite things?" "Where then?" "One may see it in other animals, and not a little in that one with which we compared our guardian. 375e For this, you know, is the natural temper of generous dogs, to be most mild towards their domestics and their acquaintance, but the reverse to those they know not." "It is so." "This then," said I, "is possible; and it is not against nature that we require our guardian to be such an one." "It seems not." "Are you, further, of this opinion, that he who is to be our guardian should, besides being spirited, be a philosopher likewise?" "How?" said he; "for I do not understand you." "This, 376a likewise," said I, "you will observe in the dogs; and it is worthy of admiration in the brute." "As what?" "He is angry at whatever unknown person he sees, though he hath never suffered any ill from him before; but he is fond of whatever acquaintance he sees, though he has never at any time received any good from him. Have you not wondered at this?" "I never," said he, "much attended to it before; 376b but, that he does this, is plain." "But, indeed, this affection of his nature seems to be an excellent disposition and truly philosophical." "As how?" "As," said I, "it distinguishes between a friendly and unfriendly aspect, by nothing else but this, that it knows the one, but is ignorant of the other. How, now, should not this be deemed the love of learning, which distinguishes what is friendly and what is foreign, by knowledge and ignorance?" "It can no way be shown why it should not." "But, however," said I, "to be a lover of learning, and a philosopher; are the same." "The same," said he. "May we not then 376c boldly settle it, That in man too, if any one is to be of a mild disposition towards his domestics and acquaintance, he must be a philosopher and a lover of learning?" "Let us settle it," said he. "He then who is to be a good and worthy guardian for us, of the city, shall be a philosopher, and spirited, and swift, and strong in his disposition." "By all means," said he. "Let then our guardian," said I, "be such an one. But in what manner shall these be educated for us, and instructed? And will the consideration of this be of any assistance 376d in perceiving that for the sake of which we consider every thing else? In what manner justice and injustice arise in the city, that we may not 220 omit a necessary part of the discourse; nor consider what is superfluous?" The brother of Glauco said: "I, for my part, greatly expect that this inquiry will be of assistance to that." "Truly," said I, "friend Adimantus, it is not to be omitted, though it should happen to be somewhat tedious." "No, truly." "Come then, let us, as if we 376e were talking in the way of fable, and at our leisure, educate these men in our reasoning." "It must be done."

"What then is the education? Or, is it difficult to find a better than that which was found long ago, which is, gymnastic for the body, and music for the mind?" "It is indeed." "Shall we not then, first, begin with instructing them in music, rather than in gymnastic?" "Why not?" "When you say music, you mean discourses, do you not?" "I do: but of discourses there are two kinds; the one true, and the other 377a false." "There are." "And they must be educated in them both, and first in the false." "I do not understand," said he, "what you mean." "Do not you understand," said I, "that we first of all tell children fables? And this part of music, somehow, to speak in the general, is false; yet there is truth in them; and we accustom children to fables before their gymnastic exercises." "We do so." "This then is what I meant, when I said that children were to begin music before gymnastic." "Right," said he. "And do you not know that the beginning of every work is of the greatest importance, especially to any one young and tender? for then truly, in the easiest manner, is 377b formed and taken on the impression which one inclines to imprint on every individual." "It is entirely so." "Shall we then suffer the children to hear any kind of fables composed by any kind of persons; and to receive, for the most part, into their minds, opinions contrary to those we judge they ought to have when they are grown up?" "We shall by no means suffer it." "First of all, then, we must preside over 377c the fable-makers. And whatever beautiful fable they make must be chosen; and what are otherwise must be rejected; and we shall persuade the nurses and mothers to tell the children such fables as shall be chosen; and to fashion their minds by fables, much more than their bodies by their hands. But the most of what they tell them at present must be thrown out." "As what?" said he. "In the greater ones," said I, "we shall see the lesser likewise. For the fashion of them must be the same; and both the greater and the lesser must have the 377d same kind of power. Do not you think so?" "I do," said he: "but I do not at all understand which you call the greater one." "Those," said I, 221 "which Hesiod and Homer tell us, and the other poets. For they composed false fables to mankind, and told them as they do still." "Which," said he, "do you mean, and what is it you blame in them?" "That," said I, "which first of all and most especially ought to be blamed, when one does not falsify handsomely." "What is that?" 377e "When one, in his composition, gives ill representations of the nature of Gods and heroes: as a painter drawing a picture in no respect resembling what he wished to paint." "It is right," said he, "to blame such things as these. But how have they failed, say we, and as to what?" "First of all, with reference to that greatest lie, and matters of the greatest importance, he did not lie handsomely, who told how Heaven did what Hesiod says he did; and then again how Saturn

378a punished him, and what Saturn did, and what he suffered from his son: For though these things were true, yet I should not imagine they ought to be so plainly told to the unwise and the young, but ought much rather to be concealed. But if there were a necessity to tell them, they should be heard in secrecy, by as few as possible; after they had sacrificed not a hog, but some great and wonderful sacrifice, that thus the fewest possible might chance to hear them."

"These fables," said he, "are indeed truly hurtful." "And not to be
378b mentioned, Adimantus," said I, "in our city. Nor is it to be said in the hearing of a youth, that he who does the most extreme wickedness does nothing strange; nor he who in every shape punishes his unjust father, but that he does the same as the first and the greatest of the Gods." "No truly," said he, "these things do not seem to me proper to be said." "Nor, universally," said I, "must it be told how Gods war with Gods, and plot and fight against one another, (for such
378c assertions are not true,)—if, at least, those who are to guard the city for us ought to account it the most shameful thing to hate one another on slight grounds. As little ought we to tell in fables, and embellish to them, the battles of the giants; and many other all various feuds, both of the Gods and heroes, with their own kindred and relations. But if we are at all to persuade them that at no time
378d should one citizen hate another, and that it is unholy; such things as these are rather to be said to them immediately when they are
222 children, by the old men and women, and by those well advanced in life; and the poets are to be obliged to compose agreeably to these things. But Juno fettered by her son, and Vulcan hurled from heaven by his father for going to assist his mother when beaten, and all those battles of the Gods which Homer has composed, must not be admitted into the city; whether they be composed in the way of allegory, or without allegory; for the young person is not able to judge what is allegory and what is not: but whatever opinions he receives at
378e such an age are with difficulty washed away, and are generally immoveable. On these accounts, one would imagine, that, of all things, we should endeavour that what they are first to hear be composed in the most handsome manner for exciting them to virtue." "There is reason for it," said he. "But, if any one now should ask us concerning these, what they are, and what kind of fables they

are, which should we name?" And I said: "Adimantus, you and I are not poets at present, but founders of a city; and it belongs to the founders to know the models according to which the poets are to compose their fables; contrary to which if they compose, they are not to be tolerated; but it belongs not to us to make fables for them." "Right," said he. "But, as to this very thing, the models concerning theology, which are they?" "Some such as these," said I. "God is always to represented such as he is, whether one represent him in epic, in song, or in tragedy." "This ought to be done." "Is not God essentially good, and is he not to be described as such?" "Without doubt." "But nothing which is good is hurtful is it?" "I does not appear to me that it is." "Does, then, that which is not hurtful ever do hurt?" "By no means." "Does that which does no hurt do any evil?" "Nor this neither." "And what does no evil cannot be the cause of any evil." "How can it?" "But what? Good is beneficial." "Yes." "It is, then, the cause of welfare?" "Yes." "Good, therefore, is not the cause of all things, but the cause of those things which are in a right state; but is not the cause of those things which are in a wrong." "Entirely so," said he. "Neither, then, can God," said I, "since he is good, be the cause of all things, as the many say, but he is the cause of a few things to men; but of many things he is not the cause; for our good things are much fewer than our evil: and no other than God is the cause of our good things; but of our evils we must not make God the cause, but seek for some other." "You seem to me," said he, "to speak most true." "We must not, then," said I, "either admit Homer or any other poet trespassing so foolishly with reference to the Gods, and saying, how

> Two vessels on Jove's threshold ever stand,
> The source of evil one, and one of good.
> The man whose lot Jove mingles out of both,
> By good and ill alternately is rul'd.
> But he whose portion is unmingled ill,
> O'er sacred earth by famine dire is driv'n.[9]

Nor that Jupiter is the dispenser of our good and evil. Nor, if any one say that the violation of oaths and treaties by Pandarus was effected by Minerva and Jupiter, shall we commend it. Nor that dissension among the Gods, and judgment by Themis and Jupiter. Nor yet must

379a

379b

379c

223

379d

379e

380a

we suffer the youth to hear what Æschylus says; how,

> Whenever God inclines to raze
> A house, himself contrives a cause.

But, if any one make poetical compositions, in which are these iambics, the sufferings of Niobe, of the Pelopides, or the Trojans, or others of a like nature we must either not suffer them to say they are the works of God; or, if of God, we must find that reason for them
380b which we now require, and we must say that God did what was just and good; and that they were benefited by being chastised: but we must not suffer a poet to say, that they are miserable who are punished; and that it is God who does these things. But if they say that the wicked, as being miserable, needed correction; and that, in being punished, they were profited by God, we may suffer the assertion. But, to say that God, who is good, is the cause of ill to any one, this we must by all means oppose, nor suffer any one to say so in his city; if he
380c wishes to have it well regulated. Nor must we permit any one, either young or old, to hear such things told in fable, either in verse or prose; as they are neither agreeable to sanctity to be told, nor profitable to us, nor consistent with themselves."

"I vote along with you," said he, "in this law, and it pleases me."
224 "This, then," said I, "may be one of the laws and models with reference to the Gods: by which it shall be necessary that those who speak, and who compose, shall compose and say that God is not the cause of all things, but of good." "Yes, indeed," said he, "it is
380d necessary." "But what as to this second law? Think you that God is a buffoon, and insidiously appears, at different times, in different shapes; sometimes like himself; and, at other times, changing his appearance into many shapes; sometimes deceiving us, and making us conceive false opinions of him? Or, do you conceive him to be simple, and departing the least of all things from his proper form?" "I cannot, at present, at least," replied he, "say so." "But what as to this? If any thing be changed from its proper form, is there not a necessity that it
380e be changed by itself, or by another?" "Undoubtedly." "Are not those things which are in the best state, least of all changed and moved by any other thing? as the body, by meats and drinks, and labours: and every vegetable by tempests and winds, and such like accidents. Is not

the most sound and vigorous least of all changed?" "Why not?" "And ₃₈₁ₐ as to the soul itself, will not any perturbation from without, least of all disorder and change the most brave and wise?" "Yes." "And surely, somehow, all vessels which are made, and buildings, and vestments, according to the same reasoning, such as are properly worked, and in a right state, are least changed by time, or other accidents?" "They are so, indeed." "Every thing then which is in a good state, either by nature, or art, or both, receives the smallest change from any thing ₃₈₁ᵦ else." "It seems so." "But God, and every thing belonging to divinity, are in the best state." "Why not?" "In this way, then, God should least of all have many shapes." "Least of all, truly." "But should he change and alter himself?" "It is plain," said he, "if he be changed at all." "Whether then will he change himself to the better, and to the more handsome, or to the worse, and the more deformed?" "Of necessity," ₃₈₁ᵧ replied he, "to the worse, if he be changed at all; for we shall never at any time say, that God is any way deficient with respect to beauty or excellence." "You say most right," said I. "And this being so; do you imagine, Adimantus, that any one, either of Gods or men, would willingly make himself any way worse?" "It is impossible," said he. "It is impossible, then," said I, "for a God to desire to change himself; but each of them, being most beautiful and excellent, continues always, to the utmost of his power, invariably in his own form." "This ₂₂₅ appears to me, at least," said he, "wholly necessary." "Let not, then," said I, "most excellent Adimantus, any of the poets tell us, how the ₃₈₁ᵨ Gods,

> . . . . . at times resembling foreign guests,
> Wander o'er cities in all-various forms.[10]

Nor let any one belie Proteus and Thetis. Nor bring in Juno, in tragedies or other poems, as having transformed herself like a priestess, and collecting for the life-sustaining sons of Inachus the Argive River. Nor let them tell us many other such lies. Nor let the ₃₈₁ₑ mothers, persuaded by them, affright their children, telling the stories wrong; as, that certain Gods wander by night,

> resembling various guests, in various forms,

that they may not, at one and the same time, blaspheme against the Gods, and render their children more dastardly." "By no means," said he. "But are the Gods," said I, "such as, though in themselves they never change, yet make us imagine they appear in various forms, deceiving us, and playing the mountebanks?" "Perhaps," said he. "But 382a what," said I, "can a God cheat; holding forth a phantasm, either in word or deed?" "I do not know," said he. "Do not you know," said I, "that what is truly a cheat, if we may be allowed to say so, both all the Gods and men abhor?" "How do you say?" replied he. "Thus," said I: "That to offer a cheat to the most principal part of themselves, and that about their most principal interests, is what none willingly incline to do; but, of all things, every one is most afraid of possessing a cheat there." "Neither as yet," said he, "do I understand you." 382b "Because," said I, "you think I am saying something venerable: but I am saying, that to cheat the soul concerning realities, and to be so cheated, and to be ignorant, and there to have obtained and to keep a cheat, is what every one would least of all choose; and a cheat in the soul is what they most especially hate." "Most especially," said he. "But this, as I was now saying, might most justly be called a true cheat,— 226 ignorance in the soul of the cheated person: since a cheat in words is 382c but a kind of imitation of what the soul feels; and an image afterwards arising, and not altogether a pure cheat. Is it not so?" "Entirely." "But this real lie is not only hated of the Gods, but of men likewise." "So it appears." "But what now? With respect to the cheat in words, when has it something of utility, so as not to deserve hatred? Is it not when employed towards our enemies; and some even of those called our friends; when in madness, or other distemper, they attempt to do some mischief? In that case, for a dissuasive, as a drug, it is 382d useful. And in those fables we were now mentioning, as we know not how the truth stands concerning ancient things, making a lie resembling the truth, we render it useful as much as possible." "It is," said he, perfectly so." "In which then of these cases is a lie useful to God? Whether does he make a lie resembling the truth, as being ignorant of ancient things?" "That would be ridiculous," said he. 382e "God is not then a lying poet." "I do not think it." "But should he make a lie through fear of his enemies?" "Far from it." "But on account of the folly or madness of his kindred?" "But," said he, "none of the foolish and mad are the friends of God." "There is then no occasion at all for God to make a lie." "There is none." "The divine and godlike nature is then, in all respects, without a lie?" "Altogether," said he. "God then is simple and true, both in word and deed; neither is he changed himself, nor does he deceive others; neither by visions, nor by discourse, nor by the pomp of signs; neither when we are awake, nor when we sleep." "So it appears," said he, "to me, at least whilst you are speaking." "You agree then," said I, "that this shall be the second model, by which we are to speak and to compose concerning the Gods: that they are neither mountebanks, to change themselves; nor to mislead us by lies, either in word or deed?" "I agree." "Whilst then we commend many other things in Homer, this we shall not commend, the dream sent by Jupiter to Agamemnon; neither shall we commend Æschylus, when he makes Thetis say that Apollo had sung at her marriage, that 383b

> A comely offspring she should raise,
> From sickness free, of lengthen'd days:
> Apollo, singing all my fate,
> And praising high my Godlike state,
> Rejoic'd my heart and 'twas my hope,
> That all was true Apollo spoke:
> But he, who, at my marriage feast, 227
> Extoll'd me thus, and was my guest;
> He who did thus my fate explain,
> Is he who now my son hath slain.

When any one says such things as these of the Gods, we shall show 383c displeasure, and not afford the chorus: nor shall we suffer teachers to make use of such things in the education of the youth; if our guardians are to be pious, and divine men, as far as it is possible for man to be." "I agree with you," said he, "perfectly, as to these models; and we may use them as laws."

THE END OF THE SECOND BOOK.

BOOK III.

"These things indeed then," said I, "and such as these, are, as it 386a
seems, what are to be heard, and not heard, concerning the Gods,
immediately from childhood, by those who are to honour the Gods
and their parents, and who are not to despise friendship with one
another." "And I imagine," replied he, "that these things have
appeared right." "But, what now? If they are to be brave, must not
these things be narrated to them, and such other likewise as may
render them least of all afraid of death? Or, do you imagine that any 386b
one can ever be brave whilst he has this fear within him?" "Not I,
truly," said he. "But what? do you think that any one can be void of a
fear of death, whilst he imagines that there is Hades, and that it is
dreadful; and, that in battles he will choose death before defeat and
slavery?" "By no means."

"We ought then, as it seems, to give orders likewise to those who
undertake to discourse about fables of this kind; and to entreat them
not to reproach thus in general the things in Hades, but rather to
commend them; as they say neither what is true, nor what is 386c
profitable to those who are to be soldiers." "We ought indeed," said
he. "Beginning then," said I, "at this verse, we shall leave out all of
such kind, as this;

> I'd rather, as a rustic nave, submit
> To some mean man, who had but scanty fare,
> Than govern all the wretched shades below.[1]

And that,

386d   The house, to mortals and immortals, seems
        Dreadful and squalid; and what Gods abhor;

229 And,

        O strange! in Pluto's dreary realms to find
        Soul and its image, but no spark of mind.

And,

        He's wise alone, the rest are flutt'ring shades.

And,

        The soul to Hades from its members fled;
        And, leaving youth and manhood, wail'd its fate.

387a And,

        . . . . the soul, like smoke, down to the shades
        Fled howling² . . . .

And,

        As, in the hollow of a spacious cave,
        The owls fly screaming; if one chance to fall
        Down from the rock, they all confus'dly fly;
        So these together howling went³ . . . .

387b We shall request Homer and the other poets not to be indignant if we raze these things, and such as these; not that they are not poetical, and pleasant to many to be heard; but, the more poetical they are, the less ought they to be heard by children, and men who ought to be free, and more afraid of slavery than of death." "By all means, truly."

"Further, are not all dreadful and frightful names about these
387c things likewise to be rejected? Cocytus, and Styx, those in the infernal regions, and the dead, and such other appellations, in this form, such as terrify all who hear them. These may perhaps, serve some other purpose: but we are afraid for our guardians; lest, by such a terror, they be rendered more effeminate and soft than they ought to be." "We are rightly afraid of it," said he. "Are these then to be taken away?" "They are." "And they must speak and compose on a contrary model."
387d "That is plain." "We shall take away likewise the bewailings and lamentations of illustrious men." "This is necessary, if what is above

be so." "Consider then," said I, "whether we rightly take away, or not. And do not we say, that the worthy man will imagine that to die is not a dreadful thing to the worthy man whose companion he is?" "We say so." "Neither then will he lament over him, at least, as if his friend suffered something dreadful." "No, indeed." "And we say this likewise, that such an one is most of all sufficient in himself, for the 387e purpose of living happily, and that, in a distinguished manner from 230 others, he is least of all indigent." "True," said he. "It is to him, then, the least dreadful to be deprived of a son, a brother, wealth, or any other of such like things." "Least of all, indeed." "So that he will least of all lament; but endure, in the mildest manner, when any such misfortune befalls him." "Certainly." "We shall rightly then take away the lamentations of famous men, and assign them to the women, but not to the better sort, and to such of the men as are 388a dastardly; that so those whom we propose to educate for the guardianship of the country may disdain to make lamentations of this kind." "Right," said he. "We shall again then entreat Homer, and the other poets, not to say in their compositions, that Achilles, the son of a goddess,

> Lay sometimes on his side, and then anon
> Supine; then grov'ling; rising then again,
> Lamenting wander'd on the barren shore.[4]

Nor how 388b

> . . . . . With both his hands
> He pour'd the burning dust upon his head.[5]

Nor the rest of his lamentation, and bewailing; such and so great as he has composed. Nor that Priam, so near co the Gods, so meanly supplicated, and rolled himself in the dirt: 'Calling on every soldier by his name.'[6]

"But still much more must we entreat them not to make the Gods, at least, to bewail, and say,

> Ah wretched me! unfortunately brave 388c
> A son I bore.

"And if they are not thus to bring in the Gods, far less should they dare to represent the greatest of the Gods in so unbecoming a manner as this:

> How dear a man, around the town pursu'd,
> Mine eyes behold! for which my heart is griev'd:
> Ah me! 'tis fated that Patroclus kill
> Sarpedon; whom, of all men, most I love.[7]

388d

231   For, if, friend Adimantus, our youth should seriously hear such things as these, and not laugh at them as spoken most unsuitably, hardly would any one think it unworthy of himself, of himself being a man, or check himself, if he should happen either to say or to do any thing of the kind; but, without any shame or endurance, would, on small

388e sufferings, sing many lamentations and moans." "You say most true," replied he. "They must not, therefore, do in this manner, as our reasoning now has evinced to us; which we must believe, till some one persuade us by some better." "They must not, indeed." "But, surely, neither ought we to be given to excessive laughter; for, where a man gives himself to violent laughter, such a disposition commonly requires a violent change." "It seems so," said he. "Nor, if any one

389a shall represent worthy men as overcome by laughter, must we allow it, much less if he thus represent the Gods." "Much less, indeed," said he. "Neither, then, shall we receive such things as these from Homer concerning the Gods:

> Vulcan ministrant when the Gods beheld,
> Amidst them laughter unextinguish'd rose.[8]

This is not to be admitted, according to your reasoning." "If you

389b incline," said he, "to call it my reasoning; this, indeed, is not to be admitted." "But surely the truth is much more to be valued. For; if lately we reasoned right, and if indeed a lie be unprofitable to the Gods, but useful to men, in the way of a drug, it is plain that such a thing is to be entrusted only to the physicians, but not to be touched by private persons." "It is plain," said he. "It belongs then to the governors of the city, if to any others, to make a lie, with reference either to enemies or citizens, for the good of the city; but none of the

389c rest must venture on such a thing. But for a private person to tell a lie to such governors; we will call it the same, and even a greater offence, than for the patient to tell a lie to the physician; or for the man who learns his exercises, not to tell his master the truth as to the indispositions of his body: or for one not to tell the pilot the real state of things, respecting the ship and sailors, in what condition himself and the other sailors are." "Most true," said he. "But if you find in, the 389d city any one else making a lie,

> . . . . . . of those who artists are, 232
> Or prophet, or physician, or who make
> The shafts of spears . . . . . .

you shall punish them, as introducing a practice subversive and destructive of the city, as of a ship." "We must do so; if indeed it is upon speech that actions are completed." "But what? shall not our youth have need of temperance?" "Certainly." "And are not such things as these the principal parts of temperance? that they be obedient to their governors; that the governors themselves be temperate in drinking, feasting, and in venereal pleasures. And we 389e shall say, I imagine, that such things as these are well spoken, which Diomed says in Homer:

> Sit thou in silence, and obey my speech.[9]

And what follows; thus,

> The Greeks march'd on in silence, breathing force;
> Revering their commanders;[10] . . . .

and such like." "Well spoken." "But what as to these? 'Thou drunkard 390a with dog's eyes, and heart of deer;'[11] and all of this kind, are these, or such other juvenile things, which any private person may say against their governors, spoken handsomely?" "Not handsomely." "For I do not imagine that when they are heard they are fit to promote temperance in youth; and though they may afford a pleasure of a different kind, it is no wonder. But what do you think?" "Just the same way," said he. "But what of this? To make the wisest man say, that it appears to him to be the most beautiful of all things,

> . . . . . . To see the tables full 390b
> Of flesh and dainties, and the butter bear
> The wine in flagons, and fill up the cup:[12]

is this proper for a youth to hear, in order to obtain a command over himself? Or yet this?

...... most miserable it is,
To die of famine, and have adverse fate.[13]

₂₃₃
_{390c} Or that Jupiter, through desire of venereal pleasures, easily forgetting all those things which he alone awake revolved in his mind, whilst other Gods and men were asleep, was so struck, on seeing Juno, as not even to be willing to come into the house, but wanted to embrace her on the ground; and at the same time declaring that he is possessed with such desire, as exceeded what he felt on their first connection with each other,

...... Hid from their parents dear.[14]

_{390d} Nor yet how Mars and Venus were bound by Vulcan, and other such things." "No, by Jupiter," said he. "These things do not seem fit." "But if any instances of self-denial," said I, "with respect to all these things be told, and practised by eminent men, these are to be beheld and heard. Such as this:

He beat his breast, and thus reprov'd his heart:
Endure, my heart! thou heavier fate hast borne."

_{390e} "By all means," said he, "we should do thus." "Neither must we suffer men to receive bribes, nor to be covetous." "By no means." "Nor must we sing to them, that

Gifts gain the Gods and venerable kings.

_{391a} Nor must we commend Phœnix, the tutor of Achilles, as if he spoke with moderation, in counselling him to accept of presents, and assist the Greeks; but, without presents, not to desist from his wrath. Neither shall we commend Achilles, nor approve of his being so covetous as to receive presents from Agamemnon; and likewise a ransom to give up the dead body of Hector, but not incline to do it otherwise." "It is not right," said he, "to commend such things as these." "I am unwilling," said I, "for Homer's sake, to say it, That neither is it lawful that these things, at least, be said against Achilles, nor that they be believed, when said by others; nor, again, that he spoke thus to Apollo:

Me thou halt injur'd, thou, far-darting God!
Most baneful of the powers divine! But know,

Were I poss'est of power, then vengeance should be mine.[15] 234

And how disobedient he was to the river, though a divinity, and was 391b
ready to fight; and again, he says to the river Sperchius, with his sacred
locks,

> Thy lock to great Patroclus I could give,
> Who now is dead . . . .

Nor are we to believe he did this. And again, the dragging Hector
round the sepulchre of Patroclus, and the slaughtering the captives at
his funeral pile,—that all these things are true, we will not say; nor 391c
will we suffer our people to be persuaded that Achilles, the son of a
goddess, and of Peleus the most temperate of men and the third from
Jupiter, and educated by the most wise Chiron was full of such
disorder as to have within him two distempers opposite to one
another,—the illiberal and covetous disposition, and a contempt
both of Gods and of men." "You say right," replied he. "Neither," said
I, "let us be persuaded of these things; nor suffer any to say that
Theseus the son of Neptune, and Pirithous the son of Jupiter, were 391d
impelled to perpetrate such dire rapines; nor that any son of another
deity, nor any hero, would dare to do horrible and impious deeds;
such as the lies of the poets ascribe to them: but let us compel the poets
either to say that these are not the actions of these persons, or that
these persons are not the children of the Gods; and not to say both.

"Nor let us suffer them to attempt to persuade our youth that the
Gods create evil; and that heroes are in no respect better than men.
For, as we said formerly, these things are neither holy nor true: for we 391e
have else where shown, that it is impossible that evil should proceed
from the Gods." "Why not?" "And these things are truly hurtful, to
the hearers, at least. For every one will pardon his own depravity,
when he is persuaded that even the near relations of the Gods do and
have done things of the same kind: such as are near to Jupiter,

> Who, on the top of Ida, have up-rear'd
> To parent Jupiter an altar;—

And,

> Whose blood derived from Gods is not extinct.

On which accounts all such fables must be suppressed; lest they create 392a

235   in our youth a powerful habit of wickedness." "We must do so," replied he, "by all means." "What other species of discourses," said I, "have we still remaining, now whilst we are determining what ought to be spoken, and what not? We have already mentioned in what manner we ought to speak of the Gods, and likewise of dæmons and heroes; and of what relates to Hades." "Yes, indeed." "Should not, then, what yet remains seem to be concerning men?" "It is plain." "But it is impossible for us, friend, to regulate this at present." "How?"

392b   "Because, I think, we shall say that the poets and orators speak amiss concerning the greatest affairs of men: as, That most men are unjust, and, notwithstanding this, are happy; and that the just are miserable; and that it is profitable for one to do unjustly, when he is concealed; and that justice is gain indeed to others, but the loss of the just man himself: these, and innumerable other such things, we will forbid them to say; and enjoin them to sing, and compose in fable, the contrary to these. Do not you think so?" "I know it well," said he. "If then you acknowledge that I say right, shall I not say that you have

392c   acknowledged what all along we seek for?" "You judge right," said he. "Shall we not then grant that such discourses are to be spoken concerning men, whenever we shall have discovered what justice is; and how in its nature it is profitable to the just man to be such, whether he appear to be such or not?" "Most true," replied he.

"Concerning the discourses, then, let this suffice. We must now consider, as I imagine, the manner of discourse. And then we shall have completely considered, both what is to be spoken, and the manner how." Here Adimantus said, "But I do not understand what

392d   you say." "But," replied I, "it is needful you should. And perhaps you will rather understand it in this way. Is not every thing told by the mythologists, or poets, a narrative of the past, present, or future?" "What else?" replied he. "And do not they execute it, either by simple narration, or imitation, or by both?" "This too," replied he, "I want to understand more plainly." "I seem," said I, "to be a ridiculous and

392e   obscure instructor. Therefore, like those who are unable to speak, I will endeavour to explain, not the whole, but, taking up a particular part, show my meaning by this particular. And tell me, Do not you know the beginning of the Iliad? where the poet says that Chryses entreated Agamemnon to set free his daughter; but that he was displeased that Chryses, when he did not succeed, prayed against the Greeks to the God." "I know." "You know, then, that down to these verses, 393a

———The Grecians all he pray'd;
But chief the two commanders, Atreus' sons—

the poet himself speaks, and does not attempt to divert our attention elsewhere; as if any other person were speaking: but what he says after this, he says as if he himself were Chryses, and endeavours as much as possible to make us imagine that the speaker is not Homer, but the priest, an old man; and that in this manner he has composed almost the whole narrative of what happened at Troy, and in Ithaca, and all the adventures in the whole Odyssey." "It is certainly so," replied he. "Is it not then narration, when he tells the several speeches? and likewise when he tells what intervenes between the speeches?" "Why not?" "But when he makes any speech in the person of another, do not we say that then he assimilates his speech, as much as possible, to each person whom he introduces as speaking?" "We say so, do we not?" "And is not the assimilating one's self to another, either in voice or figure, the imitating him to whom one assimilates himself?" "Why not?" "In such a manner as this, then, it seems, both he and the other poets perform the narrative by means of imitation." "Certainly." "But if the poet did not at all conceal himself, his whole action and narrative would be without imitation. And that you may not say you do not again understand how this should be, I shall tell you, If Homer, after relating how Chryses came with his daughter's ransom, beseeching the Greeks, but chiefly the kings, had spoken afterwards, not as Chryses, but still as Homer, you know it would not have been imitation, but simple narration. And it would have been somehow thus: (I shall speak without metre, for I am no poet:) 393b 393c 393d

"The priest came and prayed, that the Gods might grant they should take Troy, and return safe; and begged them to restore him his daughter, accepting the presents, and revering the God. When he had said this, all the rest showed respect, and consented; but Agamemnon was enraged, charging him to depart instantly, and not to return again; lest his sceptre and the garlands of the God should be of no avail; and told him, that before he would restore his daughter she 393e

should grow old with him in Argos; but ordered him to be gone, and
394a not to irritate him, that he might get home in safety. The old man
upon hearing this was afraid, and went away in silence. And when he
was retired from the camp he made many supplications to Apollo,
rehearsing the names of the God, and reminding him and beseeching
him, that if ever he had made any acceptable donation in the
building of temples, or the offering of sacrifices,—for the fake of
these, to avenge his tears upon the Greeks with his arrows. "Thus,"
394b said I, "friend, the narration is simple, without imitation." "I
understand," said he.

"Understand then," said I, "that the opposite of this happens, when
one, taking away the poet's part between the speeches, leaves the
speeches themselves." "This," said he, "I likewise understand, that a
thing of this kind takes place respecting tragedies." "You apprehend
perfectly well," said I. "And I think that I now make plain to you
what I could not before; that in poetry, and likewise in mythology,
394c one kind is wholly by imitation, such as you say tragedy and comedy
are; and another kind by the narration of the poet himself: and you
will find this kind most especially in the dithyrambus: and another
again by both; as in epic poetry, and in many other cases besides, if
you understand me." "I understand now," replied he, "what you
meant before." "And remember too, that before that we were saying
that we had already mentioned what things were to be spoken; but
that it yet remained to be considered in what manner they were to be
394d spoken." "I remember, indeed." "This then, is what I was saying, that
it were necessary we agreed whether we shall suffer the poets to make
narratives to us in the way of imitation; or, partly in the way of
imitation, and partly not; and, what in each way; or, if they are not to
use imitation at all." "I conjecture," said he, "you are to consider
whether we shall receive tragedy and comedy into our city, or not."
"Perhaps," replied I, "and something more too; for I do not as yet
know, indeed; but wherever our reasoning, as a gale, bears us, there we
394e must go." "And truly," said he, "you say well." "Consider this now,
Adimantus, whether our guardians ought to practise imitation, or
not. Or does this follow from what is above? That each one may
handsomely perform one business, but many he cannot: or, if he shall
attempt it, in grasping at many things, he shall fail in all; so as to be

remarkable in none." "Why shall he not?" "And is not the reason the   *238*
same concerning imitation? That one man is not so able to imitate
many things well, as one." "He is not." "Hardly then shall he perform
any part of the more eminent employments, and at the same time   395a
imitate many things, and be an imitator; since the same persons are
not able to perform handsomely imitations of two different kinds,
which seem to resemble each other; as, for instance, they cannot
succeed both in comedy and tragedy: or, did you not lately call these
two, imitations?" "I did; and you say true, that the same persons
cannot succeed in them." "Nor can they, at the same time, be
rhapsodists and actors." "True." "Nor can the same persons be actors   395b
in comedies and in tragedies. And all these are imitations, are they
not?" "Imitations."

"The genius of man seems to me, Adimantus, to be shut up within
still lesser bounds than these; so that it is unable to imitate
handsomely many things, or do these very things, of which even the
imitations are the resemblances." "Most true," said he. "If therefore
we are to hold to our first reasoning, that our guardians, unoccupied
in any manufacture what ever, ought to be the most accurate   395c
manufacturers of the liberty of the city, and to mind nothing but
what has some reference to this; it were surely proper, they neither did
nor imitated any thing else; but, if they shall imitate at all, to imitate
immediately from their childhood such things as are correspondent
to these; brave, temperate, holy, free men, and all such things as these;
—but neither to do, nor to be desirous of imitating, things illiberal
or base, lest from imitating they come to be really such. Or have you   395d
not observed, that imitations, if from earliest youth they be
continued onwards for a long time, are established into the manners
and natural temper, both with reference to the body and voice, and
likewise the dianoëtic power?" "Very much so," replied he. "We will
not surely allow," said I, "those we profess to take care of, and who
ought to be good men, to imitate a woman, either young or old,
either reviling her husband, or quarrelling with the Gods, or speaking
boastingly when she imagines herself happy; nor yet to imitate her in
her misfortunes, sorrows, and lamentations, when sick, or in love, or   395e
in child-bed labour. We shall be far from permitting this." "By all
means," replied he. "Nor to imitate man or maid-servants in doing

what belongs to servants." "Nor this neither." "Nor yet to imitate
239   depraved men, as it seems, such as are dastardly, and do the contrary
of what we have now been mentioning; reviling and railing at one
another; and speaking abominable things, either intoxicated or
396a   sober, or any other things such as persons of this sort are guilty of,
either in words or actions, either with respect to themselves or one
another. Neither must they accustom themselves to resemble madmen, in words or actions. Even the mad and wicked are to be known,
both the men and the women; but none of their actions are to be
done, or imitated." "Most true," said he. "But what?" said I, "are they
to imitate such as work in brass, or any other handicrafts, or such as
are employed in rowing boats, or such as command these; or any
396b   thing else appertaining to these things?" "How can they," said he, "as
they are not to be allowed to give application to any of those things?"
"But what? shall they imitate horses neighing, or bulls lowing, or
rivers murmuring, or the sea roaring, or thunder, and all such like
things?" "We have for bidden them," said he, "to be mad, or to
resemble madmen."

"If then I understand," replied I, "what you say, there is a certain
396c   kind of speech, and of narration, in which he who is truly a good and
worthy man expresses himself when it is necessary for him to say any
thing; and another kind again unlike to this, which he who has been
born and educated in an opposite manner always possesses, and in
which he expresses himself." "But of what kind are these?" said he. "It
appears to me," said I, "that the worthy man, when he comes in his
narrative to any speech or action of a good man, will willingly tell it
as if he were himself the man, and will not be ashamed of such an
396d   imitation; most especially when he imitates a good man acting
prudently and without error, and failing seldom, and but little,
through diseases, or love, intoxication, or any other misfortune. But
when he comes to any thing unworthy of himself, he will not be
studious to resemble himself to that which is worse, unless for a short
time when it produces some good; but will be ashamed, both as he is
unpractised in the imitation of such character as these, and likewise as
he grudges to degrade himself and stand among the models of baser
396e   characters, disdaining it in his dianoëtic[16] part, and doing it only for
amusement." "It is likely," said he.

"He will not then make use of such a narrative as we lately mentioned, with reference to the compositions of Homer: but his composition will participate of both imitation and the other *240* narrative; and but a small part of it will be imitation, in a great quantity of plain narrative, Do I seem to say any thing, or nothing at all?" "You express," replied he, "perfectly well what ought to be the model of such an orator." "And, on the other hand, will not the *397a* man," said I, "who is not such an one, the more depraved he is, be the readier to rehearse every thing whatever; and not think any thing unworthy of him? so that he will undertake to imitate every thing in earnest, and likewise in the presence of many; and such things also as we now mentioned; thunderings, and noises of winds and tempests, and of axles, and wheels, and trumpets, and pipes, and whistles, and sounds of all manner of instruments, and voices of dogs too, and of sheep, and of birds. And the whole expression of all these things shall be by imitation in voices and gestures, having but a small part of it *397b* narration." "This too," said he, " happen of necessity." "These now," said I, "I called the two kinds of diction." "They are so," replied he. "But has not the one of these small variations? And if the orator afford the becoming harmony and measure to the diction, where he speaks with propriety, the discourse is almost after one and the same manner, and in one harmony; for the variations are but small, and in *397c* a measure which accordingly is somehow similar." "It is indeed," replied he, "entirely so." "But what as to the other kind? Does it not require the contrary, all kinds of harmony, all kinds of measure, if it is to be naturally expressed, as it has all sorts of variations?" "It is perfectly so." "Do not now all the poets, and such as speak in any kind, make use of either one or other of these models of diction, or of one compounded of both?" "Of necessity," replied he. "What then *397d* shall we do?" said I. "Whether shall we admit into our city all of these; or one of the unmixed, or the one compounded?" "If my opinion," replied he, "prevail, that uncompounded one, which is imitative of what is worthy." "But surely, Adimantus, the mixed is pleasant, at least. And the opposite of what you choose is by far the most pleasant to children and pedagogues, and the crowd." "It is most pleasant." "But you will not, probably," said I, "think it suitable to our *397e* government, because with us no man is to attend to two or more employments, but to be quite simple, as every one does one thing." "It is not indeed suitable."

"Shall we not then find that in such city alone, a shoe-maker is only a shoemaker, and not a pilot along with shoe-making, and that the husbandman is only a husbandman, and not a judge along with husbandry; and that the soldier is a soldier, and not a money-maker besides: and all others in the same way?" "True," replied he. "And it would appear, that if a man, who, through wisdom, were able to become every thing, and to imitate every thing, should come into our city, and should wish to show us his poems, we should revere him as a sacred, admirable, and pleasant person: but we should tell him, that there is no such person with us, in our city, nor is there any such allowed to be: and we should send him to some other city, pouring oil on his head, and crowning him with wool: but we use a more austere poet, and mythologist, for our advantage, who may imitate to us the diction of the worthy manner; and may say whatever he says, according to those models which we established by law and first, when we undertook the education of our soldiers." "So we should do," replied he, "if it depended on us."

"It appears," said I, "friend, that we have now thoroughly discussed that part of music respecting oratory and fable; for we have already told what is to be spoken, and in what manner." "It appears so to me likewise," said he. "Does it not yet remain," said I, "that we speak of the manner of song, and of melodies?" "It is plain." "May not any one discover what we must say of these things; and of what kind these ought to be, if we are to be consistent with what is above mentioned?" Here Glauco laughing said: "But I appear, Socrates, to be a stranger to all these matters, for I am not able at present to guess at what we ought to say: I suspect, however." "You are certainly," said I, "fully able to say this in the first place, that melody is composed of three things; of sentiment, harmony, and rhythm." "Yes," replied he, "this I can say." "And that the part which consists in the sentiment differs in nothing from that sentiment which is not sung, in this respect, that it ought to be performed upon the same models, as we just now said, and in the same manner." "True," said he. "And surely, then, the harmony and rhythm ought to correspond to the sentiment." "Why not?" "But we observed there was no occasion for wailings and

₂₄₁

_{398a}

_{398b}

_{398c}

_{398d}

lamentations in compositions." "No occasion, truly." "Which then are the querulous harmonies? Tell me, for you are a musician." "The mixed Lydian," replied he, "and the sharp Lydian; and some others of this kind." "Are not these, then," said I, "to be rejected? for they are unprofitable even to women, such as are worthy, and much more to men." "Certainly." "But intoxication is most unbecoming our guardians; and effeminacy and idleness." "Why not?" "Which then are the effeminate and convivial harmonics?" "The sonic," replied he, "and the Lydian, which are called relaxing." "Can you make any use of these, my friend, for military men?" "By no means," replied he. "But, it seems, you have yet remaining the Doric, and the Phrygian." "I do not know," said I, "the harmonies; but leave that harmony, which may, in a becoming manner, imitate the voice and accents of a truly brave man, going on in a military action, and every rough adventure; and bearing his fortune in a determinate and persevering manner, when he fails of success, rushes on wounds, or deaths, or falls into any other distress: and leave that kind of harmony likewise, which is suited to what is peaceable; where there is no violence, but every thing is voluntary; where a man either persuades or beseeches any one, about any thing, either God by prayer, or man by instruction and admonition: or, on the other hand, where one submits himself to another, who beseeches, instructs, and persuades; and, in all these things, acts according to intellect, and does not behave haughtily; demeaning himself soberly and moderately; gladly embracing whatever may happen: leave then these two harmonies, the vehement and the voluntary; which, in the most handsome manner, imitate the voice of the unfortunate and of the fortunate, of the moderate and of the brave." "You desire," replied he, "to leave no others but those I now mentioned." "We shall not then," said I, "have any need of a great many strings, nor of the panarmonion in our songs and melodies." "It appears to me," replied he, "we shall not." "We shall not nourish, then, such workmen as make harps and spinets, and all those instruments which consist of many strings, and produce a variety of harmony." "We shall not, as it appears." "But what? Will you admit into your city such workmen as make pipes, or pipers? for, are not the instruments which consist of the greatest number of strings, and those that produce all kinds of harmony, imitations of

398e

242

399a

399b

399c

399d

the pipe?" "It is plain," replied he. "There are left you still," said I, "the lyre and the harp, as useful for your city, and there might likewise be some reed for shepherds in the fields." "Thus reason," said

399e he, "shows us." "We then," replied I, "do nothing dire, if we prefer

243 Apollo, and Apollo's instruments, to Marsyas, and the instruments of that eminent musician." "Truly," replied he, "we do not appear to do it." "And by the dog," said I, "we have unawares cleansed again our city, which we said was become luxurious." "And we have wisely done it," replied he.

"Come then," said I, "and let us cleanse what remains; for what concerns rhythm should be suitable to our harmonies; that our citizens pursue not such rhythms as are diversified, and have a variety of cadences; but observe what are the rhythms of a decent and manly

400a life, and, which they observe these, make the foot and the melody subservient to sentiment of such a kind; and not the sentiment subservient to the foot and melody. But what these rhythms are, is your business to tell, as you have done the harmonies." "But by Jupiter," replied he, "I cannot tell. That there are three species of which the notes are composed, as there are four in sounds, whence the whole of harmony, I can say, as I have observed it: but which are the imitations of one kind of life, and which of another, I am not able to

400b tell." "But these things," said I, "we must consider with Damon's assistance: what notes are suitable to illiberality and insolence, to madness or other ill disposition; and what notes are proper for their opposites. And I remember, but not distinctly, to have heard him calling a certain warrior, composite, a dactyl, and heroic measure; ornamenting him I do not know how, making him equal above and below, in breadth and length: and he called one, as I imagine,

400c Iambus, and another Trochæus. He adapted, besides, the lengths and shortnesses; and, in some of these, I believe, he blamed and commended the measure of the foot, no less than the numbers themselves, or something compounded of both; for I can not speak of these things; because, as I said, they are to be thrown upon Damon. To speak distinctly, indeed, on these matters, would require no small discourse: do not you think so?" "Not a small one, truly." "But can you determine this, that the propriety or impropriety corresponds to the

400d good or ill rhythm?" "Why not?" "But, with respect to the good or ill rhythm, the one corresponds to handsome expression, conforming itself to it; and the other to the reverse. And, in the same way, as to the harmonious, and the discordant: since the rhythm and harmony are subservient to the sentiment, as we just now said; and not the sentiment to these." "These, indeed," said he, "are to be subservient to the sentiment." "But what?" said I, "As to the manner of expression, and as to the sentiment itself, must it not correspond to the temper of 244 the soul?" "Why not?" "And all other things correspond to the expression." "Yes." "So that the beauty of expression, fine consonancy, and propriety, and excellence of numbers, are subservient to the good 400e disposition; not that stupidity, which in complaisant language we call good temper; but the dianoëtic part, truly adorned with excellent and beautiful manners." "By all means," replied he. "Must not these things be always pursued by the youth, if they are to mind their business?" "They are indeed to be pursued." "But painting too is somehow full of these things; and every other workmanship of the 401a kind; and weaving is full of these, and carving, and architecture, and all workmanship of every kind of vessels: as is moreover the nature of bodies, and of all vegetables: for in all these there is propriety, and impropriety; and the impropriety, discord, and dissonance, are the sisters of ill expression, and depraved manners; and their opposites are the sisters, and imitations, of sober and worthy manners." "'Tis entirely so," replied he.

"Are we then to give injunctions to the poets alone, and oblige 401b them to work into their poems the image of the worthy manners, or not to compose at all with us? or are we to enjoin all other workmen likewise; and refrain this ill, undisciplined, illiberal, indecent manner, that they exhibit it neither in the representations of animals, in buildings, nor in any other workmanship? or, that he who is not able to do this, be not suffered to work with us? lest our guardians, being educated in the midst of ill representations, as in an ill pasture, 401c by every day plucking and eating much of different things, by little and little contract, imperceptibly, some mighty evil in their soul. But we must seek for such workmen as are able, by the help of a good natural genius, to investigate the nature of the beautiful and the decent: that our youth, dwelling as it were in a healthful place, may be profited on all sides; whence, from the beautiful works, something

will be conveyed to the sight and hearing, as a breeze bringing health
401d from salutary places; imperceptibly leading them on directly from
childhood, to the resemblance, friendship, and harmony with right
reason." "They should thus," said he, "be educated in the most
handsome manner by far." "On these accounts therefore, Glauco,"
said I, "is not education in music of the greatest importance, because
rhythm and harmony enter in the strongest manner into the inward
245 part of the soul, and most powerfully affect it, introducing at the same
time decorum, and making every one decent if he is properly
401e educated, and the reverse if he is not? And moreover, because the man
who has here been educated as he ought, perceives in the quickest
manner whatever workmanship is defective, and whatever execution
is unhandsome, or whatever productions are of that kind; and being
disgusted in a proper manner, he will praise what is beautiful,
rejoicing in it; and, receiving it into his soul, be nourished by it, and
402a become a worthy and good man: but whatever is base, he will in a
proper manner despise, and hate, whilst yet he is young, and before he
is able to be a partaker of reason; and when reason comes, such an one
as has been thus educated will embrace it, recognizing it perfectly
well, from its intimate familiarity with him." "It appears to me,"
replied he, "that education in music is for the sake of such things as
these." "Just as, with reference to letters," said I, "we are then
sufficiently instructed when we are not ignorant of the elements,
which are but few in number, wherever they are concerned; and when
402b we do not despise them more or less as unnecessary to be observed, but
by all means endeavour to understand them thoroughly, as it is
impossible for us to be literary men till we do thus." "True." "And if
the images of letters appeared any where, either in water or in
mirrors, should we not know them before we knew the letters
themselves? or does this belong to the same art and study?" "By all
means." "Is it indeed then according as I say? that we shall never
402c become musicians, neither we ourselves, nor those guardians we say
we are to educate, before we understand the images of temperance,
fortitude, liberality, and magnificence, and the other sister virtues;
and, on the other hand again, the contraries of these, which are every
where to be met with; and observe them wheresoever they are, both
the virtues themselves, and the images of them, and despise them

neither in small nor in great instances; but let us believe that this belongs to the same art and study." "There is," said he, "great necessity for it." "Must not then," said I, "the person who shall have in his soul beautiful manners, and in his appearance whatever is proportionable, and corresponding to these, partaking of the same impression, be the most beautiful spectacle to any one who is able to behold it?" "Exceedingly so." "But what is most beautiful is most lovely." "Why not?" "He who is musical should surely love those men who are most eminently of this kind; but if one be unharmonious he shall not love him." "He shall not," replied he, "if the person be any way defective as to his soul: if indeed it were in his body, he would bear with it, so as to be willing to associate with him."

"I understand," said I, "that your favourites are or have been of this kind. And I agree to it. But tell me this, is there any communion between temperance and excessive pleasure?" "How can there?" said he, "for such pleasure causes a privation of intellect no less than grief." "But has it communion with any other virtue?" "By no means." "But what, has it communion with insolence and intemperance?" "Most of all." "Can you mention a greater and more acute pleasure than that respecting venereal concerns?" "I cannot," said he, "nor yet one that is more insane." "But the right love is of such a nature as to love the beautiful, and the handsome, in a temperate and a musical manner." "Certainly." "Nothing then which is insane, or allied to intemperance, is to approach to a right love. Neither must pleasure approach to it; nor must the lover, and the person he loves, have communion with it, where they love and are beloved in a right manner." "No truly," said he; "they must not, Socrates, approach to these." "Thus then, as appears, you will establish by law, in the city which is to be established, that the lover is to love, to converse, and associate with the objects of his love, as with his son, for the sake of virtue, if he gain the consent: and as to every thing besides, that every one so converse with him whose love he solicits, as never to appear to associate for any thing beyond what is now mentioned; and that otherwise he shall undergo the reproach of being unmusical, and unacquainted with the beautiful." "It must be thus," replied he. "Does then," said I, "the discourse concerning music seem to you to be finished? For it has terminated where it ought to terminate, as the

402d

246

402e

403a

403b

403c

affairs of music ought, somehow, to terminate in the love of the beautiful." "I agree," said he.

"But, after music, our youth are to be educated in gymnastic. But what? It is sorely necessary that in this likewise they be accurately
403d disciplined, from their infancy through the whole of life. For the matter, as I imagine, is somehow thus: but do you also consider. For it does not appear to me that whatever body is found, doth, by its own virtue, render the soul good; but contrariwise, that a good soul, by its virtue, renders the body the best which is possible: but how does it
247 appear to you?" "In the same manner to me likewise," replied he. "If then, when we have sufficiently cultivated the dianoëtic part, we shall commit to it the accurate management of the concerns of the body;
403e shall not we, as we are only laying down models, (that we may not enlarge) act in a right manner?" "Entirely so." "We say then, that they are to abstain from intoxication; for it is more allowable to any, than to a guardian, to be intoxicated, and not to know where he is." "It would be ridiculous," said he, "that the guardian should stand in need of a guardian." "But what as to meats? For these men are wrestlers in the noblest combat: are they not?" "They are." "Would not then the bodily plight of the wrestlers be proper for such as
404a these?" "Probably." "But," said I, "it is of a drowsy kind, and dubious as to health: or, do you not observe, that they sleep out their life? and, if they depart but a little from their appointed diet, such wrestlers become greatly and extremely diseased." "I perceive it." "But some more elegant exercise," said I, "is requisite for our military wrestlers; who, as dogs, ought to be wakeful, and to see, and to hear in the most
404b acute manner; and, in their expeditions, to endure many changes of water and of food, of heat and of cold, that so they may not have a dubious state of health." "To me it appears so."

"Is not then the best gymnastic a kind of sister to the simple music, which we a little before described?" "How do you say?" "That the gymnastic is to be simple and moderate, and of that kind most especially which pertains to war." "Of what kind?" "Even from Homer," said I, "one may learn these things: for you know, that in their warlike expeditions, at the entertainments of their heroes, he
404c never feasts them with fishes, and that even whilst they were by the sea at the Hellespont, nor yet with boiled flesh, but only with roast, as

what soldiers can most easily procure: for, in short, one can every where more easily make use of fire, than carry vessels about." "Yes, indeed." "Neither does Homer, as I imagine, any where make mention of seasonings: and this is what the other wrestlers understand, that the body which is to be in good habit must abstain from all these things." "They rightly understand," said he, "and 404d abstain." "You do not then, friend, as appears, approve of the Syracusian table, and the Sicilian variety of meats, since this other appears to you to be right?" "I do not, as appears." "You will likewise disapprove of a Corinthian girl, as a mistress, for those who are to be of a good habit of body." "By all means, truly." "And likewise of those delicacies, as they are reckoned, of Attic confections." "Of necessity." 248 "For all feeding and dieting of this kind, if we compare it to the melody and song produced in the panarmonion, and in all rhythms, 404e shall not the comparison be just?" "Why not?" "And does not the diversity in that case create intemperance, and here disease? But simplicity, as to music, creates in the soul temperance; and, as to gymnastic, health in the body." "Most true," said he. "And when intemperance and diseases multiply in the city, shall we not have 405a many halls of justice and of medicine opened? And will not the arts of justice and of medicine be in request, when many free persons shall earnestly apply to them?" "Why not?"

"But can you adduce any greater argument of an ill and base education in a city, than that there should be need of physicians and supreme magistrates, and that not only for the contemptible and low handicrafts, but for those who boast of having been educated in a liberal manner? Or, does it not appear to be base, and a great sign of 405b want of education, to be obliged to observe justice pronounced on us by others, as our masters and judges, and to have no sense of it in ourselves?" "Of all things, this," replied he, "is the most base." "And do you not," said I, "deem this to be more base still; when one not only spends a great part of life in courts of justice, as defendant and plaintiff; but, from his ignorance of the beautiful, imagines that he becomes renowned for this very thing; as being dexterous in doing injustice, and able to turn himself through all sorts of windings, and, 405c using every kind of subterfuge, thinks to escape so as to evade justice; and all this for the sake of small and contemptible things; being ignorant how much better and more handsome it were so to regulate his life as not to stand in need of a sleepy judge?" "This," replied he, "is still more base than the other."

"And to stand in need of the medicinal art," said I, "not on 405d account of wounds, or some incidental epidemic distempers, but through sloth, and such a diet as we mentioned, being filled with rheums and wind, like lakes; obliging the skilful sons of Æsculapius to invent new names for diseases, such as dropsies and catarrhs. Do not you think this abominable?" "These are truly," replied he, "very new and strange names of diseases." "Such," said I, "as were not, I imagine, in the days of Æsculapius: and I conjecture so from this, that when 405e Eurypylus was wounded at Troy, and was getting Pramnian wine to 406a drink with much flour in it, with the addition of cheese; (all which 249 seem to be phlegmatic,) the sons of Æsculapius neither blamed the woman who presented it, nor reprehended Patroclus, who had presented the cure." "And surely the potion," said he, "is absurd for one in such a case." "No," said I, "if you consider, that, as they tell us, the descendants of Æsculapius did not, before the days of Herodicus, practice this method of cure now in use, which puts the patient on a regimen: but Herodicus being a teacher of youth, and at the same 406b time infirm in his health, mixing gymnastic and medicine together, he made himself most uneasy in the first place, and afterwards many others besides." "After what manner?" said he. "In procuring to himself," said I, "a lingering death; for, whilst he was constantly attentive to his disease, which was mortal, he was not able, as I imagine, to cure himself; though, neglecting every thing besides, he was still using medicines; and thus he passed his life, still in the greatest uneasiness if he departed in the least from his accustomed diet; and through this wisdom of his, struggling long with death, he arrived at old age." "A mighty reward," said he, "he reaped of his art!" 406c "Such as became one," said I, "who did not understand that it was not from ignorance or inexperience of this method of cure that Æsculapius did not discover it to his descendants; but because he knew that, in all well regulated states, there was some certain work enjoined every one in the city, which was necessary to be done, and that no one was to be allowed to have the leisure of being sick through the whole of life, and to be attentive only to the taking of medicines. This we may pleasantly observe in the case of labouring people; but we do not observe it in the case of the rich, and such as are counted happy." "How?" said he. "A smith," replied I, "when he falls sick, thinks it fit 406d to take from the physician some potion, to throw up his disease, or purge it downwards, or, by means of caustic or amputation, to be freed from the trouble: but if any one prescribe for him a long regimen, putting caps on his head, and other such things, he quickly tells him that he has not leisure to lie sick, nor does it avail him to live in this manner, attentive to his trouble, and negligent of his proper work; and so, bidding such a physician farewell, he returns to 406e his ordinary diet; and, if he recovers his health, he continues to manage his own affairs; but if his body be not able to support the disease, he dies, and is freed from troubles." "It seems proper," said he, "for such an one to use the medicinal art in this manner." "Is it not," 250 said I, "because he has a certain business, which if he does not 407a perform, it is not for his advantage to live?" "It is plain," replied he. "But the rich man, as we say, has no such work allotted him, from which if he be obliged to refrain, life is not worth the having." "He is surely said at least to have none." "For you do not," said I, "attend to what Phocylides says; that one ought still, whilst there is life, to practise virtue." "I think," replied he, "we attended to that formerly." "Let us by no means," said I, "differ from him in this. But let us inform ourselves whether this excessive attention to one's disease is to be the business of the rich; and that life is not worth keeping, if he 407b does not give this attention; for that such a life is indeed a hindrance of the mind's application to masonry and other arts; but, with respect to the exhortation of Phocylides, it is no hindrance." "Yes, by Jupiter," said he, "it is, and that in the greatest degree when this excessive care of the body goes beyond gymnastic. Neither does it agree with attention to private economy, or military expeditions, or sedentary magistracies in the city." "But what is of the greatest moment is, that such application to health is ill fitted for any sort of learning, and inquiry, and study, by one's self, whilst one is 407c perpetually dreading certain pains and swimmings of the head, and blaming philosophy as occasioning them; so that where there is this attention to health it is a great obstacle to the practice of virtue and improvement in it; for it makes us always imagine that we are ill, and

always complain of the body." "That is likely," said he. "And shall we not say that Æsculapius too understood these things, when to persons
407d of a healthful constitution, and such as used a wholesome diet, but were afflicted by some particular disease, to these and to such a constitution he prescribed medicine, repelling their diseases by drugs and incisions, and enjoined them their accustomed diet, that the public might suffer no damage. But he did not attempt, by extenuating or nourishing diet, to cure such constitutions as were wholly diseased within; as it would but afford a long and miserable life to the man himself, and the descendants which would spring
407e from him would probably be of the same kind: for he did not imagine the man ought to be cured who could not live in the ordinary course, as he would be neither profitable to himself nor to the state." "You
251 make Æsculapius," said he, "a politician." "It is plain," said I. "And his sons may show that he was so. Or do you not see, that at Troy they
408a excelled in war, and likewise practised medicine in the way I mention? Or do not you remember, that when Menelaus was wounded by Pandarus, they

Wash'd off the blood, and soft'ning drugs applied?

But, as to what was necessary for him to eat or drink afterwards, they prescribed for him no more than for Eurypylus; deeming external applications sufficient to heal men, who, before they were wounded,
408b were healthful and moderate in their diet, whatever mixture they happened to have drunk at the time. But they judged, that to have a diseased constitution, and to live an intemperate life, was neither profitable to the men themselves nor to others; and that their art ought not to be employed on these, nor to minister to them, not even though they were richer than Midas." "You make," said he, "the sons of Æsculapius truly ingenious."

"It is proper," replied I; "though in opposition to us the writers of tragedy, and Pindar, call indeed Æsculapius the son of Apollo, but say
408c that he was prevailed on by gold to undertake the cure of a rich man, who was already in a deadly state; for which, truly, he was even struck with a thunderbolt: but we, agreeably to what has been formerly said, will not believe them as to both these things; but will aver, that if he was the son of the God, he was not given to filthy lucre; or, if he were

given to filthy lucre, he was not a son of the God." "These things," said he, "are most right. But what do you say, Socrates, as to this? Is it not necessary to provide good physicians for the state? and must not these, most likely, be such who have been conversant with the greatest number of healthy and of sickly people? and these, in like manner, be 408d the best judges, who have been conversant with all sorts of dispositions?" "I mean now," said I, "those who are very good. But do you know whom I deem to be such?" "If you tell me," replied he. "I shall endeavour to do it," said I; "but you inquire in one question about two different things." "As how?" said he. "Physicians," replied I, "would become most expert, if, beginning from their infancy, they would, in learning the art, be conversant with the greatest number of 252 bodies, and these the most sickly; and laboured themselves under all 408e manner of diseases, and by natural constitution were not quite healthful; for it is not by the body, I imagine, that they cure the body; (else their own bodies could at no time be admitted to be of an ill constitution,) but they cure the body by the soul; which, whilst it is of an ill constitution, is not capable to perform well any cure." "Right," said he.

"But the judge, friend, governs the soul by the soul; which, if from 409a its childhood it has been educated with depraved souls, has been conversant with them, and has itself done all manner of evil, it is not able to come out from among them, so as accurately, by itself, to judge of the evils of others, as happens in the diseases of the body; but it must in its youth be inexperienced and unpolluted with evil manners, if it means to be good and beautiful itself, and to judge soundly of what is just. And hence the virtuous in their youth appear simple, and easily deceived by the unjust, as they have not within 409b themselves dispositions similar to those of the wicked." "And surely this at least," said he, "they do often suffer extremely." "For which reason," said I, "the good judge is not to be a young man, but an old, having been late in learning wickedness, what it is; perceiving it not as a kindred possession, residing in his own soul, but as a foreign one, in the souls of others, which he has for a long time studied, and has understood what sort of an evil it is, by the help of science rather than 409c by proper experience." "Such an one," said he, "is like to be the most noble judge." "And likewise a good one," said I; "which was what you required. For he who has a good soul is good. But the other notable and suspicious man, who has committed much of iniquity himself, when indeed he converses with his like, being thought to be subtle and wise, he appears a notable man, being extremely cautious, having an eye to those models which he has within himself; but when he 409d approaches the good, and the more aged, he appears foolish, suspicious out of season, and ignorant of integrity of manners, as having within no models of such a kind: but however, being more frequently conversant with the wicked than with the wise, he appears, both to himself and others, to be more wise, rather than more ignorant." "This," said he, "is perfectly true."

"We must not, therefore," said I, "look for such an one to be a wise and good judge, but the former one; for indeed vice can never at all 253 know both itself and virtue. But virtue, where the temper is instructed 409e by time, shall attain to the knowledge of both itself and depravity. This one, then, and not the wicked, as it appears to me, is the wise man." "And I," replied he, "am of the same opinion." "Will you not then establish in the city such a method of medicine as we have mentioned, along with such a method of judicature as shall carefully preserve for you those of your citizens who are naturally well disposed 410a both in mind and in body? and with respect to those who are otherwise, such as are so in their bodies, they shall suffer to die; but such as are of an evil nature, and incurable with respect to their soul, these they shall themselves put to death?" "This, said he, "has appeared to be best, both for those who suffer it and for the city." "And it is plain," said I, "that your youth will be afraid of needing this justiciary, whilst they are employed in that simple music, which, we say, generates temperance." "Why will they not?" said he. "And, 410b according to the very same steps of reasoning, the musician who is willing to pursue gymnastic, will choose to do it so as not to require any medicine unless there be necessity." "It appears so to me." "And he will perform his exercises, and his labours, rather looking to the irascible part of his nature, and exciting it by labour, than to strength; and not as the other wrestlers, who eat and drink and engage in labours for the sake of bodily strength." "Most right," said he. "Why then," said I, "Glauco, they who propose to teach music and 410c gymnastic, propose these things, not, for what some imagine, to cure the body by the one, and the soul by the other." "What then?" replied he. "They seem," said I, "to propose them both chiefly on the soul's account." "As how?" "Do not you perceive," said I, "how those are affected as to their dianoëtic part, who have all their life been conversant with gymnastic, but have never applied to music? or how those are affected who have lived in a method the reverse of this?" "What," said he, "do you speak of?" "Of rusticity," said I, "and 410d fierceness, and again of softness and mildness." "I know," said he, "that those who apply themselves immoderately to gymnastic, become more rustic than is proper; and those again who attend to music alone, are more soft than is becoming for them to be." "And surely," said I, "this rusticity, at least, may impart an irascibility of nature, and, when rightly disciplined, may become fortitude; but, when carried further than is becoming, may, as is likely, be both more fierce and troublesome." "So it appears to me," said he. "But 254 what? does not the philosophic temper partake of the mild? And when 410e this disposition is carried too far, may it not prove more soft than is becoming; but, when rightly disciplined, be really mild and comely?" "These things are so." "But we say that our guardians ought to have both these dispositions." "They ought." "Ought not then these to be adapted to one another?" "Why not?" "And the soul in which they are thus adapted is temperate and brave." "Certainly." "But the soul in 411a which they are not adapted, is cowardly and savage." "Extremely so."

"And when one yields up himself to be soothed with the charms of music, and pours into his soul through his ears, as through a pipe, those we denominated the soft, effeminate, and plaintive harmonies, and spends the whole of his life chanting and ravished with melody; such an one, at the first, if he has any thing irascible, softens it like 411b iron, and, from being useless and fierce, renders it profitable. But when still persisting he does not desist, but enchants his soul, after this, it melts and dissolves him, till it liquefies his anger, and cuts out, as it were, the nerves of his soul, and renders him an effeminate warrior." "It is certainly so indeed," said he. "But if," said I, "he had from the beginning a temper void of irascibility, this he quickly effectuates; but, if irascible, it renders the mind weak, and easily turned, so as instantly to be enraged at trifles, and again the rage is 411c extinguished: so that, from being irascible, they become outrageous and passionate, and full of the morose." "So indeed it happens." "But what now? If one labour much in gymnastic, and feast extremely well, but apply not to music and philosophy; shall he not, in the first place, having his body in a good condition, be filled with prudence and courage, and become more brave than he was before?" "Certainly so."

"But what, when he does nothing else; nor participates in any thing 411d which is music-like, though there were any love of learning in his soul, as it neither tastes of any study, nor bears a share in any inquiry nor reasoning, nor any thing besides which is musical, must it not become feeble, and deaf, and blind, as his perceptions are neither awakened, nor nourished, nor refined?" "Just so." "Such an one then becomes, as I imagine, a reason-hater, and unmusical; and by no means can be persuaded to any thing by reasoning, but is carried to 411e every thing by force and savageness, as a wild beast; and thus he lives in ignorance and barbarity, out of measure, and unpolished." "It is," said he, "entirely so."

255 "Corresponding then to these two tempers, I would say, that some God, as appears, has given men two arts, those of music and gymnastic, in reference to the irascible and the philosophic temper; not for the soul and body, otherwise than as a by-work, but for that other purpose, that those two tempers might be adapted to one 412a another; being stretched and slackened as far as is fit." "So indeed it appears." "Whoever then shall in the most handsome manner mingle gymnastic with music, and have these in the justest measure in his soul, him we shall most properly call the most completely musical, and of the best harmony; far more than the man who adjusts to one another musical strings." "Most reasonably," said he, "Socrates." "Shall we not then, Glauco, always have need of such a president for 412b our state, if our government is to be preserved?" "We shall most especially have need of this."

"Those then may be the models of education and discipline. For why should one go over the dances, the huntings of wild beasts, both with dogs and with nets, the wrestlings and the horse-races proper for such persons? for it is nearly manifest that these naturally follow of course, and it is no difficult matter to find them." "It is indeed," said he, "not difficult." "Be it so," said I. "But what follows next? What was 412c next to be determined by us. Was it, which of these shall govern, and be governed?" "What else?" "Is it not plain that the elder ought to be governors, and the younger to be the governed?" "It is plain." "And is it not likewise plain, that the best of them are to govern?" "This too is plain." "But are not the best husbandmen the most assiduous in agriculture?" "They are." "If now our guardians are the best, will they not be most vigilant over the city?" "They will." "Must we not for this purpose make them prudent, and able, and careful likewise of the 412d city?" "We must do so." "But one would seem to be most careful of that which he happens to love." "Undoubtedly." "And one shall most especially love that to which he thinks the same things are profitable which are so to himself, and with whose good estate he thinks his own connected; and where he is of a contrary opinion, he will be contrariwise affected." "Just so." "We must choose then from the other guardians such men as shall most of all others appear to us, on observation, to do with the greatest cheerfulness, through the whole of life, whatever they think advantageous for the state, and what 412e appears to be disadvantageous they will not do by any means." "These are most proper," said he.

"It truly appears to me, that they ought to be observed through 256 every stage of their life, if they be tenacious of this opinion, so as that neither fraud nor force make them inconsiderately throw out this opinion, that they ought to do what is best for the state." "What throwing out do you mean?" said he. "I will tell you," said I. "An opinion seems to me to depart from the dianoëtic part voluntarily or involuntarily. A false opinion departs voluntarily from him who 413a unlearns it; but every true opinion departs involuntarily." "The case of the voluntary one," replied he, "I understand; but that of the involuntary I want to learn." "What now? Do not you think," said I, "that men are involuntarily deprived of good things; but voluntarily of evil things? Or, is it not an evil to deviate from the truth, and a good to form true opinion? Or, does it not appear to you, that to conceive of things as they really are, is to form true opinion?" "You say rightly indeed," replied he. "They do seem to me to be deprived unwillingly of true opinion." "Do they not then suffer this, either in the way of theft, enchantment, or force?" "I do not now," said he, "understand you." "I seem," said I, "to speak theatrically. But, I say, 413b those have their opinions stolen away, who are persuaded to change their opinions, and also those who forget them; in the one case, they are imperceptibly taken away by time, and in the other by reasoning. Do you now understand in any measure?" "Yes." "And those, I say, have their opinions forced from them, whom grief or agony obliges to change them." "This," said he, "I understand, and you say right." "And those, I imagine, you will say, are enchanted out of their opinions, who change them, being bewitched by pleasure, or seduced by fear, being afraid of something." "It seems," said he, "that every thing magically beguiles which deceives us."

413c

"That then which I was now mentioning must be sought for: who are the best guardians of this opinion; that that is to be done which is best for the state: and they must be observed immediately from their childhood, setting before them such pieces of work in which they may most readily forget a thing of this kind, and be deluded; and he who is mindful, and hard to be deluded, is to be chosen, and he who is otherwise is to be rejected. Is it not so?" "Yes." "And we must appoint them trials of labours and of pains, in which we must observe the same thing." "Right," said he. "Must we not," said I, "appoint them a third contest, that of the mountebank kind; and observe them as those do, who, when they lead on young horses against noises and tumults, observe whether they are frightened? So must they, whilst young, be led into dreadful things, and again be thrown into pleasures, trying them more than gold in the fire, whether one is hard to be beguiled with mountebank tricks, and appear composed amidst all, being a good guardian of himself, and of that music which he learned, showing himself in all these things to be in just measure and harmony. Being of such a kind as this, he would truly be of the greatest advantage both to himself and to the state. And the man who in childhood, in youth, and in manhood, has been thus tried, and has come out pure, is to be appointed governor and guardian of the state; and honours are to be paid him whilst alive, and when dead he should receive the highest rewards of public funeral and other memorials. And he who is not such an one is to be rejected. Of such a kind, Glauco," said I, "as it appears to me, is to be the choice and establishment of our governors and guardians, as in a sketch, and not accurately." "And I," said he, "am of the same opinion." "Is it not then truly most just, to call these the most complete guardians, both

413d

257

413e

414a

414b

with reference to enemies abroad, and to friends at home; so as that the one shall not have the will, nor the other have the power to do any mischief? And the youth (whom we now called guardians) will be allies and auxiliaries to the decrees of the governors." "I imagine so," replied he.

"What now," said I, "may be the contrivance of those lies, which are made on occasion, and of which we were lately saying that it is a most generous part, in making lies, to persuade the governors themselves most especially; or, if not these, the rest of the state?" "What sort do you mean?" "Nothing new," said I, "but somewhat Phœnician, which has frequently happened heretofore, as the poets tell us, and have persuaded us, but has not happened in our times, nor do I know if ever it shall happen: to persuade one of it surely requires a subtle persuasion." "How like you are," said he, "to one who is averse to speak!" "I shall appear," said I, "to be averse with very good reason, after I tell it." "Speak," said he, "and do not fear." "I speak then, though I know not with what courage, and using what expressions,, I shall tell it. And I shall attempt, first of all, to persuade the governors themselves, and the soldiers, and afterwards the rest of the state, that, whatever we educated and instructed them in, all these particulars seemed to happen to them and to befall them as dreams; but that they were in truth at that time formed and educated within the earth; both they themselves, and their armour and their other utensils, being there likewise fabricated. And after they were completely fashioned, that the earth, who is their mother, brought them forth; and now they ought to be affected towards the country where they are, as to their mother and nurse; to defend her, if any invade her; and to consider the rest of the citizens as being their brothers, and sprung from their mother earth." "It was not without reason," said he, "that some time since you were ashamed to tell this falsehood." "I had truly reason," said I. "But hear however the rest of the fable. All of you now in the state are brothers (as we shall tell them in way of fable); but the God, when he formed you, mixed gold in the formation of such of you as are able to govern; therefore are they the most honourable. And silver, in such as are auxiliaries; and iron and brass in the husbandmen and other handicrafts. As you are all of the same kind, you for the most part resemble one another: and it sometimes happens, that of the gold is generated the silver, and of the silver there is a golden descendant; and thus every different way are they generated of one another. The God gives in charge, first of all, and chiefly to the governors, that of nothing are they to be so good guardians, nor are they so strongly to keep watch over any thing, as over their children; to know what of those principles is mixed in their 415c soul; and if their descendant shall be of the brazen or iron kind, they shall by no means have compassion; but, assigning him honour proportioned to his natural temper, they shall push him down to the craftsmen or husbandmen. And if again any from among these shall be born of a golden or silver kind, they shall pay them honour, and prefer them; those to the guardianship, and these to the auxiliary rank: it being pronounced by the oracle, that the state is then to perish when iron or brass shall have the guardianship of it. Have you now any contrivance to persuade them of this fable?"

415d   "None," said he, "to persuade these men themselves; but I can contrive how that their sons and posterity, and all mankind afterwards, shall believe it." "Even this," said I, "would do well towards making them more concerned about the state, and one another; for I almost understand what you say. And this truly will lead the same way as the oracle. But let us, having armed these earth-born 259 sons, lead them forwards under their leaders; and when they are come 415e into the city, let them consider where it is best to place their camp, so as best to keep in order those who are within, if any one should want to disobey the laws; and likewise defend against those without, if any enemy, as a wolf, should come upon the fold. And when they have marked out their camp, and performed sacrifices to the proper divinities, let them erect their tents: or, how are they to do?" "Just so," said he. "Shall they not be such as may be sufficient to defend them, both from winter and summer?" "Why not? for you seem," said he, "to mean houses." "Yes," said I, "but military ones; not such as are 416a costly." "What do you say," replied he, "is the difference between the one and the other?" "I will endeavour," said I, "to tell you; for, of all things, it is the most dreadful, and the most shameful to shepherds, to breed such kind of dogs, and in such a manner, as auxiliaries of the flocks, as either through intemperance or famine, or some other ill disposition, the dogs themselves should attempt to hurt the sheep;

and, instead of dogs, resemble wolves." "That is dreadful," said he, "why is it not?" "Must we not then, by all means, take care lest our 416b allies do such a thing towards our citizens, as they are more powerful; and, instead of generous allies, resemble savage lords?" "We must take care," said he. "Would they not be prepared, as to the greatest part of the care, if they were really well educated?" "But they are so at least," replied he. And I said: "That is not proper to be confidently affirmed, friend Glauco; but that is proper which we were now saying, that they 416c ought to have good education, whatever it is, if they are to have what is of the greatest consequence towards rendering them mild, both among themselves and towards those who are guarded by them." "Very right," said he. "Besides then this education, any one of understanding would say, that their houses, and all their other substance, ought to be so contrived, as not to hinder their guardians from being the very best of men, and not to stir them up to injure the other citizens." "And he will say true." 416d

"If then they intend to be such, consider," said I, "whether they ought to live and dwell in some such manner as this: First, then, let none posses any substance privately, unless there be the greatest necessity for it: next, let none have any dwelling, or store-house, into which whoever inclines may not enter: as for necessaries, let them be such as temperate and brave warriors may require; and as they are 416e instituted by the other citizens, let them receive such a reward of their guardianship, as to have neither over-plus nor deficiency at the year's 260 end. Let them have public meals, as in encampments, and live in common. They must be told, that they have from the Gods a divine gold and silver at all times in their souls; and have no need of the human. And that it would be profane to pollute the possession of the divine kind, by mixing it with the possession of this mortal gold; because the money of the vulgar has produced many impious deeds, but that of these men is incorruptible. And of all the men in the city, 417a they alone are not allowed to handle or touch gold and silver; nor to bring it under their roof; nor carry it about with them; nor to drink out of silver or gold: and that thus they are to preserve themselves and the state. But whenever they shall possess lands, and houses, and money, in a private way, they shall become stewards and farmers instead of guardians, hateful lords instead of allies to the other 417b citizens: hating and being hated, plotting and being plotted against, they shall pass the whole of their life; much oftener and more afraid of the enemies from within than from without, they and the rest of the state hastening speedily to destruction. For all which reasons," said I, let us affirm, that our guardians are thus to be constituted with reference both to their houses and to other things. And let us settle these things by law. Shall we?" "By all means," said Glauco.

THE END OF THE THIRD BOOK.

BOOK IV.

Adimantus hereupon replying, "What now, Socrates," said he, "will you say in your own defence, if one shall say that you do not make these men very happy? for, though it is owing to these men that the city really exist, yet they enjoy no advantage in the city, such as others do who possess lands, build beautiful and large houses, purchase suitable furniture, offer sacrifices at their own expense, give public entertainments to strangers, and posses what you were now mentioning, gold and silver, and every thing which is reckoned to contribute towards the rendering men happy. But one may readily say, that, like hired auxiliaries, they seem to possess nothing in the city but the employment of keeping guard."

"Yes," said I; "and that too only for their maintenance, without receiving, as all others do, any reward besides. So that they are not allowed so much as to travel privately any where abroad, though they should incline to it; nor to bestow money on others, nor to spend it in such other methods as those do who are counted happy. These and many such things you leave out of the accusation." "But let these things too," said he, "be charged against them." "You ask then, what we shall say in our defence?" "I do." "Whilst we go on in the same road, we shall find, as I imagine, what may be said: for we shall say, that it would be nothing strange if these men, even in these circumstances, should be the happiest possible. Yet it was not with an eye to this that we established the city; to have any one tribe in it remarkably happy beyond the rest; but that the whole city might be

in the happiest condition; for we judged, that in such an one we
420c should most especially find justice, and injustice in the city the worst
established: and that, upon thoroughly examining these, we should
determine what we have for some time been in search of. Now then,
262 as I imagine, we are forming a happy state, not selecting some few
persons to make them alone happy; but are establishing the universal
happiness of the whole: and we shall next consider a state which is the
reverse. As if then we were painting human figures, and one
approaching should blame us, saying, that we do not place the most
beautiful colours on the most beautiful parts of the creature; for that
the eyes, the most beautiful part, were not painted with purple, but
420d with black; should we not seem to apologize sufficiently to him, by
saying, Wonderful critic! do not imagine that we ought to paint the
eyes beautiful, in such a way as that they would not appear to be eyes;
and so with reference to all other parts. But consider, whether, in
giving each particular part its due, we make the whole beautiful. And
so now, do not oblige us to confer such a happiness on our guardians
420e as shall make them any thing rather than guardians: for we know too,
how to array the husbandmen in rich and costly robes, and to enjoin
them to cultivate the ground only with a view to pleasure; and in like
manner, those who make earthen ware, to lie at their ease by the fire,
to drink and feast, neglecting the wheel, and working only so much
as they incline: and we know how to confer a felicity of this nature on
every individual, in order to render the whole state happy. But do not
421a advise us to act after this manner; since, if we obey you, neither would
the husbandman really be a husbandman, nor the potter be a potter;
nor would any other really be of any of those professions of which the
city is composed. But, as to others, it is of less consequence; for, when
shoemakers become bad, and are degenerate, and profess to be
shoemakers when they are not, no great mischief happens to the state:
but when the guardians of the law and of the state are not so in
reality; but only in appearance, you see how they entirely destroy the
whole constitution; if they alone shall have the privilege of an
affluent and happy life. If we then are for appointing men who shall
421b be really guardians of the city, the least of all hurtful to it; and he who
makes the objection is for having them rather as certain farmers, and
as in a festival-meeting, not in a city, certain public entertainers,

indulging in jollity, he must mean something else than a city: we must then consider whether we establish guardians with this view, that they may have the greatest happiness; or if we establish them with a view to the happiness of the whole city, let us see whether this takes place; and let us oblige these allies and guardians to do this, and we must persuade them they shall thus become the best performers of their own particular work; and we must act towards all others in the same manner. And thus the whole city being increased, and well constituted, let us allow the several tribes to participate of happiness as their natures admit."

"You seem to me," said he, "to say well." "Shall I appear to you," said I, "to speak right in what is akin to this?" "What is that?" "Consider whether other artificers are corrupted by these things, so as to be made bad workmen." "What things do you mean?" "Riches," said I, "and poverty." "As how?" "Thus: Does the potter, after he becomes rich, seem still to mind his art?" "By no means," said he. "But will he not become more idle and careless than formerly?" "Much more so." "Shall he not then become a more skilful potter?" "Much more so, likewise," said he. "And surely, being unable through poverty to furnish himself with tools, or any thing else requisite to his art, his workmanship shall be more imperfectly executed, and his sons, or those others whom he instructs, shall be inferior artists." "How should they not?" "Through both these, now, poverty and riches, the workmanship in the arts is rendered less perfect, and the artists themselves become less expert." "It appears so." "We have then, it seems, discovered other things, which our guardians must by all means watch against, that they may in no respect escape their notice, and steal into the city." "What kind of things are these?" "Riches," said I, "and poverty: as the one is productive of luxury, idleness, and a love of novelty; and the other, besides a love of novelty, is illiberal, and productive of mischief." "They are entirely so," said he. "But consider this, Socrates. How shall our city be able to engage in war, since she is possessed of no money, especially if she be obliged to wage war against a great and opulent state?" "It is plain," said I, "that to fight against one of this kind is somewhat difficult; but to fight against two is a more easy matter." "How say you?" replied he.

"First of all, now," said I, "if they have at all occasion to fight, will

they not, being expert in the art of war, fight against rich men?"
"They will," said he. "What then," said I, "Adimantus, do not you
think that one boxer who is fitted out in the best manner possible for
this exercise, is easily able to fight against two who are not expert
boxers, but, on the contrary, are rich and unwieldy?" "He would not
perhaps easily fight with both at once," said he. "Would he not," said
I, "though he had it in his power to retire a little, and then turn on
the one who should be the furthest advanced towards him, and strike
him, and by doing this frequently in the sun and heat? Might not a
person of this kind easily defeat many such as these?" "Certainly," said
he; "that would be no great wonder." "But do not you think that the
rich have more knowledge and experience of boxing than of the
military art?" "I do," said he. "Easily then, as it plainly appears, will
our athletics combat with double and triple their number." "I will
agree with you," said he; "for you seem to me to say right." "But what
if they should send an embassy to an other state, informing them of
the true situation of the affair, telling them, We make no use of gold
or silver, neither is it lawful for us to use them, but with you it is
lawful; if then you become our allies in the war, you will receive the
spoils of all the other states: do you imagine that any, on hearing
these things, would choose to fight against strong and resolute dogs,
rather than in alliance with the dogs to fight against fat and tender
sheep?" "I do not think it; but, if the riches of others be amassed in to
one state, see that it does not endanger that which is poor." "You are
happy," said I, "that you imagine any other deserves to be called a
state besides such an one as we have established." "Why not?" said he.
"We must give others," said I, "a more magnificent appellation; for
each of them consists of many states, and is not one, as is said in way
of irony: for there are always in them two parties at war with each
other, the poor and the rich; and in each of these again there are very
many: to which if you apply as to one, you are mistaken entirely; but
if, as to many, you put one part in possession of the goods and power
of another, or even deliver up the one to the other, you shall always
have the many for your allies, and the few for enemies; and, so long as
your state shall continue temperately, as now established, it shall be
the greatest. I do not say it shall be accounted so, but shall be really
the greatest, though its defenders were no more than one thousand;

for one state so great you will not easily find, either among the Greeks 423b
or Barbarians, but many which are accounted many times larger than
such an one as this. Are you of a different opinion?" "No, truly," said
he.

"Might not this, then," said I, "be the best mark for our rulers how
large to make the city, and what extent of ground to mark off for it
in proportion to its bulk, without attending to any thing further?"
"What mark?" said he. "I imagine," said I, "this: So long as the city, 265
on its increase, continues to be one, so long it may be increased, but 423c
not beyond it." "Very right," said he. "Shall we not then lay this
further injunction on our guardians, to take care by all means that
the city be neither small nor great, but of moderate extent, and be
one city?" "We shall probably," said he, "enjoin them a trifling
affair." "A more trifling affair still than this," said I, "is that we
mentioned above, when we observed, that if any descendant of the
guardians be depraved, he ought to be dismissed to the other classes;
and if any descendant of the others be worthy, he is to be raised to the 423d
rank of the guardians; and this was intended to show that all the
other citizens ought to apply themselves each to that particular art for
which he has a natural genius, that so every one minding his own
proper work may not be many, but be one; and so likewise the whole
state may become one, and not be many." "This indeed," said he, "is
still a more trifling matter than the other."

"We do not here," said I, "good Adimantus, as one may imagine,
enjoin them many and great matters; but such as are all trifling, if 423e
they take care of one grand point, as the saying is, or rather that
which is sufficient in place of the grand." "What is that?" said he.
"Education," said I, "and nurture; for if, being well educated, they
become temperate men, they will easily see through all these things,
and such other things as we omit at present, respecting women,
marriages, and the propagation of the species. For these things ought 424a
all, according to the proverb, to be made entirely common among
friends." "That," said he, "would be most right." "And surely," said I,
"if once a republic is set a-going, it proceeds happily, increasing as a
circle. And whilst good education and nurture are preserved, they
produce good geniuses; and good geniuses, partaking of such
education, produce still better than the former, as well in other 424b

respects as with reference to propagation, as in the case of other animals." "It is likely," said he. "To speak then briefly, this the guardians of the state must oppose, that it may not, escaping their notice, hurt the constitution; nay, above all things, they must guard against this, not to make any innovations in gymnastic and music, contrary to the established order of the state, but to maintain this order as much as possible; being afraid lest, whilst a man adopts that poetical expression,

. . . . . Men most admire that song,
Which most partakes of novelty,

266

424c one should frequently imagine, that the poet means not new songs, but a new method of the song, and should commend this. Such a thing is neither to be commended nor admitted; for, to receive a new kind of music is to be guarded against, as endangering the whole of the constitution: for never are the measures of music altered without the greatest politic laws, according to Damon, with whom I agree." "You may place me likewise," said Adimantus, "among those who are 424d of that opinion." "We must erect then," said I, "same barrier, as would seem, somewhere here, for our guardians themselves, with regard to music." "A transgression here," said he, "easily indeed steals in imperceptibly." "It does," said I, "in the way of diversion, and as productive of no mischief." "For neither indeed does it produce any other," said he, "but that becoming familiar by degrees it insensibly runs into the manners and pursuits; and from thence, in intercourse 424e of dealings one with another, it becomes greater; and from this intercourse it enters into laws and policies with much impudence, Socrates, till at last it overturns all things, both private and public." "Well," said I, "let it be allowed to be so." "It appears so to me," replied he.

"Ought not then our children, as I said at the beginning, to receive directly from their infancy an education more agreeable to the laws of the constitution? because, if their education be such as is contrary to 425a law, and the children be of such a nature themselves, it is impossible that they should ever grow up to be worthy men, and observant of the laws." "Why, is it not?" said he. "But when handsome amusements are appointed them from their infancy, and when, by means of the music, they embrace that amusement which is according to law (contrariwise to those others), this music attends them in every thing else, and grows with them, and raises up in the city whatever formerly was fallen down." "It is true, indeed," said he. "And these men," said I, "discoverer those establishments which appear trifling, and which those others destroyed altogether." "What establishments?" "Such as these: Silence of the younger before the elder, which is proper; and the 425b giving them place, and rising up before them, and reverence of parents; likewise what shaving, what clothes and shoes are proper, with the whole dress of the body, and every thing else of the kind. Are you not of this opinion?" "I am." "But to establish these things by law, would, I imagine, be a silly thing, nor is it done any where; nor would it stand, though established both by word and writing." "For, *267* how is it possible?"

"It seems then," said I, "Adimantus, that a man's character and conduct will always be according to his education, let him apply 425c himself afterwards to what he will: or, does not the like always produce the like?" "Why not?" "And we may say, I imagine, that at last it arrives at somewhat complete and vigorous, either good, or what is the reverse." "Why not?" said he. "I would not then," said I, "for these reasons, as yet, undertake to settle by law such things as these." "Right," said he. "But what now, by the gods," said I, "as to those laws relative to matters of exchange, and to their traffic one with another in the forum, and, if you please, their traffic likewise 425d among their handicrafts, their scandals, bodily hurt, and raising of lawsuits; their institution of judges, and likewise such imposts and payments of taxes as may be necessary either in the forum or at shores; or in general whatever laws are municipal, civil, or marine, or what other laws there may be of this kind; shall we dare to establish any of these?" "It is improper," said he, "to prescribe these to good and worthy men; for they will easily find out the most of them, such as ought to be established by law." "Yes," said I, "friend, if at least God 425e grant them the preservation of the laws we formerly explained." "And if not," said he, "they will spend the whole of their life making and amending many such laws as these, imagining that they shall thus attain to that which is best." "You say that such as these shall lead a life," said I, "like those who are sick, and at the same time unwilling,

426a through intemperance, to quit an unwholesome diet." "Entirely so."
"And these truly must live very pleasantly; for, though they deal with
physicians, they gain nothing, but render their diseases greater and
more complex; and they still hope, that when any one recommends
any medicine to them, they shall, by means of it, be made whole."
"This is entirely the situation of such diseased persons as these." "But
what," said I, "is not this pleasant in them? to count that man the
most hateful of all, who tells them the truth; that, till one give over
426b drunkenness and gluttony, and unchaste pleasure, and laziness,
neither drugs nor caustics, nor amputations, nor charms, nor
applications, nor any other such things as these, will be of any avail."
"That," said he, "is not quite pleasant; for to be enraged at one who
tells us what is right, has nothing pleasant in it." "You are no
admirer," said I, "as it would seem, of this sort of men." "No, truly."

268   "Neither then, though the whole of the city (as we were lately
saying) should do such a thing, would you commend them: or, is not
the same thing which is done by these people, done by all those cities,
426c which, being ill-governed, enjoin their citizens not to alter any part
of the constitution, for that whoever shall do such a thing is to be put
to death; but, that whoever shall with the greatest cheerfulness
reverence those who govern in this fashion, and shall gratify them in
the most obsequious manner; and, anticipating their desires, be most
dexterous in satisfying them, shall be reckoned both worthy and wise
in matters of highest importance; and be held by them in the greatest
honour?" "They seem to me at least," said he, "to do the very same
426d thing, and by no means do I commend them." "But what again as to
those who desire to have the management of such states, and are even
fond of it, are you not delighted with their courage and dexterity?" "I
am," said he; "excepting such as are imposed on by them, and fancy
that they are really politicians, because they are commended as such
by the multitude." "How do you mean? Do you not pardon those
men?" said I. "Or do you even think it is possible for a man who
cannot measure himself, when he hears many other such men telling
426e him that he is four cubits, not to believe this of himself?" "It is
impossible," said he. "Then be not angry in this case; for such men as
these are of all the most ridiculous, since, always making laws about
such things as we now mentioned, and always amending, they

imagine that they shall find some period of these frauds respecting commerce, and those other things I now spoke of, being ignorant that they are in reality attempting to destroy a hydra." "They are 427a surely," said he, "doing nothing else." "I imagine then," said I, "that a true lawgiver ought not to give himself much disturbance about such a species of laws and police, either in an ill or well-regulated state; in the one, because it is unprofitable and of no avail; in the other, because any one can find out some of the laws, and others of them flow of course from the habits arising from their early education."

"What part then of the institutions of law," said he, "have we yet 427b remaining?" And I said, that "to us indeed there is nothing remaining; but, however, to the Delphian Apollo there remains the greatest, noblest, and most important of legal institutions." "Of what kind?" said he. "The institutions of temples, sacrifices, and other worship of the Gods, dæmons, and heroes; likewise the depositing the 267 dead, and what other rites ought to be performed to them, so as to make them propitious. For truly such things as these, we ourselves 427c neither know; nor, in founding the state, will we entrust them to any other, if we be wise; nor will we make use of any other interpreter, except the God of the country. For this God is the interpreter in every country to all men in these things, who interprets to them sitting in the middle of the earth." "And it is well established," said he, "and we must do accordingly."

"Thus now, son of Aristo," said I, "is the city established for you. 427d And, in the next place, having procured somehow sufficient light, do you yourself observe, and call on your brother and on Polemarchus and these others to assist us, if by any means we may at all perceive where justice is, and where injustice; and in what respect they differ from each other: and which of them the man ought to acquire, who proposes to himself to be happy, whether he be concealed or not concealed both from Gods and men." "But you say nothing to the purpose," replied Glauco; "for you yourself promised to inquire into this, deeming it impious for you not to assist the cause of justice by 427e every possible means." "It is true," said I, "what you remind me of, and I must do accordingly. But it is proper that you too should assist in the inquiry." "We shall do so," said he. "I hope then," said I, "to discover it in this manner. I think that our city, if it be rightly established, is perfectly good." "Of necessity," said he. "Then it is plain, that it is wise, and brave, and temperate, and just." "It manifestly is so." "Whichever then of these we shall find in it, shall

428a there not remain behind that which is not found?" "Why not?"

"For as if we were in quest of one, of any other four, in any thing whatever, if we discovered this one at the first, we would be satisfied; but if we should first discover the other three from this itself, that which we were inquiring after would be known; for it is plain it would be no other but that which remained." "You say right," said he. "Since then there are in our state those four above mentioned, shall we not inquire about them, according to the same manner?" "It is

428b plain we ought." "First of all, then, to me at least, wisdom appears to be conspicuous in it; and concerning it there appears something very uncommon." "What is that?" said he. "Surely this city which we have described appears to me to be wise, for its councils are wise; are they

270 not?" "They are." "And surely this very thing, the ability of counselling well, is plainly a certain science; for men nowhere counsel well through ignorance, but through science." "It is plain." "But there are many and various species of science in the state." "Why, are there

428c not?" "Is it then from the science of the carpenters, that the state is to be denominated wise and well-counselled?" "By no means from this," said he, "is it said to be wise, but to be mechanical." "Is then the state to be denominated wise, when it consults wisely through its knowledge in utensils of wood, how to have these in the best manner possible?" "Nor this neither." "But what, is it for its knowledge of these in brass, or for any thing else of this kind?" "For none of these," said he. "Nor yet for its knowledge of the fruits of the earth is it said to be wise, but to be skilled in agriculture." "It seems so to me." "But what," said I, "is there any science among any of the citizens in this city which we have founded, which deliberates, not about any

428d particular thing in the city, but about the whole, how it may, in the best manner, behave towards itself, and towards other cities?" "There is truly." "What is it," said I, "and among whom is it to be found?" "This very guardianship," said he, "is it, and it is among these governors, whom we lately denominated complete guardians." "What now do you denominate the state on account of this knowledge?"

"Well-counselled," said he, "and really wise."

"Whether then," said I, "do you imagine the brass-smiths, or these 428e true guardians, will be most numerous in the state?" "The brass-smiths," said he, "will be much more numerous." "And of all," said I, "as many as, having any knowledge, are of any account, will not these guardians be the fewest in number?" "By much." "From this smallest tribe then, and part of the state and from that presiding and governing science in it, is the whole city wisely established according to nature; and this tribe, as it appears, is by nature the smallest, to 429a whom it belongs to share in this science, which of all others ought alone to be denominated wisdom." "You say," replied he, "perfectly true." "This one, then, of the four, we have found, I know not how, both what it is, and in what part of the state it resides." "And it seems to me," said he, "to be sufficiently described."

"But surely as to fortitude, at least, it is no difficult matter, both to find out itself, and the particular part of the city in which it resides, on account of which virtue the city is denominated brave." "As how?" 271 "Doth any one," said I, "call a city brave or cowardly, with reference 429b to any other than that particular part of it which makes war and fights in its defence?" "No one," said he, "calls it such, with reference to any other part." "For I do not think," said I, "that the other tribes who are in it, whether they be cowardly or brave, have power to render the city either the one or the other." "No, indeed." "The city then is brave likewise in one particular part of itself, because it has within it a power of such a nature as shall always preserve their opinions about things which are dreadful, that they are both these 429b very things, and of the very same kind which the lawgiver inculcated on them in their education? Do not you call this fortitude?" "I have not," said he, "entirely comprehended what you say; but tell it over again." "I call fortitude," said I, "a certain preservative." "What sort of preservative?" "A preservative of opinion formed by law in a course of education about things which are dreadful, what these are, and of what kind: I called it a preservative at all times, because they were to retain it in pains and in pleasures, in desires and fears, and never to 429c call it off; and, if you are willing, I shall liken it to what in my opinion it bears a near resemblance." "I am willing."

"Do not you know then," said I, "that the dyers, when they want to

dye their wool, so as to be of a purple colour, out of all the colours they first make choice of the white; and then, with no trifling apparatus, they prepare and manage it, so as best of all to take on the
429e purest colour, and thus they dye it; and whatever is tinged in this manner is of an indelible dye; and no washing, either without or with soap, is able to take away the pure colour: but such wool as is not managed in this manner, you know what sort it proves, whether one is dyeing other colours, or this, without the due preparation beforehand." "I know," said he, "that they are easily washed out, and are ridiculous." "Imagine then, that we too, according to our ability, were aiming at such a thing as this, when we were choosing out our
430a soldiers, and were instructing them in music and gymnastic: and do not imagine we had any thing else in view, but that, in obedience to us, they should in the best manner imbibe the laws as a colour; in order that their opinion about what is dreadful, and about other things, might be indelible, both by means of natural temper and suitable education: and that these washes, however powerful in
272 effacing, may not be able to wash away their dye, pleasure, which is
430b more powerful in effecting this than all soap and ashes, pain and fear, and desire, which exceed every other cosmetic. Such a power now, and perpetual preservation of right opinion, and such as is according to law, about things which are dreadful, and which are not, I call and constitute fortitude, unless you offer something else." "But I offer," said he, "nothing else: for you seem to me to reckon that such right opinion of these things, as arises without education, is both savage and servile, and not at all according to law, and you call it something
430c else than fortitude." "You say most true," said I. "I admit then, that this is fortitude." "Admit it further," said I, "to be political fortitude, and you shall admit rightly: but, if you please, we shall inquire about it more perfectly another time; for, at present, it is not this, but justice we were seeking; and with regard to the inquiry concerning this, it has, in my opinion, been carried far enough." "You speak very well," said he.

430d   "There yet remain," said I, "two things in the city which we must search out: both temperance, and that for the sake of which we have been searching after all the rest, to wit, justice." "By all means." "How now can we find out justice, that we may not be further troubled about temperance?" "I truly neither know," said he, "nor do I wish it to appear first, if we are to dismiss altogether the consideration of temperance; but, if you please to gratify me, consider this before the other." "I am indeed pleased," said I, "if I be not doing an injury." 430e "Consider then," said he. "We must consider," replied I; "and as it appears from this point of view, it seems to resemble a certain symphony and harmony more than those things formerly mentioned." "How?" "Temperance," said I, "is somehow a certain ornament, and a government, as they say, of certain pleasures and desires; and to appear superior to oneself, I know not how, and other such things, are mentioned as vestiges of it; are they not?" "These are the principal vestiges of it," said he. "Is not then the expression, 'superior to oneself,' ridiculous? For he who is superior to himself must somehow be likewise inferior to himself, and the inferior be the 431a superior; for the same person is spoken of in all these cases." "Why not?" "But to me," said I, "the expression seems to denote, that in the same man, with respect to his soul, there is one part better, and another worse; and that when the part more excellent in his nature is that which governs the inferior part, this is called being superior to himself; and expresses a commendation; but when through ill education, or any kind of converse, that better part, which is smaller, 273 is conquered by the crowd, the worse part; this, by way of reproach, 431b both expresses blame, and denotes the person thus affected to be inferior to himself, and altogether licentious." "So it appears," said he.

"Observe then," said I, "our new city, and you shall find one of these in it: for you will own, it may justly be said to be superior to itself, if, where the better part governs the worse, that state is said to be temperate, and superior to itself." "I observe," said he, "and you say true." "And surely one may find a great many and various desires and 431c pleasures and pains more especially among children and women and domestics, and among the greatest and most depraved part of those who are called free." "It is perfectly so." "But the simple and the moderate desires, and such as are led by intellect, and the judgment of right opinion, you will meet with both in the few, and those of the best natural temper, and of the best education." "True," said he. "And do not you see those things in our city, that there too the desires of the 431d many, and of the baser part, are governed by the desires and by the prudence of the smaller and more moderate part?" "I see it," said he.

"If then any city ought to be called superior to pleasures and desires, and to itself, this one is to be called so." "By all means," said he. "And is it not on all these accounts temperate?" "Very much so," said he.

431e "And if, in any other city, there is the same opinion in the governors and the governed about this point, who ought to govern, it is to be found in this, do not you think so?" "I am strongly of that opinion." "In whom then of the citizens will you say that temperance resides, when they are thus affected, in the governors, or the governed?" "In both of them somehow," said he. "You see then," said I, "that we justly conjectured of late, that temperance resembles a kind of harmony." "For what?" "Because not as fortitude and wisdom, which

432a reside each of them in a certain part, the one of them making the city wise, and the other courageous, not after this manner doth it render the city temperate; but it is naturally diffused through the whole, connecting the weakest, and those in the middle, all in one symphony, either as to wisdom if you will, or if you will in strength, or in substance, or in any other of those things; so that most justly may we say, that this concord is temperance: a symphony of that

432b which is naturally the worse and the better part, with reference to this, which of them ought to govern in the city, and in every

274 individual." "I am entirely," said he, "of the same opinion." "Be it so then," said I. "There are now three things in the city, it would seem, clearly discovered: but with respect to that other species which remains, by which the city partakes of virtue; what at all can it be? Is it not plain that it is justice?" "It is plain." "Ought we not now, Glauco, like some huntsmen, to surround the thicket, carefully attending lest

432c justice somehow escape, and, disappearing, remain undiscovered? For it is plain that she is somewhere here. Look, therefore and be eager to perceive her, if any how you see her sooner than I, and point her out to me." "I wish I could," said he; "but if you employ me as an attendant rather, and one who is able to perceive what is pointed out to him, you will treat me perfectly well." "Follow," said I, "after you have offered prayers along with me." "I will do so; only," said he, "lead you the way."

"To me this seems," said I, "to be a place somehow of difficult access, and shady: It is therefore dark, and difficult to be scrutinized; 432d we must however go on." "We must go," said he. I then perceiving, said, "Iö! Iö! Glauco, we seem to have somewhat which appears to be a footstep; and I imagine that something shall not very long escape us." "You tell good news," said he. "We are truly," said I, "of a slow disposition." "As how?" "It appears, so blessed man! to have been long since rolling at our feet, from the beginning, and we perceived it not, but made the most ridiculous figure, like those who seek sometimes 432e for what they have in their hand; so we did not perceive it, but were looking somewhere off at a distance, and in this why perhaps it escaped us." "How do you say?" replied he. "Thus," said I, "that we seem to me to have been speaking and hearing of it long since, and not to understand ourselves, that in some measure we expressed it." "A long preamble," said he, "to one who is eager to hear."

"Hear then," said I, "if I say any thing. For that which we at first 433a established, when we regulated the city, as what ought always to be done, that, as it appears to me, or a species of it, is justice. For we somewhere established it, and often spoke of it, if you remember; that every one ought to apply himself to one thing, relating to the city, to which his genius was naturally most adapted." "We did speak of it." "And that to do one's own affairs, and not to be pragmatical, is justice. This we have both heard from many others, and have often 433b spoken of it ourselves." "We have indeed spoken of it." "This then, friend," said I, "appears to be in a certain manner justice; to do one's own affairs. Do you know whence I conjecture this?" "No; but tell," 275 said he. "Besides those things we have already considered in the city, *viz.* temperance, fortitude, and wisdom; this," said I, "seems to remain, which gives power to all these, both to have a being in the state, and, whilst they exist in it, to afford it safety; and we said too, 433c that justice would be that which would remain, if we found the other three." "There is necessity for it," said he.

"But if," said I, "it be necessary to judge which of these, when subsisting in the city, shall in the greatest measure render it good; it would be difficult to determine whether the agreement between the governors and the governed, or the maintaining of sound opinion by the soldiers about what things are dreadful, and what are not or wisdom and guardianship in the rulers; or whether this, when it exists 433d in the city, renders it in the greatest measure good, *viz.* when child and woman, bond and free, artificer, magistrate and subject, when every one does their own affairs, and is not pragmatical." "It is difficult to deter mine," said he: "How should it not be so?" "This power then, by which every one in the city performs his own office, is co-rival it seems for the perfection of the city, along with its wisdom, temperance, and fortitude." "Extremely so," said he. "Will you not 433e then constitute justice to be this co-rival with these, for the perfection of the city?" "By all means."

"Consider it likewise in this manner, whether it shall thus appear to you. Will you enjoin the rulers to give just decisions in judgment?" "Why not?" "But will they give just judgment, if they aim at any thing preferable to this, that no one shall have what belongs to others, nor be deprived of his own?" "No; but they can only give just judgment, when they aim at this." "And do they not aim at this as being just?" "Yes." "And thus justice is acknowledged to be the 434a habitual practice of one's own proper and natural work." "It is so." "See then if you agree with me. If a carpenter take in hand to do the work of a shoemaker, or a shoemaker the work of a carpenter, or exchange either their utensils or prices; or if the same man take in hand to do both, and all else be exchanged; do you imagine the state would be any way greatly injured?" "Not very much," said he. "But I imagine, that when one who is a craftsman, or who is born to any 434b lucrative employment, shall afterwards being puffed up by riches, by the mob, or by strength, or any other such thing, attempt to go into the rank of counsellor and guardian, when unworthy of it; and when 276 these shall exchange utensils and rewards with one another; or when the same man shall take in hand to do all these things at once; then I imagine you will be of opinion that this interchange of these things, and this variety of employments practised by one, is the destruction of the state." "By all means." "Pragmaticalness then in these three 434c species, and their change into one another, is the greatest hurt to the state, and may most justly be called its depravity." "It may so truly." "But will not you say that injustice is the greatest ill of the state?" "Why not?"

"This then is injustice. But let us again speak of it in this manner. When the craftsman, the auxiliary and the guardian-band do their proper work, each of them doing their own work in the city; this is the contrary of the other, that is justice, and renders the city just." "It 434d seems to me," said he, "to be no otherwise than thus." "But let us not," said I, "affirm it very strongly: but if it shall be allowed us that this species of these, when it enters into any individual, is likewise justice in him, we shall then be agreed; (for what shall we say?) if not, we shall consider something else. But now let us finish that speculation, which we thought proper, when we judged that, if we attempted first to contemplate justice in some of the greater objects which possess it, it would more easily be seen in one man; and a city 434e appeared to us to be the most proper object of this kind. And so we established the very best we could, well knowing that justice would be in a good one. Let us now transfer and apply to a single person what has there appeared to us with respect to a whole city: and, if the same things correspond, it shall be well; but, if any thing different appear in the individual, going back again to the city, we shall put it to the proof; 435a and, instantly considering them, when placed by one another, and striking them, we shall make justice shine out as from flints; and, when it is become manifest, we shall firmly establish it among ourselves." "You say quite in the right way," said he, "and we must do so."

"Why then," said I, "when we denominate any thing the same, though different in degrees, is it dissimilar in that respect in which we call it the same, or is it similar?" "It is similar," said he. "The just man then," said I, "will differ nothing from the just city, according to the 435b idea of justice, but will be similar to it." "He will be similar to it," said he. "But indeed with respect to this inquiry, the city at least appeared then to be just, when the three species of dispositions in it did each of them its own work, *viz.* the temperate, the brave, and the wise, by virtue of their own proper natures, and not according to any other 277 affections and habits." "True," said he. "And shall we not, friend, judge it proper, that the individual, who has in his soul the same principles (*viz.* temperance, fortitude, wisdom), shall, from having 435c the same affections with those in the city, be called by the same names?" "By all means," said he.

"We have again, O wonderful man! fallen into no mean speculation concerning the soul; whether it contain in itself those these principles or not." "Into no mean one, as I imagine," said he. "And it is likely,

Socrates, that the common saying is true, that things excellent are
435d difficult." "It appears so," said I. "But know well, Glauco, that,
according to my opinion, we shall never comprehend this matter
accurately, in the methods we are now using in these reasonings, for
the road leading to it is greater and longer: we may however, it is
likely, speak of it in such a manner as may be worthy of our former
disquisitions and speculations." "Is not that desirable?" said he. "This
would satisfy me for my own part, at present, at least." "This," said I,
"shall to me too be quite sufficient." "Do not then give over," said he,
435e "but pursue your inquiry." "Are we not, then, under a necessity," said
I, "of acknowledging that there are in every one of us the same forms
and manners which are in the city? for from no where else did they
arrive thither. For it would be ridiculous if one should imagine that
the irascible disposition did not arise from the individuals in cites,
who have this blemish, as those of Thrace, Scythia, and, in some
measure, almost all the higher region; and the same thing may be said
with respect to the love of learning, which one may chiefly ascribe to
436a this country; or with reference to the love of riches, which we may say
prevailed especially among the Phœnicians and the inhabitants of
Egypt." "Very much so," said he. "This then is so," said I; "nor is it
difficult to be known." "No, indeed."

"But this is difficult to determine, whether we perform each of
these by the same power; or, as they are three, we perform one by one
power, and another by another; that is, we learn by one, we are angry
by another, and by a certain third we desire those pleasures relating to
436b nutrition and propagation, and the other pleasures of affinity to these.
Or do we, in each of these, when we apply to them, act with the whole
soul? These things are difficult to be determined in a manner worthy
of the subject." "So it seems to me," said he. "Let us then, in this
278 manner, attempt to determine these things, whether they are the
same with one another, or different." "How are we to do it?" "It is
plain, that one and the same thing cannot, at one and the same time,
do or suffer contrary things in the same respect, and with reference to
the same object; so that, if we any where find these circumstances
436c existing among them, we shall know that it was not one and the same
thing, but several." "Be it so." "Consider then what I am saying."
"Proceed," replied he.

"Is it possible for the same thing to stand and to be moved at once in the same respect?" "By no means." "Let us determine this more accurately still; lest, as we proceed, we be any way uncertain about it. For, if one should say that when a man stands, yet moves his hands and his head, that the same person at once stands and is moved, we should not, I imagine, think it proper to speak in this manner; but that one part of him stood, and another part was moved. Should we not speaking this manner?" "In this manner." "But if one who says these things should, in a more jocose humour still, and facetiously cavilling, allege that tops stand wholly, and are at the same time moved, when their centre is fixed on one point, and they are whirled about,—or that any thing else going round in a circle in the same position doth this,—we should not admit it, as it is not in the same respect that they stand still and are moved: but we should say, that they have in them the straight line and the periphery; and that, with relation to the straight line, they stood; (for towards no side they declined); but with relation to the periphery, they moved in a circle. But, when its perpendicularity declines either to the right or left hand, forwards or backwards, whilst it is at the same time whirling round; then in no respect doth it stand." "Very right," said he. "Nothing then of this kind shall move us, when it is said: nor shall any one persuade us, as if any thing, being one and the same thing, could do and suffer contraries at one and the same time, with reference to the same object, and in the same respect." "He shall not persuade me," said he. "But however," said I, "that we may not be obliged to be tedious in going over all these quibbles, and in evincing them to be false, let us proceed on this supposition, that so it is; after we have agreed that, if at any time these things appear otherwise than as we now settle them, we shall yield up again all we shall gain by it." "It is necessary," said he, "to do so."

"Would not you then," said I, "deem these things among those which are opposite to one another; whether they be actions or passions, for in this there is no difference; to assent, to wit, and to dissent, to desire to obtain a thing, and to reject it; to bring towards oneself, and to push away?" "I would deem these," said he, "among the things which are opposite to each other." "What then," said I, "with respect to thirsting, to hungering, and in general with respect

436d

436e

437a

437b
279

to all the passions; and further, to desire, to will, and all these, may
437c they not somehow be placed among those species which have now
been mentioned? As for example, will you not always say that the soul
of one who has desire goes out after that which it desires, or brings
near to it that which it wishes to have? Or again, in so far as it wants
something to be afforded it, like one who only sees an object, that it
intimates by signs, to have it brought near, desiring the actual
possession of it?" "I would say so." "But what, to be unwilling, not to
wish, nor to desire, shall we not deem these of the same kind, as to
437d push away from the soul, and drive off, and every thing else which is
opposite to the former?" "Why not?"

"This being the case, shall we say there is a certain species of the
desires? and that the most conspicuous are those which we call thirst
and hunger?" "We shall say so," replied he. "Is not the one the desire
of drinking, and the other of eating?" "Yes." "Is it then, when
considered as thirst, a desire in the soul of something further than of
drink?" "It is according to the nature of the thirst." "Is there then a
thirst of a hot drink, or of a cold, of much or of little, or in short of
437e some particular kind of drink? for, if there be any heat accompanying
the thirst, it readily occasions a desire of a cold drink; but if cold
accompanies it, then there is excited a desire of a warm drink: if the
thirst be great, through many circumstances, it occasions a desire of
much drink, but if small, a desire of a little drink: but the desire itself
to thirst never creates the desire of any thing else, but of drink itself,
as its nature prompts; and in like manner of the appetite of hunger
with relation to meat." "Thus every desire," said he, "in itself, is of
that alone of which it is the desire; but to be a desire of such or such a
438a particular species, are adventitious circumstances." "Let not then any
one," said I, "create us any trouble, as if we were inadvertent; that no
one desired drink, but good drink; or meat, but good meat: for
indeed all men desire that which is good. If then thirst be a desire, it is
of what is good; whether it be of drink, or of whatever else it is the
279 desire. And in the same way of all the other desires." "Perhaps,"
replied he, "the man who should mention these things would seem to
438b say something material." "But however," said I, "whatever things are
of such a nature as to belong to any genus, have a general reference to
the genus; but each particular of these refers to a particular species of

that genus." "I have not understood you," said he. "Have you not understood," said I, "that greater is of such a kind as to be greater than somewhat?" "Yes, indeed." "Is it not greater than the lesser?" "Yes." "And that which is considerably greater than that which is considerably lesser; is it not?" "Yes." "And that which was formerly greater than that which was formerly lesser; and that which is to be greater than that which is to be lesser?" "What else?" said he. "And 438c after the same manner, what is more numerous with respect to what is less numerous, and what is double with reference to what is half, and all such like things; and further, what is heavier with respect to lighter, and swifter to slower, and further still, hot to cold; and all such like things, are they not after this manner?" "Entirely so."

"But what as to the sciences? Is not the case the same? For, science itself is the science of learning itself, or of whatever else you think proper to make it the science: but a certain particular science, and of such a particular kind, refers to a certain particular object, and of such a kind. What I mean is this. After the science of building houses arose, 438d did it not separate from other sciences, so as to be called architecture?" "What else?" "Was it not from its being of such a kind as none of others were?" "Yes." "Was it not then from its being the art of such a particular thing, that itself became such a particular art? And all other arts and sciences in like manner?" "They are so."

"Allow then," said I, "that this is what I wanted to express, if you have now understood it; where things are considered as having reference to other things, generals alone refer to generals, and 438e particulars to particulars. I do not however say that the science altogether resembles that of which it is the science; (as if, for example, the science of healthy and sickly were itself healthy and sickly; or that the science of good and evil were itself good and evil.) But as science is not constituted the science of that thing in general of which it is the science, but only of a certain quality of it (to wit, of its healthy and sickly state), so itself comes to be a certain particular science; and this causes it to be called no longer simply a science, but the medicinal science; the particular species to which it belongs being superadded." *281* "I have understood you," said he, "and it appears to me to be so."

"But will not you," said I, "make thirst now, what ever it be, to be 439a one of those things which respect somewhat else, considered as what it is, and it is surely thirst?" "I will," said he, "and it respects drink." "And does not a particular thirst desire a particular drink? But thirst in general is neither of much nor of little, nor of good nor bad, nor, in one word, of any particular kind; but of drink in general alone is thirst in general naturally the desire." "Entirely so, indeed." "The soul of the man then who thirsts, so far as he thirsts, inclines for nothing

439b further than to drink; this he desires, to this he hastens." "It is plain." "If then at any time any thing draw back the thirsting soul, it must be some different part of it from that which thirsts, and leads it as a wild beast to drink: for, have we not said that it is impossible for the same thing, in the same respects, and with the same parts of it, to do at once contrary things?" "It is indeed impossible." "In the same manner, I imagine, as it is not proper to say of an archer, that his hands at once push out and likewise pull in the bow; but that the one hand is that which pushes out, and the other that which pulls in."

439c "Entirely so," said he. "But whether may we say, that there are some who when athirst are not willing to drink?" "Yes, indeed," said he, "there are many, and many times that is the case." "What now," said I, "may one say of these persons? Might it not be said, that there was in their soul somewhat prompting them to drink, and likewise something hindering them, different from the other, and superior to the prompting principle?" "It seems so to me," said he. "Does not

439d then the restraining principle arise from reason when it arises; but those which push, and drive forwards, proceed from passions and diseases?" "It appears so." "We shall then," said I, "not unreasonably account these to be two, and different from one another; calling the one part which reasons, the rational part of the soul; but that part with which it loves, and hungers, and thirsts, and those other appetites, the irrational and concupiscible part, the friend of certain gratifications and pleasures." "We shall not," said he; "but we may

439e most reasonably consider them in this light." "Let these then," said I, "be allowed to be distinct species in the soul. But as to that of anger, is it a third principle, or has it affinity to one of those two?" "Perhaps it has," said he, "to the concupiscible part." "But I believe," said I, "what

282 I have somewhere heard, how that Leontius, the son of Aglaion, as he returned from the Pyræum, perceived some dead bodies lying in the sewer, below the outside of the north wall, and had both a desire to

look at them and at the same time was averse from it, and tu 440a
himself away; and for a while he struggled with his desire, and covered
his eyes; but, at last, being overcome by his appetite, with eager eyes,
running towards the dead bodies, 'Lo now,' said he, 'you wretched
eyes! glut yourselves with this fine spectacle.'" "I too," said he, "have
heard it." "This speech now," said I, "shows that anger sometimes
opposes the appetites, as being different one from another." "It shows
it, indeed," said he.

"And do not we often perceive," said I, "when, the appetites compel
any one contrary to reason, that he reproaches himself, and is angry at 440b
the compelling principle within him? And when the rational and
concupiscible are in a state of sedition, anger in such a person becomes
as it were an ally to reason: but when the appetite goes along with
reason; then anger gives no opposition. You will say, I imagine, that
you have perceived nothing of this kind in yourself at any time, nor
yet in another." "No, by Jupiter," said he. "What now," said I, "when 440c
one imagines he does an injury, the more generous he is, is he not so
much the less apt to be angry, when he suffers hunger and cold, or any
other such things, from one who inflicts, as he imagines, these things
with justice? And, as I have said, his anger will not incline him to rise
up against such an one." "True," said he. "But what? when a man
imagines he is injured, does not anger in such an one burn? is he not
indignant? and does he not fight, as an ally, on the side of what 440d
appears to be just? and under all the sufferings of hunger, cold, and
such like, does he not bear up and conquer; and cease not from his
generous toils, till either he accomplish them, or die, or be restrained
by the rational principle within him, like a dog by the shepherd, and
is rendered mild?" "It perfectly resembles," said he, "what you say; for,
in our city, we appointed the auxiliaries to be obedient, as dogs, to the
rulers of the city, as to shepherds." "You rightly understand," said I,
"what I would say. But have you besides considered this?" "As what?" 440e
"That here the reverse appears concerning the irascible from that in
the former case: for there we were deeming it the same with the
concupiscible; but now we say it is far from it; or that, in the sedition
of the soul, it much rather joins its arms with the rational part."
"Entirely so," said he. "Is it then as something different from it, or as 283
a species of the rational? so as that there are not three species, but only

two in the soul, the rational and concupiscible. Or, as there were three
441a species which completed the city, the lucrative, the auxiliary, the
legislative; so, in the soul, this irascible is a third thing, naturally an
auxiliary to the rational, if it be not corrupted by bad education?" "Of
necessity it is," said he, "a third." "Yes," said I, "if at least it appear to
be any way different from the rational, as it appeared to be distinct
from the concupiscible." "But that is not difficult," said he, "to be
seen. For one may see this, even in little children, that immediately
441b from their infancy they are full of anger; but some appear, to me at
least, never at all to participate of reason; and the most arrive at it but
late." "Yes, truly," said I, "you say right. And one may yet further
observe in the brute creatures, that what you say is really the case: and
besides this, it is likewise attested by what we formerly mentioned
from Homer,[1]

His breast he struck, and thus his heart reproved.

For, in that passage, Homer has plainly made one part reprehend
441c another; the part which reasons about good and evil, reprehend the part
which is unreasonably angry." "You say perfectly right," said he.

"These things," said I, "we have with difficulty agreed to; and it is
now sufficiently acknowledged, that the same species of principles as
are in a city are in every individual, and in the same number." "They
are so." "Must it not therefore of necessity follow, that after what
manner the city was wise, and in what respect, after the same manner,
and in the same respect, is the individual wise also." "Why not?" "And
441d in what respects, and after what manner, the individual is brave, in
the same respect, and after the same manner, is a city brave, and so in
all other respects, both of them are the same as to virtue." "Of
necessity." "And I think, Glauco, we shall say that a man is just in the
same way as we said a city was so?" "This likewise is quite necessary."
"But have we not somehow forgot this, that the city was just, when
every one of the three species in it did each its own work?" "We do not
284 appear to me," said he, "to have forgot it." "We must then remember
441e likewise, that each one of us will be just, and do his own work, when
he doth his own affairs within himself." "We must," said he,
"carefully remember it."

"Is it not then proper that the rational part should govern, as it is wise, and hath the care of the whole soul? and that the irascible part should be obedient, and an auxiliary of the other?" "Certainly." "Shall not then the mixture, as we observed, of music and gymnastic make these two harmonious, raising and nourishing the one with ₄₄₂a beautiful reasonings and disciplines, and unbending the other, soothing and rendering it mild by harmony and rhythm?" "Most perfectly," said he. "And when those two are in this manner nourished, and have been truly taught, and instructed in their own affairs, let them be set over the concupiscible part, which in every one is the greater part of the soul, and in its nature most insatiably desirous of being gratified: and let them take care of this part, lest, being filled with these bodily pleasures, as they are called, it become great and vigorous, and do not its own work, but attempt to enslave ₄₄₂b and rule over those it ought not, and overturn the whole life of all in general." "Entirely so," said he. "And might he not," said I, "by this principle, guard likewise in the best manner against enemies from without, by its influence both over the whole soul and body likewise, the one deliberating, and the other fighting in obedience to its leader, and executing with fortitude the things deliberated?" "It is so."

"And I think that we call a man brave, when through all the pains ₄₄₂c and pleasures of life, the irascible part preserves the opinion dictated by reason concerning what is terrible, and what is not." "Right," said he. "And we call him wise, from that small part which governs in him, and dictates these things, having in it the knowledge of what is advantageous for each one, and for the whole community of the three themselves." "Perfectly so." "But what, do we not call him temperate, moreover, from the friendship and harmony of these very things, ₄₄₂d when the governing and governed agree in one, that reason ought to govern, and when they do not raise sedition?" "Temperance," said he, "is no other than this, both as to the city and the individual." "But, as we have often said, he shall be just, by these things, and in this manner." "It is quite necessary." "What then," said I, "has any thing blunted us, that we should think justice to be any thing else than what it has appeared to be in a city?" "Nothing appears to me at least," said he, "to have done it.

"But in this maimer, let us, by all means, confirm ourselves, if there ₄₄₂e yet remain any doubt in the soul, that can be an objection to this principle, by bringing the man into difficult circumstances." "As what?" "Such as this: if we were obliged to declare concerning such a city, and concerning a man born and educated conformably to it, whether we thought such a one, when entrusted with gold or silver, would embezzle it; do you imagine that any one would think such a

443a one would do it sooner than those who are not of such a kind?" "No one," said he. "Will not such a one then be free of sacrileges, thefts, treacheries, against companions in private, or the city in public?" "He will be free." "Nor will he ever, in any shape, be faithless, either as to his oaths, or other declarations." "How can he?" "Adulteries, and neglect of parents, impiety against the Gods, will belong to every one else, sooner than to such an one." "They will belong to every one else,

443b truly," said he. "And is not this the cause of all these things, that, of all the parts within him, each one thing does its own work, as to governing and being governed?" "This is it, and nothing else." "Do you desire justice to be any thing else, but such a power as produces such men and cities?" "Not I, truly," said he, "for my part."

"Our dream then which we conjectured is at last accomplished; that when we first began to build our city, we seemed, by some God's

443c assistance, to have got to a beginning and pattern of justice." "Entirely so." "And that, Glauco, was a certain image of justice, according to which, it behoved the man who was fitted by nature for the office of a shoe-maker, to perform properly that office, and to do nothing else, and he who is a carpenter to perform that office, and all

443d others in the same way." "It appears so." "And of such a kind truly was justice, as it appeared to us, I do not mean as to external action, but concerning that which is really internal, relating to the man himself, and those things which are properly his own; not allowing any principle in himself to attempt to do what belongs to others, nor the principles to be pragmatical, engaging in one another's affairs; but in reality well establishing his own proper affairs, and holding the government of himself, adorning himself and becoming his own friend, and attuning those three principles in the most natural

443e manner, as three musical strings, base, tenor, and treble, or whatever others may chance to intervene. Thus he will be led to combine all

286 these together, and become of many an entire one, temperate and attuned, and in that manner to perform whatever is done, either in

the way of acquiring wealth, or concerning the management of the body, or any public affair or private bargain; and in all these cases to account and call that action just and handsome, which always sustains and promotes this habit; and to call the knowledge which presides over 444a this action, wisdom: but to call that an unjust action which dissolves this habit, and the opinion which presides over this, folly." "You say perfectly true, Socrates," said he. "Be it so," said I. "If then we should say that we have found out a just man and city, and what justice is in them, I do not think we should seem to be altogether telling a lie." "No, by Jupiter," said he. "May we say so?" "We may say it."

  "Be it so," said I. "But we were next, I think, to consider injustice." "That is plain." "Must it not then be some sedition among the three 444b principles, some pragmaticalness and intermeddling in things foreign to their proper business, and an insurrection of some one principle against the whole soul, to govern in it when it does not belong to it, but which is of such a nature, as what really ought to be in subjection to the governing principle? I imagine then we shall call their tumult and mistake by such names as these, injustice, intemperance, cowardice and folly, and in general all vice." "These things," said he, "are so." "To do injustice then," said I, "and to be injurious, and 444c likewise to do justly, all these must be very manifest, if, to wit, injustice and justice are so." "As how?" "Because they are no way different from what is salutary or noxious: as these are in the body, so are the others in the soul." "How?" said he. "Such things as are healthy constitute health, and such as are noxious produce disease." "Yes." "And must not the doing justly produce justice, and doing 444d unjustly produce injustice?" "Of necessity." "But to produce health, is to establish all in the body according to nature; to govern and to be governed of one another; and to produce disease, is to govern and be governed, one part by another, contrary to nature." "It is indeed." "Then again, to produce justice, is it not to establish all in the soul according to nature, to govern and be governed by one another? And injustice is to govern and be governed by one another, contrary to nature." "Plainly so," said he. "Virtue then, it seems, is a sort of health, and beauty and good habit of the soul; and vice the disease, 444e and deformity, and infirmity." "It is so." "Do not then honourable pursuits lead to the acquisition of virtue? but dishonourable ones to that of vice?" "Of necessity."

"What remains then for us, as seems, to consider, is, whether it be
445a profitable to do justly, and to pursue what is honourable, and to be
just; whether a man under such a character be unknown or not? Or to
do unjustly, and to be unjust, though one be never punished, nor by
chastisement become better?" "But," said he, "Socrates, this
speculation seems now, to me at last, to be ridiculous. For if, when the
nature of the body is corrupted, it be thought that life is not worth
having, not even though one had all kinds of meats and drinks, all
kind of wealth, all kind of dominion; when the nature of that by
445b which we live is disordered, and thoroughly corrupted, shall life then
be worth having, though one can do every thing else which he
inclines, except ascertaining, how he shall be liberated from vice and
injustice, and acquire justice and virtue, since, to wit, both these
things have appeared as we have represented them?" "It would be truly
ridiculous," said I. "But, however, as we have arrived at such a point as
enables us most distinctly to perceive that these things are so, we must
not be weary." "We must, by Jupiter," said he, "the least of all things
445c desist." "Come then," said I, "that you may likewise see how many
principles vice possesses, principles which, as I imagine, are worthy of
attention." "I attend," said he, "only tell me."

"And truly now," said I, "since we have reached this part of our
discourse it appears to me as from a lofty place of survey, that there is
one principle of virtue, but those of vice are infinite. Of which there
are four, which deserve to be mentioned." "How do you say?" replied
445d he. "There seem to be as many species of soul as there are of republics."
"How many then?" "There are five," said I, "of republics, and five of
the soul." "Tell," said he, "what these are." "I say," replied I, "that
this, which we have gone through, is one species of a republic; and it
may have a two-fold appellation; for, if among the rulers there be one
surpassing the rest, it may be called a Monarchy; if there be several, an
Aristocracy." "True," said he. "I call this then," said I, "one species;
445e for, whether they be several, or but one, who govern, they will never
alter the principal laws of the city; observing the nurture and
education we have described." "It is not likely," said he.

THE END OF THE FOURTH BOOK.

BOOK V.

"I denominate then indeed both such a city and republic, and such
a man as we have described, good and upright; and if this republic be
an upright one, I deem the others bad and erroneous, both as to the
regulations in cities, and the establishing the temper of soul of
individuals, and that in four species of depravity." "Of what kind are
these?" said he. I was then proceeding to mention them in order, as
they appeared to me to rise out of one another: but Polemarchus
stretching out his hand (for he sat a little further off than Adimantus)
caught him by the robe at his shoulder, and drew him near; and,
bending himself towards him, spoke something in a whisper, of
which we heard nothing but this: "Shall we let pass then?" said he, "or
what shall we do?" "Not at all," said Adimantus, speaking now aloud.
And I replied, "What then will not you let pass?" "You," said he, "for
it was to you I alluded." "You seem to us to be growing negligent, and
to steal a whole branch of the discourse, and that not the least
considerable, that you may not have the trouble of going through it;
and you imagine that you escaped our notice, when you made this
speech so simply, *viz.* that, both as to wives and children, it is
manifest to every one that these things will be common among
friends." "Did not I say right, Adimantus?" "Yes," said he: "but this,
which was rightly said, like other parts of your discourse, requires
explanation: to show what is the manner of their being common; for
there may be many kinds of it. Do not omit then to tell which is the
method you spoke of; for we have been in expectation for some time

past, imagining you would, on some occasion, make mention of the propagation of children, in what way they should be propagated; and, when they are born, how they should be nurtured; and every thing relative to what you spoke concerning wives and children being in common; for we imagine, that it is of considerable, nay, of the utmost importance to the state, when this is rightly performed, or otherwise. But now when you are entering on the consideration of another constitution, before you have sufficiently discussed these things, it seemed proper to us what you now heard, not to let you pass, before you went over all these things, as you did the others." "And you may count me too," said Glauco, "as joining in this vote." "You may easily judge, Socrates," said Thrasymachus, "that this is the opinion of us all."

"What is this," said I, "you have done, laying hold of me? What a mighty discourse do you again raise, as you did at the beginning, about a republic, in which I was rejoicing as having now completed it, being pleased if any one would have let these things pass, and been content with what was then said! But you know not what a swarm of reasonings you raise by what you now challenge, which I foreseeing passed by at that time, lest it should occasion great disturbance." "What then," said Thrasymachus, "do you imagine that these are now come hither to melt gold, and not to hear reasonings?" "Yes," said I, "but in measure." "The whole of life, Socrates," said Glauco, "is with the wise, the measure of hearing such reasonings as these. But pass what relates to us, and do not at all grudge to explain your opinion concerning the object of our inquiry,—What sort of community of wives an children is to be observed by our guardians, and concerning the nurture of the latter while very young, in the period between their generation and their education, which seems to be the most troublesome of all. Endeavour then to tell us in what manner it should be done."

"It is not easy, happy Glauco," said I, "to go through these things; for there are many of them hard to be believed, whether the things we say be possible; and though they could easily be effected, whether they would be for the best might still be doubted: wherefore, dear companion, I grudge somewhat to touch on these things, lest our reasonings appear to be rather what were to be wished for, than what

Margin references: 289, 450a, 450b, 450c, 450d

could take place." "Do not at all grudge," said he; "for your hearers
are neither stupid, nor incredulous, nor ill-affected towards you."
Then I said, "Do you say this, most excellent Glauco, with a desire to
encourage me?" "I do," said he. "Then your discourse has a quite
contrary effect," said I; "for, if I trusted to myself, that I understood
what I am to say, your encouragement would do well. For one who 450e
understands the truth, about the greatest and the most interesting *290*
affairs,speaks with safety and confidence among the wise and friendly;
but to be diffident of oneself, and doubtful of the truth, and at the
same time to be haranguing as I do now, is both dreadful and 451a
dangerous; not only lest he should be exposed to ridicule (for that is
but a trifling thing), but lest that, mistaking the truth, I not only fall
myself, but draw my friends along with me into an error about things
in which we ought least of all to be mistaken. I adore therefore
Adrastia, for the sake of what, Glauco, I am going to say. For I trust it
is a smaller offence to be a man-slayer without intention, than to be
an impostor with regard to what is good and excellent, just and
lawful: and it were better to hazard such a thing among enemies than 451b
friends; so that you must give me better encouragement." Then
Glauco, laughing: "But, Socrates," said he, "if we suffer any thing
amiss from your discourse, we shall acquit you as clear of any man-
slaughter, and as no impostor: so proceed boldly." "But indeed," said
I, "he who is acquitted at a court of justice is deemed clear of the
crime, as the law says; and if it be so in that case, 'tis reasonable it
should be so in this." "For this reason then," said he, "proceed."

"We must now," said I, "return again to what it seems should,
according to method, have been recited before; and perhaps it is right 451c
to proceed in this manner, that, after having entirely finished the
drama respecting the men, we go over that which concerns the
women; especially since you challenge me to proceed in this manner.
For, in my opinion, men who have been born and educated in such a
manner as we have described, can have no right possession and
enjoyment of children and wives, but in pursuing the same track in
which we have proceeded from the beginning; for we have
endeavoured, in our reasoning, to form somehow men as the
guardians of a flock." "We have." "Let us proceed then, having 451d
established likewise affairs relating to propagation and education in a

manner similar to that of the males; and let us consider whether it be proper for us to do so or not." "How do you mean?" replied he. "Thus: Whether shall we judge it proper for the females of our guardian dogs, to watch likewise in the same manner as the males do, and to hunt along with them, and do every thing else in common? Or shall we judge it proper for them to manage domestic affairs within doors, as being unable for the other exercises, because of the bringing forth and the nursing the whelps; and the males to labour, and to have the whole care of the flocks?" "They are to do all," said he, "in common. Only we are to employ the females as the weaker, and the males as the stronger." "Is it possible then," said I, "to employ any creature for the same purposes with another, unless you give it the same nurture and education as you give the other?" "It is not possible." "If then we shall employ the women for the same purposes as we do the men, must we not likewise teach them the same things?" "We must." "Were not both music and gymnastic bestowed on the males?" "They were." "These two arts therefore, and those likewise relating to war, must be bestowed also on the women, and they must be employed about the same things." "It is reasonable," said he, "from what you say." "Yet as these things," said I, "are contrary perhaps to custom, many of these things we are now speaking of may appear ridiculous, if practised in the way we mention." "Extremely so," replied he.

"What," said I, "do you perceive as the most ridiculous part? Or is it plainly because that you see the women naked in the Palæstra wrestling with the men, and not only the young women, but even the more advanced in years, in the same manner as old men in the wrestling-schools, when they are wrinkled, and not at all handsome to the eye, yet still fond of the exercises?" "Yes, by Jupiter," said he. "Because it might indeed appear ridiculous, at least as matters stand at present." "Must we not therefore," said I, "since we have entered upon this discourse, be afraid of the railleries of the men of pleasantry, whatever things they may say with regard to such a revolution being introduced, as well in gymnastic as in music, and particularly in the use of arms, and the management of horses?" "You say right," replied he. "But since we have entered on this discourse, we must go to the rigour of the law, and beg these men not to follow their own customs, but to think seriously, and remember, that it is not long ago since

291
451e
452a

452b

452c

these things appeared base and ridiculous to the Greeks, which are only so now to the most of the barbarians: such as to see naked men. And when first the Cretans, and afterwards the Lacedæmonians, 452d began their exercises, it was in the power of the men of humour of that time to turn all these things into ridicule. Do not you think so?" "I do." "But I imagine, that when upon experience it appeared better to strip themselves of all these things, than to be wrapped in them, what was ridiculous indeed to the eye, was removed by the idea of the best, mentioned in our reasoning; and this too showed manifestly, that he is a fool who deems anything ridiculous but what is bad, and 292 attempts to rally upon any other idea of the ridiculous but that of the 452e foolish and the vicious, or to be serious in any other pursuit but that of the good." "By all means," said he.

"Is not this then first of all to be agreed on, whether these things be possible or not? And we must allow it to be a matter of dispute, if any one, either in jest or earnest, incline to doubt, whether the human 453a nature in the female sex be able, in every thing, to bear a share with the male? or if it be not in any one thing? or if it be able in some things, but not in others? and among which of these are the affairs of war? Would not the man who thus sets out in the most handsome manner conclude too, as it seems, most handsomely?" "By far," said he. "Are you willing, then," said I, "that we ourselves, instead of others, dispute about these things, that the opposite side may not be destitute of a defence?" "Nothing hinders," said he. 453b

"Let us then say this for them: that 'there is no need, Socrates and Glauco, of others to dispute with you about this matter; for yourselves in the beginning of your establishment, when you established your city, agreed, that it was necessary for each individual to practise one business, according to their several genius.' 'I think we acknowledged it; for why should they not?' 'Does not then the genius of the male differ widely from that of the female?' 'Why does it not differ?' 'And is it not fit to enjoin each a different work, according to their genius?' 453c 'Why not?' 'Are not you then in the wrong now, and contradict yourselves, when you say that men and women ought to do the same things, whilst their nature is extremely different?' Can you in answer to these objections, admirable Glauco, make any defence?"

"It is not quite an easy matter," said he, "to do it immediately; but I will entreat you, and do now entreat you, to go through the arguments on our side, whatever they may be." "These are the things, Glauco," replied I, "and many other such like, which I long ago foreseeing, was both afraid and backward to touch on the law concerning the possession of wives, and the education of children." "It is not easy, by Jupiter," replied he. "It is not," said I. "But the case is thus: If a man fall into a small fish-pond, or into the middle of the greatest sea, he must still swim in the one no less than in the other." "Entirely so." "Must not we swim then, and endeavour to escape from this reasoning, expecting that either some dolphin is to carry us out, or that we shall have same other remarkable deliverance?" "It seems we must do so," replied he. "Come then," said I, let us see if we can anywhere find an out-gate; for we did acknowledge that different natures ought to study different things; but the nature of man and woman is different; yet now we say that different natures ought to study the same things: these are the things which you accuse us of." "Certainly."

"How generous, Glauco," said I, "is the power of the art of contradicting!" "How?" "Because," replied I, "many seem to fall into it unwillingly, and imagine that they are not cavilling, but reasoning truly, because they are not able to understand the subject by dividing it into its proper parts; and under this arguing will pursue the opposite of their subject, using cavilling instead of reasoning." "This is indeed," said he, "the case with many; but does it at present extend likewise to us?" "Entirely so," said I. "We seem then unwillingly to have fallen into a contradiction." "How?" "Because we have very strenuously and very keenly asserted, that when the nature is not the same, they ought not to have the same employments; but we have not in any respect considered what is the characteristic of the sameness or diversity of nature, nor to what it points we stopped then, when we had assigned different pursuits to different natures, and to the same natures the same pursuits." "We have never indeed," said he, "considered it."

"It is therefore," replied I, "still in our power, as appears, to question ourselves, whether the nature of the bald, or of those who wear their hair, be the same, and not different? And after we should agree that it was different, whether, if the bald made shoes, we should allow those who wear hair to make them? or, if those who wear hair made them, whether we should allow the others?" "That would be ridiculous," replied he. "Is it in any other respect," said I, "ridiculous then, that we did not wholly determine the sameness and diversity of nature, but attended only to that species of diversity and sameness 454d which respects the employments themselves; just as we say that the physician, and the man who has a medical soul, have one and the same nature? Do not you think so?" "I do." "But that the physician and architect have a different nature." "Entirely."

"And so," replied I, "of the nature of men and of women, if it appear different, in respect to any art; or other employment, we shall say, that this different employment is to be assigned to each separately. But if their nature appear different only in this, that the female brings forth, and the male begets, we shall not say that this has 454e at all shown the men to be different from the woman in the respect we speak of. But we shall still be of opinion, that both our guardians 294 and their wives ought to pursue the same employments." "And with reason," said he. "Shall we not then henceforth desire any one who says the contrary, to instruct us in this point, what is that art or study 455a respecting the establishment of a city, where the nature of the man and woman is not the same, but different?" "It is reasonable, truly."

"Possibly some one may say, as you was saying some time since, that it is not easy to tell this sufficiently on the sudden, but that it is not difficult to one who has considered it." "One might indeed say so." "Are you willing then that we desire such an opponent to listen to us, if by any means we shall show him that there is in the administration 455b of the city no employment peculiar to the women?" "By all means." "Come on then, (shall we say to him) answer us. Is not this your meaning? That one man has a good genius for any thing, and another a bad, in this respect, that the one learns any thing easily, and the other with difficulty; and the one with a little instruction discovers much in what he learns; but the other, when he obtains much instruction and care, does not retain even what he has learned: with the one, the body is duly subservient to the mind; with the other, it 455c opposes its improvement: are there any other marks than these by which you would determine one to have a good genius for any thing, and another to have a bad one?" "No one," said he, "would mention any other." "Know you then of any thing which is managed by mankind, with reference to which the men have not all these marks in a more excellent degree than the women? Or, should we not be 455d tedious, if we mentioned particularly the weaving art, and the dressing pot-herbs and victuals, in which the the male genius seems to be somewhat considerable, and is most ridiculous where it is surpassed?" "You say true," said he, "that in the general, in every thing the one genius is superior to the other, yet there are many women who in many things excel many men: but, on the whole, it is as you say." "There is not then, my friend, any office among the whole inhabitants of the city peculiar to the woman, considered as woman, nor to the man, considered as man; but the geniuses are indiscriminately diffused through both: the woman is naturally fitted 455e for sharing in all offices, and so is the man; but in all the woman is weaker than the man." "Perfectly so."

"Shall we then commit every thing to the care of the men, and no thing to the care of the women?" "How shall we do so?" "It is 295 therefore, I imagine, as we say, that one woman too is fitted by natural genius for being a physician, and another is not; one is naturally a musician, and another is not?" "What else?" "And one is 456a naturally fitted for gymnastic, and another is not; one is fitted for war, and another is not." "I at least am of this opinion." "And is not one likewise a lover of philosophy, and another averse to it; one of high spirits, and another of low?" "This likewise is true." "And has not one woman a natural genius for being a guardian, and another not? And have not we made choice of such a genius as this for our guardian men?" "Of such a genius as this." "The nature then of the woman and of the man for the guardianship of the city is the same, only that the one is weaker, and the other stronger." "It appears so."

456b "And such women as these are to be chosen to dwell with these men, and be guardians along with them, as they are naturally fit for them, and of a kindred genius." "Entirely so." "And must not the same employments be assigned to the same natures?" "The same." "We are now arrived by a circular progression at what we formerly mentioned; and, we allow that it is not contrary to nature, to appoint 456c for the wives of our guardians music and gymnastic." "By all means." "We are not then establishing things impossible, or such as can only be wished for, since we establish the law according to nature; and what is at present contrary to these things, is contrary to nature rather, as appears." "It seems so." "Was not our inquiry to hear of what was possible and best?" "It was." "And we have agreed, that these things are possible." "We have." "And we must next agree, that they are best." "It is plain we must."

"In order therefore to make a guardian woman, at least the education will not be different from that of the men, especially as she 456d has received the same natural genius." "It will not be different." "What do you think then of such an opinion as this" "Of what?" "That of imagining with yourself one man to be better, and another worse,—or do you deem them to be all alike?" "By no means." "In the city now which we establish, whether do you judge, that our guardians with this education we have described, or shoe-makers with education in their art, will be rendered the better men?" "The question," replied he, is ridiculous." "I understand you," said I. "But what? Of all the 456e other citizens, are not they the best?" "By far." "But what? Will not these women too be the best of women?" "They will be so," replied he, "by far." "Is there any thing better in a city than that both the 296 women and the men be rendered the very best?" "There is not." "This then will be effected by music and gymnastic, being afforded them 457a according as we have described." "Why will it not?" "We have then established a law which is not only possible, but moreover best for the state." "We have." "The wives, then, of our guardians must be unclothed, since they are to put on virtue for clothes; and they must bear a part in war, and the other guardianship of the city, and do nothing else. But the lightest part of these services is to be allotted to the women rather than to the men, on account of the weakness of 457b their sex. And the man who laughs at naked women, whilst performing the exercises for the sake of what is best, reaps the empty fruit of a ridiculous wisdom, and in no respect knows, as appears, at what he laughs, nor why he does it. For that ever was and will be deemed a noble saying, That what is profitable is beautiful, and what is hurtful is base." "By all means." "Let us say then, that we have escaped one wave, as it were, having thus settled the law with respect to the women, without being wholly overwhelmed, ordaining that 457c our male and female guardians are to manage all things in common:

but our reasoning has been consistent with itself, as it respects both what is possible and likewise advantageous."

"It is truly no small wave you have escaped," said he. "You will not," replied I, "call it a great one, when you see what follows." "Mention it," said he, "that I may see." "That law," replied I, "and those others formerly mentioned, are adopted, as I imagine, by the following." "Which?" "That these women must all be common to all these men, 457d and that no one woman dwell with any man privately, and that their children likewise be common; that neither the parent know his own children, nor the children their parent." "This is much greater than the other, as to the incredibility, both of its being possible, and at the same time advantageous." "I do not believe," replied I, "that any one will doubt of its utility, at least, as if it were not the greatest good to have the women and children in common, if it were but possible. But 457e I think the greatest question will be, whether it be possible or not?" "One may very readily," said he, "dispute as to both." "You mention," replied I, "a crowd of disputes. But I thought that I should at least have escaped from the one, if its utility had been agreed on, and that 297 it should have only remained to consider its possibility." "But you have not," said he, "escaped unobserved; give then an account of both." "I must then," said I, "submit to a trial. But, however, indulge 458a me thus far: allow me to feast myself, as those are wont to feast themselves who are sluggish in their dianoëtic part, when they walk alone. For men of this sort, sometimes before they find out how they shall attain what they desire; waving that inquiry, that they may not fatigue themselves in deliberating about the possibility or impossibility of it, suppose they have obtained what they desire, and then go through what remains. And they delight in running over what they will do when their desire is obtained, rendering their soul, otherwise indolent, more indolent still. I am now effeminate after 458b this manner, and wish to defer those debates, and to inquire afterwards whether these things be possible. But at present, holding them possible, if you allow me, I will consider in what manner our rulers shall regulate these things, when they take place, that they may be done in the most advantageous manner, both to the state and the guardians. These things I shall endeavour, in the first place, to go over with your assistance, and the others afterwards, if you allow me." "I allow," said he, "and inquire accordingly."

"I imagine then," said I, "that if our rulers are worthy of that 458c
name, and in like manner these who are their auxiliaries, their
ministers in the government, the latter will be disposed to do
whatever is enjoined them, and the former will be ready to command;
enjoining them some things in direct obedience to the law, and
imitating the law in whatever things are entrusted to them." "It is
likely," said he. "Do you now," said I, "who are their lawgiver, in the
same manner as you have chosen out the men, choose out likewise the
women, making their genius as similar as possible: and as they dwell
and eat together in common; and as no one possesses any of these
things privately, they will meet together; and being mingled in their 458d
exercises and other conversation, they will be led from an innate
necessity, as I imagine, to mutual embraces. Do not I seem to say what
will necessarily happen?" "Not," replied he, "by any geometrical, but
amatory necessity, which seems to be more pungent than the other,
to persuade and draw the bulk of mankind."

"Much more," said I. "But after this, Glauco, to mix together in a
disorderly manner, or to do any thing else, is neither holy in a city of 458e
happy persons, nor will the rulers permit it." "It would not be just,"
said he. "It is plain then, that after this we must make marriages as 298
much as possible sacred; but the most advantageous would be sacred."
"By all means." "How then shall they be most advantageous? Tell me 459a
that, Glauco, for I see in your houses dogs of chase, and a great many
excellent birds. Have you then indeed ever attended at all, in any
respect, to their marriages and the propagation of their species?"
"How?" said he. "First of all, that among these, although they be
excellent themselves, are there not some who are most excellent?"
"There are." "Whether then do you breed from all of them alike? or
are you careful to breed chiefly from the best?" "From the best." "But 459b
how? From the youngest or from the oldest, or from those who are
most in their prime?" "From those in their prime." "And if the breed
be not of this kind, you reckon that the race of birds and dogs greatly
degenerates." "I reckon so," replied he. "And what think you as to
horses," said I, "and other animals? is the case any otherwise with
respect to these?" "That," said he, "would be absurd."

"Strange," said I, "my friend! What extremely perfect governors

must we have, if the case be the same with respect to the human race!"
459c "However, it is so," replied he; "but what then?" "Because there is a necessity," said I, "for their using many medicines for where bodies have no occasion for medicines, but are ready to subject themselves to a regimen of diet, we reckon that a weaker physician may suffice; but when there is a necessity for medicines, we know that a more able physician is then requisite." "True; but with what view do you say this?" "With this view," replied I. "It appears that our rulers are
459d obliged to use much fiction and deceit for the advantage of the governed; and we said somewhere, that all these things were useful in the way of medicines." "And rightly," said he. "This piece of right now seems not to be the most inconsiderable in marriages, and the propagation of children." "How now?"

"It is proper," said I, "from what we have acknowledged, that the best men embrace for the most part the best women; and the most
459e depraved men, on the contrary, the most depraved women and the offspring of the former is to be educated, but not that of the latter, if you desire to have the flock of the most perfect kind; and this must be performed in such a manner as to escape the notice of all but the governors themselves, if you would have the whole herd of the guardians to be as free from sedition as possible." "Most right," said
299 he. "Shall there not then be some festivals by law established, in which we shall draw together the brides and bridegrooms? Sacrifices
460a too must be performed, and hymns composed by our poets suitable to the marriages which are making. But the number of the marriages we shall commit to the rulers, that as much as possible they may preserve the same number of men, having an eye to the wars, diseases, and every thing else of this kind, and that as far as possible our city may be neither too great nor too little." "Right," said he. "And certain lots too, I imagine, should be made so artificial, that the depraved man may, on every embrace, accuse his fortune, and not the governors." "By all means," said he.
460b   "And those of the youth who distinguish themselves, whether in war or any where else, ought to have rewards and prizes given them, and the most ample liberty of embracing women, that so, under this pretext likewise, the greatest number of children may be generated of such persons." "Right." "And shall the children always as they are

born be received by magistrates appointed for these purposes, whether men or women, or both? for the magistracies are in common to women as to men." "They are so." "And when they receive the _{460c} children of worthy persons, they will carry them, I imagine, to the nursery, to certain nurses dwelling apart in a certain place of the city. But the children of the more depraved, and such others as are any way lame, they will hide in some secret and obscure place, as is proper." "If they want," said he, "the race of guardians to be pure." "And shall not these take care likewise of their nursing, in bringing to the nursery the mothers when their breasts are full, practising every art, that no _{460d} one know her own child, and in providing others who have milk, if these shall prove insufficient? And they shall likewise take care of these nurses, that they suckle a competent time: and they shall appoint the nurses and keepers to be wakeful, and to take every other necessary toil." "You speak," said he, "of great ease to the wives of our guardians, in the breeding of children."

"It is fit," replied I. "But let us in the next place discuss that which we chiefly intended. We said that true offspring ought to be generated of persons in their prime. Are you then of opinion with me, that the _{460e} proper season of vigour is twenty years to a woman, and thirty to a man?" "Of what continuance are these seasons?" said he. "The woman," replied I, "beginning at twenty, is to bear children to the state until the age age of forty; and the man, after he has passed the ₃₀₀ most raging part of his course, from that period, is to beget children to the state until the age of fifty-five." "This indeed is the acme," _{461a} replied he, "in both sexes, both of body and of mind."

"If then any one who is older or younger than these shall meddle in generating for the public, we shall say the trespass is neither holy nor just, as he begets to the state a child, which, if it be concealed, is born and grows up not from sacrifices and prayers, (which, upon every marriage, the priestesses and priests, and the whole of the city, shall offer, that the descendants of the good may be still more good, and from useful descendants still more useful may arise); but is born from _{461b} darkness, and with a dreadful intemperance." "Right," said he. "And the law," said I, "must be the same. If any of those men, who are yet of the age for generating, shall touch women of a proper age, without the concurrence of the magistrate, we shall consider him as having raised to the state a bastardly, illegitimate and unhallowed child." "Most right," said he. "And I imagine, that when the women and men exceed the age of generating, we shall permit the men to cohabit with any woman they incline, besides their daughter and mother, and those who are the children of their daughters, or those upwards from their mother: and so likewise the women to embrace any but a son and father, and the children of these, either downwards or upwards: all this liberty we will allow them, after we have enjoined them to attend carefully, in the first place, if any thing should be conceived, not to bring it to the light; but if, by any accident, it should be brought forth, to expose it as a creature for which no provision is made." "All these things," said he, "are reasonably said. But how shall fathers and daughters, and those other relations you now mentioned, be known of one another?"

461c

461d

"They shall not be known at all," said I. "But from the day on which any one is a bride groom, whatever children are born in the tenth or in the seventh month; after it, all these he shall call, the male his sons, and the female his daughters, and they shall call him father. And in the same way again, he shall call the children of these grandchildren, and they again shall call them grandfathers and grandmothers: and those who were born in that period in which their fathers and mothers were begetting children, they shall call sisters and brothers, so as not to touch each other, as I just now said. But the law shall allow brothers and sisters to live together, if their lot so fall out, and the Pythian oracle give consent." "Most right," said he.

461e

301

"This, Glauco, and such as this, is the community of women and children, among your city guardians: and that it is both consonant to the other parts of our polity, and by far the best, we must, in the next place, establish from reason; or how shall we do?" "Just so, by Jupiter," said he. "Did not we then agree on this at the beginning? to inquire what we can mention as the greatest good with relation to the establishment of a state, with an eye to which the lawgiver ought to enact the laws, and what is the greatest evil; and then to inquire, whether what we have hitherto gone over contributes towards leading us in the steps of this good, and away from that evil?" "By all means," said he. "Is there, then, any greater ill to a city than that which lacerates it; and, instead of one, makes it many? Or, is there any

462a

462b

greater good than that which binds it together, and makes it one?" "There is not." "Does not then the communion of pleasure and pain bind them together, when the whole of the citizens as much as possible rejoice and mourn in the same manner, for the same things when they are obtained, and when they are lost?" "By all means so," replied he. "But a separate feeling of these things destroys it, when some of the citizens are extremely grieved, and others extremely glad, at the same sufferings of the city, or of those who are in it." "Why 462c not?" "Does not then such an evil as the following arise from this, when they do not all jointly in the state pronounce these words, mine, and not mine? And will not that city be best regulated, when every individual, with regard to the concerns of another, in the same way with him, pronounces these words, mine, and not mine?" "By far." "And it is such as comes nearest to one man. As when our finger is any how hurt the whole common feeling spread through the body to the soul, with one coordination of its governing part, perceives it, and the 462d entire whole mourns along with the distressed part: and so we say that the man is distressed in his finger: and the reasoning is the same as to any other part of a man, both with respect to grief, when any part is in pain; or with respect to pleasure, when any part is at ease." "It is the same," said he. "And to return to your question, the city which comes nearest to this is governed in the best manner: and when any one of the citizens receives any good or ill, such a city, I imagine, will most 462e especially say, that she herself receives it, and the whole city rejoice or mourn together." "Of necessity," said he, "this must prevail in a city 302 governed by good laws."

"It may be time for us to go back to our city, and consider how those things are in it which we have agreed on in our reasoning, whether they prevail most in our city, or more in some other." "We must do so," replied he. "What now? Are there not, in other cities, 463a governors and people? And are there not likewise in this?" "There are." "And will not all these call one another citizens?" "Why not?" "But besides this of citizens, what do the people call their governors in other states?" "Masters or lords in most states, and, in democracies, this very name, governors." "But in our city, besides that of citizens, what do the people call their governors?" "Their preservers," said he, 463b "and helpers." "And what do they call the people?" "Rewarders," replied he, "and nourishers." "And in other cities, what do the governors call their people?" "Slaves," replied he. "And what do the governors call one another?" "Fellow rulers," said he. "And ours, what?" "Fellow guardians." "Can you tell, whether any one of the governors in other cities can address one of their fellow governors as his kinsman, and another as a stranger?" "Very many so." "Does he not then reckon and call the kindred one his own, and the stranger one as not his own?" "Just so." "But how is it with your guardians? Is there so much as any one of them, who can deem and call any one of

463c their fellow guardians a stranger?" "By no means," replied he; "for, with whomsoever any one meets, he reckons he meets with a brother or sister, a father or mother, a son or daughter, or the descendants or ancestors of these."

"You speak most beautifully," replied I. "But further, tell me this

463d likewise, whether will you only establish among them, by law, these kindred names? or will you also enjoin them to perform all their actions in conformity to these names? With respect to parents, whatever the law enjoins to be performed to parents, such as reverence, and care, and obedience. And that otherwise it will not be for his advantage, neither in the sight of Gods nor of men, as he acts what is neither holy nor just, if he do other things than these. Shall these, or any other speeches from all our citizens, resound directly in the ears of our children, both concerning their parents, whom any

463e one shall point out to them, and concerning other relations?" "These things shall be said," replied he; "for it would be ridiculous, if friendly names alone resounded, without any actions accompanying them."

"Of all cities, then, there will be the greatest harmony in it, when any

303 one individual is either well or ill, as to the expression we lately mentioned, *viz.* mine is well, or mine is ill." "Most true," said he.

464a "Did not we say too, that their common pleasures and pains will accompany this opinion and expression?" "And we said rightly." "Will not then our citizens most especially have this in common which they call my own; and, having this in common, they will of all others most especially have in common pleasure and pain?" "Extremely so." "And along with the other parts of the constitution, is not the community of women and children among the guardians the cause of these things?" "This is it most especially," replied he.

"But we agreed, that this was the greatest good of a city, likening a 464b well established city to a body, in its being affected with the pleasure and pain of any part." "And we rightly," said he, "agreed on this." "This community, then, of women and children among our auxiliaries, has appeared to us to be the cause of the greatest good to the city." "Extremely so," replied he. "And surely we agree at least with what went before; for we somewhere said, that they ought neither to have houses of their own, nor land, nor any possession; but, 464c receiving their subsistence from others, as a reward for their guardianship, they should all spend it in common, if they intended really to be guardians." "Right," said he. "Do not therefore, as I say, both these things which were formerly mentioned, and still more what we now speak of, render them real guardians, and prevent the city from being lacerated, by their not at all calling one and the same thing their own; but one one thing, and another another; one drawing to his own house whatever he can possess, separate from others, and another to his, which is different from the other; and 464d having both wives and children different, which occasion different pleasures and pains, which are private, as belonging to private persons: but being of an opinion concerning their home, and all of them pointing towards the same thing, as far as possible, to have one common feeling of pleasure and pain?" "Extremely so," replied he. "But what? shall law-suits and accusations against one another be banished from among them, so to speak, by their possessing nothing as private property but their body, and every thing else being common, from whence they shall be liberated from all those 464e disturbances which men raise about money, children or relations?" "They will of necessity be liberated from these." "Neither indeed can there be reasonably among them any actions raised for violence or unseemly treatment. For, making the protection of their persons a 304 necessary thing, we will own it to be handsome and just for those of equal age to help one another." "Right," said he. "And this law," said 465a I, "hath this right in it likewise: that if any one be in a passion, gratifying his passion in this manner, he is less apt to raise greater seditions." "It is entirely so."

"The elder shall be enjoined both to govern and to chastise the younger." "That is plain." "And surely the younger, as becomes them,

shall never attempt to beat the elder, or in any other way to offer violence to him, unless appointed by the governors; nor will they, I imagine, in any sort, dishonour them; for there are sufficient
465b guardians to hinder it, both fear and reverence;—reverence on the one hand refraining them from assaulting, as it were, their parents, and fear on the other; lest others shall assist the sufferer; some as sons, others as brothers, and others as fathers." "It happens so," said he. "In every respect then, as far as relates to the laws, the men shall live peaceably with one another." "Very much so." "And while these have no seditions among themselves, there is no danger of any other city railing disturbance against these, or that they shall split into
465c factions." "There is not." "As for the lesser evils, from which surely they will be freed, I do not choose, because of the impropriety of it, so much as to mention them. That flattery of the rich; that indigence and solicitude in the education of their children, and in procuring money for the necessary support of their family, which is the portion of the poor; sometimes borrowing, and sometimes being despised, and sometimes using all manner of shifts, in procuring provisions, which they give to the management of their wives and domestics: how many slavish and mean things, my friend, they suffer in all these
465d respects, are not even worthy to be mentioned." "And they are manifest," said he, "to one blind."

"They will be delivered from all these things and will live more blessedly than that most blessed life which those live who gain the prize in the Olympic games." "How?" "Those are esteemed happy, on account of a small part of what these enjoy. But the victory of these is more noble, and their maintenance from the public is more complete; for the victory they gain is the safety of the whole city; and
465e both they and their children are crowned with their maintenance, and all the other necessaries of life, as laurels, and receive honour from their city while alive, and at their death an honourable funeral."
305 "The most noble rewards!" said he. "Do you remember then," said I, "that in our former reasonings, I do not know who it was objected to
466a us, that we were not making our guardians happy, who, though they had it in their power to have the whole wealth of their citizens, had nevertheless nothing at all? and we proposed to consider of this afterwards, if it fell in our way; but that at the present we were

making our guardians only guardians, and the city itself as happy as possible, but without regarding one particular tribe in it, with a view to make it happy." "I remember it," said he. "What think you now of the life of our auxiliaries, which appears far more noble and happy than that of those who gain the prize at the Olympic games? It does 466b not at all appear to resemble the life of the leather-cutter, the handicraft, or farmer." "I do not think it," said he.

"But however, it is proper that I mention here what I likewise said on a former occasion, that if the guardian shall attempt to be happy in such a way as to be no longer a guardian, nor be content with this moderate, and steady, and, as we say, best life; but, being seized with a foolish and youthful opinion about happiness, shall, because he has it in his power, be driven to make himself the master of every thing in 466c the city, he shall know that Hesiod was truly wise, in saying that the half is somehow more than the whole." "If he take me," said he, "for his counsellor, he will remain in such a life." "You allow then," said I, "that the women act in common with the men, as we have explained, with respect to education and the breeding of children, and the guardianship of the other citizens; both in remaining in the city and in going forth to war; and that along with the men they ought to keep guard, and to hunt like dogs, and in every case to take a share in 466d all things as far as they can; and that while they do these things they will do what is best, and no way contrary to the nature of the female, with respect to the male, by which nature they are made to act jointly with one another." "I agree," said he.

"Does not then this," said I, "remain to be discussed, whether it be possible that this community take place among men likewise, as among other animals? and how far it is possible." "You have prevented me," said he, "in mentioning what I was going to ask." "For, with relation to warlike affairs, it is plain, I imagine," said I, "how they 466e will fight." "How?" said he. "That they will jointly go out on their military expeditions, and besides will carry along with them such of their children, as are grown up, that, like those of other artists, they 306 may see what if will be necessary for them to practise when they are grown up; and, besides seeing, that they may serve and administer in 467a every thing with relation to the war, and assist both their fathers and mothers. Or, have you not observed what happens in the common arts? as for instance, that the children of the potters, ministering to them for a long time, look on before they apply themselves to the making earthen ware?" "Yes, indeed." "Whether now are these or our guardians to instruct their children with greater care, by the practice and view of what belongs to their office?" "To suppose those," replied he, "should take greater care than our guardians, would be 467b ridiculous." "But every creature fights more remarkably in the presence of its offspring." "The case is so; but there is no small danger, Socrates, when they are defeated, as is often the case in war, that when their children, as well as themselves, are cut off, it shall be impossible to raise an other city." "You say true," replied I; "but you imagine we ought, first of all, to take care never to run any risk." "No, by no means." "What then, if they are at all to hazard themselves in any case, is it not where, if they succeed, they shall become better men?" 467c "That is plain." "But do you imagine it a small matter, and not worthy of the risk, whether children, who are destined to be military men, see affairs relating to war, or not?" "No; it in a matter of consequence with respect to what you mention." "We must, then, first endeavour to make our children spectators of the war, but contrive for them a place of safety—and then it shall do well, shall it not?" "Yes."

"And shall not then," said I, "our parents, in the first place, as 467d being men, not be ignorant, but understand which of the camps are, and which are not dangerous?" "It is likely," said he. "And they shall bring them into the one, but with respect to the other they will be on their guard." "Right." "And they will probably set governors over them," said I; "not such as are the most depraved, but such as by experience and years are able leaders and pedagogues." "It is very proper." "But we will say many things have happened contrary to expectation." "Very many." "With reference therefore to such events as these, it is proper that whilst they are children they procure wings, 467e that so, in any necessity, they may escape by flight." "How do you mean?" said he. "They must, when extremely young, be mounted on horses, and taught to ride on horseback, and brought to see the 307 battle, not on high-mettled and warlike horses, but on the fleetest, and those that are the most obedient to the rein; for thus they shall, in the best manner, observe their proper work, and, on any necessity, shall escape with the greatest safety, following the aged leaders." "You seem to me," said he, "to say right."

"But what," said I, "as to the affairs of war? how are you to manage 468a your soldiers, both with respect to one another and their enemies? have I imagined rightly or not?" "As to what?" said he. "That whoever of them," said I, "leaves his rank, throws away his arms, or does any such thing from cowardice, must he not be made a handicraft, or land-labourer?" "By all means." "And shall not the man who is taken alive by the enemy be given gratis to any who incline to employ him in the country just as they please?" "By all means." "And are you of 468b opinion, that he who gains a character, and excels, ought, in the first place, in the expedition itself, to be crowned in some measure by every one of the youths and boys who are his fellow soldiers? or think you otherwise?" "I am of opinion, for my part, they ought to be crowned." "But what, and get the right hand likewise?" "This likewise." "But this further, I imagine," said I, "you are not yet satisfied about." "What?" "That they embrace and be embraced by every one." "They should most of all others," said he: "and I will add to this law, that whilst they are upon this expedition no one shall be allowed to refuse 468c them, whoever they incline to embrace, that if any happen to be in love with any one, male or female, he may be the more animated to win the prizes." "Very well," said I; "for we have already said that there are more marriages provided for the good citizen than for others, and more frequent choice in such matters allowed them than others, that the descendants of such an one may be as numerous as possible." "We have already said so," replied he.

"But surely, even according to Homer's opinion, it is just that such 468d of the youth as are brave be honoured in this way. For Homer says that Ajax, who excelled in war, was rewarded with a large share at the entertainments, this being the most natural reward to a brave man in the bloom of youth, by which he at the same time acquired honour and strength." "Most right," said he. "We shall then obey Homer," said I, "at least, in these things. And we shall honour the good, both at our sacrifices, and on all such occasions, in as far as they appear to be deserving, with hymns likewise, and with those things we lately *308* mentioned; and besides these things, with seats, and dishes; and full 468e cups; that at the same time we may both honour and exercise the

virtue of worthy men and women." "You say most admirably well,"
replied he. "Be it so. If any one of those who die in the army shall have
distinguished himself, shall we not, in the first place, say that he is of
the golden race?" "Most especially." "And shall we not believe Hesiod
telling us, that when any of these die,

469a
> Good, holy, earthly dæmons, they become,
> Expelling evils, guardians of mankind?"[1]

"We shall believe him." "And we shall ask the oracle in what manner
we ought to bury dæmoniacal and divine men, and with what marks
of distinction; and thus shall we bury them in that very manner
which shall be explained." "Why shall we not?" "And we shall in all
469b after time reverence and worship their tombs as those of dæmons.
And we shall enact by law, that the same things be performed, and in
the same manner, to any who shall have been deemed to have
remarkably distinguished themselves in life, when they die of old age,
or any thing else?" "It is right," said he. "But what now? How shall
our soldiers behave towards enemies?" "As to what?" "First, as to
bringing into slavery. Do you think it just that Greeks should enslave
Greek cities? or rather, as far as they are able, not suffer any other to
469c do it, and accustom themselves to this, to be sparing of the Grecian
tribe, being greatly on their guard against being enslaved by the
Barbarians?" "It is," said he, "in general, and in every particular case
best to be sparing." "Are they not to acquire any Grecian slave
themselves, and to counsel the other Greeks to act in the same
manner?" "By all means," said he. "They will the more, at least, by
such a conduct, turn themselves against the Barbarians, and abstain
from one another." "But what? To strip the dead," said I, "of any
thing but their arms after they conquer them, is it handsome or not?
469d It gives a pretence to cowards not to go against the enemy who is
alive, as being necessarily occupied when they are thus employed
about the one who is dead; and many armies have been lost by this
309 plundering." "Very many." "And does it not appear to you to be
illiberal and sordid, and the part of a womanish and little mind, to
strip the dead body, and deem the body of the deceased an enemy,
when the enemy is fled off, and there is only left behind that with
469e which he fought? Or, do you imagine that they who act in this

manner do any way different from dogs, who are in a rage at the stones which are thrown at them, not touching the man who throws them?" "Not in the least," said he. "We must let alone then this stripping the dead, and these hindrances arising from the carrying off booty." "Truly," said he, "these must be banished."

"Nor shall we at any time bring the arms into the temples, as if we were to dedicate them, at least not the arms of Grecians, if we have 470a any concern to obtain the benevolence of the other Greeks: but we shall rather be afraid, lest it should be a kind of profanation to bring into the temple such things as these from our own kinsman, unless the oracle shall say otherwise." "Most right," replied he. "But what, with reference to the laying waste Grecian lands, and burning of houses, how shall your soldiers behave towards their enemies?" "I should be glad," said he, "to hear you signifying your opinion." "Truly then," said I, "in my opinion, neither of these ought to be 470b done, but only one year's produce to be carried off. And would you have me tell you the reason why this should be done?" "By all means." "It appears to me, that as these two words, war and sedition, are different, so they are two different things which are signified by them: I call them two different things, because the one is domestic and akin, the other foreign and strange. When hatred is among ourselves, it is called sedition; when it respects foreigners, it is called war." "What you say," replied he, "is no way unreasonable."

"But consider now, if I say this likewise reasonably: for I aver that 470c the Greek nation is friendly and akin to itself, but is foreign and strange to the Barbarian." "This too is right." "When then the Greeks fight with the Barbarians, and the Barbarians with the Greeks, we shall say they wage war, and are naturally enemies; and this hatred is to be called war. But when Greeks do any such thing to Greeks, we shall say that they are friends by nature, and that Greece in such a case is distempered, and in sedition; and such a hatred is to be called a 470d sedition." "I agree," said he, "to account for it in the same manner." "Consider then," said I, "that in the sedition now mentioned, wherever such a thing happens, and the city is disjointed, if they sequester the lands, and burn the houses of one another, how destructive the sedition appears, and neither of them seem to be lovers 310 of their country: for otherwise they would never dare to lay waste

470e their nurse and mother; but it would suffice the victors to carry off the fruits of the vanquished, and to consider they are to be reconciled, and not perpetually to be at war." "This indeed is by much a more mild sentiment than the other." "But what now?" said I. "Is not this city you are establishing a Greek one?" "It should be so," replied he. "And shall not they be good and mild?" "By all means." "And shall they not be lovers of Greeks? And shall they not account Greece akin to them? And shall they not have the same religious rites with the rest

471a of the Greeks?" "By all means." "A difference then with Greeks, as with kinsmen, will they not denominate a sedition, and not a war?" "They will." "And they will behave as those who are to be reconciled." "By all means." "They shall then be mild and moderate, not punishing so far as to enslave or destroy, since they are moderate, and not hostile." "Just so," said he. "Neither then, as they are Greeks, will they sequester Grecian lands, nor burn their houses; nor will they allow that in every city all are their enemies, men, women, and

471b children; but that always a few only are enemies, the authors of the quarrel: and on all these accounts they will neither choose to lay waste lands, as the greatest number are their friends; nor will they overturn the houses, but will carry on the war so far as till the guilty be obliged by the innocent, whom they distress, to make reparation." "I agree," said he, "that we ought to behave so towards our own citizens when we are set against one another; and to behave so towards the Barbarians as the Greeks at present do to one another." "Let us then

471c likewise establish this law for our guardians,—neither to lay waste the lands, nor burn the houses."

"Let us establish it," said he, "and this further, that these things, and those too you mentioned formerly, are right: but it appears to me, Socrates, if one is to allow you to speak in this manner, that you will never remember what you formerly passed by, when you entered on all that you have now said; viz. how far such a government is possible? and in what way it is at all possible? For, if it be at all possible, I will allow that all these good things will belong to that city, and the

471d following likewise which you have omitted;—that they will, in the best manner, fight against their enemies, and of all others least abandon one another, recognizing these names, and calling one

311 another by these,—fathers, sons, and brothers; and if the female shall

encamp along with them, whether in the same rank, or drawn up behind them, that they will strike terror into the enemies, and at the same time assist if ever there be necessity for it, I know that in this way they will entirely be invincible. And I plainly see too what advantages they have at home, which we have omitted. But speak no more about this government, as I allow that all these, and ten 471e thousand other things, will belong to it, if it actually exist. But let us endeavour to persuade one another of this itself, whether it be possible, and in what respect it is so; and let us omit those other 472a things."

"You have suddenly," said I, "made an assault on my reasoning, and make no allowance for one who is fighting; for perhaps you do not advert, that, with difficulty, I am escaped from two waves, and now you are bringing upon me the greatest and most dangerous of the three. After you have seen and heard this, you will entirely forgive me; allowing, that I with reason grudged, and was afraid to mention so great a paradox, and undertake to examine it." "The more," said he; "you mention these things, the less will you be freed from explaining 472b in what respect this government is possible. Proceed then, and do not delay." "Must not this then," said I, "in the first place, be remembered, that we are come hither in search of justice, what it is? and what injustice is?" "It must;" said he. "But what is this to the purpose?" "Nothing. But if we discover what justice is, shall we then judge that the just man ought in no respect to differ from it, but in 472c every respect to be such as justice is? and shall we be satisfied if he approach the nearest to it, and, of all others, partake of it the most?" "We shall," said he, "be thus satisfied."

"As a model then," said I, "we were inquiring into this, what kind of thing justice is; and we likewise were in quest of a just man; and considered what sort of man he should be, if he did exist. We likewise inquired what injustice is, and what too the most unjust men—in order that, looking into these two models, what kind of men they appeared with respect to happiness and its opposite, we might be obliged to acknowledge concerning ourselves, that whoever should 472d most resemble them in character shall have a fortune the most resembling theirs; and not for this end, to show that these things are possible or not." "In this," said he, "you say true." "Do you imagine

then that the painter is in any degree the less excellent, who having
312   painted a model of the most beautiful man, and brought every thing
fully into his piece, is yet unable to show that such a man does really
exist?" "By Jupiter," said he, "I do not." "What then, have we not
472e   made in our reasonings (shall we say) a model of a good city?" "Yes,
indeed." "Have we then spoken any thing the worse, do you imagine,
on this account, that we are not able to show, that it is possible for a
city to be established such as we have described?" "No, indeed," said
he. "This then," said I, "is the truth of the case. But if truly I must
now likewise, on your account, hasten to this, to show how especially,
and in what respects, it is most possible, in order to this discovery, you
must again grant the same things as formerly." "What things?"

473a   "Is it possible for any thing to be executed so perfectly as it is
described? or, is such the nature of practice, that it approaches not so
near the truth as theory, though some may think otherwise? But
whether will you allow this or not?" "I allow it," said he. "Do not
then oblige me to show you all these things, and in every respect,
existing in fact, so perfectly as we have described in our reasoning; but
if we be able to find out how a city may be established the nearest
possible to what we have mentioned, you will say we have discovered
473b   that these things which you require are possible? Or will you not even
be satisfied if this be obtained? For my own part, I should be satisfied."
"And I too," said he.

"We are now, it seems in the next place, to endeavour to find out
and to show what, at all, is the evil which is now practised in cities
through which they are not established in this manner we have
described; and what is that smallest change, which, if made, would
bring the city to this model of government; and let us chiefly see, if
this can be effected by the change of one thing, if not by the change
of two, if not that, by the change of the fewest things in number, and
473c   the smallest in power." "By all means," said he. "Upon the change
then of one thing," said I, "I am able I think to show that the state
can fall into this model of government. But the change is not indeed
small nor easy, yet it is possible." "What is it?" said he. "I am now
come," said I, "to what I compared to the greatest wave: and it shall
now be mentioned, though, like a breaking wave, it should
overwhelm us with excessive laughter and unbelief. But consider what

I am going to say." "Proceed," replied he.

"Unless either philosophers," said I, "govern in cities, or those who are at present called kings and governors philosophize genuinely and sufficiently, and these two, the political power and philosophy, unite in one; and till the bulk of those who at present pursue each of these separately are of necessity excluded, there shall be no end, Glauco, to the miseries of cities, nor yet, as I imagine, to those of the human race; nor till then shall ever this republic, which we have gone over in our reasonings, spring up to a possibility, and behold the light of the sun. But this is that which all along made me grudge to mention it, that I saw what a paradox I was to utter: for it is difficult to be convinced that no other but this republic can enjoy happiness, whether public or private." "You have thrown out, Socrates," said he, "such an expression and argument, as you may imagine will bring on you a great many, and these courageous to such a degree as to put off their clothes, and naked to snatch whatever weapon fortune affords each of them; and, as if they were to perform prodigies, rush upon you in battle array. And unless, mowing them down with argument, you make your escape, you will pay for it by suffering most severe ridicule." "And are not you the cause of all this?" said I. "But in acting handsomely at least," replied he. "However, in this affair, I will not betray you, but defend you with such things as I am able. And I am able both by my good-will and by encouraging you, and probably I will answer your questions more carefully than any other; only do you endeavour, with the help of such an assistant, to show those who are backward to believe these things, that the case really is as you represent it." "I must endeavour," said I, "since even you afford so great an alliance. And here it seems to me to be necessary, if we are any how to make our escape from those you mention, accurately to define to them what kind of men these are whom we call philosophers, when we dare to assert that they alone ought to govern, in order that, when they are made perfectly manifest, any one may be able to defend himself, when he asserts that to these it naturally belongs both to apply themselves to philosophy, and likewise to take upon them the government of the state: but others are to apply themselves neither to philosophy nor government, but to obey their leader." "It is proper," said he, "to define them." "Come then, follow

473d

313

473e

474a

474b

474c

me this way, if together any how we shall sufficiently explain this matter." "Lead on then," said he.

"Will it then be needful," said I, "to remind you, or do you remember it, that when we say of any one, that he loves any thing, when we speak with propriety, he must not appear to love one part of it, and not another, but to have an affection for the whole?" "I need, it seems," replied he, "to be put in mind; for I do not understand it perfectly." "It might become another, Glauco," replied I, "to say what you say; but it does not become a man who is a lover, to forget that all those who are in their bloom sting somehow, and give emotion to one who is amorous, and a lover, as they are deemed worthy both of respect and of being saluted. Or do you not behave in this manner towards the beautiful? One, because flat-nosed, shall be called agreeable, and be commended by you; and the hook-nose of the other, you say, is princely; and that which is in the middle of these is according to the exactest symmetry: the black are said to be manly to behold; and the fair to be the children of the Gods:—but this appellation of pale green, do you imagine it is the invention of any other than of a flattering lover, and one who easily bears with the paleness, provided it is in the bloom of youth? And, in one word, you make all kinds of pretences, and say every thing so as never to reject any one who is of a blooming age?" "If you incline," said he, "to judge by me of other lovers, that they act in this manner, I agree to it for the sake of the argument." "And what," said I, "with respect to the lovers of wine; do you not observe them acting in the same manner, cheerfully drinking every kind of wine upon every pretext?" "Yes, indeed." "And you perceive, as I imagine, that the ambitious likewise, if they cannot obtain the command of a whole army, will take the third command; and, if they cannot be honoured by greater and better men, are content if they be honoured by the lower and more contemptible, being desirous of honour at any rate?" "It is perfectly so." "Agree to this or not: if we say, one is desirous of any thing, shall we say that he desires the whole species, or that he desires one part of it, but not another?" "The whole," replied he.

"Shall we not then likewise say, that the philosopher is desirous of wisdom, and that not of one part only, but of the whole?" "True." "He then who is averse to disciplines, especially if he be young, and

314
474d

474e

475a

475b

475c

has not at all understanding to discern what is good, and what is otherwise, shall not be called a lover of learning, nor a philosopher; in the same manner as we say of one who is disgusted with meats, that he neither hungers after nor desires meats, nor is a lover but a hater of them." "And we shall say right." "But the man who readily inclines to taste of every discipline, and with pleasure enters on the study of it, and is insatiable of it, this man we shall with justice call a philosopher: shall we not?" On this Glauco said, "There will be many such 475d philosophers as those very absurd: for all your lovers of shows appear to me to be of this kind, from their taking a pleasure in learning; and 315 your story lovers are the most stupid of all to be reckoned among philosophers at least. These indeed would not willingly attend on such reasonings, and such a disquisition as this. But yet, as if they had hired out their ears to listen to every chorus, they run about to the Bacchanalia, omitting neither those of cities nor villages. Shall all these then, and others studious of such things, and those who apply to 475e the inferior arts, be called by us philosophers?" "By no means," said I, "but resembling philosophers."

"But whom," said he, "do you call the true ones?" "Those," said I, "who are desirous of discerning the truth." "This likewise," said he, "is right. But how do you mean?" "It is not easy," said I, "to tell it to another; but you, I imagine, will agree with me in this." "In what?" "That since the beautiful is opposite to the deformed, these are two things." "Why are they not?" "And if they are two, then each of them 476a is one." "This also is granted." "And the reasoning is the same concerning justice and injustice, good and evil. And concerning every other species of things the argument is the same—that each of them is one in itself, but appears to be many, being every where diversified by their communication with action and body, and with one another." "You say right," said he. "In this manner then," said I, "I separate these, and set apart those you now mentioned, the lovers of public shows, of handicrafts, and mechanics; and then apart from 476b these I set those of whom we discourse at present, whom alone we may properly call philosophers." "How do you say?" replied he. "The lovers of common stories and of spectacles delight in fine sounds, colours, and figures, and every thing which is compounded of these; but the nature of beauty itself their dianoëtic part is unable to discern and admire." "Indeed the case is so," said he. "But as to those then who are able to approach this beauty itself, and to behold it as it is in itself, 476c must they not be few in number?" "Extremely so."

"He then who accounts some things beautiful, but neither knows beauty itself, nor is able to follow if one were to lead I him to the knowledge of it, does he seem to you to live in a dream, or to be awake? Consider now, what is it to dream? Is it not this, when a man, whether asleep or awake, imagines the similitude of a thing is not the similitude, but really the thing itself which it resembles?" "I for my part would aver," replied he, "that such a person is really in a dream." 316 "But what now as to him who judges opposite to this, who 476d understands what beauty is itself, and is able to discern both it and such things as participate of it, and neither deems the participants to be beauty, nor beauty to be the participants? whether does such an one seem to you to live awake, or in a dream?" "Perfectly awake," said he.

"May we not then properly call this man's dianoëtic perception, as he really knows, knowledge, but that of the other, opinion, as he only opines?" "By all means." "But what if the person who we say only opines things, but does not really know them, be enraged at us, and 476e dispute with us, alleging that what we say is not true; shall we have any method of soothing and persuading him, in a gentle manner, by concealing that he is not in a sound state?" "At least there is need of it," replied he. "Come now, consider what we shall say to him. Or do you incline we shall thus interrogate him? telling him, that if he knows any thing, no one envies him for it, but we shall gladly see him possessed of some knowledge; but only tell us this, does the man who has knowledge, show something or nothing? Do you now answer me for him?" "I will answer," said he, "that he knows something." "Whether something which really exists, or which does not?" "What 477a does really exist: for how can that be known which has no real existence?" "We have then examined this sufficiently, though we might have considered it more fully; that what really is, may be really known; but what does not at all exist, cannot at all be known." "We have examined it most sufficiently."

"Be it so. But if there be any thing of such a kind, as both to be and not to be, must it not lie between that which perfectly is, and that which is not at all?" "Between them." "As to what really is, then, is there not knowledge? and as to that which is not at all, is there not of necessity ignorance? And for that which is between these, we must 477b seek for something between ignorance and science, if there be any such thing." "By all means." "Do we say then that opinion is any thing?" "Why not?" "Whether is it a different power from science, or the same?" "Different." "Is opinion then conversant about one thing, and science about another, by virtue of the same power, or each of them by virtue of a power of its own?" "This last." "Is not the power of science conversant about what really exists, to know that it is? Or rather it seems to me to be necessary to distinguish in this manner." "How?"

"We shall say, that powers are a certain species of real existences, by 477c which we can both do whatever we can do, and every being else whatever it can do. Thus, I say, that seeing and hearing are among 317 these powers, if you understand what I mean to call a species." "I understand," said he. "Hear then what appears to me concerning them. For I do not see any colour of a power, nor figure, nor any of such qualities, as of many other things, with reference to which I distinguish some things with myself, that they are different from one 477d another. But as to power, I regard that alone about which it is conversant, and what it effects; and on this account I have called each of these a power. And the power which is conversant about and effects one and the same thing, I call the same power, but that conversant about and effecting a different thing, I call a different power: but what say you? In what manner do you call it?" "Just so," replied he.

"But come again, excellent Glauco, whether do you say that science is itself a certain power, or to what class do you refer it?" "I refer it to 477e this class of power," said he, "as it is of all powers the most strong." "But what now? Shall we refer opinion to power, or to some other species?" "By no means to power," said he; "for that by which we form opinions is nothing else but opinion." "But you owned some time since, that science and opinion were not the same." "How," said he, "can ever any one who possesses intellect reduce under one, that which is infallible, and that which is not infallible?" "You say right," said I. "And it is plain that we have allowed opinion to be a different 478a thing from science." "We have." "Each of them then has naturally a different power over a different thing." "Of necessity." "Science has a power over being itself, in knowing real existence, how it exists." "Yes." "But we say that opinion opines." "Yes." "Whether does it know the same thing which science knows? and shall that which is known, and that which is opined, be the same? or is this impossible?" "Impossible," said he, "from what we have allowed: since they are 478b naturally powers of different things, and both of them are powers, opinion and science, and each of them different from the other, as we have said; from these things it cannot be, that what is opined is the same with that which is known." "If then being itself be known, must it not be different from the being which is perceived by opinion?" "Different." "Does he then who opines, opine that which has no existence? Or is it impossible to opine that which doth not exist at all? Consider now, does not the man who opines, refer his opinion to somewhat? Or is it possible to opine, and yet opine nothing at all?" "Impossible." "But whoever opines, opines some one thing." "Yes." 318 "But surely that which does not exist, cannot be called any one thing, 478c but most properly nothing at all." "Certainly so."

"But we necessarily referred ignorance to that which does not exist, but knowledge to real exigence." "Right," said he. "Neither therefore does he opine being, nor yet that which is not." "He does not." "Opinion then is neither knowledge, nor is it ignorance." "It appears it is not." "Does it then exceed these, either knowledge in perspicuity, or ignorance in obscurity?" "It does neither." "But does opinion," said I, "seem to you to be more obscure than knowledge, but more perspicuous than ignorance?" "By much," said he. "But does it lie 478d between them both then?" "It does." "Opinion then is in the middle of these two." "Entirely so." "And have we not already said, that if any thing appeared of such a kind, as at the same time to be, and yet not to be, such a thing would lie between that which has really an existence, and that which does not at all exist, and that neither science nor ignorance would be conversant about it, but that which appeared to be between ignorance and science?" "Right." "And now that which we call opinion, has appeared to be between them." "It has appeared."

478e   "It yet remains for us, as it seems, to discover that which participates of both these, of being, and of non-being, and which with propriety can be called neither of them perfectly, that if it appear to be that which is opined, we may justly call it so, assigning to the extremes what is extreme, and to the middle what is in the middle. Shall we not do thus?" "Thus." "These things being determined, let this worthy man, I will say, tell and answer me, he who reckons that 479a beauty, and a certain idea of beauty there is none, always the same, and in the same respects; but this lover of beautiful objects reckons there are many beautiful things, but can never endure to be told that there is one beautiful, and one just, and so of others. Of all these many things, excellent man! shall we say to him, is there any which will not appear deformed, and of those just which will not appear unjust, of those holy which will not appear profane?" "No; but of necessity," said he, "the beautiful things themselves must in some respect appear even 479b deformed, and others in like manner."

"But what? many things which are double, or two-fold, do they less really appear to be halves than doubles?" "No less." "And things great and small, light and heavy, shall they be denominated what we call them, any more than the opposite?" "No; but each of them," said he, "always participates of both." "Whether then is each of these many things that which it is said to be, or is it not?" "It is like their riddles 319 at feasts," said he, "and the riddle of children about the eunuch's 479c striking the bat, puzzling one another in what manner and how far he strikes it. For all these things have a double meaning, and it is impossible to know accurately that they are, or are not, that they are both, or neither of the two." "How can you do with them then?" said I, "or have you a better class for them than a medium between being and non-being? For nothing seems more obscure than non-being in respect of having no being at all, nor more perspicuous than being in 479d respect of real being." "Most true," said he.

"We have then discovered, it seems, that most of the maxims of the multitude concerning the beautiful, and those other things, roll somehow between being and non-being." "We have accurately discovered it." "But we formerly agreed, that if any such thing should appear, it ought to be called that which is opined, and not what is known; and that which fluctuates between the two is to be perceived by the power between the two." "We agreed." "Those then who contemplate many beautiful things, but who never perceive beauty 479e itself, nor are able to follow another leading them to it; and many just things, but never justice itself, and all other things in like manner, we will say that they opine all things, but know none of the things which they opine." "Of necessity," said he.

"But what now? Those who perceive each of the things themselves, always existing in the same manner, and in the same respect, shall we not say that they know, and do not opine?" "Of necessity this likewise." "And shall we not say, that these embrace and love the things of which they have knowledge, and the others the things of 480a which they have opinion? Or do we not remember, that we said they beheld and loved fine sounds and colour, and such things; but that beauty itself they do not admit of as any real being?" "We remember." "Shall we then act wrong in calling them lovers of opinion, rather than philosophers? and yet they will be greatly enraged at us if we call them so." "Not, if they be persuaded by me," said he; "for it is not lawful to be enraged at the truth, those then who admire every thing which has a real being, are to be called philosophers, and not lovers of opinion." "By all means."

THE END OF THE FIFTH BOOK.

BOOK VI.

"Those now who are philosophers," said I, "Glauco, and those who 484a
are not, have, through a long compass of discourse, with difficulty
discovered themselves what they severally are." "Because, perhaps, it
was not easy," said he, "in a short one." "So it appears," said I. "But I
still think they would have better discovered themselves, if it had
been requisite to speak concerning this alone, and not to have
discussed that multitude of other things, when we were to consider
what difference there is between a just life and an unjust." "What 484b
then," said he, "are we to treat of next?" "What else," said I, "but of
that which is next in order? Since those are philosophers who are able
to pass into contact with that which always subsists similarly
according to the same;¹ but those who are not able to accomplish this,
but who wander amidst many things, and such as are every way
shifting, are not philosophers; which of these ought to be the
governors of the city?" "Which way," said he, "shall we determine in
this, and determine reasonably?" "Whichever of them," said I,
"appear capable of preserving the laws and institutions of cities, these 484c
are to be made guardians." "Right," said he.

"This now," said I, "is certainly plain; whether a blind or quick-
sighted guardian be proper for guarding any thing." "Why is it not
plain?" said he. "Whether then do those appear to you to differ from
the blind, who are in reality deprived of the knowledge of each
particular being, and have neither a clear paradigm in their soul, nor
are able, as painters looking up to the truest paradigm, and always

223

484d referring themselves thither, and contemplating it in the most accurate manner possible, to establish here too in like manner just

321 maxims of the beautiful, and just, and good, if there be occasion to establish them, and to guard and preserve such as are already established?" "No, by Jupiter," said he. "They do not differ much." "Shall we then appoint those to be guardians, or those who know each being, and who in experience are nothing behind those others, nor inferior to them in any other part of virtue?" "It would be absurd," said he, "to choose others, at least if these are not deficient in other

485a things; for in this, which is almost the greatest, they excel." "Shall we not then speak to this point,—In what manner the same persons shall be able to have both the one and the other of those things?" "By all means."

"It is then first of all necessary, as we observed in the beginning of this discourse, thoroughly to understand their genius; and I think if we sufficiently agree respecting it, we shall likewise agree that the same persons be able to possess both these things, and that no others but these ought to be the governors of cities." "How so?" "Let this

485b now be agreed among us concerning the philosophic geniuses, that they are always desirous of such learning as may discover to them that essence which always is, and is not changed by generation or corruption." "Let it be agreed." "And likewise," said I, "that they are desirous of the whole of such learning, and that they will not willingly omit any part of it, neither small nor great, more honourable or more dishonourable, as we formerly observed concerning the ambitious, and concerning lovers." "You say right," said he.

"Consider then, in the next place, if, besides what we have

485c mentioned, it be necessary that this also should subsist in the genius of those who are to be such as we have described." "What?" "That they be void of falsehood, nor willingly at any time receive a lie; but hate it, and love the truth." "It is likely," said he. "It is not only likely, my friend, but is perfectly necessary, that one who is naturally in love with any thing should love every thing allied and belonging to the objects of his affection." "Right," said he. "Can you then find any thing more allied to wisdom than truth?" "How can we?" said he. "Is it possible then that the same genius can be philosophic, and at the

same time a lover of falsehood?" "By no means." "He then who is in 485d
reality a lover of learning, ought immediately from his infancy to be
in the greatest measure desirous of all truth." "By all means." "But we
know somehow, that whoever has his desires vehemently verging to
one thing, has them upon this very account weaker as to other things,
as a current diverted from its channel." "Why are they not?" "But 322
whosoever hath his desires running out after learning, and every
thing of this kind, would be conversant, I think, about the pleasure of
the soul itself, and would forsake those pleasures which arise from the
body, provided he be not a counterfeit, but same real philosopher."
"This follows by a mighty necessity." 485e

"And such an one is moderate, and by no means a lover of money.
For the reasons why money is with so much trouble anxiously sought
after, have weight with any other than such an one to make him
solicitous." "Certainly." "And surely somehow you must likewise
consider this when you are to judge what is a philosophic genius, and 486a
what is not." "What?" "That it does not without your knowledge
partake of an illiberal turn: for pusillanimity is most opposite to a soul
which is always to pursue earnestly the whole and every thing of that
which is divine and human." "Most true," said he. "Do you then
suppose that he who possesses magnificent conceptions in his
dianoëtic part, and a contemplation of the whole of time, and the
whole of being, can possibly consider human life as a thing of great
consequence." "It is impossible," said he. "Such an one then will not 486b
account death any thing terrible." "Least of all." "A cowardly and
illiberal genius, then, will not, it seems, readily participate of true
philosophy." "It does not appear to me that it will." "What now, can
the moderate man, and one who is not a lover of money, nor illiberal,
nor arrogant, nor cowardly, ever possibly be an ill co-partner, or
unjust?" "It is impossible." "And you will likewise consider this, when
you are viewing from its infancy what is the philosophic soul, and
what is not, whether it be just and mild, or unsocial and savage." "By
all means." "Neither indeed, as I think, will you omit this." "What?" 486c
"Whether it learn with facility or difficulty. Or do you expect that
ever any one will love any thing sufficiently, in performing which he
performs with uneasiness and with difficulty, making small progress?"
"It cannot be." "But what if he can retain nothing of what he learns,

being quite forgetful, is it possible for him not to be void of science?"
"How is it possible?" "And when he labours unprofitably, do you not
imagine he will be obliged at last to hate both himself and such
486d practice?" "Why must he not?" "We shall never then reckon a
forgetful soul among those who are thoroughly philosophic, but we
shall require it to be of a good memory." "By all means."

323   "But never shall we say this at least, that an unmusical and indecent
genius leads any where else but towards intemperance." "Where else?"
"But whether do you reckon truth allied to intemperance or to
temperance?" "To temperance." "Let us require then among other
things a dianoëtic part naturally temperate and graceful, as a proper
486e guide towards spontaneously attaining the idea of each particular
being." "Why not?" "What now? Do we not in some measure seem to
you to have discussed the necessary qualifications, and such as are
consequent to each other, in a soul which is to apprehend being
487a sufficiently, and in perfection?" "The most necessary," said he. "Is it
possible then for you in any measure to blame such a study as this,
which a man can never be able sufficiently to apply to, unless he be
naturally possessed of a good memory, learn with facility, be
magnificent, graceful, and the friend and ally of truth, justice,
fortitude and temperance?" "Not even Momus himself," said he,
"could find fault with such a study." "But," said I, "will it not be to
these alone, when they are perfected by education and age, that you
will entrust the city?"

487b   Here Adimantus said, "Indeed, Socrates, no one is able to
contradict you as to these things; but all who hear you at any time
advancing what you do at present, are somehow affected in this
manner. Being led off a little by your reasoning on each question,
through their inexperience in this method of question and answer,
when all these littles are collected together, at the close of your
reasonings, they reckon that the mistake appears considerable, and
the contrary of their first concessions; and like those who play at talus
with such as are dexterous, but are themselves unskilful, they are in
487c the end shut up, and can do no more; so your hearers have nothing to
say, being shut up by this other kind of game, not with pieces, but
with your reasonings. Though the truth at least is not by this any way
advanced: I say this with reference to the present inquiry; for one may

tell you that he has nothing to oppose to each of your questions by way of argument, but that in fact he sees that all those who plunge into philosophy, applying to it not with this view, that being early instructed they may be liberated from it when in their prime, but that 487d they may continue in it much longer, become the most of them quite awkward, not to say altogether depraved; and those of them who appear the most worthy, do yet suffer thus much from this study you so much commend, that they become useless to the public."   324

When I had heard this, "Do you imagine then," said I, "that such as say these things are telling a falsehood?" "I do not know," said he, but would gladly hear your opinion." "You would then hear that they 487e appear to me to say true." "How then," replied he, "is it right to say that the miseries of cities shall never have an end till they be governed by philosophers, whom we are now acknowledging to be useless to them?" "You ask a question," said I, "which needs an answer through an image." "And you," said he, "are not wont, I think, to speak through images."

"Be it so," said I. "You jest now, when you have brought me on a subject which is so difficult to be explained. But attend to the image, that you may see further with what difficulty I assimilate; for the 488a sufferings of the most worthy philosophers in the management of public affairs are so grievous, that there is not any one other suffering so severe: but in making our simile, and in apologizing for them, we must collect from many particulars, in the same manner as painters mix the figures of two different animals together, and paint a creature which is both goat and stag in one, and others of this kind. Conceive now that such an one as this is the pilot of a fleet, or of a single ship, one who exceeds all in the ship, both in bulk and in strength, but is 488b somewhat deaf, and sees in like manner but a short way, and whose skill in sea affairs is much of the same kind. Conceive likewise that the sailors are all in sedition among themselves, contending for the pilotship, each imagining he ought to be pilot, though he never learned the art, nor is able to show who was his master, nor at what time he learned it. That besides this, all of them say that the art itself cannot be taught, and are ready to cut in pieces any one who says that it can. Imagine further, that they continually surround the pilot 488c himself, begging, and doing every thing that he may put the helm

into their hands; and that even sometimes when they are not so successful in persuading him as others are, they either kill these others, or throw them overboard; and after they have by mandragora, or wine, or some other thing, rendered the noble pilot incapable, they manage the ship with the assistance of the crew, and whilst they drink and feast in this manner, they sail as it may be expected of such people. And besides these things, if any one be dexterous in assisting
488d them to get the government into their own hands, and in setting
325 aside the pilot, either by persuasion or force, they commend such an one, calling him sailor and pilot, and intelligent in navigation; but they contemn as useless every one who is not of this kind, whilst they never in the least think that the true pilot must necessarily pay attention to the year, the seasons, the heavens, and stars, and winds, and every thing belonging to the art if he intends to be a governor of
488e a ship in reality: but the art and practice of governing men, whether some be willing or not, they think impossible for a man to attain in conjunction with the art of navigation. Whilst affairs are in this situation with regard to the ships, do you not think that the true pilot will be called by the sailors aboard of ships fitted out in this manner, a
489a star-gazer, insignificant, and unprofitable to them?" "Undoubtedly," said Adimantus. "I think then," said I, "that you will not want any explanation of the image, to see that it represents how they are affected in cities towards true philosophers, but that you understand what I say." "Perfectly," said he. "First of all then with respect to this, if any one wonders that philosophers are not honoured in cities, teach him our image, and endeavour to persuade him that it would be much more
489b wonderful if they were honoured." "I will teach him so," replied he.

"And further, that it is indeed true, what you now were observing that the best of those who apply to philosophy are useless to the bulk of mankind; but however, for this, bid them blame such as make no use of these philosophers, and not these philosophers themselves. For it is not natural for the pilot to entreat the sailors to allow him to govern them, nor for the wise to be resorting to the gates of the rich. But whoever pleasantly said this was mistaken; for this is truly the natural method, that whoever is sick, whether rich or poor, must of
489c necessity go to the gates of the physician, and whoever wants to be governed must wait on him who is able to govern; for it is not natural

that the governor who is really of any value should entreat the governed to subject themselves to his government. But you will not greatly err, when you compare our present political governors to those sailors we now mentioned, and those who are called by them insignificant and star-gazers to those who are truly pilots." "Most right," said he. "From hence then it would seem that the best pursuit is not likely to be held in esteem among those who pursue studies of an opposite nature; but by far the greatest and most violent accusation 489d of philosophy is occasioned by means of those who profess to study it; *326* the most of whom, you say, your accuser of philosophy calls altogether depraved, and the very best of them of no advantage to the state; and I agreed that you say the truth, did I not?" "You did." "And have we not fully explained the cause why the best of them are of no advantage?" "We have." "Would you choose then, that we should in the next place explain the reason why the most of them must of necessity be depraved, and that we endeavour to demonstrate, that of this, philosophy is by no means the cause." "Entirely so." 489e

"Let us attend then, and begin our reasoning, calling to mind what we formerly observed concerning the natural genius which necessarily belongs to the good and worthy.—And what was a leading part in it, 490a if you remember, was truth, which he must by all means wholly pursue, or else be a vain boaster, and never partake of true philosophy." "It was so said." "Is not this one part of his character perfectly contrary to the present opinions of him?" "It is very much so," replied he. "Will it not then be no small defence, if we be able to show that the true lover of learning is naturally made to aspire to the knowledge of real being, and not to rest in the many particular things 490b which are the objects of opinion, but goes on, and is not blunted, nor ceases from his love of truth till he comes into Contact with the nature of every thing which *is*, by that part of the soul whose office it is to come into contact with a thing of this kind. But it is the office of that part of the soul which is allied to real being; to which when this true lover of learning approaches, and is mingled with it, having generated intellect and truth, he will then have true knowledge, and truly live and be nourished, and then he becomes liberated from the pains of parturition, but not before." "This," said he, "will be a most reasonable defence."

490c   "What now, will it be the part of such an one to love falsehood, or, entirely the contrary, to hate it?" "To hate it," said he. "But whilst truth indeed leads the way, we can never, I think, say that any band of evils follows in her train." How can we?" "But, on the contrary, we may aver that she is followed by sound and moderate manners, and such as are accompanied with temperance." "Right," said he. "Why, now, need we go over again and range in order the whole qualities of the philosophic genius? for you no doubt remember that there belong

327   to men of this character fortitude, magnanimity, facility of learning,

490d   and memory: and when you replied that every one would be obliged to agree to what we said, we quitted that subject, and turned to that which is the subject of discourse at present, on your saying that you observed some of the philosophers were insignificant, and many of them altogether depraved. And while we were examining into the cause of that calumny, we are now come to this, whence it is that many of them are depraved. And on this account we have gone over again the genius of true philosophers, and have necessarily defined

490e   what it is." "It is so," said he.

"It is necessary now," said I, "that we consider the corruptions of this genius, and in what manner it is destroyed in the most; but one small particular escapes us: who those are that they call not depraved,

491a   but useless. And next, what these geniuses are which counterfeit the philosophic nature, and pretend to its pursuit: and what is the nature of those souls who aspire to a pursuit which does not belong to them, and is above their reach: for these, by their manifold errors, have every where, and among all men, introduced this opinion of philosophy which you mention." "What sort of corruptions," said he, "do you mean?" "I shall endeavour to rehearse them," said I, "if I be able. And this now, I think, every one will allow us, that such a

491b   genius, with all those qualifications we have enjoined one who is to be a perfect philosopher, rarely arises among men, and that there are but few of them: do not you think so?" "Entirely so." "And of those few, consider how many and how great are the causes of corruption." "What are they?" "That which is most of all wonderful to hear, that each of those things we commended in the genius of a philosopher, corrupts the soul which possesses them, and withdraws it from philosophy; fortitude, I mean, and temperance, and all those other qualifications which we have discussed." "That is strange to hear," said he. "And further still," said I, "besides these things, all those 491c which are commonly called good, such as beauty, riches, strength of body, a powerful alliance in the city, and every thing akin to these, corrupt and withdraw it from philosophy; for you have now a specimen of what I mean." "I have," replied he, "and would gladly understand more accurately what you say." "Understand then," said I, "the whole of it aright, and it will appear manifest, and what we formerly said will not seem to be absurd." "How then," said he, "do you bid me act?" 491d

"With respect to every kind of seed, or plant," said I, "whether of 328 vegetables or animals, we know, that whatever does not meet with the proper nourishment, nor season, nor place belonging to it, the more vigorous it is by nature, the more it is defective in the excellencies of its kind; for evil is more contrary to good, than to that which is not good." "Why is it not?" "It is then reasonable, I think, that the best genius, when meeting with nourishment foreign to it, shall be more changed to what is evil, than a bad genius." "It is." "And shall we not, Adimantus," said I, "in the same manner, say that souls naturally the 491e best, when they meet with bad education, become remarkably depraved? Or do you think that great iniquity, and the extremest wickedness, arise from a weak genius, and not from a vigorous one ruined in its education; but that an imbecil genius will never be the cause either of mighty good or evil?" "I do not think it will," said he, "but the case is as you say."

"If then this philosophic genius, which we have established, meet 492a with suitable instruction, it will, I think, necessarily grow up, and attain to every virtue; but if, when sown in an improper soil, it grow up and be nourished accordingly, it will on the other hand become perfectly the reverse, unless some one of the Gods afford it assistance. Or do you think, with the multitude, that certain of the youth are corrupted by the sophists, and that the corruptors are certain private sophists, which is worthy of our notice? Or think you rather, that the persons who say these things are themselves the greatest sophists, 492b conveying their instruction in the most powerful manner, and rendering young and old, man and women, such as they wish to be?" "When do they effect this?" replied he. "When many of them," said I, "are set down, crowded together in an assembly, in their courts of

justice, the theatre, or the camp, or any other public meeting of the
people, with much tumult they blame some of the speeches and
actions, and commend others, roaring and vociferating the one and
492c the other beyond measure. And besides this, the rocks and the place
where they are resounding, the tumult is redoubled, whilst they thus
blame and applaud. In such a situation now, what kind of heart, as we
say, do you think the youth are to have? Or what private instruction
can make him withstand, so as not to be perfectly overwhelmed by
such blame or applause, and, giving way, be borne along the stream
492d wherever it carries him, and say that things are beautiful and base,
329 according as these people say, and pursue the things they pursue, and
become of the very same kind himself?" "This," said he, "must by an
abundant necessity happen, Socrates."

"But," said I, "we have not yet mentioned, what must of the
greatest necessity be the case." "What is that?" said he. "That which
these instructors and sophists superadd by action, not being able to
persuade by speech: or, do you not know, that they punish with
disgraces, and fines, and deaths, the man whom they cannot
persuade?" "I know that," said he, "extremely well." "What other
492e sophist then, or what private reasonings do you think capable,
drawing opposite to these, to overpower them?" "I know none," said
he. "But is it not besides," said I, "great folly even to attempt it? For
there neither is, nor was, nor ever can be, a different method of
attaining virtue, besides this education by these sophists. I mean a
human method, my friend; for a divine one, according to the
proverb, I keep out of the question: for you must know well, with
respect to whatever temper is preserved, and becomes such as it ought
493a to be in such a constitution of politics, that you will not say amiss
when you say that it is preserved by a divine destiny." "Nor am I," said
he, "of a different opinion."

"But further now, besides these things," said I, "you must likewise
be of this opinion." "Of what?" "That each of these private hirelings,
which these men call sophists, and deem the rivals of their art, teach
no other things but those dogmas of the vulgar, which they approve
when they are assembled together, and call it wisdom. Just as if a man
had learned what were the wrathful emotions and desires of a great
493b and strong animal he were nourishing, how it must be approached,

how touched, and when it is most fierce or most mild; and from what causes, and the sounds which on these several occasions it was wont to utter, and at what sounds uttered by another, the animal is rendered both mild and savage; and, having learned all these things by associating with the animal for a long time, should call this wisdom; and, as if he had established an art, should apply himself to the teaching it; whilst yet, with reference to these dogmas and desires, he knows not in reality what is beautiful, or base, or good, or ill, or just, or unjust, but should pronounce all these according to the opinions of the great animal, calling those things good in which it delighted, and that evil with which it was vexed, and should have no other measure as to these things. Let us likewise suppose that he calls those things which are necessary, beautiful and just, but that he hath never discovered himself, nor is able to show to another the nature of the necessary and the good, how much they really differ from each other. Whilst he is such an one, does he not, by Jupiter, appear to you an absurd teacher?" "To me he appears so," said he. *493c* *330*

"And from this man, think you, does he any way differ, who deems it wisdom to have understood the anger and the pleasures of the multitude, and of assemblies of all kinds of men, whether with relation to painting, music, or politics? For, if any one converses with these, and shows them either a poem, or any other production of art, or piece of administration respecting the city, and makes the multitude the judges of it, he is under what is called a Diomedæan[2] necessity, which is above all other necessities, of doing whatever they commend. But to show that these things are in reality good and beautiful, have you at any time heard any of them advance a reason that was not quite ridiculous?" "Nor do I think," said he, "I ever shall." *493d* *493e*

"Whilst you attend then to all these things, bear this in mind, that the multitude never will admit or reckon that there is the one beautiful itself, and not many beautifuls, one *thing itself which has a single subsistence*, and not many such things." "They will be the last to do so," replied he. "It is impossible then for the multitude to be philosophers." "Impossible." "And those who philosophize must of necessity be reproached by them." "Of necessity." "And likewise by those private persons, who, in conversing with the multitude, desire to please them." "It is plain." "From this state of things now, what *494a*

safety do you see for the philosophic genius to continue in its pursuit,
331 and arrive at perfection? And consider from what was formerly said,
494b for we have allowed that facility in learning, memory, fortitude, and
magnanimity belong to this genius." "We have." "And shall not such
an one, of all men, immediately be the first in every thing, especially
if he has a body naturally adapted to the soul?" "Why shall he not?"
said he. "And when he becomes more advanced in age, his kindred
and citizens, I think, will incline to employ him in their affairs."
494c "Why will they not?" "And making supplications to him, and paying
him homage, they will submit to him, and anticipate and flatter
beforehand his growing power." "Thus," said he, "it usually happens."

"What now," said I, "do you think such an one will do, in such a
case, especially if he happen to belong to a great city, and be rich, and
of a noble descent, and withal beautiful and of a large stature? Will he
not be filled with extravagant hopes, deeming himself capable of
494d managing both the affairs of Greek's and Barbarians, and on these
accounts carry himself loftily, without any solid judgment, full of
ostentation and vain conceit?" "Extremely so," replied he. "If one
should gently approach a man of this disposition, and tell him the
truth, that he has no judgment, yet needs it; but that it is not to be
acquired but by one who subjects himself to this acquisition, do you
think that, with all these evils about him, he would be ready to
hearken?" "Far from it," said he. "If now," said I, "through a good
494e natural temper, and an innate disposition to reason, any one should
somehow be made sensible, and be bent and drawn towards
philosophy, what do we imagine those others will do, when they
reckon they shall lose his company, and the benefit which they
received from him? Will they not by every action, and every speech,
say and do every thing to the man not to suffer himself to be
persuaded; and to his adviser, to render him incapable by ensnaring
495a him in private, and bringing him to public trial?" "This," said he,
"must of necessity happen." "Is it likely now such an one will
philosophize?" "Not altogether."

"You see then," said I, "that we were not wrong when we said that
even the very parts of the philosophic genius, when they meet with
bad education, are in some measure the cause of a falling off from this
pursuit, as well as those vulgarly reputed goods, riches, and all

furniture of this kind." "We were not," replied he, "but it was rightly said." "Such then," said I, "admirable friend! is the ruin, such and so great the corruption of the best genius for the noblest pursuit, and 495b which besides but rarely happens, as we observed; and from among 332 such as these are the men who do the greatest mischief to cities, and to private persons, and likewise they who do the greatest good, such as happen to be drawn to this side. But a little genius never did any thing remarkable to any one, neither to a private person nor to a city." "Most true," said he. "These indeed, then, whose business it chiefly 495c was to apply to philosophy, having thus fallen off, leaving her desolate and imperfect, lead themselves a life neither becoming nor genuine; whilst other unworthy persons, intruding themselves on philosophy, abandoned in a manner by her kindred, have disgraced her, and loaded her with reproaches, such as these you say her reproachers reproach her with: *viz.* that of those who converse with her, some are of no value, and most of them worthy of the greatest punishments." "These things," replied he, "are commonly said." "And with reason," replied I, "they are said. For other contemptible men seeing the field unoccupied, and that the possession of it is attended with dignities and honourable names, like persons who make their escape from 495d prisons to temples, these likewise gladly leap from their handicrafts to philosophy; I mean such of them as are of the greatest address in their own little art. For, even in this situation of philosophy, her remaining dignity, in comparison with all the other arts, still surpasses in magnificence; of which dignity many are desirous, who by natural disposition are unfit for it, and whose bodies are not only deformed by their arts and handicrafts, but whose souls also are in like manner 495e confused, and crushed by their servile works. Must it not of necessity be so?" "Undoubtedly," said he.

"Does it then appear to you," said I, "that they are any way different in appearance from a blacksmith, who has made a little money, bald and puny, recently liberated from chains, and washed in the bath, with a new robe on him, just decked out as a bridegroom, presuming to marry the daughter of his master, encouraged by the poverty and 496a forlorn circumstances with which he sees him oppressed?" "There is," said he, "no great difference." "What sort of a race must such as these produce?" "Must it not be bastardly and abject?" "By an abundant necessity. But what now? When men who are unworthy of instruction apply to it, and are conversant in it, in an unworthy manner, what kind of sentiments and opinions shall we say are produced? Must they not be such as ought properly to be termed sophisms, and which

333   possess nothing genuine, or worthy of true prudence?" "By all means so," replied he.

496b   "A very small number now," said I, "Adimantus, remains of those who worthily are conversant in philosophy, who happen either to be detained somehow in banishment, and whose generous and well cultivated disposition persists in the study of philosophy, being removed from every thing which tends to corrupt it; or else when, in a small city, a mighty soul arises, who despising the honours of the state entirely neglects them, and likewise with justice despising any small thing arising from the other arts, his well-born soul returns to philosophy. These the bridle of our friend Theagis will be sufficient to

496c   restrain; for all other things conspire to withdraw Theagis from philosophy, but the care of his health excluding him from politics makes him attentive to that alone. For as to my genius, it is not worth while to mention the dæmoniacal sign; for certainly it has happened heretofore to but one other, or to none at all. And even of these few, such as are tasting, and have tasted, how sweet and blessed the acquisition of philosophy is, and have withal sufficiently seen the madness of the multitude, and how none of them, as I may say, effects

496d   any thing salutary in the affairs of cities, and that there is no ally with whom a man might go to the assistance of the just and be safe; but that he is like one falling among wild beasts, being neither willing to join them in injustice, nor able, as he is but one, to oppose the whole savage crew; but, before he can benefit the city or his friends, is destroyed, and is unprofitable both to himself and others: reasoning on all these things, lying quiet, and attending to his own affairs, as in a tempest, when the dust is driven, and the sea agitated by winds, standing under a wall, beholding others overwhelmed in iniquity, he

496e   is satisfied if he shall himself anyhow pass his life here pure from injustice and unholy deeds, and make his exit hence in good hopes

497a   cheerful and benignant." "And he shall make his exit," said he, "after having done non of the smallest matters." "Nor the greatest neither," said I, "whilst he has not met with a republic that is suitable to him;

for, in a suitable one, he shall both make a greater proficiency himself, and shall preserve the affairs of private persons as well as of the public. It appears then, to me, that we have now sufficiently told whence it happens that philosophy is accused, and that it is so unjustly, unless you have something else to offer." "But," said he, "I say nothing further about this point. But which of the present republics do you say is adapted to philosophy?" 497b

"Not one indeed," said I; "but this is what r complain of, that there 334 is no constitution of a city at present worthy of the philosophic genius, which is therefore turned and altered, as a foreign seed sown in an improper soil, which degenerates to what is usually produced in that soil. After the same manner this race, as it has not at present its proper power, degenerates to a foreign species: but should it meet with 497c the best republic, as it is the best in itself, then shall it indeed discover that it is really divine, and that all besides are human, both as to their genius and their pursuits. But now you seem plainly to be going to ask which is this republic." "You are mistaken," said he; "for this I was not going to ask: but whether it was this which we have described in establishing our city, or another." "As to other things," said I, "it is this one, and this very thing was then mentioned, that there must always be in the city some thing which shall have the same regard for 497d the republic which you the legislator have when you establish the laws." "It was mentioned," said he. "But it was not," said I, "made sufficiently plain, through fears which preoccupied you, when you signified that the illustration of the thing would be both tedious and difficult; and it is not indeed altogether easy to discuss what remains." "What is that?" "In what manner a city shall attempt philosophy and not be destroyed; for all grand things are dangerous, and, as the saying is, fine things are truly difficult." "But however," said he, "let 497e our disquisition be completed in making this evident."

"Want of inclination," said I, "shall not hinder, though want of ability may. And being present, you shall know my alacrity, and consider now how readily and adventurously I am going to say, that a city ought to attempt this study in a way opposite to that at present." "How?" "At present," said I, "those who engage in it are striplings, 498a who immediately from their childhood, amidst their domestic affairs and lucrative employments, apply themselves to the most abstruse parts of philosophy, and then they depart most consummate philosophers. I call the most difficult part, that respecting the art of reasoning. And in all after time, if, when they are invited by others who praise this art, they are pleased to become hearers, they think it a great condescension, reckoning they ought to do it as a by-work:— but when they approach to old age, besides some few, they are 498b extinguished much more than the Heraclitean[3] sun, because they are 335 never again rekindled."

"But how should they act?" said he. "Quite the reverse. Whilst they are lads and boys they should apply to juvenile instruction and philosophy,[4] and, in taking proper care of their body, whilst it shoots and grows to firmness, provide for philosophy a proper assistant: and then, as that age advances in which the soul begins to be perfected, 498c they ought vigorously to apply to her exercises; and when strength decays, and is no longer adapted for civil and military employments, they should then be dismissed, and live at pleasure, and, excepting a by-work, do nothing else but philosophize, if they propose to live happy, and, when they die, to possess in the other world a destiny adapted to the life they have led in this."

"How truly," said he, "Socrates, do you seem to me to speak with zeal! Yet I think, the greater part of your hearers will still more zealously oppose you, and by no means be persuaded, and that Thrasymachus will be the first of them." "Do not divide," said I, 498d "Thrasymachus and me, who are now become friends; nor were we enemies heretofore. For we shall no way desist from our attempts, till we either persuade both him and the rest, or make some advances towards that life at which when they arrive they shall again meet with such discourses as these." "You have spoken," said he, "but a short time." "None at all," said I, "with respect at least to the whole of time: but that the multitude are not persuaded by what is said, is not wonderful; for they have never at any time seen existing what has now 498e been mentioned, but rather such discourses as have been industriously composed, and have not fallen in spontaneously[5] as these do at present. But as for the man who has arrived at the model of virtue, and is rendered similar to it in the most perfect manner possible both 499a in word and in deed, they have never at any time seen such a man, neither one nor more of the kind. Or do you think they have?" "By no means." "Neither yet, O blessed man! have they sufficiently attended to beautiful and liberal reasonings, so as ardently to investigate the truth, by every method, for the fake of knowing it, *336* saluting only at a distance such intricate and contentious debates, as tend to nothing else but to opinion and strife, both in their courts of justice and in their private meetings." "The case is just so," replied he.

"On these accounts then," said I, "and foreseeing these things, we *499b* were formerly afraid. However, being compelled by the truth, we did assert, that neither city nor republic, nor even a man in the same way, would ever become perfect, till some necessity of fortune oblige these few philosophers, who are at present called not depraved, but useless, to take the government of the city whether they will or not, and compel the city to be obedient to them; or till the sons of those who are now in the offices of power and magistracies, or they themselves, by some divine inspiration, be possessed with a genuine love of genuine philosophy: and I aver that no one has reason to think that *499c* either of these, or both, are impossible; for thus might we justly be laughed at, as saying things which are otherwise only similar to wishes. Is it not so?" "It is." "If then, in the infinite series of past ages, the greatest necessity has obliged men that have arrived at the summit of philosophy to take the government of a state, or such men now govern in some barbarous region, remote from our observation, or *499d* shall hereafter, we are ready in that case to contend in our reasoning, that this republic we have described has existed and subsists, and shall arise at least when this our muse shall obtain the government of the state: for this is neither impossible to happen, nor do we speak of impossibilities, though we ourselves confess that they are difficult." "I am likewise," said he, "of the same opinion."

"But you will say," replied I, "that the multitude do not think so too." "It is likely," said he. "O blessed man!" said I, "do not thus *499e* altogether accuse the multitude; but, whatever opinion they may have, without upbraiding them, but rather encouraging them, and removing the reproach thrown on philosophy, point out to them the persons you call philosophers, and define distinctly, as at present, both their genius and their pursuits, that they may not think you speak of *500a* such as they call philosophers; or, if they mean the same men, you will tell them they have conceived a different opinion of the men from what you have, and give very different answers about them from yours. Or, do you think that one man can be enraged at another, who is not in a passion? or, that a man shall envy the envious, who is himself both void of envy, and is of a mild disposition?—I will prevent you, and say that I think there is in some few such a naturally bad temper, but not in the greater part of mankind." "I likewise," said he, "think so." "Are you not then of the same opinion with me in this? That these men are the cause of the multitude being ill affected towards philosophy, who openly revile what is no way becoming them, behaving in a scoffing and distasteful manner towards the multitude, always making discourses about particular men, and doing what is least of all becoming philosophy." "Certainly, said he."

"For somehow, Adimantus, the man at least who really applies his dianoëtic part to true being, has not leisure to look down to the little affairs of mankind, and, in fighting with them, to be filled with envy and ill nature; but, beholding and contemplating such objects as are orderly, and always subsist in the same manner, such as neither injure nor are injured by each other, but are in all respects beautiful, and according to reason, these he imitates and resembles as far as possible; or, do you think it possible by any contrivance that a man should not imitate that, in convening with which he is filled with admiration?" "It is impossible," replied he. "The philosopher then who converse with that which is decorous and divine, as far as is possible for man, becomes himself decorous and divine. But calumny is powerful in every thing." "It is entirely so." "If then," said I, "he be under any necessity, not merely of forming himself alone, but likewise of endeavouring to introduce any thing he beholds there among mankind, in order to form their manners, both in private and in public life, would he prove, think you, a bad artist of temperance and of justice, and of every social virtue?" "Not at all," said he.

"But if now the multitude perceive that we say the truth of such an one, will they be angry at philosophers, and disbelieve us when we say, that the city can never otherwise be happy unless it be drawn by those painters who follow a divine original?" "They will not be angry," said he, "if they perceive so: but what method of painting do you mean?" "When they have obtained," said I, "the city and the manners of men as their canvass, they would first make it pure; which is not altogether an easy matter. But in this, you know, they differ from others, that they are unwilling to meddle either with a private man or city, or to prescribe laws, till once they either receive these pure, or purify them themselves." "And rightly," said he. "And after this, do not you think they will draw a sketch of the republic?" "Why not?" "Afterwards, I think, as they proceed in their work, they will frequently look both ways, both to what is naturally just and beautiful and temperate and the like; and likewise again to that which they can establish among mankind, blending and compounding their human form from different human characters and pursuits, drawing from this which Horner calls the divine likeness, and the divine resemblance subsisting among men." "Right," said he. "They will then, I think, strike out one thing and insert another, till they have rendered human manners, as far as is possible, dear to the Gods." "It will thus," said he, "be the most beautiful picture."

"Do we now then," said I, "any way persuade these men, who, you said, were coming upon us in battle array, that such a painter of republics is the man we then recommended to them, and on whose account they were enraged at us, that we committed cities to him, and will they now be more mild when they hear us mentioning it?" "Certainly," said he, "if they be wise: for what is there now they can further question?" "Will they say that philosophers are not lovers of real being and of truth?" "That," said he, "would be absurd." "Or that their genius, as we described it, is not allied to that which is best?" "Nor this neither." "What then? whilst their genius is such as this, and meets with suitable exercises, shall it not become perfectly good and philosophic, if any other be so? or, will you say those will be more so whom we set aside?" "Not at all." "Will they still then be enraged at us when we say that till the philosophic race have the government of the city, neither the miseries of the city nor of the citizens shall have an end, nor shall this republic, which we speak of in the way of fable, arrive in reality at perfection?" "Perhaps," said he, "they will be less enraged." "Are you willing then," said I, "that we say not of them they are less enraged at us, but that they are altogether appeased, and persuaded, that if we make no more of them, they may at least consent by their blushing?" "By all means," said he.

"Let them then," said I, "be persuaded of this. But is there any one

338

501b

501c

501d

501e

502a

who will call this into question, that those of the philosophic genius do not usually spring from kings and sovereigns?" "Not one," said he, "would allege that." "And though they were born with a philosophic genius, one may say they are under a great necessity of being corrupted; for indeed that it is a difficult matter for these geniuses to

339
502b be preserved untainted, even we ourselves agree. But that in the infinite series of time, of the whole of the human race, there should never be so much as a single one preserved pure and untainted, is there any who will contend?" "How can there be any one?" "But surely," said I, "a single one is sufficient, if he exists, and has a city subject to him, to accomplish every thing now so much disbelieved." "He is sufficient," said he. "And when the governor," said I, "has established the laws and customs we have recited, it is not at all impossible that the citizens should be willing to obey him." "Not at all." "But is it wonderful or impossible, that what appears to us should also appear to

502c others?" "I do not think it," said he. "And that these things are best, if they be possible, we have sufficiently, as I think, explained in the preceding part of our discourse." "Sufficiently indeed." "Now then it seems we are agreed about our legislation; that the laws we mention are the best, if they could exist; but that it is difficult to establish them, not, however, impossible." "We are agreed," said he.

502d　　 "After this has with difficulty been brought to a conclusion, shall we not in the next place consider what follows? In what manner, and from what disciplines and studies, they shall become the preservers of our republic? and in what periods of life they shall each of them apply to the several branches of education?" "We must indeed consider that," said he. "I acted not wisely," said I, "when in the former part of our discourse I left untouched the difficulty attending the possession of women, and the propagation of the species, and the establishing governors, knowing with what envy and difficulty they must be

502e introduced, or be carried no further than theory. For now we are under no less a necessity of discussing these things at present. What relates to women and children is already finished; and we must now go over again, as from the beginning, what refers to governors. We

503a said, if you remember, that they should appear to be lovers of the city, and be tried both by pleasures and by pains, and appear to quit this dogma neither through toils nor fears, nor any other change; and that he who was not able to do this was to be rejected; but he who came forth altogether pure, as gold tried in the fire, was to be appointed ruler, and to have honours and rewards paid him both alive and dead. Such were the things we said whilst our reasoning passed over, and concealed itself, as afraid to rouse the present argument." 503b "You say most truly," said he, "for I remember it."

"For I was averse, my friend, to say, what I must now venture to 340 assert; but now we must even dare to assert this: that the most complete guardians must be made philosophers." "Let this be agreed upon," replied he. "But consider that you will probably have but few of them: for such a genius as we said they must of necessity have, is wont but seldom in all its parts to meet in one man; but its different parts generally spring up in different persons." "How do you say?" 503c replied he. "That such as learn with facility, have a good memory, are sagacious and acute, and endued with whatever qualifications are allied to these, are not at the same time strenuous and magnificent in their dianoëtic part, so as to live orderly, with quietness and stability, but that such are carried by their acuteness wherever it happens, and every thing that is stable departs from them." "You say true," replied he. "With regard then to these firm habits of the mind, which are not all all versatile, and which one might rather employ as trusty, and 503d which are difficult to be moved at dangers in war, are they not of the same temper with reference to learning? They move heavily, and with difficulty learn, as if they were benumbed, and are oppressed with sleep and yawning, when they are obliged to labour at any thing of this kind." "It is so," replied he. "But we said that he must partake of both these well and handsomely, or else he ought not to share in the most accurate education, nor magistracy, nor honours of the state." "Right," said he. "Do not you think this will but rarely happen?" "How should it not?" "They must be tried then both in the things we 503e formerly mentioned in labours, in fears, and in pleasures; and likewise in what we then passed over, and are now mentioning; we must exercise them in various kinds of learning, whilst we consider whether their genius be capable of sustaining the greatest disciplines, or whether it fails, as those who fail in the other things." "It is proper 504a now," said he, "to consider this question at least in this manner. But what do you call the greatest disciplines?"

"You rememberer in some measure," said I, "that when we had distinguished the soul into three parts, we determined concerning justice, temperance, fortitude, and wisdom, what each of them is." "If I did not remember," said he, "it would be just I should not hear what

504b remains." "Do you likewise remember what was said before that?" "What was it?" "We somewhere said, that it was possible to behold these in their most beautiful forms, but that the journey would be

341 tedious which he must make, who would see them conspicuously; that it was possible, however, to approach towards them in the way of our demonstrations above mentioned; and you said that these were sufficient; so what was then advanced came to be spoken far short, in my own opinion, of accuracy; but, if agreeably to you, you may say so." "To me at least," said he, "they seemed to be discussed in measure;

504c and the rest seemed to think so too." "But, friend," said I, "in speaking of things of this kind, such a measure as leaves out any part whatever of the truth is not altogether in measure. For nothing that is imperfect is the measure of any thing. Though some at times are of opinion, that things are sufficiently well when thus circumstanced, and that there is no necessity for further inquiry." "Very many," said he, "are thus affected through indolence." "But the guardian of the city and of the laws," said I, "has least of all need of that passion." "It

504d appears so," replied he. "Such an one, then, my friend," said I, "must make the more ample circuit, and labour no less in learning than in the exercises: otherwise, as we were now saying, he will never arrive at the perfection of the greatest and most suitable learning."

"But are not these," said he, "the greatest? Or is there yet any thing greater than justice, and those virtues which we discussed?" "There is something greater," said I. "And even of these we must not contemplate only the rude description, but we must not omit the highest finishing. Or is it not ridiculous in other things of small

504e account to employ our whole labour, and strive to have them the most accurate and perfect, and not deem the highest and most important affairs worthy of our highest attention, in order to render them the most perfect?" "The sentiment," said he, "is very just. But, however, do you think," said he, "that any one will dismiss you without asking you, what indeed is this greatest discipline, and about what is it conversant, when you call it so?" "Not at all," said I, but do you yourself ask me; for assuredly you have not seldom heard it, and at present you either do not attend, or you intend to occasion me trouble in raising opposition. This I rather think, since you have often 505a heard at least, that the idea of the good is the greatest discipline: which idea when justice and the other virtues employ, they become useful and advantageous. You now almost know that this is what I mean to say, and besides this, that we do not sufficiently know that idea, and that without this knowledge, though we understood every 342 thing else in the highest degree, you know that it is of no advantage to us in the same manner as it would avail us nothing though we 505b possessed any thing whatever without the possession of the good: or do you think there is any greater profit in possessing all things without the possession of the good, than in knowing all things without the knowledge of the good, knowing nothing at all that is beautiful and good?" "By Jupiter, not I," said he.

"But surely this too at least you know, that to the multitude pleasure seems to be the good; and to the more elegant it seems to be prudence." "And very ridiculously," said he. "How indeed can it be otherwise?" replied I, "if, when they upbraid us that we know not 505c what is the good, they tell us that they know, and call the prudence of what is good, as if we understood what they say when they pronounce the word good." "Most true," said he. "But what? those who define pleasure to be good, do they less err than the others? or are not these too obliged to confess that pleasures are evil?" "Extremely so." "It happens then, I think, that they acknowledge the same things are 505d both good and evil, do they not?" "Undoubtedly." "Is it not evident, then, that there are great and manifold doubts about it?" "Why are there not?" "But what? is it not also evident, that with reference to things just and beautiful, the multitude choose the apparent, even though they be not really so? yet they act, and possess, and appear to possess them; but the acquisition of goods, that were only the apparent, never yet satisfied any one; but in this they seek what is real, and here every one despises what is only the apparent." "Extremely 505e so," said he. "This then is that which every soul pursues, and for the sake of this it does every thing, prophesying that it is something, but being dubious, and unable to comprehend sufficiently what it is, and to possess the same stable belief respecting it as of other things; and

506a thus are they unsuccessful also in other things, if there be in them any profit. About a thing now of such a kind, and of such mighty consequence, shall we say that even these our best men in the city, and to whom we commit the management of every thing, shall be thus in the dark?" "As little at least as possible," said he. "I think then," said I, "that whilst it is unknown in what manner the just and beautiful are good, they are not of any great value to a guardian to possess, if it be likely he shall know these, whilst he is ignorant of this; but I

343 prophesy that no one will arrive at the knowledge of these before he sufficiently knows what the good is." "You prophesy well," said he.

506b "Shall not then our republic be completely adorned, if such a guardian be placed over it as is scientifically knowing in these things?"

"It must of necessity," said he. "But with respect to yourself, whether, Socrates, do you say that the good is science, or pleasure, or something else besides these?" "You were ever," said I, "a worthy man, and manifestly showed of old that you were not to be satisfied with the opinions of others about these things." "Nor does it appear to me just, Socrates," said he, "that a man should be able to relate the dogmas of others, but not his own, after having spent so much time

506c in inquiring about these particulars." "But what," said I, "does it then appear to you just for a man to speak of things of which he is ignorant, as if he knew them?" "By no means," said he, "as if he knew them; yet however, according as he thinks, those things which he thinks he should be willing to tell us." "But what," said I, "have you not observed of opinions void of science how deformed they all are, and that the best of them are blind? Or do those who without intellect form right opinion seem to you, in any respect, to differ from those who are blind, and at the same time walk straight on the road?" "In no respect," said he. "Are you willing, then, that we should

506d examine things deformed, blind, and crooked, having it in our power to hear from others⁶ what is clear and beautiful?" "Do not, by Jupiter, Socrates," said Glauco, "desist at the end; for it will suffice us, if in the same way as you have spoken of justice and temperance, and those other virtues, you likewise discourse concerning the good." "And I too shall be very well satisfied, my friend," said I; "but I am afraid I shall not be able; and, by appearing readily disposed, I shall incur the ridicule of the unmannerly. But, O blessed man! let us at present 506e dismiss[7] this inquiry, what the good is; (for it appears to me a greater thing than we can arrive at, according to our present impulse,) but I am willing to tell you what the offspring of the good appears to be, and what most resembles it, if this be agreeable to you; and if not, I shall dismiss it." "But tell us," said he; "for you shall afterwards 344 explain to us what the father is."

"I could wish," said I, "both that I were able to give that 507a explanation, and you to receive it, and not as now the offspring only. Receive now then this child and offspring of the good itself. Yet take care however that unwillingly I deceive you not, in any respect, giving au adulterate account of this offspring." "We shall take care," said he, to the best of our ability; only tell us." "I shall tell, then," said I, "after we have thoroughly assented, and I have reminded you of what was mentioned in our preceding discourse, and has, been frequently said on other occasions." "What is it?" said he. "That there are many 507b things," said I, "beautiful, and many good, and each of these we say is so, and we distinguish them in our reasoning." "We say so." "But as to the beautiful itself, and the good itself, and in like manner concerning all those things which we then considered as many, now again establishing them according to one idea of each particular, as being one, we assign to each that appellation which belongs to it; and these indeed we say are seen by the eye, but are not objects of intellectual perception; but that the ideas are perceived by the 507c intellect, but are not seen by the eye." "Perfectly so."

"By what part then of ourselves do we see things visible?" "By the sight," said he. "And is it not," said I, "by hearing, that we perceive what is heard; and by the other senses, all the other objects of sense?" "Why not?" "But have you not observed," said I, "with regard to the artificer of the senses, how he has formed the power of sight, and of being visible, in the most perfect manner?" "I have not entirely perceived it," replied he. "But consider it in this manner. Is there any other species, which hearing and sound require, in order that the one 507d may hear, and the other be heard, which third thing if it be not present, the one shall not hear, and the other not be heard?" "There is nothing," said he. "Imagine then," said I, "that neither do many others (that I may not say none) require any such thing: or can you mention any one that does require it?" "Not I," replied he. "But with reference to the sense of seeing, and the object of sight, do not you perceive that they require something?" "How?" "When there is sight in the eyes, and when he who has it attempts to use it, and when there

507e is colour in the objects before him, unless there concur some third genus, naturally formed for the purpose, you know that the sight will see nothing, and the colours will be invisible." "What is that you

345 speak of?" said he. "What you call light," said I. "You say true," replied

508a he. "This species then is not despicable; and by no small idea are the sense of seeing, and the power of being seen, connected together; but by a bond the most honourable of all bonds, if light be not dishonourable." "But it is far," said he, "from being dishonourable."

"Whom then of the Gods in heaven can you assign as the cause of this, that light makes our sight to see, and visible objects to be seen, in the best manner?" "The same as you," said he, "and others do; for it is evident that you mean the sun." "Is not the sight then naturally formed in this manner with reference to this God?" "How?" "The sight is not the sun, nor is that the sun in which sight is ingenerated,

508b which we call the eye." "It is not." "But yet I think that of all the organs of sense it is most solar-form." "Very much so." "And the power which it possesses, does it not possess as dispensed and flowing from hence?" "Perfectly so." "Is not then the sun, which indeed is not sight itself, yet as it is the cause of it, seen by sight itself?" "It is so," said he. "Conceive then," said I, "that this is what I called the

508c offspring of *the good*, which *the good* generates, analogous to itself; and that what this is in the intelligible place, with respect to intellect, and the objects of intellect, that the sun is in the visible place with respect to sight and visible things." "How is it?" said he: "explain to me yet further."

"You know that the eyes," said I, "when they are no longer directed towards objects whose colours are shone upon by the light of day, but by the splendour of the night, grow dim, and appear almost blind, as

508d if they had in them no pure sight." "Just so," said he. "But when they turn to objects which the sun illuminates, then I think they see clearly, and in those very eyes there appears now to be sight." "There does." "Understand then, in the same manner, with reference to the soul. When it firmly adheres to that which truth and real being enlighten, then it understands and knows it, and appears to possess intellect: but when it adheres to that which is blended with darkness, which is generated, and which perishes, it is then conversant with opinion, its vision becomes blunted, it wanders from one opinion to another, and resembles one without intellect." "It has such a 508e resemblance." "That therefore which imparts truth to what is known, and dispenses the power to him who knows, you may call the idea of *the good*, being the cause of science and of truth, as being known through intellect. And as both these two, knowledge and truth, are so beautiful, when you think that *the good* is something different, and 346 still more beautiful than these, you shall think aright. Science and truth here are as light and sight there, which we rightly judged to be 509a solar-form, but that we were not to think they were the sun. So here it is right to judge, that both these partake of the form of *the good;* but to suppose that either of them is *the good*, is not right, but *the good itself* is worthy of still greater honour."

"You speak, said he, of an inestimable beauty, since it affords science and truth, but is itself superior to these in beauty. And you never any where said that it was pleasure." "Predict better things," said I, "and in this manner rather consider its image yet further." 509b "How?" "You will say, I think, that the sun imparts to things which are seen, not only their visibility, but likewise their generation, growth and nourishment, not being itself generation."[8] "Why not?" "We may say, therefore, that things which are known have not only this from *the good*, that they are known, but likewise that their being and essence are thence derived, whilst *the good* itself is not essence, but beyond essence, transcending it both in dignity and in power."[9] 509c

Here Glauco, laughing[10] very much, said, "By Apollo this is a divine 347 transcendency indeed!" "You yourself," replied I, "are the cause, having obliged me to relate what appears to me respecting it." "And 348 by no means," said he, "stop, if something does not hinder you, but again discuss the resemblance relating to the sun, if you have omitted 349 any thing." "But I omit," said I, "many things." "Do not omit," replied he, "the smallest particular." "I think," said I, "that much will be omitted: however, as far I am able at present, I shall not willingly 350 omit any thing." "Do not," said he. "Understand then," said I, "that 509d we say these are two; and that the one reigns over the intelligible 351 genus and place, and the other over the visible, not to say the heavens, lest I should seem to you to employ sophistry in the expression: you understand then these two species, the visible and the intelligible?" "I do." "As if then you took a line, cut into two unequal parts, and cut over again each section according to the same ratio, both that of the visible species, and that of the intelligible, you will then have perspicuity and obscurity placed by each other. In the visible species you will have in one section images: but I call images, in the first place, shadows, in the next, the appearances in water, and such as subsist in bodies which are dense, polished and bright, and every thing of this kind, if you understand me." "I do." "Suppose now the other section of the visible which this resembles, such as the animals around us, and every kind of plant, and whatever has a composite nature." "I suppose it," said he. "Are you willing then that this section appear to be divided into true and untrue? And that the same proportion, which the object of opinion has to the object of knowledge, the very same proportion has the resemblance to that of which it is the resemblance?" "I am, indeed," said he, "extremely willing." "But consider now again the section of the intelligible, how it was divided." "How?" "That with respect to one part of it, the soul uses the former sections as images; and is obliged to investigate from hypotheses, not proceeding to the beginning, but to the conclusion: and the other part, again, is that where the soul proceeds from hypothesis to an unhypothetical principle, and without those images about it, by the species themselves, makes its way through them." "I have not," said he, "sufficiently understood you in these things." "But again," said I, "for you will more easily understand me, these things having been premised. For I think you are not ignorant, that those who are conversant in geometry, and computations, and such like, after they have laid down hypotheses of the odd and the even, and figures, and three species of angles, and other things the sisters of these, according to each method, they then proceed upon these things as known, having laid down all these as hypotheses, and do not give any further reason about them, neither to themselves nor others, as being things obvious to all. But, beginning from these, they directly discuss the rest, and with full consent end at that which their inquiry pursued." "I know this," said he, "perfectly well." "And do you not likewise know, that when they use the visible species, and reason about them, their dianoëtic power[11] is not employed about these species, but about those of which they are the resembla $_{354}$ employing their reasonings about the square itself, and the diameter itself, and not about that which they describe? And, in the ! $_{510e}$ manner, with reference to other particulars, those very things which they form and describe, in which number, shadows and images in water are to be reckoned, these they use as images, seeking to behold those very things, which a man can no otherwise see than b $_{511a}$ dianoëtic part." "You say true," replied he.

"This then I called a species of the intelligible; but observed that the soul was obliged to use hypotheses in the investigation of it, not going back to the principle, as not being able to ascend higher than hypotheses, but made use of images formed from things below, to lead to those above, as perspicuous, as objects of opinion, and distinct from the things themselves." "I understand," said he, "that you speak $_{511b}$ of things pertaining to the geometrical, and other sister arts." "Understand now, that by the other section of the intelligible, I mean that which reason itself attains, making hypotheses by its own reasoning power not as principles, but really hypotheses, as steps and handles, that, proceeding as far as to that which is unhypothetical, *viz.* the principle of the universe, and coming into contact with it, again adhering to those things which adhere to the principle, it may thus descend to the end; using no where any thing which is sensible, $_{511c}$ but forms themselves, proceeding through some to others, and at length in forms terminating its progression."[12] "I understand," said he, "but not sufficiently. For you seem to me to speak of an arduous $_{355}$ undertaking: but you want, however, to determine that the perception of real being, and that which is intelligible, by the science of reasoning, are more conspicuous than the discoveries made by the arts, as they are called, which have hypotheses for their first principles; and that those who behold these are obliged to behold them with their dianoëtic power, and not with their senses. But as they are not $_{511d}$ able to perceive, by ascending to the principle, but from hypotheses, they appear to you not to possess intellect respecting them, though they are intelligible in conjunction with the principle. You also appear to me to call the habit of geometrical and such like concerns, the dianoëtic part, and not intellect;[13] the dianoëtic part subsisting between opinion and intellect." "You have comprehended," said I, "most sufficiently: and conceive now, that corresponding to the four sections then: are these four passions in the soul; intelligence answering to the highest, the dianoëtic part to the second; and assign faith to the third; and to the last assimilation. Arrange them likewise analogously; conceiving that as their objects participate of truth so these participate of perspicuity." "I understand," said he, "and I assent, and I arrange them as you say."

511e

THE END OF THE SIXTH BOOK

BOOK VII.

"After these things now," said I, "assimilate, with reference to 514a
erudition, and the want of erudition, our nature to such a condition
as follows. Consider men as in a subterraneous habitation, resembling
a cave, with its entrance expanding to the light, and answering to the
whole extent of the cave. Suppose them to have been in this cave from
their childhood, with chains both on their legs and necks, so as to
remain there, and only be able to look before them, but by the chain 514b
incapable to turn their heads round. Suppose them likewise to have
the light of a fire, burning far above and behind them; and that
between the fire and the fettered men there is a road above. Along
this road, observe a low wall built, like that which hedges in the stage
of mountebanks on which they exhibit their wonderful tricks." "I
observe it," said he. "Behold now, along this wall, men bearing all 514c
sorts of utensils, raised above the wall, and human statues, and other 515a
animals, in wood and stone, and furniture of every kind. And, as is
likely, some of those who are carrying these are speaking, and others
silent." "You mention," said he, "a wonderful comparison, and
wonderful fettered men." "But such, however, as resemble us," said I;
"for, in the first place, do you think that such as these see any thing of
themselves, or of one another, but the shadows formed by the fire,
falling on the opposite part of the cave?" "How can they," said he, "if
through the whole of life they be under a necessity, at least, of having 515b
their heads unmoved?" "But what do they see of what is carrying
along? Is it not the very same?" "Why not?" "If then they were able to

converse with one another, do not you think they would deem it proper to give names to those very things which they saw before them?" "Of necessity they must." "And what if the opposite part of this prison had an echo, when any of those who passed along spoke, do you imagine they would reckon that what spoke was any thing else than the passing shadow?" "Not I, by Jupiter!" said he. "Such as these then," said I, "will entirely judge that there is nothing true but the shadows of utensils." "By an abundant necessity," replied he.

"With reference then, both to their freedom from these chains, and their cure of this ignorance, consider the nature of it, if such a thing should happen to them. When any one should be loosed, and obliged on a sudden to rise up, turn round his neck, and walk and look up towards the light; and in doing all these things should be pained, and unable from the splendours, to behold the things of which he formerly saw the shadows, what do you think he would say, if one should tell him that formerly he had seen trifles, but now, being some what nearer to reality, and turned toward what was more real, he saw with more rectitude; and so, pointing out to him each of the things passing along, should question him, and oblige him to tell what it was; do not you think he would be both in doubt, and would deem what he had formerly seen to be more true than what was now pointed out to him?" "By far," said he.

"And if he should oblige him to look to the light itself, would not he find pain in his eyes, and shun it; and, turning to such things as he is able to behold, reckon that these are really more clear than those pointed out?" "Just so," replied he. "But if one," said I, "should drag him from thence violently through a rough and steep ascent, and never stop till he drew him up to the light of the sun, would he not, whilst he was thus drawn, both be in torment, and be filled with indignation? And after he had even come to the light, having his eyes filled with splendour, he would be able to see none of these things now called true." "He would not," said he, "suddenly at least." "But he would require, I think, to be accustomed to it some time, if he were to perceive things above. And, first of all, he would most easily perceive shadows, afterwards the images of men and of other things in water, and after that the things themselves. And, with reference to these, he would more easily see the things in the heavens, and the heavens

themselves, by looking in the night to the light of the stars, and the 516b
moon, than by day looking on the sun, and the light of the sun."
"How can it be otherwise?" "And, last of all, he may be able, I think,
to perceive and contemplate the sun himself, not in water, nor
resemblances of him, in a foreign seat, but himself by himself, in his 359
own proper region." "Of necessity," said he. "And after this, he would
now reason with himself concerning him, that it is he who gives the
seasons, and years, and governs all things in the visible place; and that 516c
of all those things which he formerly saw, he is in a certain manner
the cause." "It is evident," said he, "that after these things he may
arrive at such reasonings as these." "But what? when he remembers his
first habitation, and the wisdom which was there, and those who were
then his companions in bonds, do you not think he will esteem
himself happy by the change, and pity them?" "And that greatly."
"And if there were there any honours and encomiums and rewards
among themselves, for him who most acutely perceived what passed
along, and best remembered which of them were wont to pass
foremost, which latest, and which of them went together; and from 516d
these observations were most able to presage what was to happen; does
it appear to you that he will be desirous of such honours, or envy those
who among these are honoured, and in power? Or, will he not rather
wish to suffer that of Homer, and vehemently desire

> As labourer to some ignoble man.
> To work for hire . . . .

and rather suffer any thing than to possess such opinions, and live 516e
after such a manner?" "I think so," replied he, "that he would suffer,
and embrace any thing rather than live in that manner."

"But consider this further," said I: "If such an one should descend,
and sit down again in the same seat, would not his eyes be filled with
darkness, in consequence of coming suddenly from the sun?" "Very
much so," replied he. "And should he now again be obliged to give
his opinion of those shadows, and to dispute about them with those
who are there eternally chained, whilst yet his eyes were dazzled, and 517a
before they recovered their former state, (which would not be effected
in a short time) would he not afford them laughter? and would it not
be said of him, that, having ascended, he was returned with vitiated

eyes, and that it was not proper even to attempt to go above, and that whoever should attempt to liberate them, and lead them up; if ever they were able to get him into their hands; should be put to death?" *360* "They would by all means," said he, "put him to death."

"The whole of this image now," said I, "friend Glauco, "is to be *517b* applied to our preceding discourse; for, if you compare this region, which is seen by the sight, to the habitation of the prison; and the light of the fire in it, to the power of the sun; and the ascent above, and the vision of things above, to the soul's ascent into the intelligible place; you will apprehend my meaning, since you want to hear it. But God knows whether it be true. Appearances then present themselves to my view as follows. In the intelligible place, the idea of *517c* *the good* is the last object of vision, and is scarcely to be seen; but if it be seen, we must collect by reasoning that it is the cause to all of every thing right and beautiful, generating in the visible place, light, and its lord the sun; and in the intelligible place, it is itself the lord, producing truth and intellect;' and this must be beheld by him who is *361* to act wisely, either privately or in public." "I agree with you," said he, "as far as I am able." "Come now," said I, "and agree with me likewise *362* in this. And do not wonder that such as arrive hither are unwilling to *517d* act in human affairs, but their souls always hasten to converse with things above; for it is somehow reasonable it should be so, if these things take place according to our above mentioned image." "It is indeed reasonable," replied he. "But what? do you think that this is any thing wonderful, that when a man comes from divine contemplations to human evils, he should behave awkwardly and appear extremely ridiculous, whilst he is yet dazzled, and is obliged, before he is sufficiently accustomed to the present darkness, to contend in courts of justice, or elsewhere, about the shadows of justice, or those statues which occasion the shadows; and to dispute *517e* about this point, how these things are apprehended by those who have never at any time beheld justice itself?" "This is not at all wonderful," *518a* said he. "But if a man possesses intellect," said I, "he must remember, that there is a two-fold disturbance of the sight, and arising from two causes, when we betake ourselves from light to darkness, and from darkness to light: and when a man considers that these very things happen with reference also to the soul, whenever he sees any one disturbed, and unable to perceive any thing, he will not laugh in an unreasonable manner, but will consider, whether the soul, coming from a more splendid life, be darkened by ignorance, or, going from 518b abundant ignorance to one more luminous, be filled with the dazzling splendour, and so will congratulate the one on its fate and life, and compassionate the life and fate of the other. And if he wishes to laugh at the soul that goes from darkness to light, his laughter would be less improper, than if he were to laugh at the soul which descends from the light to darkness." "You say very reasonably," replied he.

"It is proper then," said I, "that we judge of them after such a manner as this, if those things be true. That education is not such a thing as some announce it to be; for they somehow say, that whilst 518c there is no science in the soul, they will insert it, as if they were inserting sight in blind eyes." "They say so," replied he. "But our present reasoning," said I, "now shows, that this power being in the soul of every one, and the organ by which every one learns, and being in the same condition as the eye, if it were unable otherwise, than 363 with the whole body, to turn from darkness to light, must, in like manner, with the whole soul, be turned from generation, till it be able to endure the contemplation of being itself, and the most splendid of being; and this we call *the good*. Do we not?" "We do." 518d "This then," said I, "would appear to be the art of his conversion, in what manner he shall, with greatest ease and advantage, be turned. Not to implant in him the power of seeing, but considering him as possessed of it, only improperly situated, and not looking at what he ought, to contrive some method by which this may be accomplished." "It seems so," replied he.

"The other virtues now then of the soul, as they are called, seem to be somewhat resembling those of the body (for when, in reality, they 518e were not in it formerly, they are afterwards produced in it by habits and exercises); but that of wisdom, as it seems, happens to be of a nature somewhat more divine than any other; as it never loses its power, but, according as it is turned, is useful and advantageous, or 519a useless and hurtful. Or have you not observed of those who are said to be wicked, yet wise, how sharply the little soul sees, and how acutely it comprehends every thing to which it is turned, as having no contemptible sight, but compelled to be subservient to wickedness: so that the more acutely it sees, so much the more productive is it of wickedness?" "Entirely so," replied he. "But however," said I, "with reference to this part of such a genius; if, immediately from childhood, it should be stripped of every thing allied to generation, as 519b leaden weights, and of all those pleasures and lusts which relate to feastings and such like, which turn the sight of the soul to things downwards; from all these, if the soul, being freed, should turn itself towards truth, the very same principle in the same men would most acutely see those things as it now does these to which it is turned." "It is likely," replied he. "But what? is not this likely," said I, "and necessarily deduced from what has been mentioned? that neither those who are uninstructed and unacquainted with truth can ever 519c sufficiently take care of the city; nor yet those who allow themselves to spend the whole of their time in learning. The former, because they have no one scope in life, aiming at which they ought to do whatever they do, both in private and in public; and the latter, because they are not willing to manage civil affairs, thinking that 364 whilst they are yet alive, they inhabit the islands of the blessed." "True," said he.

"It is our business then," said I, "to oblige those of the inhabitants who have the best geniuses, to apply to that learning which we 519d formerly said was the greatest, both to view *the good*, and to ascend that ascent; and when they have ascended and sufficiently viewed it, we are not to allow them what is now allowed them." "What is that?" "To continue there," said I, "and be unwilling to descend again to those fettered men, or share with them in their toils and honours, whether more trifling or more important." "Shall we then," said he, "act unjustly towards them, and make them live a worse life when 519e they have it in their power to live a better?" "You have again forgot, friend," said I, "that this is not the legislator's concern, in what manner any one tribe in the city shall live remarkably happy; but this he endeavours to effectuate in the whole city, connecting the citizens together; and by necessity, and by persuasion,, making them share the 520a advantage with one another with which they are severally able to benefit the community: and the legislator, when he makes such men in the city, does it not that he may permit them to go where each may incline, but that himself may employ them for connecting the city together." "True," said he "I forgot indeed."

"Consider then," said I, "Glauco, that we shall no way injure the philosophers who arise among us, but tell them what is just, when we oblige them to take care of others; and to be guardians. We will allow, 520b indeed, that those who in other cities become philosophers, with reason do not participate of the toils of public offices in the state (for they spring up of themselves, the policy of each city opposing them, and it is just, that what springs of itself, owing its growth to none, should not be forward to pay for its nurture to any one); but you have we generated both for yourselves, and for the rest of the state, as the leaders and kings in a hive, and have educated you better, and in a 520c more perfect manner than they, and made you more capable of sharing both in the rewards and labours attending public offices. Every one then must, in part, descend to the dwelling of the others, and accustom himself to behold obscure objects: for, when you are accustomed to them, you will infinitely better perceive things there, and will fully know the several images what they are, and of what, from your having perceived the truth concerning things beautiful, and just, and good. And thus, as a real vision, both to us and you, shall 365 the city he inhabited, and not as a dream, as most cities are at present inhabited by such as both fight with one another about shadows, and 520d raise sedition about governing, as if it were some mighty good. But the truth is as follows: in whatever city those who are to govern, are the most averse to undertake government, that city, of necessity, will be the best established, and the most free from sedition; and that city whose governors are of a contrary character, will be in a contrary condition." "Entirely so," replied he.

"Do you think then that our pupils will disobey us, when they hear these injunctions, and be unwilling to labour jointly in the city, each bearing a part, but spend the most of their time with one another, free from public affairs?" "Impossible," said he. "For we prescribe just 520e things to just men. And each of them enters on magistracy from this consideration beyond all others, that they are under a necessity of governing after a manner contrary to all the present governors of all other cities." "For thus it is, my companion," said I, "if you discover a life for those who are to be our governors, better than that of

521a governing, then it will be possible for you to have the city well established; for in it alone shall those govern who are truly rich, not in gold, but in that in which a happy man ought to be rich, in a good and prudent life. But if, whilst they are poor, and destitute of goods of their own, they come to the public, thinking they ought thence to pillage good, it is not possible to have the city rightly established. For the contest being who shall govern, such a war being domestic, and within them, it destroys both themselves; and the rest of the city."

521b "Most true," said he. "Have you then," said I, "any other kind of life which despises public magistracies, but that of true philosophy?" "No, by Jupiter!" said he. "But, however, they ought at least not to be fond of governing who enter on it, otherwise the rivals will fight about it." "How can it be otherwise?" "Whom else then will you oblige to enter on the guardianship of the city, but such as are most intelligent in those things by which the city is best established, and who have other honours, and a life better than the political one?" "No others," said he.

521c   "Are you willing then, that we now consider this, by what means such men shall be produced, and how one shall bring them into the light, as some are said, from Hades, to have ascended to the Gods?" "Why should I not be willing?" replied he. "This now, as it seems, is

366 not the turning of a shell;[2] but the conversion of the soul coming from some benighted day, to the true re-ascent to real being, which we say is true philosophy." "Entirely so." "Ought we not then to

521d consider which of the disciplines possesses such a power?" "Why not?" "What now, Glauco, may that discipline of the soul be, which draws her from that which is generated towards being itself? But this I consider whilst I am speaking. Did not we indeed say, that it was necessary for them, whilst young, to be wrestlers in war?" "We said so." "It is proper then, that this discipline likewise be added to that which is now the object of our inquiry." "Which?" "Not to be useless to military men." "It must indeed," said he, "be added if possible."

521e "They were somewhere in our former discourse instructed by us in gymnastic and music." "They were," replied he. "Gymnastic indeed somehow respects what is generated and destroyed, for it presides over the increase and corruption of body." "It seems so." "This then

522a cannot be the discipline which we investigate." "It cannot." "Is it music then, such as we formerly described?" "But it was," said he, "as a counterpart of gymnastic, if you remember, by habits instructing our guardians, imparting no science, but only with respect to harmony, a certain propriety, and with regard to rhythm, a certain propriety of rhythm, and in discourses, certain other habits the sisters of these, both in such discourses as are fabulous, and in such as are nearer to truth. But as to a discipline respecting such a good as you now 522b investigate, there was nothing of this in that music."

"You have, most accurately," said I, "reminded me; for it treated, in reality, of no such thing. But, divine Glauco, what may this discipline be? For all the arts have somehow appeared to be mechanical and illiberal." "How should they not? And what other discipline remains distinct from music, gymnastic, and the arts?" "Come," said I, "if we have nothing yet further besides these to take, let us take something 522c in these which extends over them all." "What is that?" "Such as this general thing, which all arts, and dianoëtic powers, and sciences employ, and which every one ought, in the first place, necessarily to learn." "What is that?" said he. "This trifling thing," said I, "to know completely one, and two, and three: I call this summarily number, 367 and computation. Or is it not thus with reference to these, that every art, and likewise every science, must of necessity participate of these?" "They must of necessity," replied he. "And must not the art of war likewise participate of them?" "Of necessity," said he.

"Palamedes then, in the tragedies, shows every where Agamemnon 522d to have been at least a most ridiculous general; or have you not observed how he says, that having invented numeration, he adjusted the ranks in the camp at Troy, and numbered up both the ships, and all the other forces which were not numbered before; and Agamemnon, as it seems, did not even know how many foot he had, as he understood not how to number them: but what kind of general do you imagine him to be?" "Some absurd one, for my part," replied he, "if this were true."

"Is there any other discipline then," said I, "which we shall 522e establish as more necessary to a military man, than to be able to compute and to number?" "This most of all," said he, "if he would any way understand how to range his troops, and still more if he is to be a man." "Do you perceive then," said I, "with regard to this

523a discipline the same thing as I do?" "What is that?" "It seems to belong to those things which we are investigating, which naturally lead to intelligence, but that no one uses it aright, being entirely a conductor towards real being." "How do you say?" replied he. "I shall endeavour," said I, "to explain at least my own opinion. With reference to those things which I distinguish with myself into such as lead towards intelligence, and such as do not, do you consider them along with me, and either agree or dissent, in order that we may more distinctly see, whether this be such as I conjecture respecting it."—"Show me," said he.

"I show you then," said I, "if you perceive some things with relation
523b to the senses, which call not intelligence to the inquiry, as they are sufficiently determined by sense, but other things which by all means call upon it to inquire, as sense does nothing sane." "You plainly mean," said he, "such things as appear at a distance, and such as are painted." "You have not altogether," said I, "apprehended my meaning." "Which then," said he, "do you mean?" "Those things,"
523c said I, "call not upon intelligence, which do not issue in a contrary sensation at one and the same time; but such as issue in this manner, I establish to be those which call upon intelligence: since here sense manifests the one sensation no more than its contrary, whether it meet with it near, or at a distance. But you will understand my
368 meaning more plainly in this manner. These, we say, are three fingers, the little finger, the next to it, and the middle finger." "Plainly so," replied he.

"Consider me then as speaking of them when seen near, and take notice of this concerning them." "What?" "Each of them alike
523d appears to be a finger, and in this there is no difference, whether it be seen in the middle or in the end; whether it be white or black, thick or slender, or any thing else of this kind; for in all these, the soul of the multitude is under no necessity to question their intellect what is a finger; for never does sight itself at the same time intimate finger to be finger, and its contrary." "It does not," replied he. "Is it not likely then," said I, "that such a case as this at least shall neither call upon
523e nor excite intelligence?" "It is likely." "But what? with reference to their being great and small, does the sight sufficiently perceive this, and makes it no difference to it, that one of them is situated in the

middle, or at the end; and in like manner with reference to their thickness and slenderness, their softness and hardness, does the touch sufficiently perceive these things; and in like manner the other senses, do they no way defectively manifest such things? Or does each of them act in this manner? First of all, must not that sense which 524a relates to hard, of necessity relate likewise to soft; and feeling these, it reports to the soul, as if both hard and soft were one and the same?" "It does." "And must not then the soul again," said I, "in such cases, of necessity be in doubt, what the sense points out to it as hard, since it calls the same thing soft likewise; and so with reference to the sense relating to light and heavy; the soul must be in doubt what is light and what is heavy; if the sense intimates that heavy is light, and that light is heavy?" "These at least," said he, "are truly absurd reports to 524b the soul, and stand in need of examination."

"It is likely then," said I, "that first of all, in such cases as these, the soul, calling in reason and intelligence, endeavours to discover, whether the things reported be one, or whether they be two." "Why not?" "And if they appear to be two, each of them appears to be one, and distinct from the other." "It does." "And if each of them be one, and both of them two, he will by intelligence perceive two distinct; for, if they were not distinct, he could not perceive two, but only 524c one." "Right." "The sight in like manner, we say, perceives great and small, but not as distinct from each other, but as something confused. Does it not?" "It does." "In order to obtain perspicuity in this affair, 369 intelligence is obliged again to consider great and small, not as confused, but distinct, after a manner contrary to the sense of sight." "True." "And is it not from hence, somehow, that it begins to question us, What then is great, and what is small?" "By all means." "And so we have called the one intelligible, and the other visible." "Very right," said he. "This then is what I was just now endeavouring 524d to express, when I said, that some things call on the dianoëtic part, and others do not: and such as fall on the sense at the same time with their contraries, I define to be such as require intelligence, but such as do not, do not excite intelligence." "I understand now," said he, "and it appears so to me."

"What now? with reference to number and unity, to which of the two classes do you think they belong?" "I do not understand," replied

he. "But reason by analogy," said I, "from what we have already said:
524e for, if unity be of itself sufficiently seen, or be apprehended by any
other sense, it will not lead towards real being, as we said concerning
finger. But if there be always seen at the same time something
contrary to it, so as that it shall no more appear unity than the
contrary, it would then require some one to judge of it: and the soul
would be under a necessity to doubt within itself, and to inquire,
525a exciting the conception within itself, and to interrogate it what this
unity is. And thus the discipline which relates to unity would be of the
class of those which lead, and turn the soul to the contemplation of
real being."

"But indeed this at least," said he, "is what the very sight of it
effects in no small degree: for we behold the same thing, at one and
the same time, as one and as an infinite multitude." "And if this be
the case with reference to unity," said I, "will not every number be
affected in the same manner?" "Why not?" "But surely both
525b computation and arithmetic wholly relate to number." "Very much
so." "These then seem to lead to truth." "Transcendently so." "They
belong then, as it seems, to those disciplines which we are
investigating. For the soldier must necessarily learn these things, for
the disposing of his ranks; and the philosopher for the attaining to
real being, emerging from generation, or he can never become a
reasoner." "It is so," replied he. "But our guardian at least happens to
be both a soldier and a philosopher." "Undoubtedly." "It would be
proper then, Glauco, to establish by law this discipline, and to
525c persuade those who are to manage the greatest affairs of the city to
370 apply to computation, and study it, not in a common way, but till by
intelligence itself they arrive at the contemplation of the nature of
numbers, not for the sake of buying, nor of selling, as merchants and
retailers, but both for war, and for facility in the energies of the soul
itself, and its conversion from generation to truth and essence."
"Most beautifully said," replied he.

"And surely now, I perceive likewise," said I, "at present whilst this
525d discipline respecting computations is mentioned, how elegant it is,
and every way advantageous towards our purpose, if one applies to it
for the sake of knowledge, and not with a view to traffic!" "Which
way?" replied he. "This very thing which we now mentioned, how

vehemently does it somehow lead up the soul, and compel it to reason about numbers themselves, by no means admitting, if a man in reasoning with it shall produce numbers which have visible and tangible bodies! For you know of some who are skilled in these 525e things, and who, if a man in reasoning should attempt to divide unity itself, would both ridicule him, and not admit it; but if you divide it into parts, they multiply them, afraid lest anyhow unity should appear not to be unity, but many parts." "You say," replied he, "most true."

"What think you now, Glauco, if one should ask them: O 526a admirable men! about what kind of numbers are you reasoning? in which there is unity, such as you think fit to approve, each whole equal to each whole, and not differing in the smallest degree, having no part in itself, what do you think they would answer?" "This, as I suppose; that they mean such numbers as can be conceived by the dianoëtic part alone, but cannot be comprehended in any other way." "You see then, my friend," said I, "that in reality this discipline appears to be necessary for us, since it seems to compel the soul to 526b employ intelligence itself in the perception of truth itself." "And surely now," said he, "it effects this in a very powerful degree." "But what? have you hitherto considered this? that those who are naturally skilled in computation appear to be acute in all disciplines; and such as are naturally slow, if they be instructed and exercised in this, though they derive no other advantage, yet at the same time all of them proceed so far as to become more acute than they were before." "It is so," replied he. "And surely, as I think, you will not easily find any 526c thing, and not at all many, which occasion greater labour to the learner and student than this." "No, indeed." "On all these accounts then, this discipline is not to be omitted, but the best geniuses are to 371 be instructed in it." "I agree," said he.

"Let this one thing then," said I, "be established among us; and, in the next place, let us consider if that which is consequent to this in any respect pertains to us." "What is it?" said he: "or, do you mean geometry?" "That very thing," said I. "As far," said he, "as it relates to 526d warlike affairs, it is plain that it belongs to us; for, as to encampments, and the occupying of ground, contrasting and extending an army, and all those figures into which they form armies, both in battles and in marches, the same man would differ from himself when he is a geometrician, and when he is not." "But surely now," said I, "for such purposes as these, some little geometry and some portion of computation might suffice: but we must inquire, 526e whether much of it, and great advances in it, would contribute any thing to this great end, to make us more easily perceive the idea of the good. And we say that every thing contributes to this, that obliges the soul to turn itself towards that region in which is the most divine of being, which it must by all means perceive." "You say right," replied he. "If therefore it compel the soul to contemplate essence, it belongs to us; but if it oblige it to contemplate generation, it does not belong 527a to us." "We say so indeed." "Those then who are but a little conversant in geometry," said I, "will not dispute with us this point at least, that this science is perfectly contrary to the common modes of speech, employed in it by those who practise it." "How?" said he. "They speak somehow very ridiculously, and through necessity: for all the discourse they employ in it appears to be with a view to operation, and to practice. Thus they speak of making a square, of prolonging, of 527b adjoining, and the like. But yet the whole of this discipline is somehow studied for the sake of knowledge." "By all means indeed," said he.

"Must not this further be assented to?" "What?" "That it is the knowledge of that which always is, and not of that which is sometimes generated and destroyed." "This," said he, "must be granted; for geometrical knowledge is of that which always is." "It would seem then, generous Glauco, to draw the soul towards truth, and to be productive of a dianoëtic energy adapted to a philosopher, so as to raise this power of the soul to things above, instead of causing it improperly, as at present, to contemplate things below." "As much 527c as possible," replied he. "As much as possible then," said I, "must we give orders, that those in this most beautiful city of yours by no means 372 omit geometry; for even its by-works are not inconsiderable." "What by-works?" said he. "Those," said I, "which you mentioned relating to war; and indeed with reference to all disciplines, as to the understanding of them more handsomely, we know somehow, that the having learned geometry or not, makes every way an entire difference." "Every way, by Jupiter!" said he. "Let us then establish this second discipline for the youth." "Let us establish it," replied he.

"But what? shall we, in the third place, establish astronomy? or are 527d
you of a different opinion?" "I am," said he, "of the same: for to be
well skilled in the seasons of months and years, belongs not only to
agriculture and navigation, but equally to the military art." "You are
pleasant," said I, "as you seem to be afraid of the multitude, lest you
should appear to enjoin useless disciplines: but this is not altogether a
contemptible thing, though it is difficult to persuade them, that by
each of these disciplines a certain organ of the soul is both purified
and exsuscitated, which is blinded and buried by studies of another 527e
kind; an organ better worth saving than ten thousand eyes, since
truth is perceived by this alone. To such therefore as are of the same
opinion, you will very readily appear to reason admirably well: but
such as have never observed this will probably think you say nothing
at all: for they perceive no other advantage in these things worthy of
attention. Consider now from this point, with which of these two you
will reason; or carry on the reasonings with neither of them, but 528a
principally for your own sake, yet envy not another, if any one shall
be able to be benefited by them." "In this manner," replied he, "I
choose, on my own account principally both to reason, and to
question and answer."

"Come then," said I, "let us go back again: for we have not rightly
taken that which is consequent to geometry." "How have we taken?"
replied he. "After a plain surface," said I, "we have taken a solid,
moving in a circle, before we considered it by itself: but if we had 528b
proceeded rightly we should have taken the third argument
immediately after the second, and that is some how the argument of
cubes, and what participates of depth." "It is so," replied he. "But these
things, Socrates, seem not yet to be discovered." "The reason of it,"
said I, "is two-fold. Because there is no city which sufficiently honours
them, they are slightly investigated, being difficult; and besides, those
who do investigate them want a leader, without which they cannot
discover them. And this leader is in the first place hard to be obtained; 373
and when he is obtained, as things are at present, those who
investigate these particulars, as they conceive magnificently of
themselves, will not obey him. But if the whole city presided over 528c
these things, and held them in esteem, such as inquired into them
would be obedient, and their inquiries, being carried on with

assiduity and vigour, would discover themselves what they were: since even now, whilst they are on the one hand despised and mutilated by the multitude, and on the other by those who study them without being able to give any account of their utility, they yet forcibly, under 528d all these disadvantages, increase through their native grace: nor is it wonderful that they do so." "Because truly," said he, "this grace is very remarkable. But tell me more plainly what you were just now saying; for somehow that study which respects a plain surface you called geometry." "I did," said I. "And then," said he, "you mentioned astronomy in the first place after it. But afterwards you drew back." "Because, whilst I am hastening," said I, "to discuss all things rapidly, I advance more slowly. For that augment by depth which was next according to method we passed over, because the investigation of it is 528e ridiculous; and after geometry we mentioned astronomy, which is the circular motion of a solid." "You say right," replied he.

"We establish then," said I, "astronomy as the fourth discipline, supposing that to subsist which we have now omitted, if the city shall enter upon it." "It is reasonable," said he. "And now that you agree with me, Socrates, I proceed in my commendation of astronomy, 529a which you formerly reproved as unseasonable. For it is evident, I conceive, to every one, that this discipline compels the soul to look to that which is above, and from the things here conducts it thither." "It is probable," said I, "that it is evident to every one but to me. For to me it does not appear so." "How then do you think of it?" replied he. "In the way it is now pursued by those who introduce it into philosophy, it entirely makes the soul to look downwards." "How do you say?" replied he. "You seem to me," said I, "to have formed with yourself no ignoble opinion of the discipline respecting things above, 529b what it is: for you seem to think, that if any one contemplates the various bodies in the firmament, and, by earnestly looking up, apprehends every thing, you think that he has intelligence of these things; and does not merely see them with his eyes; and perhaps you 374 judge right, and I foolishly. For I, on the other hand, am not able to conceive, that any other discipline can make the soul look upwards, but that which respects being, and that which is invisible; and if a man undertakes to learn any thing of sensible objects, whether he gape upwards, or bellow downwards, never shall I say that he learns;

for I aver he has no science of these things, nor shall I say that his soul looks upwards, but downwards, even though he should learn lying on 529c his back, either at land or at sea."

"I am punished," said he; "for you have justly reproved me. But which was the proper way, said you, of learning astronomy different from the methods adopted at present, if they mean to learn it with advantage for the purposes we speak of?" "In this manner," said I, "that these variegated bodies in the heavens, as they are varied in a visible subject, be deemed the most beautiful and the most accurate of 529d the kind, but far inferior to real beings, according to those orbits in which real velocity, and real slowness, in true number, and in all true figures, are carried with respect to one another, and carry all things that are within them. Which things truly are to be comprehended by reason and the dianoëtic power, but not by sight; or do you think they can?" "By no means," replied he. "Is not then," said I, "that variety in the heavens to be made use of as a paradigm for learning those real things, in the same manner as if one should meet with 529e geometrical figures, drawn remarkably well and elaborately by Dædalus, or some other artist or painter? For a man who was skilled in geometry, on seeing these, would truly think the workmanship most excellent, yet would esteem it ridiculous to consider these things seriously, as if from thence he were to learn the truth, as to what were 530a in equal, in duplicate, or in any other proportion." "Why would it not be ridiculous?" replied he. "And do not you then think, that he who is truly an astronomer is affected in the same manner, when he looks up to the orbits of the planets? And that he reckons that the heavens and all in them are indeed established by the demiurgus of the heavens, in the most beautiful manner possible for such works to be established; but would not he deem him absurd, who should imagine that this proportion of night with day, and of both these to a month, and of a month to a year, and of other stars to such like things, and towards 530b one another, existed always in the same manner, and in no way suffered any change, though they have a body, and are visible; and search by every method to apprehend the truth of these things?" "So it 375 appears to me," replied he, "whilst I am hearing you." "Let us then make use of problems," said I, "in the study of astronomy, as in geometry. And let us dismiss the heavenly bodies, if we intend truly to 530c apprehend astronomy, and render profitable instead of unprofitable that part of the soul which is naturally wise." "You truly enjoin a much harder task on astronomers," said he, "than is enjoined them at present." "And I think," replied I, "that we must likewise enjoin other things, in the same manner, if we are to be of any service as law-givers. But can you suggest any of the proper disciplines?" "I can suggest none," replied he, "at present at least."

530d "Lation," said I, "as it appears to me, affords us not one indeed, but many species of discipline. All of which any wise man can probably tell; but those which occur to me are two." "What are they?" "Together with this," said I, "there is its counter-part." "Which?" "As the eyes," said I, "seem to be fitted to astronomy, so the ears seem to be fitted to harmonious lation. And these seem to be sister sciences to one another, both as the Pythagoreans say, and we, Glauco, agree 530e with them, or how shall we do?" "Just so," replied he. "Shall we not," said I, "since this is their great work, inquire how they speak concerning them—and, if there be any other thing besides these, inquire into it likewise? But above all these things, we will still guard that which is our own." "What is that?" "That those we educate never attempt at any time to learn any of those things in an imperfect manner, and not pointing always at that mark to which all ought to 531a be directed: as we now mentioned with reference to astronomy. Or do not you know that they do the same thing with regard to harmony, as in astronomy? For, whilst they measure one with another the symphonies and sounds which are heard, they labour like the astronomers unprofitably." "Nay, by the gods," said he, "and ridiculously too, whilst they frequently repeat certain notes, and often with their ears to catch the sound as from a neighbouring place; and some of them say they hear some middle note, but that the interval which measures them is the smallest; and others again doubt this, and 531b say that the notes are the same as were sounded before; and both parties subject the intellect to the ears." "But you speak," said I, "of the lucrative musicians, who perpetually harass and torment their strings, and turn them on the pegs. But that the comparison may not 376 be too tedious, I shall say nothing of their complaints of the strings, their refusals and stubbornness, but bring the image to an end. But I say we ought not to choose these to speak of harmony, but those true musicians whom we mentioned. For these do the same things here as the others did in astronomy; for in these symphonies which are heard, they search for numbers, but they pass not thence to the problems, to inquire what numbers are symphonious, and what are not, and the reason why they are either the one or the other." "You speak," said he, "of a divine work." "It is then indeed profitable," said I, "in the search of the beautiful and good, but if pursued in another manner it is unprofitable." "It is likely," said he. 531c

"But I think," said I, "that the proper method of inquiry into all these things, if it reach their communion and alliance with each other, and reason in what respects they are akin to one another, will contribute something to what we want, and our labour will not be unprofitable; otherwise it will." "I likewise," said he, "prophesy the same thing. But you speak, Socrates, of a very mighty work." "Do you mean the introduction, or what else?" said I. "Or do we not know that all these things are introductory to the law itself? which we ought to learn; for even those that are skilled in dialectic do not appear expert as to these things." "No, by Jupiter," said he, "unless a very few of all I have met with." "But whilst they are not able," said I, "to impart and receive reason, will they ever be able to know any thing of what we say is necessary to be known?" "Never will they be able to do this," replied he. "Is not this itself then, Glauco," said I, "the law? To give perfection to dialectic; which being intelligible, may be said to be imitated by the power of sight; which power endeavours, as we observed, first to look at animals, then at the stars, and last of all at the sun himself. So when any one attempts to discuss a subject without any of the senses, by reasoning he is impelled to that which each particular is; and if he does not desist till he apprehends by intelligence what is the good itself, he then arrives at the end of the intelligible, as the other does at the end of the visible." "Entirely so," said he. 531d 531e 532a 532b

"What now? Do not you call this progression dialectic?" "What else?" "And now," said I, "as in our former comparison you had the liberation from chains, and turning from shadows towards images, and the light, and an ascent from the cavern to the sun; and when there, the looking at images in water, from an inability at first to behold animals and plants, and the light of the sun; so here you have 377 532c the contemplation of divine phantasms, and the shadows of real beings, and not the shadows of images shadowed out by another light of a similar kind, as by the sun. And all this business respecting the arts which we have discussed, has this power, to lead back again that which is best in the soul, to the contemplation of that which is best in beings; as in the former case, that which is brightest in the body is led

532d to that which is most splendid in the corporeal and visible place." "I admit," said he, "of these things; though truly it appears to me extremely difficult to admit of them, and in another respect it is difficult not to admit of them. But however (for we shall hear these things not only now at present, but often again discuss them), establishing these things as now expressed, let us go to the law itself, and discuss it as we have finished the introduction. Say then what is

532e the mode of the power of dialectic,[3] and into what species is it divided, and what are the paths leading to it? For these, it is likely, conduct us to that place, at which when we are arrived, we shall find a resting-place, and the end of the journey."

533a   "You will not as yet, friend Glauco," said I, "be able to follow; for otherwise no zeal should be wanting on my part; nor should you any longer only see the image of that of which we are speaking, but the truth itself. But this is what to me at least it appears; whether it be so in reality or not, this it is not proper strenuously to affirm; but that indeed it is somewhat of this kind may be strenuously affirmed. May it not?" "Why not?" "And further that it is the power of dialectic alone, which can discover this to one who is skilled in the things we have discussed, and that by no other power it is possible." "This also," said he, "we may strenuously affirm." "This at least no one," said I,

533b "will dispute with us: That no other method can attempt to comprehend, in any orderly way, what each particular being is; for all the other arts respect either the opinions and desires of men, or generations, and compositions, or are all employed in the culture of things generated and compounded. Those others, which we said participated somewhat of being, geometry, and such as are connected

533c with her, we see as dreaming indeed about being; but it is impossible

378 for them to have a true vision, so long as employing hypotheses they preserve[4] these immoveable, without being able to assign a reason for their subsistence. For where the principle is that which is unknown,

and the conclusion and intermediate steps are connected with that unknown principle, by what contrivance can an ascent of such a kind ever become science?" "By none," replied he.

"Does not then," said I, "the dialectic method proceed in this way alone, to the principle itself, removing all hypotheses, that it may firmly establish it, and gradually drawing and leading upwards the eye of the soul, which was truly buried in a certain barbaric mire, using as 533d assistants and circular leaders those arts we have mentioned, which through custom we frequently call sciences, but which require another appellation more clear than opinion, but more obscure than science? We have somewhere in the former part of our discourse termed it the dianoëtic power. But the controversy is not, as it appears to me, about a name, with those who inquire into things of such great 533e importance as those now before us." "It is not," said he. "Do you agree then," said I, "as formerly, to call the first part science, the second the 534a dianoëtic power, the third faith, and the fourth assimilation? and both these last opinion? and the two former intelligence? And that opinion is employed about generation, and intelligence about essence? likewise, that as essence is to generation, so is intelligence to opinion, science to faith, and the dianoëtic power to assimilation? But as for the analogy of the things which these powers respect, and the two-fold division of each, *viz.* of the object of opinion, and of intellect, these we omit, Glauco, that we may not be more prolix here than in our former reasonings." "As for me," said he, "with reference to those 534b other things, as far as I am able to follow, I am of the same opinion." "But do not you call him skilled in dialectic, who apprehends the reason of the essence of each particular? And as for the man who is not able to give a reason to himself, and to another, so far as he is not able, so far will you not say he wants intelligence of the thing?" "Why should I not say so?" replied he. "And is not the case the same with reference to *the good?* Whosoever cannot define it by reason, separating the idea of *the good* from all others, and as in a battle 534c piercing through all arguments, eagerly striving to confute, not 379 according to opinion, but according to essence, and in all these marching forward with undeviating reason,—such an one knows nothing of *the good itself*, nor of any good whatever: but if he has attained to any image of *the good*, we must say he has attained to it by

opinion, not by science; that in the present life he is sleeping, and
534d conversant with dreams; and that before he is roused he will descend
to Hades, and there be profoundly and perfectly laid asleep." "By
Jupiter," said he, "I will strongly aver all these things." "But surely you
will not, I think, allow your own children at least whom you
nourished and educated in reasoning, if ever in reality you educate
them, to have the supreme government of the most important affairs
in the state, whilst they are void of reason, as letters of the alphabet."
"By no means," replied he. "You will then lay down this to them as a
law: That in a most especial manner they attain to that part of
education, by which they may become able to question and answer in
534e the most scientific manner." "I will settle it by law," said he, "with your
assistance at least." "Does it then appear to you," said I, "that dialectic is
to be placed on high as a bulwark to disciplines? and that no other
535a discipline can with propriety be raised higher than this; but that every
thing respecting disciplines is now finished?" "I agree," said he.

"There now remains for you," said I, "the distribution: To whom
shall we assign these disciplines, and after what manner?" "That is
evident," said he. "Do you remember then our former election of
rulers, what kind we chose?" "How should I not?" said he. "As to other
things then, conceive," said I, "that such geniuses as these ought to be
selected. For the most firm and brave are to be preferred, and, as far as
535b possible, the most graceful; and besides, we must not only seek for
those whose manners are generous and stern, but they must be
possessed of every other natural disposition conducive to this
education." "Which dispositions do you recommend?" "They must
have," said I, "O blessed man! acuteness with respect to disciplines,
that they may not learn with difficulty. For souls are much more
intimidated in robust disciplines, than in strenuous exercises of the
body; for their proper labour, and which is not in common with the
535c body, is more domestic to them." "True," said he. "And we must seek
for one of good memory, untainted, and every way laborious: or how
else do you think any one will be willing to endure the fatigue of the
380 body, and to accomplish at the same time such learning and study?"
"No one," said he, "unless he be in all respects of a naturally good
disposition."

"The mistake then about philosophy, and the contempt of it, have been occasioned through these things, because, as I formerly said, it is not applied to in a manner suitable to its dignity: for it ought not to be applied to by the bastardly, but the legitimate." "How?" said he. "In the first place, he who is to apply to philosophy ought not," said I, "to be lame as to his love of labour, being laborious in some things, and averse to labour in others. But this takes place when a man loves wrestling and hunting, and all exercises of the body, but is not a lover of learning, and loves neither to hear nor to inquire, but in all these respects has an aversion to labour. He likewise is lame, in a different manner from this man, who dislikes all bodily exercise." "You say most true," replied he. "And shall we not," said I, "in like manner account that soul lame as to truth, which hates indeed a voluntary falsehood, and bears it ill in itself, and is beyond measure enraged when others tell a lie; but easily admits the involuntary lie; and, though at any time it be found ignorant, is not displeased, but like a savage sow willingly wallows in ignorance?" "By all means," said he.

And in like manner," said I, "as to temperance and fortitude, and magnanimity, and all the parts of virtue, we must no less carefully attend to what is bastardy, and what is legitimate; for when either any private person or city understands not how to attend to all these things, they unawares employ the lame and the bastardly for whatever they have occasion; private persons employ them as friends, and cities as governors." "The case is entirely so," said he. "But we," said I, "must beware of all such things; for, if we take such as are entire in body and in mind for such extensive learning, and exercise and instruct them, justice herself will not blame us, and we shall preserve both the city and its constitution: but if we introduce persons of a different description into these affairs, we shall do every thing the reverse, and bring philosophy under still greater ridicule." "That indeed would be shameful," said he. "Certainly," said I. "But I myself seem at present to be somewhat ridiculous." "How so?" said he. "I forgot," said I, "that we were amusing; ourselves, and spoke with too great keenness; for, whilst I was speaking, I looked towards philosophy; and seeing her most unworthily abused, I seem to have been filled with indignation, and, as being enraged at those who are the cause of it, to have spoken more earnestly what I said." "No truly," said he, "not to me your hearer at least." "But for me," said I, "the speaker. But let us

535d

535e

536a

536b

536c

381

not forget this, that in our former election we made choice of old men; but in this election it will not be allowed us. For we must not 536d believe Solon, that one who is old is able to learn many things; but he is less able to effect this than to run. All mighty and numerous labours belong to the young." "Of necessity," said he.

"Every thing then relating to arithmetic and geometry, and all that previous instruction which they should be taught before they learn dialectic, ought to be set before them whilst they are children, and that method of teaching observed, which will make them learn 536e without compulsion." "Why so?" "Because," said I, "a free man ought to learn no discipline with slavery: for the labours of the body when endured through compulsion render the body nothing worse: but no compelled discipline is lasting in the soul." "True," said he. "Do not 537a then," said I, "O best of men! compel boys in their learning; but train them up, amusing themselves, that you may be better able to discern to what the genius of each naturally tends." "What you say," replied he, "is reasonable." "Do not you remember then," said I, "that we said the boys are even to be carried to war, as spectators, on horseback, and that they are to be brought nearer, if they can with safety, and like young hounds taste the blood?" "I remember," said he. "Whoever then," said I, "shall appear the most forward in all these labours, disciplines, and 537b terrors, are to be selected into a certain number." "At what age?" said he. "When they have," said I, "finished their necessary exercises; for during this time, whilst it continues, for two or three years, it is impossible to accomplish anything else; for fatigue and sleep are enemies to learning; and this too none of the least of their trials, what each of them appears to be in his exercises." "Certainly," said he.

"And after this period," said I, "let such as formerly have been 537c selected of the age of twenty receive greater honours than others, and let those disciplines which in their youth they learned separately, be brought before them in one view, that they may see the alliance of the disciplines with each other, and with the nature of real being." "This discipline indeed will alone," said he, "remain firm in those in whom it is ingenerated." "And this," said I, "is the greatest trial for distinguishing between those geniuses which are naturally fitted for dialectic, and those which are not. He who perceives this alliance is 382 skilled in dialectic; he who does not, is not." "I am of the same

opinion," said he. "It will then be necessary for you," said I, "after you 537d
have observed these things, and seen who are most approved in these,
being stable in disciplines, and stable in war, and in the other things
established by law, to make choice of such after they exceed thirty
years, selecting from those chosen formerly, and advance them to
greater honours. You must likewise observe them, trying them by the
power of dialectic so as to ascertain which of them without the
assistance of his eyes, or any other sense, is able to proceed with truth
to being itself. And here, my companion, is a work of great caution."
"In what principally?" said he. "Do not you perceive," said I, "the evil 537e
which at preset attends dialectic, how great it is?" "What is it," said
he, "you mean?" "How it is somehow," said I, "full of what is contrary
to law." "Greatly so," replied he. "Do you think then," said I, "they
suffer some wonderful thing, and will you not forgive them?" "How
do you mean?" said he. "Just as if," said I, "a certain supposititious child
were educated in great opulence in a rich and noble family, and 538a
amidst many flatterers, and should perceive, when grown up to
manhood, that he is not descended of those who are said to be his
parents, but yet should not discover his real parents; can you divine
how such an one would be affected both towards his flatterers, and
towards his supposed parents, both at the time when he knew nothing
of the cheat, and at that time again when he came to perceive it? Or
are you willing to hear me while I presage it?" "I am willing," said he.

"I prophesy then," said I, "that he will pay more honour to his 538b
father and mother, and his other supposed relations, than to the
flatterers, and that he will less neglect them when they are in any
want, and be less apt to do or say anything amiss to them, and in
matters of consequence be less disobedient to them than to those
flatterers, during that period in which he knows not the truth." "It is
likely," said he. "But when he perceives the real state of the affair, I
again prophesy, he will then slacken in his honour and respect for
them, and attend to the flatterers, and be remarkably more persuaded 538c
by them now than formerly, and truly live according to their
manner, conversing with them openly. But for that father, and those
supposed relations, if he be not of an entirely good natural
disposition, he will have no regard." "You say every thing," said he,
"as it would happen." "But in what manner does this comparison

383   respect those who are conversant with dialectic?" "In this. We have
certain dogmas from our childhood concerning things just and
beautiful, in which we have been nourished as by parents, obeying and
538d   honouring them." "We have," said he. "Are there not likewise other
pursuits opposite to these, with pleasures flattering our souls, and
drawing them towards these? They do not however persuade those
who are in any degree moderate, but they honour those their
relations, and obey them." "These things are so."

     "What now," said I, "when to one who is thus affected the question
is proposed, What is the beautiful? and when he, answering what he
has heard from the lawgiver, is refuted by reason; and reason
538e   frequently and every way convincing him, reduces him to the
opinion, that this is no more beautiful than it is deformed; and in the
same manner, as to what is just and good, and whatever else he held in
highest esteem, what do you think such an one will after this do, with
regard to these things, as to honouring and obeying them?" "Of
necessity," said he, "he will neither honour nor obey them any longer
in the same manner as formerly." "When then he no longer deems,"
said I, "these things honourable, and allied to him as formerly, and
539a   cannot discover those which really are so, is it possible he can readily
join himself to any other life than the flattering one?" "It is not
possible," said he. "And from being an observer of the law, he shall, I
think, appear to be a transgressor." "Of necessity." "Is it not likely
then," said I, "that those shall be thus affected who in this situation
apply to reasoning, and that they should deserve, as I was just now
saying, great forgiveness?" "And pity too," said he. "Whilst you take
care then, lest this compassionable case befall these of the age of
thirty, ought they not by every method to apply themselves to
539b   reasoning?" "Certainly," said he. "And is not this one prudent
caution? that they taste not reasonings, whilst they are young: for you
have not forgot, I suppose, that the youth, when they first taste of
reasonings, abuse them in the way of amusement, whilst they employ
them always for the purpose of contradiction. And imitating those
who are refuters, they themselves refute others, delighting like whelps
in dragging and tearing to pieces, in their reasonings, those always
who are near them." "Extremely so," said he. "And after they have
539c   confuted many, and been themselves confuted by many, do they not

vehemently and speedily lay aside all the opinions they formerly possessed? and by these means they themselves, and the whole of *384* philosophy, are calumniated by others." "Most true," said he. "But he who is of a riper age," said I, "will not be disposed to share in such a madness, but will rather imitate him who inclines to reason and inquire after truth, than one who, for the sake of diversion, amuses himself, and contradicts. He will likewise be more modest himself, and *539d* render the practice of disputing more honorable instead of being more dishonourable." "Right," said he. "Were not then all our former remarks rightly made, in the way of precaution, as to this point, that those geniuses ought to be decent and stable, to whom dialectic is to be imparted, and not as at present, when every common genius, and such as is not at all proper, is admitted to it?" "Certainly," said he.

"Will not then the double of the former period suffice a man to remain in acquiring the art of dialectic with perseverance and application, and doing nothing else but in way of counterpart exercising himself in all bodily exercises?" "Do you mean six years," *539e* said he, "or four?" "'Tis of no consequence," said I, "make it five. After this you must compel them to descend to that cave again, and oblige them to govern both in things relating to war, and such other magistracies as require youth, that they may not fall short of others in experience. And they must be still further tried among these, whether, being drawn to every different quarter, they will continue firm, or whether they will in any measure be drawn aside." "And for *540a* how long a time," said he, "do you appoint this?" "For fifteen years," said I. "And when they are of the age of fifty, such of them as are preserved, and as have excelled in all these things, in actions, and in the sciences, are now to be led to the end, and are to be obliged, inclining the ray of their soul, to look towards that which imparts light to all things, and, when they have viewed *the good itself*, to use it as a paradigm, each of them, in their turn, in adorning both the city and private persons, and themselves, during the remainder of their *540b* life. For the most part indeed they must be occupied in philosophy; and when it is their turn, they must toil in political affairs, and take the government, each for the good of the city, performing this office, not as any thing honourable, but as a thing necessary. And after they have educated others in the same manner still, and left such as resemble themselves to be the guardians of the city, they depart to inhabit the islands of the blest. But the city will publicly erect for them monuments, and offer sacrifices, if the oracle assent, as to superior beings; and if it do not, as to happy and divine men." "You have, Socrates," said he, "like a statuary, made our governors all-beautiful." "And our governesses likewise, Glauco," said I. "For do not suppose that I have spoken what I have said any more concerning the men than concerning the women,—such of them as are of a sufficient genius." "Right," said he, "if at least they are to share in all things equally with the men, as we related."

"What then," said I, "do you agree, that with reference to the city and republic, we have not altogether spoken what can only be considered as wishes; but such things as are indeed difficult, yet possible in a certain respect, and in no other way than what has been mentioned, *viz.*, when those who are truly philosophers, whether more of them or a single one, becoming governors in a city, shall despise those present honours, considering them as illiberal and of no value; but esteeming rectitude and the honours which are derived from it above all things; accounting the just as a thing of all others the greatest, and most absolutely necessary; and ministering to it, and, increasing it, thoroughly regulate the constitution of their own city?" "How?" said he. "As many," said I, "of the more advanced in life as have lived ten years in the city they will send into the country, and, removing their children away from those habits which the domestics possess, at present, they will educate them in their own manners and laws, which are what we formerly mentioned: and the city and republic we have described being thus established in the speediest and easiest manner, it will both be happy itself, and be of the greatest advantage to that people among whom it is established." "Very much so indeed," said he. "And you seem to me, Socrates, to have told very well how this city shall arise, if it arise at all." "Are not now then," said I, "our discourses sufficient both concerning such a city as this, and concerning a man similar to it? For it is also now evident what kind of a man we shall say he ought to be." "It is evident," replied he; "and your inquiry seems to me to be at an end."

THE END OF THE SEVENTH BOOK.

BOOK VIII.

"Be it so. These things, Glauco, we have now assented to; that in 543a this city, which is to be established in a perfect manner, the women are to be common, the children common, and likewise the whole of education. In like manner, their employments both in peace and war are to be common; and their kings are to be such as excel all others both in philosophy and in the arts of war." "These things," said he, have been assented to." "And surely we likewise granted, that when 543b the governors are marching with the soldiers, and settle themselves, they shall dwell in such habitations as we formerly mentioned, which have nothing peculiar to any one, but are common to all: and besides these houses, we likewise, if you remember, agreed what sort of professions they shall have." "I remember," said he, "that we were of opinion, none of them ought to possess any thing as others do at present; but, as wrestlers in war and guardians, they were to receive a 543c reward for their guardianship from others, or a yearly maintenance on these accounts, and were to take care of themselves and the rest of the city." "You say right," said I. "But since we have finished this, let us recollect whence we made this digression; that we may now proceed again in the same way." "That is not difficult," said he: "for you were mentioning much the same things of the city with those you have done at present; saying that you considered such a city to be good, as it 543d was at that time described, and the man to be good who resembles it; whilst yet it seems you are able to describe a better city, and a better man. And you said moreover, that all the others were wrong, if this 544a was right. Of the other republics, you said, as I remember, there were four species, which deserved to be considered, and to have the errors in them, and the lawless people in them, observed; in order that when *387* we have beheld the whole of them, and when we have agreed which is the best, and which is the worst man, we may inquire whether the best man be the happiest, and the worst the most miserable, or *544b* otherwise. And when I asked you, which you call the four republics, Polemarchus and Adimantus hereupon interrupted; and you, in this manner having resumed the subject, are come to this part of the reasoning."

"You have recollected," said I, "most accurately." "Again therefore afford me the same opportunity, and, whilst I ask you the same question, endeavour to say what you then intended to assert." "If indeed I am able," said I. "And I am truly desirous," "said he, "for my *544c* part, to hear which you call the four republics." "You shall hear that," said I, "without difficulty. For they are these I mention, and they have names too. There is that which is commended by many, the Cretan and the Spartan. There is, secondly, that which has a secondary praise, called Oligarchy, a republic full of many evils; that which is different from this, and follows next in order, a Democracy; and then genuine Tyranny, different from all these, the fourth and last disease of a city. *544d* Or have you any other form of a republic belonging to any distinct species? For your little principalities and venal kingdoms, and such like republics, are somehow of a middle kind between these, and one may find of them as many among the barbarians as among the Greeks." "They are indeed," said he, "said to be very many, and very strange ones."

"Do you know now," said I, "that there is somehow a necessity that there be a many species of men as of republics? Or do you imagine that republics are generated somehow of an oak,[1] or a rock, and not of the *544e* manners of those who are in the city, to which, as into a current, every thing else likewise is drawn?" "By no means do I imagine," said he, "they are generated from any thing but from hence." "If then there be five species of cities, the species of souls in individuals shall be likewise five." "Why not?"

"We have already discussed that which resembles an Aristocracy, *545a* which we have rightly pronounced to be both good and just." "We have so." "Are we now, in the next place, to go over the worse species, the contentious and the a ambitious man, who is formed according to the Spartan republic; then him resembling an Oligarchy; and then the Democratic and the Tyrannic, that we may contemplate the most unjust:, and oppose him to the most just, that our inquiry may be completed? *viz.* how the most finished justice is in comparison of the most finished injustice, as to the happiness or misery of the possessor? that so we may either follow injustice, being persuaded by Thrasymachus, or justice, yielding to the present reasoning?" "By all means," said he, "we must do so." "Shall we then, in the same manner as we began, consider the manners in republics, before we consider them in private persons, as being there more conspicuous? And according to this method the ambitious republic is first to be considered (for I have no other name to call it by, but it may be denominated either a Timocracy,² or a Timarchy), and together with it we shall consider a man resembling it; afterwards we shall consider an Oligarchy, and a man resembling Oligarchy; then again, when we have viewed a Democracy, we shall contemplate a Democratic man; and then in the fourth place, when we come to Tyranny, and contemplate it, and likewise a tyrannic soul, we shall endeavour to become competent judges of what we proposed." "Both our contemplation and judgment," said he, "would in this manner at least be agreeable to reason."

"Come then," said I, "let us endeavour to relate in what manner a Timocracy arises out of an Aristocracy. Or is not this plain, that every republic changes, by means of that part which possesses the magistracies, when in this itself there arises sedition; but whilst this agrees with itself though the state be extremely small, it is impossible to be changed?" "It is so, indeed." "How then, Glauco, shall our city be changed? Or in what shape shall our allies and rulers fall into sedition with one another, and among themselves? Or are you willing, that, like Homer, we invoke the Muses to tell us, 'How first sedition rose?'—And shall we say, that whilst they talk tragically, playing with us, and rallying us children, they yet talk seriously and sublimely?" "In what manner?" "Somehow thus. It is indeed difficult for a city thus constituted to be changed. But as every thing which is generated is obnoxious to corruption, neither will such a constitution

388

545b

545c

545d

545e

546a

389

as this remain for ever, but be dissolved. And its dissolution is this. Not only with respect to terrestrial plants, but likewise in terrestrial animals, fertility[3] and sterility of soul as well as of body takes place, when the revolutions of the heavenly bodies complete the periphery of their respective orbits; which are shorter to the shorter lived, and contrariwise to such as are the contrary: and with reference to the

546b fertility and sterility of our race, although those are wise that you have educated to be governors of cities, yet will they never, by reason in conjunction with sense, observe the proper seasons, but overlook them, and sometimes generate children when they ought not. But the period to that which is divinely generated[4] is that which the perfect

390 number comprehends; and to that which is generated by man, that in which the augmentations surpassing and surpassed, when they shall have received three restitutions and four boundaries of things assimilating and dissimilating, increasing and decreasing, shall

546c render all things correspondent and effable; of which the sesquitertian progeny, when conjoined with the pentad, and thrice increased, affords two harmonies. One of these, the equally equal, a hundred times a hundred; but the other, of equal length indeed, but more oblong, is of a hundred numbers from effable diameters of pentads, each being deficient by unity, and from two numbers that are ineffable; and from a hundred cubes of the triad. But the whole

391 geometric number of this kind is the author of better and worse
546d generations.[5] Of which when our governors being ignorant, join our couples together unseasonably, the children shall neither be of a good

392 genius, nor fortunate. And though the former governor shall install the best of them in the office, they nevertheless being unworthy of it,

393 and coming to have the power their fathers had, will begin to be negligent of us in their guardianship, in the first place esteeming music less than they ought, and in the next place the gymnic exercises. Hence our youth will become less acquainted with music.

546e And the guardians which shall be appointed from among these will
547a not be altogether expert guardians, to distinguish, according to Hesiod and us, the several species of geniuses, the golden, the silver, the brazen, and the iron: but whilst iron is mixed with silver and brass with gold, dissimilitude arises, and unharmonious inequality. And when these arise, wherever they prevail, they perpetually generate war

and enmity. To such a race of men as this, we must suppose them to say, that sedition belongs whenever it happens to rise." "And we shall say that they have answered justly," replied he. "And of necessity," said I, "for they are Muses."

"What then," said he, "do the Muses say next?" "When sedition is 547b risen," said I, "two of the species of geniuses, the iron and the brazen, will be drawn to gain, and the acquisition of lands and houses, of gold and silver. But the golden and the silver geniuses, as they are not in want, but naturally rich, will lead souls towards virtue and the original constitution; yet as they live in a violent manner, and draw contrary to one another, they will make an agreement to divide their lands and houses between them, and to dwell apart from one another: and then enslaving those who were formerly kept by them as free 547c men, as friends, and tutors, they will keep them as domestics and slaves, for service in war and for their own protection." "This revolution," said he, "seems to me thus to arise." "Shall not then this republic," said I, "be somewhat in the middle between an Aristocracy and Oligarchy?" "Certainly."

"And the change shall happen in this manner, and on this change what sort of life shall it lead? Or is it not plain, that in some things it 547d shall imitate the former republic, and in others Oligarchy, as being in the middle of the two, and shall likewise have somewhat peculiar to itself?" "Just so," replied he. "Shall they not then, in honouring their rulers, and in this that their military abstain from agriculture, from 394 mechanical and other gainful employments, in their establishing common meals, and in studying both gymnastic exercises and contests of war, in all these things shall they not imitate the former republic?" "Yes." "But in this, that they are afraid to bring wise men 547e into the magistracy, as having no longer any such as are truly simple and inflexible, but such as are of a mixed kind; and in that they incline for those who are more forward and rough, whose natural genius is rather fitted for war than peace, and in that they esteem 548a tricks and stratagems, and spend the whole of their time in continual war, in all these respects shall it not have many things peculiar to itself?" "Yes." "And such as these," said I, "that I be desirous of wealth as those who live in Oligarchies, and in an illiberal manner, value gold and silver concealed in darkness, as having repositories of their

own, and domestic treasuries, where they hoard and hide them, and have their houses circularly enclosed, where, as in nests altogether peculiar, they squander every thing profusely, together with their
548b wives and such others as they fancy." "Most true," said he. "And will they not likewise be sparing of their substance, as valuing it highly, and acquiring it not in an open manner, but love to squander the substance of others, through their dissoluteness, and secretly indulging their pleasures? They will likewise fly from the law, as children from their father, who have been educated not by persuasion but by force, having neglected the true muse, which is accompanied
548c with reason and philosophy, and honoured gymnastic more than music." "You describe entirely," said he, "a mixed republic, compounded of good and ill." "It is indeed mixed," said I. "One thing is most remarkable in it, from the prevalence of the irascible temper, contention, and ambition." "Exceedingly," said he. "Does not then," said I, "this republic a rise in this manner? And is it not of such a kind
548d as this, as far as the form of a republic can be described in words where there is not perfect accuracy; as it suffices us to contemplate in description likewise the most just and the most unjust man; and it would be a work of prodigious length to discuss all republics, and all the various manners of men, without omitting any thing?" "Very right," said he.

"What now will the man be who corresponds to this republic? how shall he be formed, and of what kind?" "I think," said Adimantus,
548e "he will be somewhat like Glauco here, at least: in a love of contention." "Perhaps," said I, "as to this particular. But in other
395 respects he does not seem to me to have a natural resemblance of him." "In what?" "He must necessarily," said I, "be more arrogant, and inapt to music, but fond of it: and fond of hearing, but by no
549a means a rhetorician: and such an one will be rough towards certain slaves, without despising them, as he does who is sufficiently educated. He will be mild towards such as are free, and extremely submissive to governors; a lover of dominion, and a lover of honour, not thinking it proper to govern by eloquence, nor any thing of the kind, but by political management and military performances, being a lover of gymnastic and hunting." "This indeed," said he, "is the temper of
549b that republic." "And shall not such an one," said I, "despise money,

whilst he is young? But the older he grows, the more he will always value it, because he partakes of the covetous genius, and is not sincerely affected towards virtue, because destitute of the best guardian." "Of what guardian?" said Adimantus. "Reason," said I, "accompanied with music, which being the only inbred preservative of virtue, dwells with the possessor through the whole of life." "You say well," replied he.

"And surely at least such a timocratic youth," said I, "resembles such a city." "Certainly." "And such an one," said I, "is formed 549c somehow in this manner. He happens sometimes to be the young son of a worthy father, who dwells in an ill regulated city, and who shuns honours and magistracies, and lawsuits, and all such public business, and is willing to live neglected in obscurity, that he may have no trouble." "In what manner then," said he, "is he formed?" "When first of all," said I, "he hears his mother venting her indignation, because her husband is not in the magistracy, and complaining that 549d she is on this account neglected among other women, and that she observes him not extremely attentive to the acquisition of wealth, not fighting and reviling privately and publicly in courts of justice; but behaving on all these occasions indolently, and perceiving him always attentive to himself, and treating her neither with extreme respect nor contempt; on all these accounts, being filled with indignation, she tells her son that his father is unmanly, and extremely remiss, and such other things as wives are wont to cant over concerning such 549e husbands." "They are very many, truly," said Adimantus, "and very much in their spirit."

"And you know," said I, "that the domestics likewise of such families, such of them as appear good-natured, sometimes privately say the same things to the sons; and if they see any one either owing money whom the father does not sue at law, or in any other way 396 doing injustice, they exhort him to punish all such persons when he comes to be a man, and to be more of a man than his father. And 550a when he goes abroad, he hears other such like things. And he sees that such in the city as attend to their own affairs are called simple, and held in little esteem, and that such as do not attend to their affairs are both honoured and commended. The young man now hearing and seeing all these things, and then again hearing the speeches of his

father, and observing his pursuits in a near view, in comparison with
550b those of others; being drawn by both these, his father watering and
increasing the rational part in his soul, and these others the
concupiscible and irascible; and being naturally no bad man, but
spoiled by the bad conversations of others, he is brought to a mean
between the two, and delivers up the government within himself to a
middle power, that which is fond of contention and irascible, and so
he becomes a haughty and ambitious man." "You seem," said he, "to
have accurately explained the formation of such an one."

550c   "We have now then," said I, "the second republic and the second
man." "We have," said he. "Shall we not after this say with Æschylus?

'With diff'rent cities dilf'rent men accord.'

Or, rather, according to our plan, shall we first establish the cities?"
"By all means so," replied he. "It would be an Oligarchy then, I think,
which succeeds this republic." "But what constitution," said he, "is it
you call an Oligarchy?" "That republic," said I, "which is founded on
550d men's valuations, in which the rich bear rule, and the poor have no
share in the government." "I understand," said he. "Must we not
relate, first, how the change is made from a Timocracy to an
Oligarchy?" "We must." "And surely at least how this change is
made," said I, "is manifest even to the blind." "How?" "That
treasury," said I, "which every one has filled with gold destroys such a
republic; for, first of all, they find out for themselves methods of
550e expense, and to this purpose strain the laws, both they and their wives
disobeying them." "That is likely," said he. "And afterwards, I think,
one observing another, and coming to rival one another, the
multitude of them are rendered of this kind." "It is likely." "And
from hence then," said I, "proceeding still to a greater desire of
acquiring wealth, the more honourable they account this to be, the
397 more will virtue be thought dishonourable: or is not virtue so
different from wealth, that, if each of them be placed in the opposite
arm of a balance, they always weigh opposite to each other?" "Entirely
so," replied he.

551a   "But whilst wealth and the wealthy are honoured in the city, both
virtue and the good must be more dishonoured." "It is plain." "And
what is honoured is always pursued, and what is dishonoured is

neglected." "Just so." "Instead then of contentious and ambitious men, they will at last become lovers of gain and of wealth: and they will praise and admire the rich, and bring them into the magistracy, but the poor man they will despise." "Certainly." "And do they not then make laws, marking out the boundary of the Oligarchic constitution, and regulating the quantity of Oligarchic power according to the quantity of wealth, more to the more wealthy, and less to the less, intimating that he who has not the valuation settled by law is to have no share in the government? And do they not transact these things violently, by force of arms, or establish such a republic after they have previously terrified them? Is it not thus?" "Thus indeed." "This then in short is the constitution." "It is," replied he. "But what now is the nature of the republic, and what are the faults we ascribed to it?" 551c

"First of all," said I, "this very thing, the constitution itself, what think you of this? For consider, if a man should in this manner appoint pilots of ships, according to their valuations, but never entrust one with a poor man, though better skilled in piloting, what would be the consequence?" "They would," said he, "make very bad navigation." "And is it not in the same manner with reference to any other thing, or any government whatever?" "I think so." "Is it so in all cases but in a city?" said I, "or is it so with reference to a city likewise?" "There most especially," said he, "in as much as it is the most difficult, and the greatest government." "Oligarchy then would 551d seem to have this, which is so great a fault." "It appears so." "But what? Is this fault any thing less?" "What?" "That such a city is not one, but of necessity two; on consisting of the poor, and the other of the rich, dwelling in one place, and always plotting against one another." "By Jupiter," said he, "it is in no respect less." "But surely neither is this a handsome thing, to be incapable to wage any war, because of the necessity they are under, either of employing the armed multitude, and of dreading them more than the enemy themselves; or not 551e employing them, to appear in battle itself truly Oligarchic, and at the 398 same time to be unwilling to advance money for the public service, through a natural disposition of covetousness." "This is not handsome." "But what? with reference to what we long ago condemned, the engaging in a multiplicity of different things, the

same persons, at the same time, attending in such a republic to
552a agriculture, lucrative employments, and military affairs, does this
appear to be right?" "Not in any degree."

"But see now whether this form of republic be the first which
introduces this greatest of all evils." "What is that?" "That one shall
be allowed to dispose of the whole of his effects, and another to
purchase them from him, and the other be allowed to dwell in the
city, whilst he belongs to no one class in the city, and is neither called
a maker of money, nor mechanic, nor horseman, nor foot-soldier,
552b but poor and destitute." "It is the first," said he. "But yet such an one
shall not be prohibited in Oligarchic governments; for otherwise
some of them would not be over-rich, and others altogether poor."
"Right." "But consider this likewise. When such a rich man as this
spends of his substance, was it of any more advantage to the city with
reference to the purposes we now mentioned? or did he appear to be
indeed one of the magistrates, but was in truth neither magistrate of
the city, nor servant to it, but a waster of substance?" "So he
552c appeared," replied he. "He was nothing but a waster."

"Are you willing then," said I, "that we say of him, that as when a
drone is in a bee-hive, it is the disease of the swarm; in like manner
such an one, when a drone in his house, is the disease of the city?"
"Entirely so, Socrates," replied he. "And has not God, Adimantus,
made all the winged drones without any sting; but these with feet,
some of them without stings, and some of them with dreadful stings?
And of those who are without stings, are they who continue poor to
552d old age; and of those who have stings, are all these who are called
mischievous." "Most true," said he. "It is plain then," said I, "that in a
city where you observe there are poor, there are somewhere in that
place concealed thieves and purse-cutters, and sacrilegious persons,
and workers of all other such evils." "It is plain," said he. "What then?
Do not you perceive poor people in cities under Oligarchic
government?" "They are almost all so," said he, "except the
552e governors." "And do we not think," said I, "that there are many
mischievous persons in them with stings, whom the magistracy by
399 diligence and by force restrains?" "We think so indeed," said he. "And
shall we not say, that through want of education, through bad
nurture, and a corrupt constitution of state, such sort of persons are

there produced?" "We shall say so." "Is not then the city which is under Oligarchy of such a kind as this, and hath it not such evils as these, and probably more too?" "It is nearly so," said he.

"We have now finished," said I, "this republic likewise, which they 553a call Oligarchy, having its governors according to valuation. And let us now consider the man who resembles it, in what manner he arises, and what sort of man he is." "By all means," said he. "And is not the change from the Timocratic to the Oligarchic chiefly in this manner?" "How?" "When such a one has a son, first of all, he both emulates his father, and follows his steps; afterwards he sees him, on a 553b sudden, dashed on the city, as on a rock, and wasting both his substance and himself, either in the office of a general, or some other principal magistracy; then falling into courts of justice, destroyed by sycophants, and either put to death, or stripped of his dignities, disgraced, and losing all his substance." "It is likely," said he.

"When he has seen and suffered those things, friend, and has lost his substance, he instantly in a terror pushes headlong from the throne of his soul that ambitious and animated disposition, and, 553c being humbled by his poverty, turns his attention to gain, lives meanly and sparingly, and, applying to work, collects wealth. Or do you not think that such a man will then seat in that throne the covetous and avaricious disposition, and make it a mighty king within himself, begirt with tiaras,[6] and bracelets, and sceptres?" "I think so," said he. "But he, I imagine, having placed both the rational and the ambitious disposition low on the ground on either side, and 553d having enslaved them under it, the one he allows to reason on nothing, nor ever to inquire, but in what way lesser substance shall be made greater; and the other again he permits to admire and honour nothing but riches and the rich, and to receive honour on no other account but the acquisition of money, or whatever contributes towards it." "There is no other change," said he, "of an ambitious 400 youth to a covetous one so sudden and so powerful as this." "Is not 553e this, then," said I, "the Oligarchic man?" "And the change into such an one is from a man resembling that republic from which the Oligarchic republic arises." "Let us consider, now, if he any way 554a resembles it." "Let us consider."

"Does he not, in the first place, resemble it in valuing money above all things?" "Why does he not?" "And surely at least in being sparing and laborious, satisfying only his necessary desires, and not allowing of any other expenses, but subduing the other desires as foolish." "Certainly." "And being," said I, "an emaciated man, and making 554b gain of every thing, a man intent on hoarding, such as the multitude extols—will not this be the man who resembles such a republic?" "It appears so to me," replied he. "Riches then must be most valued both by the city and by such a man." "For I do not think," said I, "that such a man has attended to education." "I do not think he has," said he; "for he would not have taken a blind one⁷ to be the leader of his life." "But further still, consider this attentively," said I, "shall we not say that there are in him, from the want of education, the desires of 554c the drone, some of them beggarly, and same of them mischievous, forcibly kept in by some other pursuit?" "Entirely so," said he.

"Do you know then," said I, "where you will best observe their wickedness?" "Where?" said he. "In their tutelages of orphans, or in whatever else of this kind comes in their way, where they have it much in their power to do injustice." "True." "And is not this now manifest, that in every other commerce of life, wherever such an one acts so as to be approved, appearing to be just, and, by a certain 554d moderate behaviour, restrains the other wrong desires within him, he does so, not from any persuasion⁸ that it is not better to indulge them, nor from sober reason, but from necessity and fear, trembling for the rest of his substance." "Entirely so," said he. "And truly," said I, "friend, you shall find in most of them desires partaking of the nature of the drone, where there is occasion to spend the property of others." "Very much so," said he.

"Such a one as this, then, will not be without sedition within himself; nor be one, but a kind of double man; he will, however, have 554e for the most part desires governing other desires, the better governing 401 the worse." "It is so." "And on these accounts such a one, as I imagine, will be more decent than many others, but the true virtue of a harmonized and consistent soul would far escape him." "It appears so to me." "And the parsimonious man will, in private life, be but a poor 555a rival for any victory, or in any contest of the honourable kind. And being unwilling, for the sake of good reputation, or for any such contests, to spend his substance, being afraid to waken up expensive desires, or any alliance or contest of this kind, fighting with a small part of his forces in an Oligarchic manner, he is generally defeated, and increases his wealth." "Very true," said he. "Do we then yet hesitate," said I, "to rank the covetous and parsimonious man as most of all resembling the city under Oligarchic government?" "By no means," said he. 555b

"Democracy now, as seems, is next to be considered, in what manner it arises, and what kind of man it produces when arisen; that, understanding the nature of such a man, we may bring him to a trial." "We shall in this method," said he, "proceed consistently with ourselves." "Is not," said I, "the change from Oligarchy to Democracy produced in some such way as this, through the insatiable desire of the proposed good, *viz.* the desire of becoming as rich as possible?" "How?" "As those who are its governors govern on account of their 555c possessing great riches, they will be unwilling, I think, to restrain by law such of the youth as are dissolute from having the liberty of squandering and wasting their substance; that so, by purchasing the substance of such persons, and lending them on usury, they may still become both richer, and be held in greater honour." "They will be more unwilling than any other." "And is not this already manifest in the city, that it is impossible for the citizens to esteem riches, and at the same time sufficiently possess temperance, but either the one or 555d the other must of necessity be neglected?" "It is abundantly plain," said he.

"But whilst in Oligarchies they neglect education, and suffer the youth to grow licentious, they are sometimes under a necessity of becoming poor, and these such as are of no ungenerous disposition." "Very much so." "And these, I imagine, sit in the city, fitted both with stings and with armour, some of them in debt, others in contempt, others in both, hating and conspiring against those who possess their substance, and others likewise, being desirous of a change." 555e "These things are so." "But the money-catchers still brooding over it, and not seeming to observe these; wherever they see any of the rest 402 giving way, they wound them by throwing money into their hands, and, drawing to themselves exorbitant usury, fill the city with drones, 556a and the poor." "How is it possible they should not?" said he.

"Nor yet," said I, "when so great an evil is burning in the city, are they willing to extinguish it, not even by that method, restraining any one from spending his substance at pleasure; nor yet to take that method, by which, according to the second law, such disorder might be removed." "According to which?" "According to that, which after the other is secondary, obliging the citizens to pay attention to virtue; for, if one should enjoin them to traffic much in the way of voluntary commerce, and upon their own hazard, they would in a less shameful way make money in the city, and likewise less of those evils we have now mentioned would arise in it." "Much less," said he.

"But at present," said I, "by means of all these things, the governors render the governed of this kind. And do they not render both themselves and all belonging to them, and the youth likewise, luxurious and idle with respect to all the exercises of body and of mind, and effeminate in bearing both pleasures and pains, and likewise indolent?" "What else?" "As to themselves, they neglect every thing but the acquisition of wealth, and pay no more attention to virtue than the poor do." "They do not indeed." "After they are trained up in this manner, when these governors and their subjects meet together either on the road in their journeying, or in any other meetings, either at public spectacles,⁹ or military marches, either when fellow-sailors or fellow-soldiers, or when they see one another in common dangers, by no means are the poor in these cases contemned by the rich; but very often a robust fellow poor and sunburnt, when he has his rank in battle beside a rich man bred up in the shade, and swollen with a great deal of adventitious flesh, and sees him panting for breath and in agony, do not you imagine that he thinks it is through their own fault that such fellows grow rich, and that they say to one another, when they meet in private, that our rich men are good for nothing at all?" "I know very well," said he, "that they do so."

For, as a diseased body needs but the smallest shock from without to render it sickly, and sometimes without any impression from without is in sedition with itself, will not in like manner a city resembling it in these things, on the smallest occasion from without, when either the one party forms an alliance with the Oligarchic, or the other with the Democratic, be sickly, and fight with it itself, and, sometimes without these things from abroad, be in sedition?" "And extremely so." "A Democracy then, I think, arises when the poor prevailing over the rich kill some, and banish others, and share the places in the republic, and the magistracies equally among the remainder, and for the most part the magistracies are disposed in it by lot." "This truly," said he, "is the establishment of a Democracy, whether it arise by force of arms, or from others withdrawing themselves through fear."

"In what manner now," said I, "do these live, and what sort of a 557b republic is this? for it is plain that a man of this kind will appear some Democratic man." "It is plain," said he. "Is not then the city, in the first place, full of all freedom of action, and of speech, and of liberty, to do in it what any one inclines?" "So truly it is said at least," replied he. "And wherever there is liberty, it is plain that every one will regulate his own method of life in whatever way he pleases." "It is plain." "And I think that in such a republic most especially there 557c would arise men of all kinds." "How can it be otherwise?" "This," said I, "seems to be the finest of all republics. As a variegated robe diversified with all kinds of flowers, so this republic; variegated with all sorts of manners, appears the finest." "What else?" said he. "And it is likely," said I, "that the multitude judge this republic to be the best, like children and women gazing at variegated things." "Very likely," 557d said he. "And it is very proper at least, O blessed man!" said I, "to search for a republic in such a state as this." "How now?" "Because it contains all kinds of republics on account of liberty; and it appears necessary for any one who wants to constitute a city, as we do at present, to come to a Democratic city, as to a general fair of republics, and choose that form which he fancies." "It is likely indeed," said he, "he would not be in want of models."   557e

"But what now," said I, "is not this a divine and sweet manner of life for the present: To be under no necessity in such a city to govern, not though you were able to govern, nor yet to be subject unless you incline, nor to be engaged in war when others are, nor to live in peace 404 when others do so unless you be desirous of peace; and though there be a law restraining you from governing or administering justice, to govern nevertheless, and administer justice, if you incline?" "It is 558a likely," said he; "it is pleasant for the present at least." "But what now, is not the meekness of some of those who are condemned very curious? Or have you not as yet observed, in such a republic, men condemned to death or banishment, yet nevertheless continuing still, and walking up and down openly; and as if no one attended to or observed him, the condemned man returns like a hero?" "I have observed very many," said he. "But is not this indulgence of the city

558b very generous, not to mention the small regard, and even contempt, it shows for all those things we celebrated so much when we settled our city, as that unless a man had an extraordinary genius, he never would become a good man, unless when a child he were instantly educated in things handsome, and should diligently apply to all these things how magnanimously does it despise all these things, and not regard from what kind of pursuits a man comes to act in political

558c affairs, but honours him if he only says he is well affected towards the multitude?" "This contempt," said he, "is very generous indeed." "These now," said I, "and such things as are akin to these, are to be found in a Democracy; and it will be, as it appears, a pleasant sort of republic, anarchical, and variegated, distributing a certain equality to all alike without distinction." "What you say," replied he, "is perfectly manifest."

"Consider now," said I, "what kind of man such an one is in private; or, first, must we not consider, as we did with respect to the republic, in what manner he arises?" "Yes," said he. "And does he not in this manner arise, *viz.* from that parsimonious one, who was under

558d the Oligarchy as a son, I think, trained up by his father in his manners?" "Why not?" "Such a one by force governs his own pleasures, those of them which are expensive, and tend not to the acquisition of wealth, and which are called unnecessary." "It is plain," said he. "Are you willing then," said I, "that we may not reason in the dark, first to determine what desires are necessary, and what are not?" "I am willing," said he. "May not such be justly called necessary,

558e which we are not able to remove, and such as when gratified are of advantage to us? For both these kinds our nature is under a necessity

559a to pursue; is it not?" "Very strongly." "This then we shall justly say makes the necessary part in our desires." "Justly."

405 "But what now?" "Such desires as a man may banish, if he study it from his youth, and such as whilst they remain do no good, if we say of these that they are not necessary, shall we not say aright?" "Right

indeed." "Let us select a paradigm of each of them, that we may understand by an example what they are." "It is proper." "Is not the desire of eating, so far as is conducive to health and a good habit of body; and the desire of food and victuals, of the necessary kind?" "I 559b think so." "The desire of food at least is indeed necessary on both accounts, as meat is advantageous, and as the want of it must bring life to an end altogether." "It is." "And the desire of victuals is likewise necessary, if it anyhow contribute anything towards the good habit of the body." "Certainly." "But what? Such desire even of these things as goes beyond these purposes, or such desire as respects other meats than these, and yet is capable of being curbed in youth, and, by being disciplined, to be removed from many things, and which is hurtful both to the body, and hurtful to the soul with reference to her attaining wisdom and temperance, may not such desire be rightly 559c called unnecessary?" "Most rightly, indeed." "And may we not call these expensive likewise, and the others frugal, as they are conducive towards the actions of life?" "Why not?" "In the same manner, surely, shall we say of venereal desires, and the others." "In the same manner." "And did we not, by him whom we just now denominated the drone, mean one who was full of such desires and pleasures, and was governed by such as are unnecessary? but that he who was under the necessary 559d ones was the parsimonious and Oligarchic?" "Without doubt."

"Let us again mention," said I, "how the Democratic arises from the Oligarchic; and to me he appears to arise in great measure thus." "How?" "When a young man nurtured, as we now mentioned, without proper instruction, and in a parsimonious manner, comes to taste the honey of the drones, and associates with those vehement and terrible creatures who are able to procure all sorts of pleasures, and every way diversified, and from every quarter;—thence conceive there is somehow the beginning of a change in him from the Oligarchic to 559e the Democratic." "There is great necessity for it," said he. "And as the city was changed by the assistance of an alliance from without with one party of it with which it was akin, will not the youth be changed in the same manner, by the assistance of one species of desires from without, to another within him which resembles it, and is allied to it?" "By all means." "And I imagine at least, if by any alliance there be 406 given counter-assistance to the Oligarchic party within him, either

560a any how by his father, or by others of the family, both admonishing
and upbraiding him, then truly arises sedition, and oppression, and a
light within him with himself." "Undoubtedly." "And sometimes
indeed, I think, the Democratic party yields to the Oligarchic, and
some of the desires are destroyed, but others retire, on a certain
modesty being ingenerated in the soul of the youth, and he again
becomes cultivated." "This sometimes takes place," said he. "And
560b again, I conceive, that when some desires retire, there are others allied
to them which grow up, and, through inattention to the father's
instruction, become both many and powerful." "This is usually the
case," said he. "And do they not draw towards intimacies among
themselves, and, meeting privately together, generate a multitude?"
"What else?" "And at length, I think, they seize the citadel of the soul
of the youth, finding it evacuated both of beautiful disciplines and
560c pursuits, and of true reasoning, which are the best guardians and
preservers in the dianoëtic part of men beloved of the Gods." "Very
much so," said he. "And then indeed false and arrogant reasonings
and opinions, rushing up in their stead, possess the same place in such
a one." "Vehemently so," said he. "And does he not now again, on
coming among those Lotophagi,[10] dwell with them openly? And if
any assistance comes from his friends to the parsimonious part of his
soul, those arrogant reasonings, shutting the gates of the royal wall
560d against it, neither give entrance to this alliance, nor to the
ambassadorial admonitions of private old men; but, fighting against
these, hold the government themselves. and denominating modesty
stupidity, they thrust it out disgracefully as a fugitive, and temperance
they call unmanliness, and, abusing it most shamefully, expel it.
Persuading themselves likewise that moderation, and decent expense,
are no other than rusticity and illiberality, they banish them from
their territories, with many other and unprofitable desires."
"Vehemently so."

560e   "Having emptied and purified from all these desires the soul that is
detained by them, and is initiated in the great mysteries, they next
lead in, with encomiums and applauses, insolence and anarchy, luxury
407 and impudence, shining with a great retinue, and crowned. And
insolence, indeed, they denominate education; anarchy they call
561a liberty; luxury, magnificence; and impudence, manhood. Is it not,"

said I, "somehow in this manner, that a youth changes from one bred up with the necessary desires into the licentiousness and remissness of the unnecessary and unprofitable pleasures?" "And very plainly so," replied he. "And such a one, I think, after this leads his life, expending his substance, his labour, and his time, no more on the necessary than the unnecessary pleasures: and if he be fortunate, and not excessively debauched, when he is somewhat more advanced in years, and when the great crowd of desires is over, he admits a part of 561b those which were expelled, and does not deliver himself wholly up to such as had intruded, but regulates his pleasures by a sort of equality, and so lives delivering up the government of himself to every incidental desire as it may happen, till it be satisfied, and then to another, undervaluing none of them, but indulging them all alike." "Entirely so."

"And such a one," said I, "does not listen to true reasoning, nor admit it into the citadel, if any should tell him that there are some 561c pleasures of the worthy and the good desires, and others of the depraved, and that he ought to pursue and honour those, but to chastise and enslave these. But, in all these cases, he dissents, and says that they are all alike, and ought to be held in equal honour." "Whoever is thus affected," said he, "vehemently acts in this manner." "And does he not live," said I, "from day to day, gratifying after this manner every incidental desire, sometimes indulging himself in intoxication, and in music, sometimes drinking water, and extenuating himself by abstinence; and then again attending to the 561d gymnic exercises? Sometimes too he is quite indolent and careless about every thing; then again he applies as it were to philosophy; many times he acts the part of a politician, and in a desultory manner says and does whatever happens. If at any time he affects to imitate any of the military tribe, thither he is carried; or of the mercantile, then again hither; nor is his life regulated by any order, or any necessity, but, deeming this kind of life pleasant, and free, and blessed, he follows it throughout." "You have entirety," said he, 561e "discussed the life of one who places all laws what ever on a level."

"I imagine at least," said I, "that he is multiform, and full of very different manners; and that, like the city, he is fine, and variegated, and that very many men and women would desire to imitate his life,

408 as he contains in himself a great many patterns of republics and of
562a manners." "He does," said he. "What now? Shall such a man as this be
arranged as resembling a Democracy, as he may truly be called
Democratic?" "Let him be so arranged," said he.

"But it yet remains that we discuss," said I, "the most excellent
republic, and the most excellent man, *viz.* Tyranny, and the Tyrant."
"It does," said he. "Come then, my dear companion! in what manner
does Tyranny arise? for it is almost plain that the change is from
Democracy." "It is plain." "Does not Tyranny arise in the same
manner from Democracy, as Democracy does from Oligarchy?"
562b "How?" "What did Oligarchy," said I, "propose as its good, and
according to what was it constituted? It was with a view to become
extremely rich, was it not?" "Yes." "An insatiable desire then of
riches, and a neglect of other things, through attention to the
acquisition of wealth, destroys it." "True," said he. "And with
reference to that which Democracy denominates good, an insatiable
thirst of it destroys it likewise?" "But what is it you say it denominates
good?" "Liberty," said I. "For this you are told is most beautiful in a
562c city which is under a Democracy, and that for the sake of liberty any
one who is naturally free chooses to live in it alone." "This word
Liberty," said he, "is indeed often mentioned." "Does not then," said
I, "as I was going to say, the insatiable desire of this, and the neglect
of other things, change even this republic, and prepare it to stand in
need of a tyrant?" "How?" said he. "When a city," said I, "is under a
Democracy, and is thirsting after liberty, and happens to have bad
562d cup-bearers appointed it, and becomes intoxicated with an unmixed
draught of it beyond what is necessary, it punishes even the governors
if they will not be entirely tame, and afford abundant liberty,
accusing them as corrupted, and Oligarchic." "They do this," said he.
"But such as are obedient to magistrates they abuse," said I, "as willing
slaves, and good for nothing, and, both in private and in public,
commend and honour magistrates who resemble subjects, and
562e subjects who resemble magistrates; must they not therefore necessarily
in such a city arrive at the summit of liberty?" "How is it possible they
should not?" "And must not this inbred anarchy, my friend, descend
into private families, and in the end reach even the brutes?" "How,"
said he, "do we assert such a thing as this?" "Just as if," said I, "a father

should accustom himself to resemble a child, and to be afraid of his sons, and the son accustom himself to resemble his father, and *409* neither to revere nor to stand in awe of his parents, that so indeed he *563a* may be free, as if a stranger were to be equalled with a citizen, and a citizen with a stranger, and, in like manner, a foreigner." "It is just so," said he.

"These things," said I, "and other little things of a like nature happen. The teacher in such a city fears and flatters the scholars, and the scholars despise their teachers and their tutors in like manner: and in general the youth resemble the more advanced in years, and contend with them both in words and deeds: and the old men, sitting down with the young, are full of merriment and pleasantry, *563b* mimicking the youth, that they may not appear to be morose and despotic." "It is entirely so," replied he. "But that extreme liberty of the multitude," said I, "how great it is in such a city as this, when the men and women slaves are no less free than those who purchase them, and how great an equality and liberty the wives have with their husbands, and husbands with their wives, we have almost forgotten to mention." "Shall we not then, according to Æschylus," said he, "say *563c* whatever now comes into our mouth?" "By all means," said I; "and accordingly I do speak thus: With reference even to brutes, such of them as are under the care of men, how much more free they are in such a city, he who has not experienced it will not easily believe: for indeed even the puppies, according to the proverb, resemble their mistresses; and the horses and asses are accustomed to go freely and gracefully, marching up against any one they meet on the road, unless he give way; and many other such things thus happen full of liberty."

"You tell me," said he, "my dream; for I have often met with this *563d* when going into the country." "But do you observe," said I, "what is the sum of all these things collected together? How delicate it makes the soul of the citizens, so that, if any one bring near to them any thing pertaining to slavery, they are filled with indignation, and cannot endure it. And do you know, that at length they regard not even the laws, written or unwritten, that no one by any means *563e* whatever may become their masters?" "I know it well," said he.

"This now, friend," said I, "is that government so beautiful and youthful, whence Tyranny springs, as it appears to me." "Youthful truly," replied he; "but what follows this?" "The same thing," said I, which, springing up as a disease in an Oligarchy, destroyed it; the same arising here in a greater and more powerful manner, through its *410* licentiousness, enslaves the Democracy: and in reality, the doing any thing to excess usually occasions a mighty change to the reverse: for *564a* thus it is in seasons, in vegetable and in animal bodies, and in republics as much as in any thing." "It is probable," said he. "And excessive liberty seems to change into nothing else but excessive slavery, both with a private person and a city." "It is probable, indeed." "It is probable then," said I, "that out of no other republic is Tyranny constituted than a Democracy; out of the most excessive liberty I conceive the greatest and most savage slavery." "It is reasonable," said he, "to think so." "But this I think," said I, "was not *564b* what you were asking; but what that disease is which enslaves Democracy, resembling that which destroys Oligarchy?" "You say true," replied he.

"That then," said I, "I called the race of idle and profuse men, one part of which was more brave, and were leaders, the other more cowardly, and followed. And we compared them to drones; some to such as have stings, others to such as have none." "And rightly," said he. "These two now," said I, "springing up in any republic, raise *564c* disturbance, as phlegm and bile in a natural body. And it behoves a wise physician and law-giver of a city, no less than a wise bee-master, to be afraid of these, at a great distance principally, that they never get in; but, if they have entered, that they be in the speediest manner possible cut off, together with their very cells." "Yes, by Jupiter," said he, "by all means."

"Let us take it then," said I, "in this manner, that we may see more distinctly what we want." "In what manner?" "Let us divide in our reasoning a Democratic city into three parts, as it really is; for one *564d* such species as the above grows through licentiousness in it no less than in the Oligarchic." "It does so." "But it is much more fierce at least in this than in that." "How?" "In an Oligarchy, because it is not in places of honour, but is debarred from the magistracies, it is unexercised, and does not become strong. But in a Democracy this, excepting a few, is somehow the presiding party, and now it says and does the most outrageous things, and then again approaching courts

of justice, it makes a humming noise, and cannot endure any other to 564e
speak different from it; so that all things, some few excepted, in such a
republic, are administered by such a party." "Extremely so," said he.
"Some other party now, such as this, is always separated from the
multitude." "Which?" "Whilst the whole are somehow engaged in
the pursuit of gain, such as are naturally the most temperate become
for the most part the wealthiest." "It is likely." "And hence, I think, 411
the greatest quantity of honey, and what comes with the greatest ease,
is pressed out of these by the drones." "For how," said he, "can any
one press out of those who have but little?" "Such wealthy people, I
think, are called the pasture of the drones." "Nearly so," replied he.

"And the people will be a sort of third species, such of them as mind 565a
their own affairs, and meddle not with any others, who have not
much substance, but yet are the most numerous, and the most
prevalent in a Democracy, whenever it is fully assembled." "It is so;
but this it will not wish to do often, if it does not obtain same share of
the honey." "Does it not always obtain a share," said I, "as far as their
leaders are able, robbing those that have property, and giving to the
people that they may have the most themselves?" "They are indeed,"
said he, "sharers in this manner." "These then who are thus despoiled 565b
are obliged to defend themselves, saying and doing all they can
among the people." "Why not?" "Others then give them occasion to
form designs against the people, though they should have no
inclination to introduce a change of government, and so they are
Oligarchic." "Why not?" "But at length, after they see that the people,
not of their own accord, but being ignorant and imposed on by those 565c
slanderers, attempt to injure them,—do they not then indeed,
whether they will or not, become truly Oligarchic yet not
spontaneously, but this mischief likewise is generated by that drone
stinging them." "Extremely so, indeed." "And so they have
accusations, law-suits, and contests one with another." "Very much
so." "And are not the people accustomed always to place some one, in
a conspicuous manner, over themselves, and to cherish him, and
greatly increase his power?" "They are." "And this," said I, "is plain,
that whenever a tyrant arises it is from this presiding root, and from 565d
nothing else, that he blossoms." "This is extremely manifest."

"What is the beginning then of the change from a president into a tyrant? Or is it plain, that it is after the president begins to do the same thing with that in the fable, which is told in relation to the temple of Lycæan Jupiter, to whom was dedicated the wolf in Arcadia?" "What is that?" said he. "That whoever tasted human 565e entrails which were mixed with those of other sacrifices, necessarily became a wolf. Have you not heard the story?" "I have." "And must not he in the same manner, who being president of the people, and 412 receiving an extremely submissive multitude, abstains not from kindred blood, but unjustly accusing them, (of such things as they are wont) and bringing them into courts of justice, stains himself with bloodshed, taking away the life of a man, and, with unhallowed 566a tongue and mouth, tasting kindred blood, and besides this, banishes and slays, and proposes the abolition of debts, and division of lands,— must not such an one, of necessity, and as it is destined, be either destroyed by his enemies, or exercise tyranny, and, from being a man, become a wolf?" "Of great necessity," said he. "This is he now," said I, "who becomes seditious towards those who have property, and, when he fails, he goes against his enemies with open force, and becomes an accomplished tyrant." "It is plain."

566b   "And if they be unable to expel him, or to put him to death; on an accusation before the city, they truly conspire to cut him off privately by a violent death." "It is wont indeed," said he, "to happen so." "And, on this account, all those who mount up to tyranny invent this celebrated tyrannical demand,ⁿ to demand of the people certain guards for their person, that the assistance of the people may be 566c secured to them." "Of this," said he, "they take special care." "And they grant them, I imagine, being afraid of his safety, but secure as to their own." "Extremely so." "And when a man who has property, and who along with his property has the crime of hating the people, observes this,—he then, my friend, according to the answer of the oracle to Crœsus,

> . . . To craggy Hermus flies,
> Nor stays, nor fears to be a coward deemed . . ."

"Because he would not," said he, "be in fear again a second time." "But he at least, I imagine," said I, "who is caught, is put to death." "Of necessity." "It is plain, then, that this president of the city does not himself behave like a truly great man, in a manner truly great, but, hurling down many others, sits in his chair a consummate tyrant 566d of the city, instead of a president." "Why is he not?" said he.

"Shall we consider now," said I, "the happiness of the man, and of 413 the city in which such a mortal arises?" "By all means," said he, "let us consider it." "Does he not then," said I, "in the first days, and for the first season, smile, and salute every one he meets; says he is no tyrant, and promises many things, both in private and in public; and frees 566e from debts, and distributes land both to the people in general, and to those about him, and affects to be mild and patriotic towards all?" "Of necessity," said he. "But when, I think, he has reconciled to himself some of his foreign enemies, and destroyed others, and there is tranquillity with reference to these, he in the first place always raises some wars, in order that the people may be in need of a leader." "It is likely." "And is it not likewise with this view, that, being rendered 567a poor by payment of taxes, they may be under a necessity of becoming intent on daily sustenance, and may be less ready to conspire against him?" "It is plain." "And, I think, if he suspects that any of those who are of a free spirit will not allow him to govern,—in order to have some pretext for destroying them, he exposes them to the enemy; on all these accounts a tyrant is always under a necessity of raising war." "Of necessity." "And, whilst he is doing these things, he must readily 567b become more hateful to his citizens." "Why not?" "And must not some of those who have been promoted along with him, and who are in power, speak out freely both towards him, and among themselves, finding fault with the transactions, such of them as are of a more manly spirit?" "It is likely."

"It behoves the tyrant, then, to cut off all these, if he means to govern, till he leave no one, either of friends or foes, worth anything." "It is plain." "He must then carefully observe who is 567c courageous, who is magnanimous, who wise, who rich; and in this manner is he happy, that willing, or not willing, he is under a necessity of being an enemy to all such as these; and to lay snares till he purify the city." "A beautiful purification," said he. "Yes," said I, "the reverse of what physicians do with respect to animal bodies; for they, taking away what is worst, leave the best; but he does the contrary." "Because it seems," said he, "he must of necessity do so, if be is to govern.”

567d   “In a blessed necessity, then, truly, is be bound,” said I, “which obliges him either to live with many depraved people, and to be hated too by them, or not to live at all.” “In such necessity he is,” replied he. “And the more he is hated by his citizens whilst he does these things, shall he not so much the more want a greater number of guards, and more faithful ones?” “How is it possible he should not?” “Who then

414   are the faithful, and from whence shall he send for them?” “Many,” said he, “of their own accord, will come flying, if he give them hire.” “You seem, by the dog,” said I, “again to mention certain drones

567e foreign and multiform.” “You imagine right,” replied he. “But those at home, would he not incline to have them also as guards?” “How?” “After he has taken away the citizens, to give the slaves their liberty, and make of them guards about his person.” “By all means,” said he, “for these are the most faithful to him.” “What a blessed possession,” said I, “is this which you mention belonging to the tyrant, if he

568a employ such friends and faithful men, after having destroyed those former ones!” “But surely such at least,” said he, “he does employ.” “And such companions,” said I, “admire him, and the new citizens accompany him: but the worthy men both hate and fly from him.” “Why should they not?”

   “It is not without reason,” said I, “that tragedy in the general is thought a wise thing, and that Euripides is thought to excel in it.” “For what?” “Because he uttered this, which is the mark of a

568b condensed conception, That ‘tyrants are wise, by the conversation of the wise,’[12] and he plainly said those were wise with whom they hold converse.” “And he commends too,” said he, “Tyranny as a divine thing, and says a great many other things of it, as do likewise the other poets.” “Those composers then of tragedy,” said I, “as they are wise, will forgive us, and such as establish the government of cities in a manner nearly resembling ours, in not admitting them into our republic as being panegyrists of Tyranny.” “I think,” said he, “such of

568c them at least as are more polite will forgive us.” “But going about among other cities, I think, and drawing together the crowds, and putting to sale their fine, magnificent and persuasive words, they will draw over the republics to Tyrannies and Democracies.” “Extremely so.” “And do they not further receive rewards, and are they not honoured chiefly by Tyrants, as is natural, and in the next place by Democracy? But the further on they advance towards the republics, the reverse of these, their honour forsakes them the more, as if it were disabled by an asthma to advance." "Entirely so." 568d

"Thus far," said I, "we have digressed: but now again let us mention in what manner that army of the Tyrant, which is so beautiful, so numerous and multiform, and no way the same, shall be maintained." "It is plain," said he, "that if at any time there be any sacred things in the city, these they will spend, that so what they sell for may still answer their demands, and the people be obliged to pay in the lighter taxes." "But what will they do when these fail them?" "It is plain," said he, "that he and his intoxicated companions, and his associates, male and female, will be maintained out of the paternal inheritance." "I understand," said I, "that the people who have made the Tyrant will nourish him and his companions." "They are under great necessity," said he. "How do you say?" replied I. "What if the people be enraged, and say that it is not just, that the son who is arrived at maturity be maintained by the father, but contrariwise that the father be maintained by the son; and that they did not make and establish him for this purpose, to be a slave to his slaves when he should be grown up, and to maintain him and his slaves with their other turbulent attendants; but in order that they might be set at liberty from the rich in the city, who are also called the good and worthy, by having placed him over them? And now they order him and his companions to leave the city, as a father drives out of the house his son with his turbulent drunken companions." "Then, by Jupiter, shall the people," said he, "know what a beast they are themselves, and what a beast they have generated, and embraced, and nurtured, and that whilst they are the weaker they attempt to drive out the stronger." "How do you say?" replied I. "Will the Tyrant dare to offer violence to his father, and, if he cannot persuade him, will he strike him?" "Yes," said he, "even stripping him of his armour." 415 568e 569a 569b

"You call," said I, "the Tyrant a parricide and a miserable nourisher of old age: and yet, as it is probable, Tyranny would really seem to be of this kind; and according to the saying, the people defending themselves against the smoke of slavery amid free men, have fallen into the slavish fire of despotism; instead of that excessive and 569c unseasonable liberty, embracing the most rigorous and the most wretched slavery of bond-men." "These things," said he, "happen very much so." "What then," said I, "shall we not speak modestly, if we say that we have sufficiently shown how Tyranny arises out of Democracy, and what it is when it does arise?" "Very sufficiently," replied he.

THE END OF THE EIGHTH BOOK.

BOOK IX.

"The tyrannical man himself," said I, "remains yet to be _{571a} considered, in what manner he arises out of the Democratic, and, when he does arise, what kind of man he is, and what kind of life he leads, whether miserable or blessed." "He indeed yet remains," said he. "Do you know," said I, "what I still want?" "What is it?" "We do not appear to me to have sufficiently distinguished with respect to the desires; of what kind they are, and how many; and whilst this is defective, the inquiry we make will be less evident." "May it not be _{571b} done opportunely yet?" said he. "Certainly. And consider what it is I wish to know about them; for it is this: Of those pleasures and desires which are not necessary, some appear to me to be repugnant to law: these indeed seem to be ingenerated in every one; but being punished by the laws, and the better desires, in conjunction with reason, they either forsake some men altogether, or are less numerous and feeble; in others they are more powerful, and more numerous." "Will you _{571c} inform me what these are?" said he.

"Such," said I, "as are excited in sleep; when the other part of the soul, such as is rational and mild, and which governs in it, is asleep, and the part which is savage and rustic, being filled with meats or intoxication, frisks about, and, driving away sleep, seeks to go and accomplish its practices. In such a one you know it dares to do every thing, as being loosed, and disengaged from all modesty and prudence: for it scruples not the embraces, as it imagines, of a mother, or of any one else, whether of Gods, of men, or of beasts; nor to kill _{571d}

any one, nor to abstain from any sort of meat,—and, in one word, is wanting in no folly nor impudence." "You say most true," replied he.

"But I imagine, when a man is in health, and lives temperately, and goes to sleep, having excited the rational part, and feasted it with *417* worthy reasonings and inquiries, coming to an unanimity with *571e* himself; and allowing that part of the soul which is desiderative *572a* neither to be starved nor glutted, that it may lie quiet, and give no disturbance to the part which is best, either by its joy or grief, but suffer it by itself alone and pure to inquire, and desire to apprehend what it knows not, either some thing of what has existed, or of what now exists, or what will exist here after; and having likewise soothed the irascible part, not suffering it to be hurried by any thing, to transports of anger, and to fall asleep with agitated passion: but having quieted these two parts of the soul, and excited the third part, in which wisdom resides, shall in this manner take rest;—by such an *572b* one you know the truth is chiefly apprehended, and the visions of his dreams are then least of all repugnant to law." "I am altogether," said he, "of this opinion." "We have, indeed, been carried a little too far in mentioning these things. But what we want to be known is this, that there is in every one a certain species of desires which is terrible, savage, and irregular, even in some who entirely seem to us to be moderate. And this species becomes indeed manifest in sleep. But consider if there appear to be any thing in what I say, and if you agree with me." "But I agree."

"Recollect now what kind of man we said the Democratic one was: *572c* for he was somehow educated from his infancy under a parsimonious father, who valued the avaricious desires alone; but such as were not necessary, but rose only through a love of amusement and finery, he despised. Was he not?" "Yes." "But, being conversant with those who are more refined, and such as are full of those desires we now mentioned, running into their manner, and all sort of insolence, from a detestation of his father's parsimony;—however, having a *572d* better natural temper than those who corrupt him, and being drawn opposite ways, he settles into a manner which is situated in the middle of both; and participating moderately, as he imagines, of each of them, he leads a life neither illiberal nor licentious, becoming a Democratic from an Oligarchic man." "This was," said he, "and is our opinion of such an one."

"Suppose now again, that when such a one is become old, his young son is educated in his manners." "I suppose it." "And suppose, too, the same things happening to him as to his father; that he is drawn into 572e all kinds of licentiousness, which is termed however by such as draw him off the most complete liberty; and that his father and all the 418 domestics are aiding to those desires which are in the middle, and others also lend their assistance. But when those dire magicians and tyrant-makers have no hopes of retaining the youth in their power any other way, they contrive to excite in him a certain love which presides over the indolent desires, and such as minister readily to their 573a pleasures, which love is a certain winged and large drone; or do you think that the love of these things is any thing else?" "I think," said he, "it is no other than this."

"And when other desires make a humming noise about him, full of their odours and perfumes, and crowns, and wines, and those pleasures of the most dissolute kind which belong to such co-partnerships; and, being increased and cherished, add a sting of desire to the drone, then truly he is surrounded with madness as a life-guard, and that president of the soul rages with frenzy; and if he find in himself any opinions or 573b desires which seem to be good, and which yet retain modesty, he kills them, and pushes them from him, till he be cleansed of temperance, and is filled with additional madness." "You describe perfectly," said he, "the formation of a tyrannical man." "Is it not," said I, "on such an account as this, that, of old, Love is said to be a tyrant?" "It appears so," replied he. "And, my friend," said I, "has not a drunken man likewise somewhat of a tyrannical spirit?" "He has indeed." "And 573c surely at least he who is mad, and is disturbed in his mind, undertakes and hopes to be able to govern not only men, but likewise the Gods." "Entirely so," said he. "The tyrannical character then, O divine man! becomes so in perfection, when either by temper, or by his pursuits, or by both, he becomes intoxicated, and in love, and melancholy." "Perfectly so, indeed."

"Such a one, it seems, then, arises in this manner. But in what manner does he live?" "As they say in their plays," replied he, "that 573d you will tell me likewise." "Tell then," said I. "For I think that after this there are feastings among them, and revellings, and banquetings, and mistresses, and all such things as may be expected among those where Love the tyrant dwelling within governs all in the soul." "Of necessity," said he. "Every day and night, therefore, do there not blossom forth many and dreadful desires, indigent of many things?" "Many indeed." "And if they have any supplies, they are soon spent."

573e "What else?" "And after this there is borrowing and pillaging of substance." "What else?" "And when every thing fails them, is there not a necessity that the desires, on the one hand, nestling in the

419 mind, shall give frequent and powerful cries; and the men, on the other hand, being driven as by stings, both by the other desires, and more especially by love¹ itself, commanding all the others as its life-guards,² shall rage with frenzy, and search what any one possesses

574a which they are able, by deceit or violence, to carry away?" "Extremely so," said he.

"They must of necessity therefore be plundering from every quarter, or be tormented with great agonies and pains." "Of necessity." "And as with such a man his new pleasures possess more than his ancient ones, and take away what belonged to them, shall not he deem it proper in the same manner, that himself, being young, should have more than his father and mother, and take away from them, and, if he has spent his own portion, encroach on that of his parents?" "Why will he not?"

574b said he. "And if they do not allow him, will he not first endeavour to pilfer from and beguile his parents?" "By all means." "And where he is not able to do this, will he not in the next place use rapine and violence?" "I think so," replied he. "But, O wonderful man! when the old man and the old woman oppose and fight, will he not revere them, and beware of doing any thing tyrannical?" "I, for my part, am not quite secure," said he, "with reference to the safety of the parents of such an one." "But by Jupiter, Adimantus, do you think that, for the sake of a newly beloved and unnecessary mistress, such a one would give

574c up his anciently beloved and necessary mother; or, for the sake of a blooming youth newly beloved, and not necessary, give up his decayed, his necessary and aged father, the most ancient of all his friends, to stripes, and suffer these to be enslaved by those others, if he should bring them into the same house?" "Yes, by Jupiter, I do," said he. "It seems," said I, "to be an extremely blessed thing to beget a tyrannical son." "Not altogether so," said he.

"But what, when the substance of his father and mother fails such an one, and when now there is the greatest swarm of pleasures 574d assembled in him, shall he not first break into some house, or late at night strip some one of his coat, and after this shall he not rifle some temple; and in all these actions, those desires newly loosed from slavery, and become as the guards of love, shall along with him rule over those ancient opinions he had from his infancy, the established decisions concerning good and evil; these desires which heretofore 420 were only loose from their slavery in sleep, when he was as yet under 574e the laws, and his father when under Democratic government, now when he is tyrannized over by love, such as he rarely was when asleep, such shall he be always when awake; and from no horrid slaughter, or food, or deed of any kind, shall he abstain. But that tyrannical love 575a within him, living without any restraint of law or government, as being sole monarch itself, will lead on the man it possesses, as a city, to every mad attempt, whence he may support himself, and the crowd about him; which partly enters from without, from ill company, and, partly through their manners and his own, is be come unrestrained and licentious. Or is not this the life of such a one?" "It is this truly," said he.

"And if there be," said I, "but a few such in the city, and the rest of 575b the multitude be sober, they go out and serve as guards to some other tyrant, or assist him for hire, if there be any war; but if they remain in peace and quiet, they commit at home in the city a great many small mischiefs." "Which do you mean?" "Such as these: they steal, break open houses, cut purses, strip people of their clothes, rifle temples, make people slaves; and where they can speak they sometimes turn false informers, and give false testimony, and take gifts." "You call 575c these," said he, "small mischiefs, if there be but a few such persons." "What is small," said I, "is small in comparison of great. And all those things, with regard to the tyrant, when compared with the wickedness and misery of the city, do not, as the saying is, come near the mark; for when there are many such in the city, and others accompanying them, and when they perceive their own number, then these are they who, through the foolishness of the people, establish as tyrant the man who among them has himself most of the tyrant, and 575d in the greatest strength, within his soul." "It is probable indeed," said

he; "for he will be most tyrannical." "Will he not be so, if they voluntarily submit to him? But if the city will not allow him, in the same manner as he formerly used violence to his father and mother, so now again will he chastise his country if he be able; and bringing in other young people, he will keep and nourish under subjection to these, his formerly beloved mother- and father-country, as the
575e   Cretans say? And this will be the issue of such a man's desire." "It will be entirely this," said he. "But do not these," said I, "become such as
421   this, first in private, and before they govern? In the first place, by the company they keep, either converting with their own flatterers, and
576a   such as are ready to minister to them in every thing; or, if they need any thing themselves, falling down to those they converse with, they dare to assume every appearance as friends; but, after they have gained their purpose, they act as enemies." "Extremely so." "Thus they pass the whole of their life, never friends to any one, but always either domineering, or enslaved to another. But liberty and true friendship the tyrannic disposition never tastes." "Entirely so." "May we not then rightly call these men faithless?" "Why not?" "And surely we
576b   may call them most of all unjust, if we have rightly agreed about justice, in our former reasonings, what it is." "But we did rightly agree," said he.

"Let us finish then," said I, "our worst man. He would then seem such a one awake, as we described as asleep." "Entirely so." "And does not that man become such a one, who being most tyrannical by natural temper, is in possession of supreme power, and the longer time he lives in tyranny, the more he becomes such a one?" "Of necessity," replied Glauco, taking up the discourse. "And will not the man," said I, "who
576c   appears the most wicked, appear likewise the most wretched; and he who shall tyrannize for the longest time, and in the greatest measure, shall he not in reality, in the greatest measure, and for the longest time, be such a one? But as many men as many minds." "Of necessity," said he, "these things at least must be so." "And would this Tyrannic man differ any thing," said I, "as to similitude, when compared with the city under tyranny, and the Democratic man when compared with the city under democracy, and after the same manner with respect to others?"
"How should they?" "As city then is to city, as to virtue and happiness,
576d   will not man be to man in the same way?" "Why not?"

"What then? How is the city which is tyrannized over, in respect of that under kingly government, such as we at the first described?" "Quite the reverse," said he; "for the one is the best, and the other is the worst." "I will not ask," said I, "which you mean, for it is plain; but do you judge in the same way, or otherwise, as to their happiness and misery? And let us not be struck with admiration, whilst we regard the tyrant alone, or some few about him; but let us, as we ought to do, enter into the whole of the city, and consider it; and going through every part, and viewing it, let us declare our opinion." "You propose rightly," said he. "And it is evident to every one that there is no city more wretched than that which is under Tyranny, nor any more happy than that under regal power." 576e

422

"If now," said I, "I should propose the same things with respect to the men, should I rightly propose, whilst I account him worthy to judge about them, who is able, by his dianoëtic power, to enter within, and see through the temper of the man, and who may not, as a child beholding the outside, be struck with admiration of tyrannical pomp, which he makes a show of to those without, but may sufficiently see through him? If then I should be of opinion, that all of us ought to hear such a one, who, having dwelt with the man in the same house, and having been along with him in his actions in his family, is able to judge in what manner he behaves to each of his domestics, (in which most especially a man appears stripped of theatrical shows,) and likewise in public dangers; after he has observed all these things, we shall bid him declare, how the Tyrant is as to happiness and misery, in comparison of others." "You would advise to these things," said he, "most properly." "Are you willing then," said I, "that we pretend to be ourselves of the number of those who are thus able to judge, and that we have already met with such men, that we may have one who shall answer our questions?" "By all means." 577a

577bc

"Come then," said I, "consider in this manner. Recollect the resemblance of the city, and the man, to one another, and, thus considering each of them apart, relate the passions of each." "Which passions?" said he. "To begin first," said I, "with the city. Do you call the one under Tyranny, either free or enslaved?" "Slavish," said he, "in the greatest degree possible." "And yet, surely, at least, you see in it masters and free men." "I see," said he, "some small part so. But the 577c

whole in it, in the general, and the most excellent part, is
577d disgracefully and miserably slavish." "If then the man," said I,
"resembles the city, is it not necessary that there be the same
regulation in him likewise; and that his soul be full of the greatest
slavery and illiberality; and that these parts of his soul, which are the
noblest, be enslaved, and that some small part, which is most wicked
and frantic, is master?" "Of necessity," said he. "What now? will you
say that such a soul is slavish, or free?" "Slavish somehow, I say." "But
does not then the city which is slavish, and tyrannized over, least of
all do what it inclines?" "Very much so." "And will not the soul too,
577e which is tyrannized over, least of all do what it shall incline, to speak
423 of the whole soul;³ but, hurried violently by some stinging passion, be
full of tumult and inconstancy?" "How should not it be so?"

578a "But whether will the city which is tyrannized over be necessarily
rich or poor?" "Poor." "And the soul under Tyranny be of necessity
likewise indigent and insatiable?" "Just so," said he. "But what? must
not such a city, and such a man, of necessity be full of fear?" "Very
much so." "Do you think you will find more lamentations, and
groans, and weepings, and torments, in any other city?" "By no
means." "But with reference to a man, do you think that these things
are greater in any other than in this tyrannical one, who madly rages
by his desires and lusts?" "How can they?" said he. "It is then on
578b consideration of all these things, and other such as these, I think, that
you have deemed this city the most wretched of cities?" "And have I
not deemed right?" said he. "Extremely so," said I. "But what say you
again with reference to the tyrannical man, when you consider these
things?" "That he is by far," said he, "the most wretched of all
others." "You do not as yet say this rightly," replied I. "How?" said he.
"I do not as yet think," said I, "that he is such in the greatest degree."
"But who then is so?" "The following will probably appear to you to
578c be yet more miserable than the other." "Which?" "He," said I, "who,
being naturally tyrannical, leads not a private life, but is unfortunate,
and through some misfortune is led to become a Tyrant." "I
conjecture," said he, "from what was formerly mentioned, that you
say true." "It is so," said I. "But we ought not merely to conjecture
about matters of such importance as these, but most thoroughly to
inquire into them by reasoning of this kind: for the inquiry is

concerning a thing of the greatest consequence, a good life and a bad." "Most right," said he.

"Consider then whether there be any thing in what I say; for, in 578d considering this question, I am of opinion that we ought to perceive it from these things." "From what?" "From every individual of private men, *viz.* such of them as are rich, and possess many slaves; for those have this resemblance at least of Tyrants, that they rule over many, with this difference, that the Tyrant has a great multitude." "There is this difference." "You know then that these live securely, and are not 424 afraid of their domestics." "What should they be afraid of?" "Nothing," said I; "but do you consider the reason?" "Yes. It is because the whole city gives assistance to each particular private man." "You 578e say right," replied I. "But what now? If some God should lift a man who had fifty slaves or upwards out of the city, both him, and his wife and children, and set him down in a desert, with his other substance, and his domestics, where no freeman was to give him assistance,—in what kind of fear, and in how great, do you imagine he would be about himself, his children and wife, lest they should be destroyed by the domestics?" "In the greatest possible," said he, "I imagine." "Would he not be obliged even to flatter some of the very slaves, and 579a promise them many things, to set them at liberty when there was no occasion for it; and appear to be himself a flatterer of servants?" "He is under great necessity," said he, "to do so, or be destroyed."

"But what," said I, "if the God should settle round him many other neighbours, who could not endure if any one should pretend to lord it over another; but, if they any where found such a one, should punish him with the extremest rigour?" "I imagine," said he, "that he would 579b be still more distressed, thus beset by every kind of enemies." "And in such a prison-house is not the Tyrant bound, being such by disposition, as we have mentioned, full of many and most various fears and loves of all kinds? And whilst he has in his soul the greatest desire, he alone of all in the city is neither allowed to go any where abroad, nor to see such things as other men are desirous of; but, creeping into his house, lives mostly as a woman, envying the other 579c citizens if any of them go abroad, and see any good." "It is entirely so," said he.

"And besides such evils as these, does not the man reap still more of them, who, being under ill policy within himself, (which you just now deemed to be the most wretched Tyranny,) lives not as a private person, but through some fortune is obliged to act the tyrant, and, without holding the government of himself, attempts to govern others, as if one with a body diseased, and unable to support itself,

579d were obliged to live not in a private way, but in wrestling and fighting against other bodies?" "You say, Socrates," replied he, "what is altogether most likely and true." "Is not then, friend Glauco," said I, "this condition altogether miserable? and does not the Tyrant live

425 more miserably still, than the man deemed by you to live most miserably?" "Very much so," said he.

"True it is then, though one may fancy otherwise, that the truly
579e tyrannical an is truly slavish with respect to the greatest flatteries and slaveries; and is a flatterer of the most abandoned men; nor does he ever in the smallest degree obtain the gratification of his desires but is of all the most indigent of most things, and appears poor indeed, if a man knows how to contemplate his whole soul; and full of fear through the whole of life, being filled with anxieties and griefs, if indeed he resembles the constitution of that city which he governs.

580a But he does resemble it. Does he not?" "Extremely," said he. "And shall we not, besides these things, likewise ascribe to this man what we formerly mentioned, that he must necessarily be, and, by governing still, become more than formerly envious, faithless, unjust, unfriendly, unholy, and a general recipient and nourisher of all wickedness; and from all these things be most especially unhappy himself, and then render all about him unhappy likewise?" "No one," said he, "who hath understanding will contradict you."

580b "Come now," said I, "as a judge who pronounces, after considering all, so do you tell me, who, according to your opinion, is the first as to happiness, and who second, and the rest in order, they being five in all? The Regal, the Timocratic, the Oligarchic, the Democratic, and the Tyrannic." "But the judgment," said he, "is easy; for, as if I had entered among them, I judge of them as of public performers, by their virtue and vice, and by their happiness; and its contrary." "Shall we then hire a Herald?" said I. "Or shall I myself declare that the son of

580c Ariston hath judged the best and justest man to be the happiest; (and that this is the man who hath most of the regal spirit; and rules himself with a kingly power;) and that the worst and the most unjust is the most wretched; and that he again happens to be the man who is most tyrannical, who in the greatest degree tyrannizes over himself, and the city?" "Let it be published by you," said he. "Shall I add," said I, "whether they be unknown to be such or not both to all men and Gods?" "Add it," said he.

"Be it so," said I: "this would seem to be one proof of ours. And this, if you are of the same opinion, must be the second." "Which is it?" "Since the soul," said I, "of every individual is divided into three parts, in the same manner as the city was divided it will, in my opinion, afford a second proof." "What is that?" "It is this. Of the three parts of the soul, there appear to me to be three pleasures, one peculiar to each. And the desires and governments are in the same manner." "How do you say?" replied he. "There is one part, we said, by which a man learns, and another by which he is irascible; the third is so multiform, we are unable to express it by one word peculiar to itself, but we denominated it from that which is greatest and most impetuous in it; for we called it the desiderative, on account of the impetuosity of the desires relative to meat, drink, and venereal pleasures, and whatever others belong to these; and we called it avaricious likewise, because it is by means of wealth most especially that such desires are accomplished." "And we said rightly," replied he.

"If then we say that its pleasure and delight are in gain, shall we not best of all reduce it under one head in our discourse, so as to express something to ourselves, when we make mention of this part of the soul? and, calling it the covetous, and the desirous of gain, shall we not term it properly?" "So it appears to me," said he. "But what? Do not we say that the irascible ought to be wholly impelled to superiority, victory, and applause?" "Extremely so." "If then we term it the contentious and ambitious, will it not be accurately expressed?" "Most accurately." "But it is evident to every one, that the part of the soul, by which we learn, is wholly intent always to know the truth; and as to wealth and glory, it cares for these least of all." "Extremely so." "When we call it then the desirous of learning, and the philosophic, we shall call it according to propriety." "How should we not?" "And do not these," said I, "govern in souls, one of them in some, and in others another, as it happens?" "Just so," said he. "On

580d

426

580e

581a

581b

581c

this account then, we said there were three original species of men: the philosophic, the ambitious, and the avaricious." "Entirely so." "And that there were likewise three species of pleasures, one subject to each of these." "Certainly."

"You know then," said I, "that if you were to ask these three men, each of them apart, which of these lives is the most pleasant, each 581d would most of all commend his own. And the avaricious will say, that in comparison with the pleasure of acquiring wealth, that arising from honour, or from learning, is of no value, unless one make money by them." "True," said he. "And what says the ambitious?" said I. "Does not he deem the pleasure arising from making money a sort of burden? And likewise that arising from learning, unless learning bring him honour, does he not deem it smoke and trifling?" 427 "It is so," said he. "And we shall suppose the philosopher," said I, "to 581e deem the other pleasures as nothing in comparison of that of knowing the truth, how it is, and that whilst he is always employed in learning something of this kind, he is not very remote from pleasure; but that he calls the other pleasures truly necessary, as wanting nothing of the others, but where there is a necessity for it." "This," said he, "we must well understand."

"When, therefore," said I, "these several lives, and the respective pleasure of each, dispute among themselves, not with reference to living more worthily or more basely, or worse or better; but merely with reference to this of living more pleasantly, or on the contrary 582a more painfully,—how can we know which of them speaks most conformably to truth?" "I am not quite able," said he, "to tell." "But consider it thus. By what ought we to judge of whatever is to be rightly judged of? Is it not by experience, by prudence, and by reason? Or has any one a better criterion than these?" "How can he?" said he, "Consider now; of the three men, who is the most experienced in all the pleasures? Whether does it appear to you that the avaricious man, 582b in learning truth itself, what it is, is more experienced in the pleasure arising from knowledge, than the philosopher is in that arising from the acquisition of wealth?" "There is," said he, "a great difference: for the philosopher, beginning from his childhood, must, of necessity, taste the other pleasures; but what it is to know real beings, and how sweet this pleasure is, the lucrative man has no necessity of tasting, or of becoming experienced in; but rather, when he earnestly endeavours to effect this, it is no easy matter." "The philosopher then," said I, "far surpasses the lucrative man, at least in experience of both the pleasures." "Far indeed."

"But what with reference to the ambitious man? Is he more experienced in the pleasure arising from honour, than the philosopher is in that arising from intellectual energy?" "Honour," said he, "attends all of them, if they obtain each of them what they aim at: for the rich man is honoured by many, and so is the brave, and the wise; so as to that of honour, what sort of pleasure it is, all of them have the experience. But in the contemplation of being itself, what pleasure there is, it is impossible for any other than the philosopher to have tasted." "On account of experience then," said I, "he of all men 582d judges the best." "By far." "And surely, along with prudence at least, he alone becomes experienced." "Why should he not?"

"But even the organ by which these pleasures must be judged is not the organ of the lucrative, nor of the ambitious, but of the philosopher." "Which is it?" "We said somewhere, that they must be judged of by reason, did we not?" "Yes." "But reasoning is chiefly the organ of the philosopher." "How should it not?" "If then the things to be determined were best determined by riches and gain, what the 582e lucrative man commended, or despised, would of necessity be most agreeable to truth." "Entirely." "And if by honour, and victory and bravery, must it not be as the ambitious and contentious man determined?" "It is evident." "But since it is by experience, and prudence, and reason."—"Of necessity," said he, "what the philosopher and the lover of reason commends must be the most true."

"Of the three pleasures then, that is the most pleasant which 583a belongs to that part of the soul by which we learn most, and he among us in whom this part governs lives the most pleasant life." "How can it," said he, "be otherwise? For the wise man, being the sovereign commender, commends his own life." "But which life," said I, "does our judge pronounce the second, and which the second pleasure?" "It is plain, that of the warlike and ambitious man; for this is nearer to his own than that of the lucrative." "And that of the covetous, as it appears, is last of all." "Why not?" he. "These things 583b now have thus succeeded one another in order. And the just man has twice now overcome the unjust. The third victory now, as at the Olympic games, is sacred to Olympic Jupiter, the saviour; for consider, that the pleasure of the others is not every way genuine, but that of the wise man is: nor are they pure, but somehow shadowed over, as I appear to myself to have heard from one of the wise men. And this truly would be the greatest and most complete downfall of the unjust." "Extremely so. But how do you mean?"

583c "I shall thus trace it out," said I, "whilst in searching you answer my questions." "Ask then," said he. "Tell me then," replied I, "do we not say that pain is opposite to pleasure?" "Entirely so." "And do we not say likewise, that to feel neither pleasure nor pain is somewhat?" "We say it is." "That being in the middle of both these, it is a certain tranquillity of the soul with reference to them. Do you not thus understand it?" "Thus," replied he. "Do you not remember," said I,

429 "the speeches of the diseased, which they utter in their sickness."

583d "Which?" "How that nothing is more pleasant than health, but that it escaped their notice before they became sick, that it was the most pleasant." "I remember it," said he. "And are you not wont to hear those who are under any acute pain say, that there is nothing more pleasant than a cessation from pain?" "I am wont to hear them." "And you may perceive in men, I imagine, the same thing, when they are in many other such like circumstances, where, when in pain, they extol a freedom from pain, and the tranquillity of such a state, as being the most pleasant, and do not extol that of feeling joy." "Because this, it is likely," said he, "becomes at that time pleasant and desirable tranquillity."

583e "And when any one ceaseth," said I, "to feel joy, this tranquillity from pleasure will be painful." "It is likely," said he. "This tranquillity, then, which we just now said was between the two, will at times become each of these, pain and pleasure." "It appears so." "But is it truly possible, that what is neither of the two should become both?" "It does not appear to me that it is." "And surely at least, when any thing pleasant or any thing painful is in the soul, both sensations are a

584a certain motion; are they not?" "Yes." "But did not that which is neither painful nor pleasant appear just now to be tranquillity and in the middle of these two?" "It appears so, indeed." "How is it right then, to deem it pleasant not to be in pain, or painful not to enjoy pleasure?" "It is by no means right." "In these cases, then, tranquillity is not really so," said I, "but it appears pleasant in respect of the painful, and painful in respect of the pleasant. And there is nothing genuine in these appearances as to the truth of pleasure, but a certain magical delusion." "As our reasoning shows," said he.

"Consider then," said I, "the pleasures which do not arise from the 584b cessation of pains, that you may not frequently in the present discourse suppose that these two naturally thus subsist, *viz.* that pleasure is the cessation of pain, and pain the cessation of pleasure." "How," said he, "and which pleasures do you mean?" "There are many others," said I, "but chiefly if you wish to consider the pleasures from smells; for these, without any preceding pain, are on a sudden immensely great, and, when they cease, they leave no pain behind them." "Most true," said he. "Let us not then be persuaded that pure 584c pleasure is the removal of pain, or pain the removal of pleasure." "Let us not." "But yet," said I, "those which extend through the body to the soul, and which are called pleasures, the greatest part of them almost, and the most considerable, are of this species, certain 430 cessations of pain." "They are so." "And are not the preconceptions of pleasure and pain, which arise in the mind from the expectation of these things, of the same kind?" "Of the same."

"Do you know then," said I, "what kind they are of, and what they 584d chiefly resemble?" "What?" said he. "Do you reckon," said I, "there is any such thing in nature as this, the above, the below, and the middle?" "I do." "Do you think then that any one, when he is brought from the below to the middle, imagines any thing else than that he is brought to the above? and when he stands in the middle, and looks down whence he was brought, will he imagine he is any where else than above, whilst yet he has not seen the true above?" "By Jupiter," said he, "I do not think that such an one will imagine otherwise." "But if he should again," said I, "be carried to the below, 584e he would conjecture he was carried to the below, and would conjecture according to truth." "How should he not?" "Would he not be affected in all these respects, from his not having experience in what is really above, and in the middle, and below?" "It is plain." "Would you wonder then, that whilst men are inexperienced in the truth, they have unsound opinions about many other things,—and that as to pleasure and pain, and what is between these, they are likewise affected in this same manner? So that, even when they are 585a brought to what is painful, they imagine truly, and are truly pained; but when from pain they are brought to the middle, they strongly imagine that they are arrived at fullness of pleasure. In the same manner as those who along with the black colour look at the gray, through inexperience of the white, are deceived; so those who consider pain along with a freedom from pain, are deceived through inexperience of pleasure." "By Jupiter," said he, "I should not wonder, but much rather if it were not so."

"But consider it," said I, "in this manner. Are not hunger and 585b thirst, and such like, certain emptinesses in the bodily habit?" "What else?" "And are not ignorance and folly an emptiness in the habit of the soul?" "Extremely so." "And is not the one filled when it receives food, and the other when it possesses intellect?" "Why not?" "But which is the more real repletion, that of the less, or that of the more real being?" "It is plain, that of the more real." "Which species, then, do you think, participates most of a more pure essence; whether these which participate of bread and drink, and meat, and all such sort of 585c nourishment; or that species which participates of true opinion and 431 science, and intellect, and, in short, of all virtue? But judge not in this manner. That which adheres to what is always similar, and immortal, and true, and is so itself, and arises in what is such, does it appear to you to have more of the reality of being, than that which adheres to what is never similar, and is mortal, which is so itself, and is generated in a thing of this kind?" "This," said he, "differs much from that which is always similar."

"Does then the essence of that which is always similar participate more of essence than of science?" "By no means." "But what with relation to truth?" "Nor of this neither." "If it participate less of truth, does it not likewise do so of essence?" "Of necessity." "In short, then, 585d do not the genera relating to the care of the body participate less of truth and essence, than those relating to the care of the soul?" "By far." "And the body less than the soul; do you not think so?" "I do." "Is not that which is filled with more real beings, and is itself a more real being, in reality more truly filled than that which is filled with less real beings, and is itself a less real being?" "How should it not?"

"If then it be pleasant to be filled with what is suitable to nature, that which is in reality filled, and with more real being, must be made 585e both more really and more truly to enjoy true pleasure; but that which participates of less real being, must be less truly and firmly filled, and participates of a more uncertain and less genuine pleasure." "Most necessarily," said he. "Such then as are unacquainted with wisdom and 586a virtue, and are always conversant in feastings and such like, are carried as it appears to the below, and back again to the middle, and there they wander for life. But never, passing beyond this, do they look towards the true above, nor are carried to it; nor are they ever really filled with real being; nor have they ever tasted solid and pure pleasure; but, after the manner of brutes looking always downwards, and bowed towards earth and their tables, they live feeding and 586b coupling; and from a lull of these things, kicking and pushing at one another with iron horns and hoofs, they perish through their insatiableness, as those who are filling with unreal being that which is no real being, nor friendly to themselves." "You pronounce most perfectly, Socrates, as from an oracle," said Glauco, "the life of the multitude." "Must they not then, of necessity, be conversant with pleasures mixed with pains, images of the true pleasure, shadowed over, and coloured by their position beside each other so that both 586c their pleasures and pains will appear vehement, and engender their mad passions in the foolish. Hence also they must fight about these 432 things, as Stesichorus says those at Troy fought about the image of Helen, through ignorance of the true one." "Of necessity," said he, "something of this kind must take place."

"And what as to the irascible part of the soul? must not other such like things happen, wherever any one gratifies it, either in the way of envy, through ambition, or in the way of violence, through contentiousness, or in the way of anger, through moroseness, pursuing a glut of honour, of conquest, and of anger, both without 586d reason, and without intelligence?" "Such things as these," said he, "must necessarily happen with reference to this part of the soul." "What then," said I, "shall we boldly say concerning all the pleasures, both respecting the avaricious and the ambitious part, that such of them as are obedient to science and reason, and, in conjunction with these, pursue and obtain the pleasures of which the prudent part of the soul is the leader, shall obtain the truest pleasures, as far as it is possible for them to attain true pleasure, and in as much as they 586e follow truth, pleasures which are properly their own; if indeed what is best for every one be most properly his own?" "But surely it is most properly," said he, "his own."

"When then the whole soul is obedient to the philosophic part, and there is no sedition in it, then every part in other respects performs its proper business, and is just, and also reaps its own pleasures, and such 587a as are the best, and as far as is possible the most true." "Certainly, indeed." "But when any of the others governs, it happens that it neither attains its own pleasures, and it compels the other parts to pursue a pleasure foreign to them, and not at all true." "It does so," said he. "Do not then the parts which are the most remote from philosophy and reason most especially effectuate such things?" "Very much so." "And is not that which is most remote from law and order, likewise most remote from reason?" "It plainly is." "And have not the amorous and the tyrannical desires appeared to be most remote 587b from law and order?" "Extremely so." "And the royal and the moderate ones, the least remote?" "Yes." "The tyrant then, I think, shall be the most remote from true pleasure, and such as is most properly his own, and the other shall be the least." "Of necessity." "And the tyrant," said I, "shall lead a life the most unpleasant, and the king the most pleasant." "Of great necessity." "Do you know then," said I, "how much more unpleasant a life the tyrant leads than 433 the king?" "If you tell me," said he.

"As there are three pleasures, as it appears, one genuine, and two 587c illegitimate; the Tyrant in carrying the illegitimate to extremity, and flying from law and reason, dwells with slavish pleasures as his life-guards, and how far he is inferior is not easily to be told, unless it may be done in this manner." "How?" said he. "The Tyrant is somehow the third[4] remote from the Oligarchic character; for the Democratic was in the middle between them." "Yes." "Does he not then dwell with the third image of pleasure, distant from him with reference to truth; if our former reasonings be true?" "Just so. "But the Oligarchic 587d is the third again from the Royal, if we suppose the Aristocratic and the Royal the same." "He is the third." "The Tyrant then," said I, "is remote from true pleasure, the third from the third." "It appears so."

"A plain surface then," said I, "may be the image of tyrannical pleasure, as to the computation of length." "Certainly." "But as to power, and the third augment, it is manifest by how great a distance it is remote." "It is manifest," said he, "to the computer at least." "If now, conversely, any one shall say the King is distant from the Tyrant 587e as to truth of pleasure, as much as is the distance of 9, and 20, and 700, shall he not, on completing the multiplication, find him leading the more pleasant life, and the Tyrant the more wretched one, by this same distance?" "You have heaped up," said he, "a prodigious account of the difference between these two men, the just and the unjust, with 588a reference to pleasure and pain." "Yet the numbers are true," said I, "and corresponding to their lives, if indeed days, and nights, and months, and years, correspond to them." "But these," said he, "do correspond to them." "If then the good and just man surpasses so far the evil and unjust man in pleasure, in what a prodigious degree further shall he surpass him in decorum of life, in beauty and in 434 virtue!" "In a prodigious degree, by Jupiter," said he.

"Be it so," said I. "Since now we are come to this part of our argument, let us recapitulate what we first said, on account of which 588b we have come hither: and it was somewhere said, that it was advantageous to do injustice, if one were completely unjust, but were reputed just. Was it not so said?" "It was indeed." "Now then," said I, "let us settle this point, since we have now settled the other, with reference to acting justly and unjustly, what power each of these possesses in itself." "How?" said he. "Let us in our reasoning fashion an image of the soul, that the man who said those things may know what he said." "What kind of image?" said he. "One of those 588c creatures," said I, "which are fabled to have been of old, as that of Chimæra, of Scylla, of Cerberus; and many others are spoken of, where many particular natures existed together in one." "They are spoken of indeed," said he. "Form now one figure of a creature, various, and many-headed,⁵ having all around heads of tame creatures, and of wild, and having power in itself of changing all these heads, and of breeding them out of itself." "This is the work," said he, 588d "of a skilful former: however, as the formation is easier in reasoning, than in wax and such like, let it be formed." "Let there be now one other figure of a lion⁶ and one of a man; but let the first be by far the greatest, and the second be the second in bulk." "These are easy," said he, "and they are formed." "Conjoin now these three in one, so as to exist some how with one another." "They are conjoined," said he. "Form now around them the external appearance of one of them, that of the man; so that to one who is not able to see what is within, but who perceives only the external covering, the man may appear one creature." "This is formed around," said he.

588e

"Let us now tell him, who asserts that it is profitable to this man to do injustice, but to do justice is unprofitable, that he asserts nothing else, than that it is profitable for him to feast the multiform creature, and to make it strong; and likewise the lion, and what respects the lion, whilst the man he kills with famine, and renders weak, so as to be dragged whichever way either of those drag him; and that he will also find it advantageous never to accustom the one to live in harmony with the other, nor to make them friends, but suffer them to be biting one another, and to fight and devour each other." "He," said he, "who commendeth the doing injustice, undoubtedly asserts these things." "And does not he again, who says it is profitable to do justice, say that he ought to do and to say such things by which the inner man shall come to have the most entire command of the man, and, as a tiller of the ground, shall take care of the many-headed creature, cherishing the mild ones, and nourishing them, and hindering the wild ones from growing up, taking the nature of the lion as his ally, and, having a common care for all, make them friendly to one another, and to himself, and so nourish them?" "He who commends justice undoubtedly says such things as these." "In all respects, then, he who commends justice would seem to speak the truth, but he who commends injustice, to speak what is false; for, with regard to pleasure, and applause, and profit, he who commends justice speaks the truth, and he who discommends it speaks nothing genuine. Nor does he discommend with understanding what he discommends." "Not at all," said he, "as appears to me at least."

589a

435

589b

589c

"Let us then in a mild manner persuade him (for it is not willingly he errs), asking him, O blessed man! do not we say that the maxims of things beautiful and base become so, upon such accounts as these? those are good which subject the brutal part of our nature most to the man, or rather perhaps to that which is divine: but those are evil

589d

which enslave the mild part of our nature to the brutal. Will he agree with us? or how?" "He will, if he be advised by me," said he. "Is there then any one," said I, "whom it avails, from this reasoning, to take gold unjustly, if something of this kind happens, if, whilst he takes the money, he at the same time subjects the best part of himself to the worst? Or, if, taking gold, he should enslave a son or daughter, and 589e that even to savage and wicked men, shall we not say this would not avail him, not though he should receive for it a prodigious sum? But if he enslaves the most divine part of himself to the most impious and most polluted part, without any pity, is he not wretched? and does he 590a not take a gift of gold to his far more dreadful ruin, than Euriphyle did when she received the necklace for her husband's life?" "By far," said Glauco; "for I will answer you for the man."

"And do you not think that to be intemperate, has of old been discommended on such accounts as these, because that in such a one that terrible, great and multiform beast was indulged more than was meet?" "It is plain," said he. "And are not arrogance and moroseness 590b blamed, when the lion and the serpentine disposition increases and 436 stretches beyond measure?" "Entirely so." "And are not luxury and effeminacy blamed because of the remissness and looseness of this disposition, when it engenders in the man cowardice?" "What else?" "Are not flattery and illiberality blamed, when any one makes this irascible part itself subject to the brutal crew, and, for the sake of wealth and its insatiable lust, accustoms the irascible to be affronted from its youth, and instead of a lion to become an ape?" "Entirely so," 590c said he. "But why is it, do you think, that mechanical arts and handicrafts are despicable? Shall we say it is on any other account than this, that when a man, has the form of that which is best in his soul naturally weak, so as not to be able to govern the creatures within himself, but to minister to them, he is able only to learn what flatters them?" "It is likely," said he.

"In order then that such a one may be governed in the same manner as the best man is, do we not say that he must be the servant of one who is the best, and who has within him the divine governor? 590d not at all conceiving that he should be governed to the hurt of the subject (as Thrasymachus imagined) but, as it is best for every one to be governed, by one divine and wise, most especially possessing it as

his own within him, if not subjecting himself to it externally; that as far as possible we may all resemble one another and be friends,
590e governed by one and the same?" "Rightly, indeed," said he. "And law at least," said I, "plainly shows it intends such a thing, being an ally to all in the city; as does likewise the government of children, in not allowing them to be free till we establish in them a proper government, as in a city; and having cultivated that in them which is
591a best, by that which is best in ourselves, we establish a similar guardian and governor for youth, and then truly we set it free." "It shows indeed," said he.

"In what way then shall we say, Glauco, and according to what reasoning, that it is profitable to do injustice, to be intemperate, or to do any thing base, by which a man shall indeed become more wicked, but yet shall acquire more wealth, or any kind of power?" "In no way," said he. "But how shall we say it is profitable for the unjust to be
591b concealed, and not to suffer punishment? or does he not indeed, who is concealed, still become more wicked? but he who is not concealed, and is punished, has the brutal part quieted, and made mild, and the mild part set at liberty. And the whole soul being settled in the best temper, in possessing temperance and justice, with wisdom, acquires a
437 more valuable habit than the body does, in acquiring vigour and beauty, with a sound constitution; in as far as the soul is more valuable than the body." "Entirely so," said he.

591c   "Shall not every one then, who possesses intellect, regulate his life in extending the whole of his powers hither, in the first place, honouring those disciplines which will render his soul of this kind, and despising all other things?" "It is plain," said he. "And next," said I, "with reference to a good habit of body and its nourishment, he will spend his life in attention to these, not that he may indulge the brutal and irrational pleasure; nor yet with a view to health, nor, principally regarding this, to become strong and healthy, and beautiful, unless by means of these he is to become temperate likewise:
591d but he always appears to adjust the harmony of the body for the sake of the symphony which is in the soul." "By all means," said he, "if indeed he is to be truly musical." "That arrangement then," said I, "and symphony arising from the possession of wealth, and that vulgar magnificence, he will not, in consequence of being astonished with

the felicity of the multitude, increase to infinity, and bring on himself infinite evils." "I do not think it," said he.

"But looking," said I, "to that polity within himself and taking 591e care that nothing there be moved out of its place, through the greatness or smallness of his property, governing in this manner as far as he is able, he will add to his substance, and spend out of it." "Entirely so," said he. "He will regard honours likewise in the same manner; some he will willingly partake of, and taste, which he judges 592a will render him a better man, but those which he thinks would dissolve that habit of soul which subsists within him, he will fly from both in private and in public." "He will not then," said he, "be willing to act in polities, if he takes care of this." "Yes truly," said I, "in his own city, and greatly too. But not probably in his country, unless same divine fortune befall him." "I understand," said he. "You mean in the city we have now established, which exists in our reasoning, since it is nowhere on earth, at least, as I imagine." "But in 592b heaven, probably, there is a model of it," said I, "for any one who inclines to contemplate it, and on contemplating to regulate himself accordingly; and it is of no consequence to him, whether it does exist any where, or shall ever exist here. He does the duties of this city alone, and of no other." "It is reasonable," said he.

THE END OF THE NINTH BOOK.

BOOK X.

"I observe," said I, "with reference to many other things, that we 595a have established a city in a right manner, beyond what all others have done, and among these establishments, I mean that respecting poetry[1] as none of the least." "Which?" said he. "That no part of it which is 439 imitative be by any means admitted. For it appears, now most of all, 440 and with greatest perspicuity, that it is not to be admitted, since the 595b several forms of the soul have been distinguished apart from one another." "How do you mean?" "That I may tell it as to you, (for you 441 will not accuse me to the composers of tragedy, and the rest of the imitative kind) all such things as these seem to be the ruin of the 442 dianoëtic part of the hearers, viz. of such of them as have not a medicine to enable them to discern their peculiar nature." "From 443 what consideration," said he, "do you say so?" "It must be spoken," said I, "although a certain friendship, at least, and reverence for Homer, which I have had from my childhood, restrains me from 444 telling it; for he seems truly both to have been the first teacher and 595c leader of all these good composers of tragedy: but the man must not 445 be honoured preferably to the truth. But what I mean must be spoken." "By all means," said he.

"Hear me then, or rather answer me." "Ask." "Can you tell me 446 perfectly, what at all imitation is? for I do not myself altogether understand what it means." "And shall I then any how understand 447 it?" said he. "That would be no way strange," said I; "since those who 596a are dim-sighted perceive many things sooner than those who see more clearly." "The case is so," said he; "but whilst you are present, I should not be able to adventure to tell, even though something did appear to me. But consider it yourself." "Are you willing then, that we hence begin our inquiry in our usual method? for we were wont to suppose a certain species with respect to many individuals, to which we give the same name; or do you not understand me?" "I understand."

596b "Let us suppose now such among the many, as you please; as, for example, there are many beds and tables, if you please." "Why are there not?" "But the ideas,² at least respecting these pieces of furniture,

448 are two; one of bed, and one of table." "Yes." "And are we not wont to say, that the workmen of each of these species of furniture, looking towards the idea, make in this manner, the one the beds, and the other the tables which we use? and all other things after the same manner. For no one of the artists makes, at least, the idea itself; for

596c how can he?" "By no means." "But see now whether you call such a one as this an artist?" "Which?" "One who does all such things, as each manual artificer does." "You mention some skilful and wonderful man." "Not yet, at least; but you will much more say so presently; for this same mechanic is not only able to make all sorts of utensils, but he makes also every thing which springs from the earth, and he makes all sorts of animals, himself as well as others: and besides these things, he makes the earth, and heaven, and the Gods, and all things in heaven, and in Hades under the earth." "You mention," said he, "a perfectly wonderful sophist."

596d "You do not believe me; but tell me, does it appear to you that there is not any such artist? or that, in one respect, he is the maker of all these things, and in another he is not? or do you not perceive that even you yourself might be able to make all these things, in a certain manner at least?" "And what," said he, "is this manner?" "It is not difficult," said I, "but is performed in many ways, and quickly; but in the quickest manner of all, if you choose to take a mirror, and carry it

596e round every where; for then you will quickly make the sun, and the things in the heavens, quickly the earth, quickly yourself, and the other animals, and utensils, and vegetables, and all that was now mentioned." "Yes," said he, "the appearances, but not however the real things." "You come well," said I, "and seasonably, with your remark; for I imagine that the painter too is one of these artists. Is he not?" "How is it possible he should not?" "But you will say, I think, that he does not make what he makes, true, although the painter too, in a certain manner, at least, makes a bed, does he not?" "Yes," said 449 he, "he too makes only the appearance."

"But what with reference to the bed-maker: Did you not indeed 597a say, just now, that he does not make the form which we say exists, which is bed, but a particular bed?" "I said so indeed." "If then he does not make that which is, he does not make real being, but some such thing as being, but not being itself: but if any one should say, that the work of a bed-maker, or of any other handicraft, were real being, he would seem not to say true." "He would," said he, "as it must appear to those who are conversant in such kind of reasonings." "Let us not then at all wonder if this likewise happen to be somewhat obscure with reference to the truth." "Let us not." 597b

"Are you willing then," said I, "that, with reference to these very things, we inquire concerning the imitator, who he really is?" "If you are willing," said he. "Are there not then these three sorts of beds? One which exists in nature, and which we may say, as I imagine, God made, or who else?" "None, I think." "And one which the joiner makes." "Yes," said he. "And one which the painter makes. Is it not so?" "Be it so." "Now the painter, the bed-maker, God, these three preside over three species of beds." "They are three, indeed." "But 597c God, whether it were that he was not willing, or whether there was some necessity for it, that he should not make but one bed in nature, made this one only, which is really bed; but two such, or more, have never been produced by God, nor ever will be produced." "How so?" said he. "Because," said I, "if he had made but two, again one would have appeared, the form of which both these two would have possessed and that form would be, that which is bed, and not those two." "Right," said he. "God then, I think, knowing these things, and willing to be the maker of bed, really, and really existing, but not of 597d any particular bed, nor to be any particular bed-maker, produced but one in nature." "It appears so."

"Are you willing, then, that we call him the planter of this, or something of this kind?" "It is just," said he, "since he has, in their nature, made both this, and all other things." "But what as to the joiner? Is not he the workman of a bed?" "Yes." "And is the painter,

too, the workman and maker of such a work?" " By no means." "But
597e what will you say he is with relation to bed?" "This," said he, "as it
appears to me, we may most reasonably call him, the imitator of what
these are the workmen of." "Be it so," said I; "you call him then the
imitator who makes what is generated the third from nature?"
450 "Entirely so," said he. "And this the composer of tragedy shall be
likewise, since he is an imitator, rising as a sort of third from the King
and the truth; and in like manner all other imitators." "It seems so."

598a   "We have agreed then as to the imitator; but tell me this
concerning the painter, whether do you think he undertakes to
imitate each particular thing in nature, or the works of artists?" "The
works of artists," said he. "Whether, such as they really are, or such as
they appear? Determine this further." "How do you say?" replied he.
"Thus. Does a bed differ any thing from itself, whether he view it
obliquely, or directly opposite, or in any particular position? or, does it
differ nothing, but only appears different, and in the same way as to
other things?" "Thus," said he, "it appears, but differs nothing."
598b "Consider this too, with reference to which of the two does painting
work, in each particular work; whether with reference to real being,
to imitate it as it really is, or with reference to what is apparent, as it
appears; and whether is it the imitation of appearance, or of truth?"
"Of appearance," said he.

    "The imitative art, then, is far from the truth: and on this account,
it seems, he is able to make these things, because he is able to attain
but to some small part of each particular, and that but an image. Thus
we say that a painter will paint us a shoemaker, a joiner, and other
598c artists, though he be skilled in none of those arts; yet he will be able
to deceive children and ignorant people, if he be a good painter, when
he paints a joiner, and shows him at a distance, so far as to make them
imagine he is a real joiner." "Why not?" "But this, I think, my friend,
we must consider with reference to all these things; that when any
one tells us of such a painter, that he has met with a man who is
skilled in all manner of workmanship, and every thing else which
598d every several artist understands, and that there is nothing which he
does not know more accurately than any other person, we ought to
reply to such an one, that he is a simple man, and that it seems,
having met with some magician, and mimic, he has been deceived; so

that he has appeared to him to know every thing, from his own incapacity to distinguish between science, and ignorance, and imitation." "Most true," said he.

"Ought we not then," said I, "in the next place, to consider tragedy, and its leader, Homer? since we hear from some, that these poets understand all arts, and all human affairs, respecting virtue and 598e vice, and likewise all divine things; for a good poet must necessarily *451* compose with knowledge, if he means to compose well what he composes, else he is not able to compose. It behoves us then to consider whether these who have met with those imitators have been deceived, and on viewing their works have not perceived that they are 599a the third distant from real being, and that their works are such as can easily be made by one who knows not the truth (for they make phantasms, and not real beings); or whether they do say something to the purpose, and that the good poets in reality have knowledge in those things which they seem to the multitude to express with elegance." "By all means," said he, "this is to be inquired into."

"Do you think then, that if any one were able to make both of these, that which is imitated, and likewise the image, he would allow himself seriously to apply to the workmanship of the images, and propose this to himself as the best thing in life?" "I do not." "But if he 599b were in reality intelligent in these things which he imitates, he would far rather, I think, seriously apply himself to the things than to the imitations, and would endeavour to leave behind him many and beautiful actions, as monuments of himself, and would study rather to be himself the person commended than the encomiast." "I think so," said he; "for neither is the honour nor the profit equal." "As to other things, then, let us not call them to account, asking Homer or 599c any other of the poets, whether any of them were any way skilled in medicine, and not an imitator only of medical discourses, for which of the ancient or latter poets is said to have restored any to health, as Æsculapius did? or what students in medicine has any left behind him, as he did his descendants? Nor let us ask them concerning the other arts, but dismiss them: but with reference to those greatest and most beautiful things which Homer attempts to speak of, concerning wars and armies, and constitutions of cities, and the education 599d belonging to men, it is just, somehow, to question him, whilst we demand of him: Friend Homer, if you be not the third from the truth with regard to virtue, being the workman of an image (which we have defined an imitator to be), but the second, and are able to discern what pursuits render men better or worse, both in private and public, tell us which of the cities has been by you better constituted, as

599e Lacedæmon was by Lycurgus, and many other both great and small cities by many others, but what city acknowledges you to have been a

452 good lawgiver, and to have been of advantage to them. Italy and Sicily acknowledge Charondas, and we Solon; but will any one acknowledge you as the benefactor of any city?" "I think not," said Glauco. "It is not then pretended even by the Homerics themselves."

600a   "But what war in Homer's days is recorded to have been well conducted by him as leader, or counsellor?" "Not one." "But what are his discoveries? as among the works of a wise man there are many discoveries and inventions spoken of, respecting the arts, and other affairs; as of Thales the Milesian, and of Anacharsis the Scythian." "By no means is there any such thing." "But if not in a public manner, is Homer said to have lived as a private tutor to any who delighted in his

600b conversation, and have delivered down to posterity a certain Homeric manner of life? in like manner as Pythagoras was remarkably beloved on this account, and, even to this day, such as denominate themselves from the Pythagorean manner of life appear to be somehow eminent beyond others." "Neither is there," said he, "any thing of this kind related of Homer. For Creophilus,[3] Socrates, the companion of Homer, may probably appear more ridiculous still in his education, than in his name, if what is said of Homer be true. For it is said that he was greatly neglected when he lived under Homer's tuition."

600c   "It is said indeed," replied I. "But do you think, Glauco, that if Homer had been able to educate men, and to render them better, as being capable not only to imitate with respect to these things, but to understand them, would he not then have procured himself many companions, and have been honoured and beloved by them? But Protagoras the Abderite, and Prodicus the Chian, and many others,

600d are able to persuade the men of their times, conversing with them privately, that they will neither be able to govern their family, nor yet their city, unless they themselves preside over their education; and for this wisdom of theirs, they are so exceedingly beloved, that their companions almost carry them about on their heads. Would then the men of Homer's time have left him or Hesiod to go about singing their songs, if he had been able to profit men in the way of virtue; and not rather have retained him with gold, and obliged him to stay with *453* them? or, if they could not persuade him, would they not as scholars *600e* have followed him every where, till they had obtained sufficient education?" "You seem to me," said he, "Socrates, to say what is in every respect true."

"Shall we not then establish this point,—That all the poetical men, beginning with Homer, are imitators of the images of virtue, and of other things about which they compose, but that they do not attain to the truth: but as we just now said, a painter who himself knows *601a* nothing about the making of shoes, will draw a shoemaker, who shall appear to be real to such as are not intelligent, but who view according to the colour and figure?" "Entirely so." "In the same manner, I think, we shall say that the poet colours over with his names and words certain colours of the several arts, whilst he understands nothing himself, but merely imitates, so as to others such as himself who view things in his compositions, he appears to have knowledge: and if he says any thing about shoemaking in measure, *601b* rhythm and harmony, he seems to speak perfectly well, and in like manner if of an expedition, or of any thing else: so great an enchantment have these things naturally, since you know, I think, in what manner poetical things appear when stripped of musical colouring, and expressed apart by themselves, for you have somewhere beheld it." "I have," said he. "Do they not," said I, "resemble the faces of people who are in their prime, but who are not beautiful, such as they appear when their bloom forsakes them?" "Entirely," said he.

"Come now, and consider this. The maker of the image, whom we call the imitator, knows nothing of real being, but only of that which is apparent. Is it not so?" "Yes." "Let us not then leave it expressed by *601c* halves, but let us sufficiently perceive it." "Say on," replied he. "A painter, we say, will paint reins, and a bridle." "Yes." "And the leather-cutter, and the smith, will make them." "Certainly." "Does then the painter understand what kind of reins and bridle there ought to be? or not even he who makes them, the smith, nor the leather-cutter, but he who knows how to use them, the horseman

601d alone?" "Most true." "Shall we not say it is so in every thing else?" "How?" "That with reference to each particular thing, there are these three arts, That which is to use it, that which is to make it, and that which is to imitate it." "Yes." "Are then the virtue, and the beauty, and the rectitude of every utensil, and animal, and action, for

454 nothing else but for the use for which each particular was made, or generated?" "Just so."

"By a great necessity, then, he who uses each particular must be the most skilful, and be able to tell the maker what he makes good or bad,

601e with reference to the use for which he uses it: thus, for example, a player on the pipe tells the pipe-maker concerning pipes, what things are of service towards the playing on the pipe, and he will give orders how he ought to make them, but the workman does not so." "How should it be otherwise?" "Does not the one then, being intelligent, pronounce concerning good and bad pipes, and the other, believing him, make accordingly?" "Yes." "With reference then to one and the same instrument, the maker shall have right opinion concerning its beauty or deformity, whilst he is conversant with one who is intelligent, and is

602a obliged to hear from the intelligent; but he who uses it shall have science." "Entirely so." "But whether shall the imitator have science from using the things he paints, whether they be handsome and right, or otherwise? or shall he have right opinion from his being necessarily conversant with the intelligent, and from being enjoined in what manner he ought to paint?" "Neither of the two." "The imitator then shall have neither knowledge, nor right opinion about what he imitates with reference to beauty or deformity." "It appears not." "The imitator then should be very agreeable in his imitation, with regard to

602b wisdom, concerning what he paints." "Not entirely." "But however he will imitate at least, without knowing concerning each particular in what respect it is ill or good; but it is likely that he will imitate such as appears to be beautiful to the multitude, and those who know nothing." "What else?" "We have now, indeed, sufficiently, as it appears, at least, settled these things: That the imitator knows nothing worth mentioning in those things which he imitates, but that imitation is a sort of amusement, and not a serious affair. And likewise that those who apply to tragic poetry in iambics and heroics, are all imitators in the highest degree." "Entirely so."

"But, by Jupiter," said I, "this of imitation is somehow in the third 602c degree from the truth. Is it not?" "Yes." "To what part then of man does it belong, having the power it possesses?" "What part do you speak of?" "Of such as this. The same magnitude perceived by sight, does not appear in the same manner, near, and at a distance." "It does not." "And the same things appear crooked and straight, when we look at them in water, and out of water, and concave and convex, 455 through the error of the sight, as to colours. All this disturbance is 602d manifest in the soul; and this infirmity of our nature painting attacks, and leaves nothing of magical seduction unattempted, together with the wonder-working art, and many other such-like devices." "True." "And have not the arts of measuring, numbering, and weighing, appeared to be most ingenious helps in these things, that so the apparent greater or less, the apparent more or heavier, may not govern us, but the numbered, the measured, and the weighed?" "How should 602e it be otherwise?" "But this again is, at least, the work of the rational part in the soul." "It is so, indeed." "But whilst reason often measures and declares some things to be greater or less than other things, or equal, the contrary appears at the same time with reference to these things." "Yes." "But did not we say that it was impossible for the same person to have contrary opinions about the same things at the same time?" "And thus far we said rightly." 603a

"That part of the soul, then, which judges contrary to the measure, would seem not to be the same with that which judges according to the measure." "It would not." "But surely, at least, that which trusts to measure and computation would seem to be the best part of the soul." "Why not?" "That then which opposes itself to this will be some one of the depraved parts of us." "Of necessity." "It was this then I wished should be agreed upon, when I said that painting, and in short imitation, being far from the truth, delight in their own work, conversing with that part in us which is far from wisdom, and are its 603b companion and friend, to no sound nor genuine purpose." "Entirely so," said he. "Imitation then, being depraved in itself, and joining with that which is depraved, generates depraved things." "It seems so." "Whether," said I, "is the case thus, with reference to the imitation which is by the sight only, or is it likewise so with reference to that by hearing, which we call poetry?" "Likely as to this also," said

he. "We shall not therefore," said I, "trust to the appearance in
603c painting, but we shall proceed to the consideration of the dianoëtic
part with which the imitation through poetry is conversant, and see
whether it is depraved or worthy." "It must be done."

"Let us proceed then thus: Poetic imitation, we say, imitates men
acting either voluntarily or involuntarily; and imagining that in their
acting they have done either well or ill, and in all these cases receiving
456 either pain or pleasure: Does it any more than this?" "No more." "In
603d all these, now, does the man agree with himself? or, as he disagreed
with reference to sight, and had contrary opinions in himself of the
same things at one and the same time, does he, in the same manner,
disagree likewise in his actions, and fight with himself? But I recollect
that there is no occasion for us to settle this at least; for, in our
reasonings above, we sufficiently determined all these things, that our
soul is full of a thousand such contrarieties existing in it." "Right,"
said he. "Right indeed," said I; "but it appears to me necessary to
603e discuss now, what was then omitted." "As what?" said he. "We said
somewhere formerly," said I, "that a good man, when he meets with
such a fortune as the loss of a son, or of any thing else which he values
the most, will bear it of all men the easiest." "Certainly." "But let us
now consider this further,—whether will he not grieve at all, or is
this indeed impossible, but he will, however, moderate his grief?"
604a "The truth," said he, "is rather this last." "But tell me this now
concerning him, whether do you think that he will struggle more
with grief and oppose it, when he is observed by his equals, or when he
is in solitude, alone by himself?" "Much more," said he, "when he is
observed." "But when alone, he will venture, I think, to utter many
things, which, if any one heard him, he would be ashamed of, and he
will do many things which he would not wish any one saw him
doing." "It is so," said he.

604b   "Is it not then reason and law which command him to restrain his
grief,—but what drags him to grief is the passion itself?" "True." "As
then there is in the man an opposite conduct, with regard to the same
thing, at one and the same time, we must necessarily say that he has
two conductors." "What else?" "And shall we not say that one of them
is ready to obey the law wherever law leads him?" "How?" "Law in a
manner says that it is best in misfortunes to have the greatest

tranquillity possible, and not to bear them ill; since the good and evil
of such things as these is not manifest, and since no advantage follows
the bearing these things ill; and as nothing of human affairs is worthy 604c
of great concern; and, besides, their grief proves a hindrance to that
in them which we ought to have most at hand." "What is it," said he,
"you speak of?" "To deliberate," said I, "on the event; and, as on a
throw of the dice, to regulate his affairs according to what casts up, in
whatever way reason shall declare to be best: and not as children when 457
they fall, to lie still, and waste the time in crying; but always to 604d
accustom the soul to apply in the speediest manner to heal and rectify
what was fallen and sick, dismissing lamentation." "One would thus,"
said he, "behave in the best manner in every condition."

"And did not we say that the best part is willing to follow this
which is rational?" "It is plain." "And shall not we say that the part
which leads to the remembrance of the affliction, and to wailings,
and is insatiably given to these, is irrational, and idle, and a friend to
cowardice?" "We shall say so truly." "Is not then the grieving part that 604e
which admits of much and of various imitation? But the prudent and
tranquil part, which is always uniform with itself, is neither easily
imitated, nor, when imitated, easily understood, especially by a popular
assembly, where all sorts of men are assembled together in a theatre.
For it is the imitation of a disposition which is foreign to them." 605a
"Entirely so." "It is plain, then, that the imitative poet is not made for
such a part of the soul as this. Nor is his skill fitted to please it, if he
means to gain the applause of the multitude. But he applies to the
passionate and the multiform part, as it is easily imitated." "It is plain."

"May we not then, with justice, lay hold of the imitative poet, and
place him as correspondent to the painter? for he resembles him, both
because, as to truth, he effects but depraved things, and in this too he
resembles him, in being conversant with a different part of the soul
from that which is best. And thus we may, with justice, not admit 605b
him into our city which is to be well regulated, because he excites and
nourishes this part of the soul, and, strengthening it, destroys the
rational. And as he who in a city makes the wicked powerful, betrays
the city, and destroys the best men, in the same manner we shall say
that the imitative poet establishes a bad republic in the soul of each
individual, gratifying the foolish part of it, which neither discerns 605c

what is great, nor what is little, but deems the same things sometimes great, and sometimes small, forming little images in its own imagination, altogether remote from the truth." "Entirely so."

"But we have not however as yet brought the greatest accusation against it: for that is, somehow, a very dreadful one, that it is able to corrupt even the good, if it be not a very few excepted." "How should it not, since it acts in this manner?" "But hear now, and consider; for somehow, the best of us, when we hear Homer, or any of the tragic 605d writers, imitating some of the heroes when in grief, pouring forth 458 long speeches in their sorrow, bewailing and beating their breasts, you know we are delighted; and, yielding ourselves, we follow along, and, sympathizing with them, seriously commend him as an able poet whoever most affects us in this manner." "I know it." "But when any domestic grief befalls any of us, you perceive, on the other hand, that we value ourselves on the opposite behaviour, if we can be quiet, and 605e endure, this being the part of a man, but that of a woman, which in the other case we commended." "I perceive it," said he. "Is this commendation then," said I, "a handsome one, when we see such a man as one would not deign to be oneself, but would be ashamed of, not to abominate but to delight in him, and commend him?" "No, 606a by Jupiter," said he; "it appears unreasonable." "Certainly," said I, "if you consider it, in this manner." "How?"

"If you consider that the part of us, which in our private misfortunes is forcibly restrained, and is kept from weeping and bewailing to the full, being by nature of such a kind as is desirous of these, is the very part which is by the poets filled and gratified: but that part in us, which is naturally the best, being not sufficiently instructed, either by reason or habit, grows remiss in its guardianship 606b over the bewailing part, by attending to the sufferings of others, and deems it no way disgraceful to itself, to commend and pity one who grieves immoderately, whilst he professes to be a good man. But this it thinks it gains, even pleasure, which it would not choose to be deprived of, by despising the whole of the poem. For, I think, it falls to the share of few to be able to consider, that what we feel with respect to the fortunes of others, must necessarily be felt with respect to our own. Since it is not easy for a man to bear up under his own misfortunes, who strongly cherishes the bewailing disposition over those of others." "Most true," said he. "And is not the reasoning the 606c same with reference to the ridiculous? For when you hear, in imitation by comedy, or in private conversation, what you would be ashamed to do yourself to excite laughter, and are delighted with it, and imitate it, you do the same thing here as in the tragic: for that part, which, when it wanted to excite laughter, was formerly restrained by reason from a fear of incurring the character of scurrility, by now letting loose, and allowing there to grow vigorous, you are often imperceptibly brought to be in your own behaviour a 606d buffoon." "Extremely so," said he. "And the case is the same as to venereal pleasures, and anger, and the whole of the passions, as well 459 the sorrowful as the joyful, which truly, we have said, attend us in every action; that the poetical imitation of these has the same effect upon us; for it nourishes and waters those things which ought to be parched, and constitutes as our governor, those which ought to be governed, in order to our becoming better and happier, instead of being worse and more miserable." "I can say no otherwise," said he.

"When therefore, Glauco," said I, "you meet with the encomiasts 606e of Homer, who tell how this poet instructed Greece, and that he deserves to be taken as a master to teach a man both the management and the knowledge of human affairs; and that a man should regulate the whole of his life according to this poet, we should indeed love and 607a embrace such people, as being the best they are able; and agree with them that Homer is most poetical, and the first of tragic writers: but they must know, that hymns to the Gods, and the praises of worthy actions, are alone to be admitted into the city. But if it should admit the pleasurable muse likewise, in songs, or verses, you would have pleasure and pain reigning in the city, instead of law, and that reason which always appears best to the community." "Most true," said he.

"Let these things now," said I, "be our apology, when we recollect 607b what we have said with reference to poetry, that we then very properly dismissed it from our republic, since it is such as is now described: for reason obliged us. And let us tell it further, lest it accuse us of a certain roughness, and rusticity, that there is an ancient variance between philosophy and poetry; for such verses as these,

That bawling bitch, which at her mistress barks,

607c And

> He's great in empty eloquence of fools,

And

> On trifles still they plod, because they're poor;

and a thousand such like, are marks of an ancient opposition between them. But nevertheless let it be said, that if any one can assign a reason why the poetry and the imitation which are calculated for pleasure ought to be in a well regulated city, we, for our part, shall gladly admit them, as we are at least conscious to ourselves that we are charmed by them. But to betray what appears to be truth, would be an 607d unholy thing. For are not you yourself, my friend, charmed by this 460 imitation, and most especially when you see it performed by Homer?" "Very much so." "Is it not just, then, that we introduce it apologizing for itself, either in song, or in any other measure?" "By all means."

"And we may at least grant, somehow, even to its defenders, such as are not poets, but lovers of poetry, to speak in its behalf, without verse, and show that it is not only pleasant, but profitable for 607e republics, and for human life; and we shall hear with pleasure, for we shall gain somewhat if it shall appear not only pleasant but also profitable." "How is it possible we should not gain?" said he. "And if it happen otherwise, my friend, we shall do as those who have been in love when they deem their love unprofitable,—they desist, though with violence: so we in like manner, through this inborn love of such 608a poetry that prevails in our best republics, shall be well pleased to see it appear to be the best and truest: and we shall hear it till it is able to make no further apology. But we shall take along with us this discourse which we have held, as a counter-charm, and incantation, being afraid to fall back again into a childish and vulgar love. We may perceive then that we are not to be much in earnest about such poetry as this, as if it were a serious affair, and approached to the truth; 608b but the hearer is to beware of it, and to be afraid for the republic within himself, and to entertain those opinions of poetry which we mentioned." "I entirely agree," said he. "For great, friend Glauco," said I, "mighty is the contest, and not such as it appears, to become a good or a bad man: so as not to be moved, either through honour, or riches, or any magistracy, or poetic imitation, ever to neglect justice, and the other virtues." "I agree with you, from what we have discussed, and so I think will any other."

"But we have not yet," said I, "discussed the greatest prize of virtue, 608c and the rewards laid up for her." "You speak of some prodigious greatness," said he, "if there be other greater than those mentioned." "But what is there," said I, "can be great in a little time? for all this period from infancy to old age is but little in respect of the whole." "Nothing at all indeed," said he. "What then? Do you think an immortal being ought to be much concerned about such a period, and not about the whole of time?" "I think," said he, "about the 608d whole. But why do you mention this?" "Have you not perceived," said I, "that our soul is immortal, and never perishes?" On which he, looking at me, and wondering, said, "By Jupiter, not I indeed. But are you able to show this?" "I should otherwise act unjustly," said I. "And 461 I think you yourself can show it, for it is in no respect difficult." "To me at least," said he, "it is difficult; but I would willingly hear from you this which is not difficult." "You shall hear then," said I. "Only speak," replied he.

"Is there not some thing," said I, "which you call good, and 608e something which you call evil?" "I own it." "Do you then conceive of them in the same manner as I do?" "How?" "That which destroys and corrupts every thing is the evil, and what preserves and profits it is the good." "I do," said he. "But what? Do you not say, there is something which is good, and something which is bad, to each particular? as 609a blindness to the eyes, and disease to every animal body, blasting to corns, rottenness to wood, rust to brass and iron, and, as I am saying, almost every thing has its connate evil, and disease?" "I think so," replied he. "And when any thing of this kind befalls any thing, does it not render that which it befalls base, and in the end dissolves and destroys it?" "How should it not?" "Its own connate evil then and baseness destroys each particular; or, if this does not destroy it, nothing else can ever destroy it. For that which is good can never destroy any 609b thing, nor yet that which is neither good nor evil." "How can they?" said he. "If then we shall be able to find, among beings, any one which has indeed some evil which renders it base, but is not however able to dissolve and destroy it, shall we not then know that a being thus constituted cannot be destroyed at all?" "So," replied he, "it appears."

"What then?" said I. "Is there not something which renders the soul evil?" "Certainly," replied he; "all these things which we have now 609c mentioned, injustice, intemperance, cowardice, ignorance."

"But does then any of these dissolve and destroy it? And attend now, that we may not be imposed on, in thinking that an unjust and foolish man, when he is detected acting unjustly, is then destroyed through his injustice, which is the baseness of his soul: but consider it thus. As disease, which is the baseness of animal body, dissolves and destroys body, and reduces it to be no longer that body; so all those things we mentioned, being destroyed by their own proper evil 609d adhering to them and possessing them, are reduced to a non-existence. Is it not so?" "Yes.""Consider now the soul in the same manner. Does injustice, or other vice, possessing it, by possessing, and adhering to it, corrupt and deface it, till, bringing it to death, it separates it from the body?" "By no means," said he. "But it would be 462 absurd," said I, "that any thing should be destroyed by the baseness of 609e another, but not by its own." "Absurd." "For consider, Glauco," said I, "that neither by the baseness of victuals, whether it be their mouldiness, or rottenness, or whatever else, do we imagine our body can be destroyed; but if this baseness in them create in the body a depravity of the body, we will say that, through their means, the body 610a is destroyed by its own evil, which is disease. But we will never allow that by the baseness of food, which is one thing, the body, which is another thing, can ever by this foreign evil, without creating in it its own peculiar evil, be at any time destroyed." "You say most right," replied he.

"According to the same reasoning, then," said I, "unless the baseness of the body create a baseness of the soul, let us never allow that the soul can be destroyed by an evil which is foreign, without its own peculiar evil, one thing by the evil of another." "There is reason 610b for it," said he. "Let us then either refute these things as not good reasoning; or, so long as they are unrefuted, let us at no time say, that the soul shall be ever in any degree the more destroyed, either by burning fever, or by any other disease, or by slaughter, not even though a man should cut the whole body into the smallest parts possible, till some one show that, through these sufferings of the body, the soul herself becomes more unjust and unholy. But we will never allow it to be said, that when a foreign evil befalls any thing, whilst its own proper evil is not within it, either the soul or any thing else is destroyed." "But this at least," said he, "no one can ever show, that the souls of those who die are by death rendered more unjust." "But if any one," replied I, "shall dare to contend with us in reasoning; and, in order that he may not be obliged to own that souls are immortal, should say, that when a man dies he becomes more wicked and unjust, we shall somehow justly demand of him to show, if he says true in telling us this, that injustice is deadly to the possessor, as a disease; and that those who embrace it are destroyed by it as by a disease destructive in its own nature—those most speedily who embrace it most, and those more slowly who embrace it less. And not as at present, where the unjust die having this punishment inflicted on them by others." "By Jupiter," said he, "injustice would not appear perfectly dreadful, if it were deadly to him who practises it (for that would be a deliverance from evil); but I rather think it will appear to be altogether the reverse, destroying others as far as it can, but rendering the unjust extremely alive, and, in conjunction with being alive, wakeful likewise; so far, as it seems, does it dwell from being deadly." "You say well," replied I; "for, when a man's own wickedness and peculiar evil is insufficient to kill and destroy the soul, hardly can that evil, which aims at the destruction of another, destroy a soul, or any thing else but what it is aimed against." "Hardly indeed," said he, "as appears to me at least." "Since therefore it is destroyed by no one evil, neither peculiar nor foreign, is it not plain that, of necessity, it always is? and, if it always is, it is immortal?" "Of necessity," replied he.

"Let this then," said I, "be fixed in this manner. And if it be, you will perceive that the same souls will always remain, for their number will never become less, none being destroyed, nor will it become greater; for if anyhow, the number of immortals was made greater, you know it would take from the mortal, and in the end all would be immortal." "You say true." "But let us not," said I, "think that this will be the case, (for reason will not allow of it) nor yet that the soul in its truest nature is of such a kind as to be full of much variety, dissimilitude, and difference, considered in itself." "How do you say?" replied he. "That cannot easily," said I, "be eternal which is compounded of many things, and which has not the most beautiful

610c

610d

610e

611a

611b

composition, as hath now appeared to us to be the case with reference to the soul." "It is not likely." "That the soul then is something immortal, both our present reasonings, and others too, may oblige us to own: but in order to know what kind of being the soul is, in truth, 611c one ought not to contemplate it as it is damaged both by its conjunction with the body, and by other evils, as we now behold it, but such as it is when become pure, such it must by reasoning be fully contemplated; and he (who does this) will find it far more beautiful at least, and will more plainly see through justice and injustice, and every thing which we have now discussed. We are now telling the truth 611d concerning it, such as it appears at present. We have seen it, indeed, in the same condition in which they see the marine Glaucus,[4] where 464 they cannot easily perceive his ancient nature, because the ancient members of his body are partly broken off, and others are worn away; and he is altogether damaged by the waves: and, besides this, other things are grown to him, such as shell fish, sea weed, and stones: so that he in every respect resembles a beast, rather than what he naturally was. In such a condition do we behold the soul under a thousand evils. But we ought, Glauco, to behold it there." "Where?" said he.

611e   "In its philosophy; and to observe to what it applies, and what intimacies it affects, as being allied to that which is divine, immortal, and eternal; and what it would become, if it pursued wholly a thing of this kind, and were by this pursuit brought out of that sea in which it 612a now is, and had the stones and shell fish shaken off from it, which, at present, as it is fed on earth, render its nature, in a great measure, earthy, stony, and savage, through those aliments, which are said to procure felicity. And then might one behold its true nature, whether multiform, or uniform, and every thing concerning it. But we have, I think, sufficiently discussed its passions, and forms in human life." "Entirely so," replied he.

612b   "Have we not now," said I, "discussed every thing else in our reasonings, though we have not produced those rewards and honours of justice (as you say Hesiod and Homer do)? but we find justice itself to be the best reward to the soul; and that it ought to do what is just, whether it have or have not Gyges' ring, and, together with such a ring, the helmet[5] likewise of Pluto." "You say most true," said he. "Will it not now then, Glauco," said I, "be attended with no envy, if,

besides these, we add those rewards to justice and the other virtues, 612c
which are bestowed on the soul by men and Gods, both whilst the
man is alive, and after he is dead?" "By all means," said he. "Will you
then restore me what you borrowed in the reasoning?" "What,
chiefly?" "I granted you, that the just man should be deemed unjust,
and the unjust be deemed to be just. For you were of opinion, that
though it were not possible that these things should be concealed
from Gods and men, it should however be granted, for the sake of the
argument, that justice in itself might be compared with injustice in 612d
itself; or do you not remember it?" "I should, indeed, be unjust," said 465
he, "if I did not."

"Now after the judgment is over, I demand again, on behalf of
justice, that as you allow it to be indeed esteemed both by Gods and
men, you likewise allow it to have the same good reputation, that it
may also receive those prizes of victory, which it acquires from the
reputation of justice, and bestows on those who possess it; since it has
already appeared to bestow those good things which arise from really
being just, and that it does not deceive those who truly embrace it."
"You demand what is just," said he. "Will you not then," said I, "in 612e
the first place, restore me this? That it is not concealed from the Gods,
what kind of man each of the two is." "We will grant it," said he.
"And if they be not concealed, one of them will be beloved of the
Gods, and one of them hated,[6] as we agreed in the beginning." "We
did so." "And shall we not agree, that as to the man who is beloved of
the Gods, whatever comes to him from the Gods will all be the best 613a
possible, unless he has some necessary ill from former miscarriage."
"Entirely so."

"We are then to think in this manner of the just man, That if he
happen to be in poverty, or in diseases, or in any other of those
seeming evils, these things to him issue in something good, either
whilst alive, or dead. For never at any time is he neglected by the Gods
who inclines earnestly to endeavour to become just, and practises
virtue as far as it is possible for man to resemble God." "It is 613b
reasonable," replied he, "that such an one should not be neglected by
him whom he resembles." "And are we not to think the reverse of
these things concerning the unjust man?" "Entirely." "Such, then,
would seem to be the prizes which the just man receives from the

Gods." "Such they are indeed in my opinion," said he. "But what," said I, "do they receive from men? Is not the case thus? (if we are to suppose the truth) Do not cunning and unjust men do the same thing as those racers, who run well at the beginning, but not so at the end? 613c for at the first they briskly leap forward, but in the end they become ridiculous, and, with their ears on their neck, they run off without any reward. But such as are true racers, arriving at the end, both receive the prizes, and are crowned. Does it not happen thus for the most part as to just men? that at the end of every action and 466 intercourse of life they are both held in esteem, and receive rewards from men." "Entirely so."

613d "You will then suffer me to say of these what you yourself said of the unjust. For I will aver now, that the just, when they are grown up, shall arrive at power if they desire magistracies, they shall marry where they incline, and shall settle their children in marriage agreeably to their wishes; and every thing else you mentioned concerning the others, I now say concerning these. And on the other hand I will say of the unjust, that the most of them, though they may be concealed whilst they are young, yet being caught at the end of the race, are ridiculous, and, when they become old, are wretched and 613e ridiculed, and shall be scourged both by foreigners and citizens, and they shall afterwards be tortured, and burnt; which you said were terrible things, and you spoke the truth. Imagine you hear from me that they suffer all these things. But see if you will admit of what I say." "Entirely," said he, "for you say what is just."

"Such as these now," said I, "are the prizes, the rewards and gifts, 614a which a just man receives in his life-time, both from Gods and men; besides those good things which justice contains in itself." "And they are extremely beautiful," said he, "and likewise permanent." "But these now," said I, "are nothing in number or magnitude, when compared with those which await each of the two at death. And these things must likewise be heard, that each of them may completely have what is their due in the reasoning." "You may say on," replied 614b he, "not as to a hearer who has heard much, but as to one who hears with pleasure." "But, however, I will not," said I, "tell you the apologue of Alcinus; but that, indeed, of a brave man, Erus the son of Armenius, by descent a Pamphylian; who happening on a time to die in battle, when the dead were on the tenth day carried off, already corrupted, he was taken up sound; and being carried home, as he was about to be buried on the twelfth day, when laid on the funeral pile, he revived;[7] and being revived, he told what he saw in the other state, *467* and said: That after his soul left the body, it went with many others, 614c and that they came to a certain dæmoniacal place, where there were *468* two chasms in the earth, near to each other, and two other openings in the heavens opposite to them, and that the judges sat between *469* these. That when they gave judgment, they commanded the just to go to the right hand, and upwards through the heaven, fixing before them the accounts of the judgment pronounced; but the unjust they commanded to the left, and downwards, and these likewise had behind them the accounts of all they had done. 614d

"But on his coming before the judges, they said, it behoved him to be a messenger to men concerning things there, and they commanded him to hear, and to contemplate every thing in the place. And that he saw here, through two openings, one of the heaven, and one of the earth, the souls departing, after they were there judged; and through the other two openings he saw, rising through the one out of the earth, souls full of squalidness and dust; and through the other, he saw other souls descending pure from heaven; and that always on their 614e arrival they seemed as if they came from a long journey, and that they gladly went to rest themselves in the meadow, as in a public assembly, and saluted one another, such as were acquainted, and that those who rose out of the earth asked the others concerning the things above, and those from heaven asked them concerning the things below, and *470* that they told one another; those wailing and weeping whilst they 615a called to mind, what and how many things they suffered and saw in their journey under the earth; (for it was a journey of a thousand years) and that these again from heaven explained their enjoyments, and spectacles of immense beauty.

"To narrate many of them, Glauco, would take much time; but this, he said, was the sum, that whatever unjust actions any had committed, and how many soever any one had injured, they were punished for all these separately tenfold, and that it was in each, according to the rate of an hundred years, the life of man being 615b considered as so long, that they might suffer tenfold punishment for the injustice they had done. So that if any had been the cause of many deaths, either by betraying cities or armies, or bringing men into slavery, or being confederates in any other wickedness, for each of all these they reaped tenfold sufferings; and if, again, they had benefited

615c any by good deeds, and had been just and holy, they were rewarded according to their desserts. Of those who died very young, and lived but a little time, he told what was not worth relating in respect of other things. But of impiety and piety towards the Gods and parents, and of suicide, he told the more remarkable retributions. For he said he was present when one was asked by another, where the great Aridæus was? This Aridæus had been tyrant in a certain city of Pamphylia a thousand years before that time, and had killed his aged

615d father, and his elder brother, and had done many other unhallowed deeds, as it was reported: and he said, the one who was asked, replied: He neither comes, said he, nor ever will come hither.

"For we then surely saw this likewise among other dreadful spectacles: When we were near the mouth of the opening, and were about to ascend after having suffered every thing else, we beheld both him on a sudden, and others likewise, most of whom were tyrants,

615e and some private persons who had committed great iniquity, whom, when they imagined they were to ascend, the mouth of the opening did not admit? but bellowed when any of those who were so polluted with wickedness, or who had not been sufficiently punished, attempted to ascend. And then, said he, fierce men, and fiery to the

471 view,[8] standing by, and understanding the bellowing, took them and
616a led them apart, Aridæus and the rest, binding their hands and their feet, and, thrusting down their head, and pulling off their skin, dragged them to an outer road, tearing them on thorns; declaring always to those who passed by, on what accounts they suffered these things, and that they were carrying them to be thrown into Tartarus.

"And hence, he said, that amidst all their various terrors, this terror surpassed, lest the mouth should bellow, and that when it was silent every one most gladly ascended. And that the punishments and

616b torments were such as these, and their rewards were the reverse of these. He also added, that every one, after they had been seven days in the meadow, arising thence, it was requisite for them to depart on the eighth day, and arrive at another place on the fourth day after, whence they perceived from above through the whole heaven and earth, a light extended as a pillar, mostly resembling the rainbow, but more splendid and pure; at which they arrived in one day's journey; and thence they perceived, through the middle of the light from heaven, the extremities of its ligatures extended; as this light was the belt of heaven, like the transverse beams of ships keeping the whole circumference united. That from the extremities the distaff of necessity is extended, by which all the revolutions were turned round, whose spindle and point were both of adamant, but its whirl mixed of this and of other things; and that the nature of the whirl was of such a kind, as to its figure, as is any one we see here.

"But you must conceive it, from what he said, to be of such a kind as this: as if in some great hollow whirl, carved throughout, there was such another, but lesser, within it, adapted to it, like casks fitted one within another; and in the same manner a third, and a fourth, and four others, for that the whirls were eight[9] in all, as circles one within another, having their lips appearing upwards, and forming round the spindle one united convexity of one whirl; that the spindle was driven through the middle of the eight; and that the first and outmost whirl had the widest circumference in the lip, that the sixth had the second wide, and that of the fourth is the third wide, and the fourth wide that of the eighth, and the fifth wide that of the seventh, the sixth wide that of the fifth, and the seventh wide that of the third, and the eighth wide that of the second. Likewise that the circle of the largest is variegated, that of the seventh is the brightest, and that of the eighth hath its colour from the shining of the seventh; that of the second and fifth resemble each other, but are more yellow than the rest. But the third hath the whitest colour, the fourth is reddish; the second in whiteness surpasses the sixth; and that the distaff must turn round in a circle with the whole it carries; and whilst the whole is turning round, the seven inner circles are gently turned round in a contrary motion to the whole. Again, that of these, the eighth moves the swiftest; and next to it, and equal to one another, the seventh, the sixth, and the fifth; and that the third went in a motion which as appeared to them completed its circle in the same way as the fourth. The fourth in swiftness was the third, and the fifth was the second, and it was turned round on the knees of necessity. And that on each

616c

616d

616e

472

617a

617b

of its circles there was seated a Siren on the upper side, carried round,
and uttering one voice variegated by diverse modulations. But that the
whole of them, being eight, composed one harmony. That there were
617c other three sitting round at equal distance one from another; each on
473 a throne, the daughters of necessity, the Fates,[10] in white vestments,
and having crowns on their heads; Lachesis, and Clotho, and
Atropos, singing to the harmony of the Sirens; Lachesis singing the
past, Clotho the present, and Atropos the future. And that Clotho, at
474 certain intervals, with her right hand laid hold of the spindle, and
along with her mother turned about the outer circle. And Atropos, in
like manner, turned the inner ones with her left hand. And that
617d Lachesis touched both of these, severally, with either hand.

"After they arrive here, it is necessary for them to go directly to
Lachesis. That then a certain prophet first of all ranges them in order,
and afterwards taking the lots, and the models of lives, from the
knees of Lachesis, and ascending a lofty tribunal, he says:—The
speech of the virgin Lachesis, the daughter of Necessity: Souls of a day!
617e The beginning of another period of men of mortal race. The dæmon
shall not receive you as his lot, but you shall choose the dæmon: He
who draws the first, let him first make choice of a life, to which he
must of necessity adhere: Virtue is independent, which every one shall
partake of, more or less, according as he honours or dishonours her:
the cause is in him who makes the choice, and God is blameless. That
when he had said these things, he threw on all of them the lots, and
that each took up the one which fell beside him, and that he was
allowed to take no other. And that when he had taken it, he knew
618a what number he had drawn. That after this he placed on the ground
before them the models of lives, many more than those we see at
present. And that they were all-various. For there were lives of all sorts
of animals, and human lives of every kind. And that among these
there were tyrannies also, some of them perpetual, and others
475 destroyed in the midst of their greatness, and ending in poverty,
banishment, and want. That there were also lives of renowned men,
618b some for their appearance as to beauty, strength, and agility; and
others for their descent, and the virtues of their ancestors. There were
the lives of renowned women in the same manner. But that there was
no disposition of soul among these models, because of necessity, on

choosing a different life, it becomes different itself. As to other things, riches and poverty, sickness and health, they were mixed with one another, and some were in a middle station between these.

"There then, as appears, friend Glauco, is the whole danger of man. And hence this of all things is most to be studied, in what manner 618c every one of us, omitting other disciplines, shall become an inquirer and learner in this study, if, by any means, he be able to learn and find out who will make him expert and intelligent to discern a good life, and a bad; and to choose every where, and at all times, the best of what is possible, considering all the things now mentioned, both compounded and separated from one another, what they are with respect to the virtue of life. And to understand what good or evil beauty operates when mixed with poverty, or riches, and with this or 618d the other habit of soul; and what is effected by noble and ignoble descent, by privacy, and by public station, by strength and weakness, docility and indocility, and every thing else of the kind which naturally pertains to the soul, and likewise of what is acquired, when blended one with another; so as to be able from all these things to compute, and, having an eye to the nature of the soul, to comprehend both the worse and the better life, pronouncing that to be the worse 618e which shall lead the soul to become more unjust, and that to be the better life which shall lead it to become more just, and to dismiss every other consideration. For we have seen, that in life, and in death, this is the best choice. But it is necessary that a man should have this 619a opinion firm as an adamant in him, when he departs to Hades, that there also he may be unmoved by riches, or any such evils, and may not, falling into tyrannies, and other such practices, do many and incurable mischiefs, and himself suffer still greater: but may know how to choose always the middle life, as to these things, and to shun the extremes on either hand, both in this life as far as is possible, and in the whole of hereafter. For thus man becomes most happy. 619b

"That then the messenger from the other world further told, how that the prophet spoke thus: Even to him who comes last, choosing *476* with judgment, and living consistently, there is prepared a desirable life; not bad. Let neither him who is first be negligent in his choice, nor let him who is last despair. He said, that when the prophet had spoken these things, the first who drew a lot ran instantly and chose

619c the greatest tyranny, but through folly and insatiableness had not sufficiently examined all things on making his choice, but were ignorant that in this life there was this destiny, the devouring of his own children, and other evils; and that afterwards, when he had considered it at leisure he wailed and lamented his choice, not having observed the admonitions of the prophet above mentioned. For that he did not accuse himself, as the author of his misfortunes, but fortune and the dæmons, and every thing instead of himself. He added, that he was one of those who came from heaven, who had in

619d his former life lived in a regulated republic, and had been virtuous by custom without philosophy. And that, in short, among these there were not a few who came from heaven, as being unexercised in trials. But that the most of those who came from earth, as they had endured hardships themselves, and had seen others in hardships, did not precipitantly make their choice. And hence, and through the fortune of the lot, to most souls there was an exchange of good and evil things. Since, if one should always, whenever he comes into this life,

619e soundly philosophize, and the lot of election should not fall on him the very last, it would seem, from what has been told us from thence, that he shall be happy not only here, but when he goes hence, and his journey hither back again shall not be earthy, and rugged, but smooth and heavenly.

"This spectacle, he said, was worthy to behold, in what manner the

620a several souls made choice of their lives. For it was pitiful and ridiculous and wonderful to behold, as each for the most part chose according to the habit of their former life. For he told, that he saw the soul which was formerly the soul of Orpheus making choice of the life of a swan, through hatred of woman-kind, being unwilling to be born of woman on account of the death he suffered from them. He saw likewise the soul of Thamyris making choice of the life of a nightingale. And he saw also a swan turning to the choice of human

620b life; and other musical animals in a similar manner, as is likely: And that he saw one soul, in making its choice, choosing the life of a lion; and that it was the soul of Telamonian Ajax, shunning to become a

477 man, remembering the judgment given with reference to the armour. That after this he saw the soul of Agamemnon, which, in hatred also of the human kind, on account of his misfortunes, exchanged it for

the life of an eagle. And that he saw the soul of Atalante choosing her lot amidst the rest, and, having attentively observed the great honours paid an athletic man, was unable to pass by this lot, but took it. Next to this, he saw the soul of Epæus the Panopean going into 620c the nature of a skilful workwoman. And that far off, among the last, he saw the soul of the buffoon Thersites assuming[11] the ape. And that by chance he saw the soul of Ulysses, who had drawn its lot last of all, going to make its choice: that in remembrance of its former toils, and tired of ambition, it went about a long time seeking the life of a private man of no business, and with difficulty found it lying somewhere, neglected by the rest. And that on seeing this life, it said, 620d that it would have made the same choice even if it had obtained the first lot,—and joyfully chose it. That in like manner the souls of wild beasts went into men, and men again into beasts: the unjust changing into wild beasts, and the just into tame; and that they were blended by all sorts of mixtures.

"After therefore all the souls had chosen their lives according as they drew their lots, they all went in order to Lachesis, and that she gave to every one the dæmon[12] he chose, and sent him along with him 620e to be the guardian of his life, and the accomplisher of what he had chosen.—That first of all he conducts the soul to Clotho, to ratify under her hand, and by the whirl of the vortex of her spindle, the destiny it had chosen by lot: and after being with her, he leads it back again to the spinning of Atropos, who makes the destinies irreversible. And that from hence they proceed directly under the throne of necessity; and that after he had passed by it, as all the others 621a passed, they all of them marched into the plain of Lethe[13] amidst dreadful heat and scorching, for he said that it is void of trees and *478* every thing that the earth produces. That when night came on, they encamped beside the river Amelete, whose water no vessel contains. Of this water all of them must necessarily drink a certain measure, and such of them as are not preserved by prudence drink more than the measure, and that he who drinks always forgets every thing. But 621b after they were laid asleep, and it became midnight, there was thunder, and an earthquake, and they were thence on a sudden carried upwards, some one way, and some another, approaching to generation like stars. But that he himself was forbidden to drink of the water. Where, however, and in what manner, be came into his body, he was entirely ignorant; but suddenly looking up in the morning, he saw himself already laid on the funeral pile. And this

621c fable, Glauco, hath been preserved, and is not lost, and it may preserve us, if we are persuaded by it; for thus we shall happily pass over the river Lethe, and shall not contaminate the soul.

"But if the company will be persuaded by me; considering the soul to be immortal, and able to bear all evil, and all good, we shall always persevere in the road which leads above; and shall by all means pursue justice in conjunction with prudence, in order that we may be friends both to ourselves, and to the Gods, both whilst we remain here, and

621d when we receive its rewards, like victors assembled together; and we shall, both here, and in that journey of a thousand years which we have described, enjoy a happy life.

THE END OF THE TENTH AND LAST BOOK OF THE REPUBLIC.

Additional Notes

on

The Republic

BOOK I.

Page 104. *Are they to have torches, and give them to one another?*

In the Panathenæan, Hephæstian, and Promethean festivals, it was customary for young men to run with torches or lamps: and in this contest he alone was victorious, whose lap remained unextinguished in the race. As a lamp or torch, therefore, from the naturally ascending nature of fire, may be considered as a proper image of our rational part, this custom perhaps was intended to signify that he is the true conqueror in the race of life, whose rational part is not extinguished, or, in other words, does not become dormant in the career.

Page 105. Note. *This nocturnal solemnity was the lesser Panathenæa.*

As in the greater Panathenæa the veil of Minerva was carried about in which the Giants were represented vanquished by the Olympian God,, so in the lesser Panathenæa another veil was exhibited, in which the Athenians, who were the pupils of Minerva, were represented victorious in the battle against the inhabitants of the

Atlantic island.' these festivals signified the beautiful order which proceeds into the world from intellect, and the unconfused distinction of mundane contrarieties. The veil of Minerva is an emblem of that one life or nature of the universe, which the goddess weaves by those intellectual vital powers which the contains. The battle of the Giants against the Olympian Gods signifies the opposition between the last demiurgic powers of the universe (or those powers which partially fabricate and proximately preside over mundane natures) and such as are first. Minerva is said to have vanquished the Giants, because she rules over these ultimate artificers of things by her unifying powers. And the battle of the Atlantics against the Athenians represents the distribution of the world according to the two coordinate oppositions of things. And as in this battle the Athenians were victorious, so in the universe the better coordination subdues the worse. See Procl. in Tim. p. 26, and Schol. Græc. in Plat. p. 143.

Page 107. *The Seriphian.*

Seriphus, one of the islands of the Cyclades, and a city in it; whence its inhabitants were called Seriphians. Schol. Græc. in Plat. p. 144.

Page 108. *As Pindar says.*

These verses of Pindar are only to be found in the fragments ascribed to him.

Page 113. *Thrasymachus.*

This Thrasymachus was a sophist, and is mentioned by Aristotle in the last book of his *Sophistical Arguments*. Nothing can more clearly show the Herculean strength of the reasoning which Socrates here employs, than that it was able to tame this savage sophist. The ability of effecting is renders Socrates *truly great*.

BOOK II.

Page 222. *Is not God essentially good?*

It is well observed by Proclus (in Plat. Polit. p. 355.), that when Plato says in this place, God is essentially good, he means every God; for the addition of the article either alone signifies transcendency, as when we say *the* poet (ὁ ποιητης), assigning this prerogative to the chief of poets, or the whole multitude, as when we say *the* rational man, adding the article as a substitute for every. Since Plato therefore says ὁ θεος αγαθος, he either means the first, or every God. But that he does not means the first only, is evident from his concluding after this, that *every God* is as much as possible most beautiful and excellent. This also shows the ignorance of modern scribblers, who pretend that Plato secretly ridiculed the doctrine of polytheism; which the reader must always remember signifies the existence of divine nature, the progeny of, and consequently subordinate to, one supreme deity.

BOOK III.

Page 241. *And we should send him to same other city, pouring oil on his heard, and crowning him with wool.*

The Greek Scholium on this part is as follows:

παροιμια επι των απο της χρειας αφιεμενων· και γαρ επι των ἑορτων εοικασιν ὁι ανθρωποι μυρῳ κατα της κεφαλης καταχεισθαι, ὡς αν σχολαζοντες απο των εργων, και μονον σχολαζοντες θυμηδια· και παλιν, τοις απο δουλειας μεταγομενοις επ᾽ ελευθεριαν, εριου καταγμα κατα της κεφαλης, ενδεσμουμενον το επισημον. Αλλως· μυρου καταχεειν των εν τοις ἁγιωτατοις ιεροις αγαλματων θεμις ην, εριῳ τε στεφειν αυτα, και τουτο κατα τινα ιερατικον νομον, ὡς ὁ μεγας Προκλος φησιν.

i.e. "This is a proverb applied to those who are dismissed from business. For in festivals men poured oil on their head, as then resting from their usual avocations, and being alone at leisure for delight. Slaves also, when manumitted, wore wool rolled round their head, as a sign of their manumission. Or thus: It was lawful to pour oil on the statues in the most holy temples, and to crown them with wool, and this according to a certain sacred law, as the great Proclus says."

Page 258. But the God when he formed you, mixed gold in the formation of such of you as are able to govern, etc.

Plato here alludes to the different ages of mankind, which are celebrated by Hesiod, in his *Works and Days*, and which signify the different lives passed through by the individuals of the human species. Among these, the *golden age* indicates an intellectual life. For such a life is pure, impassive, and free from furrow; and of this impassivity a and purity gold is an image, from never being subject to rust or putrefaction. Such a life, too, is very properly said to be under Saturn, because Saturn, as will be shown in the note to the Cratylus, is an intellectual God. By the *silver age* a rustic and natural life is implied, in which the attention of the rational soul is entirely directed to the care of the body, but without proceeding to the extremity of vice. And by the *brazen age*, a dire, tyrannic, and cruel life, is implied, which is entirely passive, and proceeds to the very extremity of vice.

BOOK IV.

523

The following extract from the exposition of the more difficult questions in the Republic, by Proclus, (p. 407) will, I doubt not, from its great excellence be very acceptable to the reader. It is concerning the demonstrations in the fourth book of the Republic, that there are three parts of the human soul, and four virtues in it. The scientific accuracy of division, solidity of judgment, and profundity of conception which Proclus has displayed in this discussion can never be sufficiently admired; and it was not without reason, though doubtless without much acquaintance with the works of this wonderful man, that a certain scurrilous writer,[2] who appears to be a man of no science, moderately learned, and an indifferent poet, calls him the animated rival of Plato.

"I here consider virtue not ambiguously, and in the same manner as when we ascribe virtues to things inanimate, but that which is properly so denominated. This therefore we say is vital, is the perfection of life, and is the cause of well-being, and not of being to those by whom it is possessed. But since life is two-fold, one kind being gnostic, and the other orectic, or appetitive, virtue will be a certain perfection both of the orectic and of the gnostic form of life. Hence it is requisite that there should not be one virtue only, nor yet more than one of the same species, the one not being so divided as similar parts are divided from each other, differing only in quantity; but it is necessary that there should be many and dissimilar virtues, For such as is the condition of subjects, such also must be their perfections. Hence the virtues of things differing in species must also be specifically different; but of things possessing the same species, there is one specific virtue: for there is one perfection of one essence, whether the cause of being is the same with that of well-being to things, since such as is the being which it imparts, such also is the well-being, or whether it is different. Hence Socrates in his Republic makes a distribution into three genera, *viz.* into guardians, auxiliaries, and mercenaries, before he indicates what the different kinds of virtue are in the best polity; and before he distributes the virtues analogously in one soul, he shows that there are three parts of the soul essentially different, *viz.* reason, anger, and desire, knowing that perfections themselves are changed together with the diversities of subjects, and on this account that there are many virtues dissimilar in species.

"To these things also it is requisite to add, for the purpose of facilitating the objects of discussion, that there is one perfection and energy of a thing considered by itself, and another according to its habitude to something else; so that the hyparxis of a thing (or the summit of its essence) is different from the proximity or alliance which it has with another. For there is not the same perfection of man, and of a man who is a despot, as neither is man the same with a despot; nor is it the same thing to behold the soul simply, and the soul as governing the body. Hence it is not the same thing to consider the essential and the relative perfection of a thing. Neither, therefore, must we consider the energy of a thing essentially originating from itself, and solely directed to itself in the same manner as the energy of that which governs or is governed; for government, and the being governed, are certain habitudes. Nothing indeed hinders but that the same thing may perform a certain action, not as governing or as governed, but as possessing a certain essence by itself, and an energy which it is allotted consequent to its essence. Thus for instance, the rational power in us when it lives cathartically,[3] performs its proper work theoretically, being naturally adapted thus to live according to its essence; but in this case it does not perform the office of a governor, as the irrational parts contribute nothing to that energy which is directed to itself. Rightly, therefore, does Socrates show that every governing art imparts good to the governed; so that when the rational part extends good to itself alone, purifying and investigating itself, it does not then possess the life of a governor. Thus also when anger acts conformably to its nature, being alone moved as an appetite avenging incidental molestations, it does not then preserve the habitude of that which is governed, with respect to reason, but alone acts as anger: for the desire of vengeance is the work of anger, and not to energize in obedience to reason. In like manner the desiderative part of the soul, when it immoderately aspires after pleasure, then lives according to its own nature: for this is the work of desire, to love pleasure, not some particular, but every, pleasure, and this not as governed by reason, whose province it is to measure its appetite. So that each of these three may be said to act after this manner, when each performs its proper work, without any reference to a governing principle.

"Since however all the parts are conjoined with each other, and give completion to one life, it is necessary to consider them according to their relative energy, and thus to perceive the virtue and the vice of each. Hence we must define political virtue to be a habit perfective of the relative life of the parts of the soul; and its contrary, political vice, to be a habit corruptive of the vital habitude of the parts to each other. Beginning from hence also, it is requisite to see that, in the different kinds of polities, the life of every individual is two-fold, one pertaining to himself, and the other relative; and again, that in these virtue and vice have a similar subsistence. For let the guardian be one who contemplates real beings, and ascends by intellectual energy as far as to *the good itself.* He therefore so far as man performs an energy adapted to himself, but abandons a governing life. Hence Socrates does not permit him to abide in such an energy, but brings him down again to a providential care of the city, that he may be a true guardian, leaving a life according to intellect as his last energy. Again, let the auxiliary, because he is the lord of all in the city, pay no attention to the governors, but act in every thing according to casual impulse, and use his power immoderately. This man indeed, as a soldier, will accomplish the energy which is adapted to him; for this consists in fighting; but he will no longer act as one governed. For it is requisite that the governed should look to the conceptions of the governor. Hence the soldier when obedient to the governor, preserves the virtue proper to one governed, but when he opposes the governor, he corrupts his own relative virtue. Lastly, let the mercenary be one who only lives for himself, and who is alone busily employed in the acquisition of wealth. This man therefore performs his proper work, so far as he is what he is said to be, a mercenary, but he has not yet the vice or the virtue of one governed. But if he becomes a member of political society, and ranks as one who is governed, he will now live with habitude to this: and when he is obedient to the governors according to this habitude, and accumulates wealth conformably to their will, and after the manner which they define, he will possess virtue adapted to a governed mercenary; but when he deviates from the will of the governors, and does not observe their mandates, he is, so far as one governed, a depraved mercenary. In the political genera, therefore, there is a two-fold proper work, one essential, and the other relative, as in the parts of the soul. But, if in both there are, governors and the governed, virtues and vices, it is requisite to consider how the virtues and vices in the one subsist with relation to those in the other, and to show that the virtues and vices of the soul presubsist as the paradigms of those in the political genera. For, the parts of the soul energizing internally, render the soul better or worse; but proceeding externally, and terminating in actions, they adorn the political genera, or fill them with disorder. Hence Socrates very properly makes a transition from the parts in one soul to those in whole polities, as proceeding to things more known. For it is not possible to know in a proper manner all the inward habits of souls, and all their inward abiding energies, in any other way than by their externally proceeding energies. This then is evident. For, the guardian governing the auxiliaries, energizes externally, imitating inward reason governing anger. And, in a similar manner, the auxiliary governs the mercenary tribe, imitating in his external energy, the inward dominion of anger over desire. All dominions therefore are habitudes, both those belonging to the soul, and those that are political; but the external are imitations of the internal; and the former are secondary energies of the latter, which are primary. The true political science, therefore, subsists about the habitudes of the soul, this being that which adorns both the governors and the governed; or rather it is one habit possessing two-fold energies, the inward governing and being governed, and the external adorning political affairs.

"These things being determined, let us now consider how we shall introduce all the four virtues; and let us endeavour to make it apparent to the learner that they are four. Since, therefore, there are three parts of the soul (for from hence we must begin); but these have not an equal order, one being allied to intellect, another being naturally adapted to body, and another being arranged in the middle of both; hence, that alone governs which is naturally allied to intellect, *viz.* reason, and, which itself spontaneously knows, intellect; and that is alone governed, which, according to its proper order, is allied to body. This is the desiderative part of the soul, which aspires after corporeal possessions, just as reason desires intellectual good. But the irascible part is that which both governs and is governed. This part, because it is irrational, is present also with irrational animals, like the desiderative part, is destitute of knowledge, and naturally requires to be governed by that which is allied to intellect; but, because it is always present with, when desire opposes reason, it is more allied to the rational part than desire, which is more remote from reason, and remarkably sympathizes with the body. For this always adheres to the body, and never abandons its life; but anger often despises the body and a life in conjunction with it, aspiring after another object of desire, which does not pertain to the body. These then, being three, one of which, reason, ought to govern only, but another, as body, to be governed only, and another to govern, and at the same time to be governed, according to an order in the middle of the extremes,—hence, the governors are two, the one primary, and the other secondary, and the things governed according to the same reasoning are also two. It is requisite, therefore, that the part which alone and primarily governs should possess one virtue perfective of governing habitude; but that the part which governs secondarily, and is governed primarily, should possess two-fold virtues perfective of two habitudes. For, as the perfections of different hyparxes are different, so also the perfections of different habitudes. But it is necessary that the part which is alone governed should possess one perfective virtue. Reason, therefore, which, as we have shown, ought only to govern, has for its ruling virtue prudence, according to which it bounds both for itself and others the measures of actions. Desire, which ought only to be governed, has for its virtue temperance, according to which it measures its appetites, converting itself to reason, from which it receives a rational impulse, through custom and discipline. But anger, which naturally governs and is governed, possesses, so far as it governs, fortitude, through which it humiliates the desiderative part, and presents itself invulnerable from its attacks; but, so far as it is governed, it possesses temperance, through which it also desires to be disciplined by the measures of reason. If reason, however, as governing both, and as the cause of conversion to itself, and of their submitting to measure, comprehends the principle which it imparts to them, this principle will be temperance, beginning indeed from reason, but ending in desire through anger as a medium; and thus the harmony diapason[4] will be produced from the three, *viz.* from reason, anger, and desire. But of these, anger being the middle, in one part produces the symphony called diatessaron,[5] and in another that which is denominated diapente;[6] the symphony of reason to anger forming the diapente, and that of anger to desire the diatessaron. This latter the Pythagoreans denominate a syllable, as not being a perfect symphony; but they assert that the diapente ought rather to be called a symphony than this; just as we must assert that anger has a greater symphony with reason, than desire has with anger, though the interval between the latter is less than that which subsists between the former: for both these are appetites, but the other two are reason and appetite. There is more symphony, therefore, between anger and reason, though the interval is greater, than between desire and anger, though the interval is lesser. For, as we have before observed, anger naturally co-arranges itself with reason, and is more disposed to

528

league with it in battle than with desire, when reason and desire war on each other. And hence, a greater symphony must be assigned to anger and reason, than to desire and anger. But from all these it must be said that a diapason is produced, which the Pythagoreans denominate by far the sweetest and the purest of all symphonies. For this, indeed, is truly a symphony, since among all others it alone possesses the peculiarity of which Timæus speaks, *viz.* that the motions of the sharper sounds ceasing, embrace those that are more flat, and embracing them conjoin the beginning with the end, and produce one motion gradually terminating from the sharp in the flat. Since, therefore, of all symphonies the diapason is alone allotted this prerogative, it will be adapted to the harmony of the soul, pervading through all the parts, conjoining the superior with the inferior motions, connascently harmonizing the intentions of the one with the remissions of the other, and truly producing one life from many. And thus in the way of digression we have shown how Socrates denominates temperance the harmony diapason.

"But if prudence is alone the virtue of the governor, but temperance is the virtue of the governed, and both temperance and fortitude form the virtue of that which governs and is at the same time governed, it is evident that the remaining virtue, justice, must belong to all the parts, to one as governing, to another as that which is governed, and to another as that which both governs and is governed; so that through this each part energizes according to its proper order, the one as governing, the other as governed, and a third as both. And here it may be inquired how anger, since it both governs and is governed, has the virtue of temperance in common with desire so far as it is governed, but has not any virtue in common with reason so far as it governs, but possesses fortitude as its proper virtue. To this it may be replied, that there is, as we have said, a greater interval between anger and reason, according to essence, than between desire and anger, though when reason and desire oppose each other, anger is by no means the ally of the latter, but takes the part of the former. But it does this through the pertinacity of desire, through which it often contumaciously excites reason against desire, and not through any alliance with reason. So that on this account it has a common virtue with desire, so far as it is governed, but a different virtue from reason, so far as governing. For the governing power of anger is perfectly different from that of reason, which begins its government from itself. For reason first governs itself, and adorns itself, prior to other things, and does not suffer its proper appetite to remain dubious, and to tend to that which is worse. After this, it measures the appetites of the irrational parts, and recalls them to its own judgment and appetite. But anger is not governed by itself, but supernally issues its mandates to the worst part alone. For, that which is irrational is never at any time able to govern itself, nor to bound and be converted to itself. That anger, however, is more allied to desire than to reason, according to Plato, is evident: for both these are from the same fathers,[7] but reason is the offspring of a different father; both are mortal, and rise and perish in conjunction, but reason is immortal; both are destitute of knowledge, but reason is naturally gnostic. As therefore to be governed is common both to anger and desire, for so far as both are irrational, and require to be adorned by another, they are governed, hence they possess a common virtue which converts them to a desire of that which governs. But as the government of reason is different from that of desire in t he manner above mentioned, as governors they possess a different ruling virtue; the one gnostic, for it is reason; the other vital, for it is appetite. When therefore, appetite governs appetite, there is need of fortitude in order to preserve appetite uninjured; but when reason rules over appetite, there is need of prudence, preparing reason to judge rightly. And on this account prudence is the ruling virtue of reason, whose province it is to know and to judge rightly, and to govern natures which possess the power of judging. Fortitude is the ruling virtue of anger, which is alone vital, and is destitute of judgment, but is an appetite wishing to have dominion over a worse appetite, the opposition of which it cannot endure. But if, as we have before observed, there is a greater interval between the higher than between the lower of these, and a greater harmony arises from the former than the latter, it is by no means wonderful: for the brevity of life obscures the harmony; since in natures whose life is more extended it is greater, and in those whose life is less extended it is evidently less. We have therefore shown that the virtues are only four, and what is the work of each. It will now, therefore, be manifest how they are to be arranged in republics. For it

530

is evident that prudence must be especially placed in the governor who consults for the good of the city. For, of what can he who consults be in greater need than of prudence, the province of which is to perceive the good and ill in every action? But in the warring and guardian genus fortitude is requisite. For fame calls those men brave who intrepidly endure dangers, resist adversaries, and despise death. That they may subdue, therefore, all those that endeavour to subvert the republic, it is fit that they should be brave; but they ought to receive the measures of their energies from those that are the true governors, and in this be temperate, looking to their will. And in him who ranks in the last place, and provides all that is necessary, temperance is requisite, lest, being inflated by affluence, he should arrogate to himself dominion, thinking that he is sufficient to himself with respect to felicity, and should thus despise the governors, in consequence of an abundance in things necessary imparting a representation of good. Temperance, therefore, is requisite to this character, that he may be obedient to the governors, and may submit to them; as in the universe, according to Timæus, necessity follows intellect. But, all of them thus receiving their proper virtue, the one acting prudently, the other temperately, and the other bravely, the employment of justice will now be known. For it prepares each, in the coordination with each other, to do its own work alone, and not, by engaging in employments foreign to its nature, to usurp the prerogatives of others, but to live in such a manner as the political science enjoins. So that the guardian may not attempt to engage in war or in agriculture, thus falling into a life unworthy of himself; nor the auxiliary to undertake the province of the merchant or the governor; nor the mercenary to occupy the place of the auxiliary or the guardian, because he provides arms for the former and necessaries for the latter. So that in the political genera all the virtues have the same relation to each other as those in the parts of the soul.

"These things, therefore, being admitted, let us consider how Socrates again transfers his discourse to the virtues in the political genera, and says, that he is willing to behold, as it were, in larger, what is written in smaller letters: for virtue in the habitation of one soul is more impartible than in cities, and the virtues of a whole city are images of those in one soul; and reason, as he says, requires that things more impartible in power should have dominion over those which are extended into a numerous division, and that things less according to number should yield to the power of things more according to quantity. In the political genera, therefore, Socrates wishing to behold all the virtues, in the first place orderly arranges the political genera,—I say orderly, because he first considers men solely employed about necessaries, without war, unskilled in discipline, living according to nature, satisfied with as little as possible, and conducting themselves temperately: and, in the second place, he shows that when their possessions are increased, they are necessarily led through their external enemies to direct their attention to military affairs. In consequence of this, he shows that discipline then becomes necessary, men passing from a physical to a defensive life, as they could not otherwise defend themselves when unjustly injured by their neighbours. It is requisite, therefore, that there should be those who may fight in defence of the husbandmen; for the same person cannot accomplish both these, since an aptitude for agriculture is different from an aptitude for war. But as aptitudes differ, so also perfections, and it is requisite that every one should be perfected according to his own nature, if he is not to possess an adulterated and unnatural life. To which we may add, that if one and the same person were a soldier and a husbandman, he could not attend to the seasons of his proper works, being compelled to take up arms when he ought to cultivate the land, to plough or plant when he should engage in war, to carry rural instead of warlike implements, the spade for the shield, and to be in want of necessaries by neglecting the concerns of agriculture. If, therefore, the auxiliary is one person, and he who attends to the necessaries of life another, two political genera must be established, the auxiliary and the mercenary, the latter supplying things necessary, and the former defending both himself and the other. But each of these requires a different discipline, for the manners of each are different. Socrates, therefore, instructs us in a two-fold kind of discipline, one pertaining to the soul, and the other to the body. For soldiers require a robust body, in order to endure the necessary labours of war. And as there are two kinds of discipline, one according to music and the other according to gymnastic, it appears to me that Socrates considers those to be most

532

adapted to universal government, whose nature is more adapted to
music, and who are better skilled in it than others. For it makes us
more prudent, teaching us concerning gods, dæmons, heroes, and
illustrious men; but this gymnastic is unable to effect. Of the truth of
which I consider this to be an argument, that the whole polity, as
Socrates says, is dissolved, not through a neglect of gymnastic, but of
music. So that we shall not err in asserting, that those who are
naturally adapted, and are more propense to music than others, are
chosen as guardians by Socrates, though he alone says that the most
excellent characters are to be chosen as governors, but does not add in
what it is that they are most excellent.

"Socrates, therefore, having established these three genera, in order
to give completion to the city, indicates whence we may call the city
wise, whence brave, temperate, and just. And the guardian genus,
indeed, on account of its being most musical, possesses the science of
good and ill; for, as we before observed, it has learnt from the
discipline of music in what manner it is requisite to be wise respecting
superior natures, and respecting human felicity. Hence, he says, poets
also are to be compelled to compose such verses as have a tendency to
these types. And if it also learns the mathematical disciplines and
dialectic, it will be in a still greater degree wise and scientific. The
auxiliary genus, on account of its living in arms, and in the exercise
and study of warlike affairs, especially possesses fortitude. And the
mercenary genus requires temperance: for an affluence of things
necessary is especially in want of this virtue, since an abundance of
these leads to an intemperate life. These three genera therefore
mutually according with each other, and preserving their own energy
with respect to governing and being governed, justice is the result of
such a subsistence. For all men, as well those that praise as those that
revile justice, say that just conduct consists in not desiring the
possessions of others. Hence its enemies reprobate it, because it is
content with its own property, when at the same time it ought to
possess all things. And thus far, indeed, Socrates, considering justice as
the founder of cities, does not reprobate its accusers: for they say that
justice is that which is beautiful by law; and they honour it as a thing
necessary; since no one is willing to be injured contrary to the laws,
because this is the extremity of evils. But, according to these men, to

act unjustly is the greatest good; and justice, having a middle subsistence, is neither good nor evil, but necessary. As we have said, therefore, though Socrates considers justice as a plenitude of good, yet he does not reprobate its accusers: for it is admitted to be that which is beautiful by law. Now, therefore, inculcating that it is truly good, and that it is beautiful by nature, he adds, that it also imparts strength to the other virtues: for each through this performs its own proper work, and none of the rest preserves a city so much as this. It is shown therefore by Socrates, that a permutation of the pursuits of the guardian, the auxiliary, and the mercenary, is the most perfect destruction of a polity.

"If, therefore, justice is a standard to each of the other virtues, which the accusers of justice acknowledge to be naturally beautiful, as, for instance, to prudence, for all men naturally desire its possession, and those that blame prudence either blame it prudently, and in this case prudence is not to be blamed, rightly blaming itself, or they blame it imprudently, and in this case prudence is not blameable, not being rightly blamed,—this being admitted, it necessarily follows that justice is naturally good in the same manner as prudence, and that it is not beautiful only by law. Socrates, having indicated these particulars respecting the virtues in the political genera, passes on to the virtues of the parts of the soul, which we have said are prior to these, and discourses in a three-fold respect concerning them. For, in the first place, he shows that the diversities of men arise from no other cause than the difference in their lives; and that neither does the difference in one city, nor in whole nations, originate from any thing else than from a diversity in the life pertaining to the soul: for it is not, says he, either from an oak, or a rock, *viz.* it is not from the lowest nature, of which an oak is the image,[8] nor from an inanimate and solid body, so far as body, for this is indicated by a rock. And the Greeks indeed have a greater aptitude to wisdom (when we speak of the whole nation), the Thracians are more irascible, and the Phœnicians more mercenary than either of these. But this arises from the soul, through which in some nations reason has dominion, in others anger, and in others desire. For the character of individuals arises from their life, and a whole nation is denominated rational or irascible from that part of the soul which principally flourishes in it.

534

They possess these diversities, therefore, either from the body or from the soul. They cannot, however, posses them from the body: for men become hot or cold, white or black, from the body, but not prudent, or brave, or temperate, or the contraries of these. It is from the soul, therefore, that they derive these distinguishing characteristics. And this is what Socrates first demonstrates.

"Some one however, perhaps, may say that the differences in souls are corporeal; for they follow the temperaments of the body, though these different powers are in the soul. It is evident, however, that he who makes this assertion grants that these diversities are in souls, though they blossom forth in consequence of the soul following the temperaments of bodies. The reasoning of Socrates therefore remains, and these lives originate from the soul, though they should be rooted in the temperament of the body. We should however be careful not to subject the soul to the nature of the body: for, in the undisciplined,[9] the powers of the soul follow the temperaments; but nature, as Plato says in the Phædo, formed the soul to govern, and the body to be governed, in order that the whole of the desiderative or irascible part might not be co-passive with the temperaments. But, in those that are well disciplined, the powers of the soul govern the temperament, so that it either is not moved by it from the beginning, or, if moved, it renders the excitation inefficacious. Socrates, therefore, as I have said, shows, in the first place, that in souls themselves there are diversities with respect to these forms of life; and, in the second place, he demonstrates as necessary to the proposed object of inquiry, that in the soul the rational, the irascible, and the desiderative parts are not one thing. But this was necessary that he might show that those three political characters are analogous to these three parts of the soul, and that both differ from each other by the same boundaries of life. This therefore he demonstrates in the second place, previously assuming as a thing universally acknowledged, that it is impossible for the same thing, according to the same, and with reference to the same, to do or suffer contraries; but that this may be accomplished by the same thing in a different respect. Thus, the same thing may be heated and refrigerated, be at rest and be moved, impart heat and cold, according to different parts. And the same thing, not with reference to the same but to different things, may be able to do and suffer contraries. Thus, the same thing may be capable of being illuminated and darkened with reference to other things, being illuminated by one thing and darkened by another. This, too, the same thing may be the cause of increase and diminution, according to the same, *i.e.* so far as it is the same, with reference to different things; as nutriment, which, at the same time that it nourishes the members of the body, is itself diminished.

"This being granted, Socrates considers the lives of the continent and incontinent, in which either reason and anger, or reason and desire, oppose each other. For these things take place in those who generously contend in battle through a love of honour, though desire is averse to the undertaking, and from the impulse of hunger urges to fight, but reason at the same time persuades to endurance. But, prior to these, this opposition is seen in the diseased, reason admonishing them not to drink if the body is hot with a fever, but desire calling on them to drink, and the two parts thus opposing each other. Prior to both these, however, it is seen in those that are injured, but do not revenge the injury, though they are incited to vengeance by anger, as in the instance which Homer presents us with in Ulysses, when he says, *536*

Endure, my heart! thou heavier ills hast borne.

"In short, reason and anger may at the same time suffer contraries with respect to the same, when, in consequence of an injury being sustained, the latter persuades to vengeance, and the former to endurance. Reason therefore and anger are not the same: for it is impossible that the same thing can do or suffer contraries, according to the same with relation to the same. Again, reason and desire exclaim contraries, as in the instance above mentioned, with respect to drinking in a fever; but it is impossible for the same thing to do or suffer contraries according to the same with reference to the same. Reason therefore and desire are not the same. Again, anger and desire, with respect to the same thing, speak oppositely in those engaged in battle, and oppressed with hunger; but as the same thing cannot be contrarily affected with respect to the same, anger and desire are not the same. Hence these three differ from each other essentially.

"Perhaps, however, some one may say that the irrational motions

are energies, and another perhaps may say that they are passions; and I
have heard some asserting that these motions when moderately
moved are energies, but, when immoderately moved, passions. The
position, however, which we have established as universally adopted,
comprehends the motions of these. So that, if it should be said, one of
these acts, and the other suffers, and that action and passion oppose
each other, it is evident that the motions themselves must much more
differ from each other: for a contrary effect is the cause of a contrary
passion. So that, if any passion has an effect contrary to that of any
other, the passion of the one will be contrary to that of the other. But
what shall we say concerning the love of riches, and the love of
pleasure? Whether do these essentially differ, or have they the same
essence, but are different orective powers? For that these oppose each
other, is testified by the avaricious man and the glutton; for the latter
is continually gratifying himself with whatever may satisfy his
appetite, and the former lives sparingly, and suffers the pain of
hunger, that be may not diminish his wealth. If therefore these
essentially differ, why do we not make four parts of the soul? But if
these, though they oppose each other, and suffer contraries, do not
essentially differ, neither will the others necessarily differ, because
they are passive to contraries.

"In thus doubting, however, we forget that desire is called by
Socrates a many headed beast, because the irrational life is both one
and many, as being proximate to the body, which is entirely manifold
and divisible; just as that which is allied to the rational[10] intellect is
more impartible than any other of the parts belonging to the soul.
The desiderative part, therefore, is essentially one and many, and on
this account possesses warring powers proceeding from different
essences, that through this it may be connascent with body: for this
also consists from contraries. Hence this part is one, so far as it
possesses one appetite, the love of body, according to which it also
differs from the rational parts. For the irascible part is adverse to
body, in consequence of aspiring after victory and honour, and
through these often calling aside the body, and despising a life in
conjunction with it. Nor is the rational part a lover of body, because
the object of its appetite is true good. It remains therefore that the
desiderative part alone is attached to body, whether it aspires after

537

pleasures or riches: for both these are corporeal. For we are compelled, as Socrates says in the Phædo, to acquire riches, in consequence of being subservient to the body and the desires of the body; and the lover of riches never despises the body, though it may sometimes happen that he may die through his attention to wealth. So that the desiderative part, so far as it is simply a lover of body, is one; but, so far as it is a lover of riches and pleasure, is not one. Hence Plato does not say that it is many animals, but calls it one animal having many heads, and living at different times according to its different heads, but being always a lover of body. The desiderative part therefore is, as we have said, the third, as the rational part which aspires after intellect is the first, and the irascible which desires power ranks as a medium. For power subsists between intellect and the summit of essence; and a representation of this summit proceeds into the third part of the soul; whence he who alone participates of this is a lover of body. A representation of power is seen in the part prior to this; and hence this part desires power: but the image of intellect is apparent in the first part; and hence reason aspires after intellection. The last part of the soul therefore is a lover of body, and is solely intent to the preservation of the body.

"Since, however, body is two-fold, one being that in which the soul *538* subsists, and the other that by which it is preserved, as the soul is incapable in its present state of being preserved by itself, hence it has two-fold appetites, one of leading into a natural condition the body in which it resides, and according to this appetite it becomes a lover of pleasure, all pleasure being an introduction to nature; but the other of these appetites leads it to procure that of which its containing body is indigent; and according to this appetite it becomes a lover of riches, the acquisition of wealth being desired for the sake of paying attention to the body. It is necessary, therefore, that these powers should always accord with each other,—I mean that the one should desire the preservation of the body in which it resides, and that the other should desire things necessary to its safety. But since one of these appetites aspires after that path which is natural to the body, instead of preserving it, hence through a love of pleasure it destroys it, and defiles it with ten thousand stains; but the other desires riches, not for the purpose of satisfying the necessary wants of the body, but as a principal good. This being the case, these appetites pursue different ends, which oppose each other because they are material. Hence the one by its own destruction contributes to the increase of the other. For the infinite appetite of pleasure is attended with a consumption of wealth, and an increase of wealth requires a diminution of things which contribute to the pleasures of the body. Here, therefore, in a contention concerning ends as principal goods, these appetites differ from each other. For the appetite of desire is not directed to one thing, *viz.* that the body may subsist according to nature, but to two things, the affluence of one of which is accomplished through the indigence of the other. Since then the end of these appetites is one according to nature, hence Socrates establishes one part of the soul in desire, though it is many-headed, which is not the case, as we have shown, with reason and anger.

"Having therefore given an essential division to the parts of the soul, let us, in the third place, consider how Socrates here disposes the four virtues. If then he had been willing to speak in a manner more known to the multitude, he would have said, that prudence is the virtue of reason, fortitude of anger, justice of the desire of riches, and temperance of the love of pleasure. But now, as he thought proper to distribute them in a manner inaccessible to the multitude, and to show the analogy in the political genera to the virtues, he evinces that prudence is a habit perfective of that which alone ought to govern the other parts of the soul; and that fortitude is a habit perfective of that which should govern secondarily in it. And having established these two principal virtues, he says that the other virtues belong to the two ruling parts. Hence, he asserts that temperance is a habit which leads the governed into concord with the governors, with respect to governing; so that the last part may consent with the other two, and the middle with the one part prior to it. But he says that justice is a habit which prescribes to each of the parts, both the governing and governed, its proper work. For it is necessary that they should accord with each other, some in governing, and others in being governed; and that the actions of some should be adapted to governors, and of others to the governed. For to govern and to be governed, are beheld in a certain form of life which justice imparts, distributing to the governor that which is alone adapted to him, to consult for the governed, and to the governed to be obedient to the governor. After this manner Socrates discourses concerning the virtues, and it is evident that they must necessarily be such and so many.

"One thing therefore only remains to be considered, *viz.* whence it becomes manifest, that there are only three parts of the soul which are the recipients of these virtues. For that these essentially differ from each other, Socrates has shown; but that there are these parts only, and neither more nor less, requires some consideration; since, if there are more than three, we shall also be in want of other virtues. It is admitted then, that if there are two things which possess contrary properties, there will be three media, as is proved to be the case in the elements," two of these being received from that which has a more proximate situation, and one from the remaining element which is more remote. This being assumed, let us see what are the peculiarities of reason and body. Reason therefore is impartible, but body partible: reason is intellective, but body is destitute of intelligence. And these things are assumed, one from the essence of reason, another from life, and another from knowledge. Hence anger is impartible indeed; for it is simple in its nature, and on this account exhibits one polity. It also possesses an appetite of power, yet is not intellective; but through the privation of intelligence is assimilated to body. But desire consists of many parts as well as body, and is multiform; and hence it is called a many-headed beast, and contributes to many polities, It is also orective, but not of the same things with anger, and is destitute of knowledge. It is necessary, therefore, that anger should be proximate to reason, but communicating in two peculiarities, in one with reason, and in the other with body; but that desire should be proximate to body. There are besides three things in these; two in which they agree,—appetite, and a privation of intellect; and one in which they differ,—the impartible, and the possession of many parts. Hence there is not any other part between the body and soul besides these.

"It may however appear, that Socrates does not leave these parts only when he says, 'Each of us is well affected when each of these three parts performs its proper office, and they are coharmonized with each other through temperance, and when this is the case with any other parts which may subsist between these.' For by this he may seem, as I have said, not to leave these parts only, but to admit that there is something in us which neither aspires after honour nor riches, but subsists between these. However, Socrates, when he indicates this, does not mean to assert that the lives of the soul are unmingled; as, for instance, that a life according to reason is unmingled with the other parts; that a life according to anger has no communion with the extremes; and that a life according to desire alone is not mingled with those prior to it; but that there are certain lives between these.—Thus, some lead a life both according to reason and anger, being lovers of learning, and at the same time ambitious. Others live according to anger and desire, being both lovers of honours and riches; and either pursue honours that they may become rich, or scatter abroad their riches that through these they may be honoured by those that admire wealth: just as those prior to these either pursue disciplines that they may be honoured for their learning,—or honour, that, being honoured by those that possess discipline, they also may partake of them. These then are the forms of life between reason and anger, and anger and desire; and are not other parts of the soul, but become, from the mixture of these, various instead of simple. For each of those three parts is itself by itself simple; one part being alone a lover of discipline, despising all honour, and every thing corporeal, and being coordinated to one thing, the knowledge of truth; but another part is ambitious and savage, despises body as a shadow, and is insatiable of one thing alone, honour; and the third part, desire, is alone attentive to body, and the things pertaining to body, but consider those honours and disciplines to be nothing more than trifles. These, therefore, being simple and unmingled, Socrates says that the lives of the soul which are mingled from these subsist between them, all which, together with the unmingled, ought to be harmonized through the best harmony, that it may be the measure of the appetite of disciplines, of honours, and of the care of the body; and that the appetite also of the other parts may become consonant, and may not dissent from reason. We must not therefore think that Socrates indicates the natures of other parts which contribute to the perfection of political virtue, but the mixture of these, and the generation of more various forms adapted to political characters.

"From what has been demonstrated, therefore, it is evident that the

541

soul is neither one, nor divided into more than the above-mentioned parts, except that the sensitive nature is different from all these. It is different from reason, because it is irrational, and is present with irrational animals; and it differs from the two irrational parts, because these are orective, but the sensitive nature is gnostic. Sense, indeed, is present with beings to whom appetite is unknown, as, for instance, to celestial natures: but the orective part necessarily requires sense; for appetites are accompanied with the senses. Hence an animal is characterized by the sensitive, and not by the orective nature. For sense is present with all animals. And hence, too, Timæus says that plants have a sensation of what is pleasant and painful, and therefore he thinks proper to call them animals: for every thing which partakes of life is an animal. Sense, therefore, as I have said, being different from the three parts of the soul, is placed under all of them.[12]

"Again: let us now consider whether the imaginative is entirely the same with the sensitive power. So far, therefore, as this power is 542 directed in its energies to externals, it is sensitive; but so far as it possess in itself what it has seen or heard, or the types which it has received from any other sense, it exerts the power of memory. Such then is imagination. Socrates also in the Philebus, when he says that the painter in us is different from the scribe, who through the senses writes in the soul imitations of the passions which the senses announce, no longer energizing after the same manner with sense, but itself by itself exciting the types received from them, when he asserts this, he indicates, by arranging the painter according to the phantastic power, but the scribe according to the common sense, that these are essentially different from each other. In the Theætetus, also, he clearly separates that which judges concerning sensible impressions, from sense in which the seals of sensibles are expressed. But whether these essentially differ from each other or not, this is evident, that memory and sense are different, though the essence of these is divided about one subject which possesses an essential multitude; and that memory is nearer to reason than sense, because it receives types from the former as well as from the latter; sense receiving no impressions from reason. And thus much concerning things useful to political virtue, and to those that are instructed in it.

"As I know, however, that Porphyry in his mixed Problems relates a certain conversation between Medius the Stoic and Longinus respecting the parts of the soul, I do not think it proper to let it pass unnoticed. Medius therefore having made the soul to consist of eight parts, and having divided it into that which governs, into the five senses, into that which is spermatic, and lastly into that which is vocal, Longinus asked him, why he divided the soul, being one, into eight parts? And Medius, in reply, asked Longinus, why, according to Plato, he made the soul, which is one, to be triple? This then deserves to be considered. For it is evident that the inquiry is not the same with the Stoics, who make the soul to consist of eight, as with Plato, who distributes it into three parts. For the Stoics make corporeal differences of parts; and hence it may be reasonably objected to them, how the soul is one, since it is divided into eight parts, without any connecting bond? But Plato, since he asserts that the soul is incorporeal, and incorporeal natures are united to each other without confusion, is not involved in the same doubt respecting the union of its three parts. Plato may also be defended after another manner by saying that, according to him, reason is of a more divine essence, but the irrational part of a much inferior nature; and that the former connects and adorns, but that the latter is connected and adorned; just as form when conjoined with matter introduces unity, and we do not require any thing else which may unite these to each other. Reason, therefore, possessing the order of form, unites the irrational life, and no other third conjoining nature is required. If, likewise, according to Plato,[13] the junior Gods produce the irrational part, and the demiurgus the rational, there can no longer be any doubt respecting the source of union to reason and the irrational nature. And thus much in defence of Plato, in answer to the noble Medius.

"In the last place, appetite and knowledge are contained in the rational soul. And its appetite is either directed to being, or to generation, through which it ascends to real being, and falls again into the regions of sense. The former appetite, therefore, is philosophic, and the latter is enamoured with generation. In like manner, with respect to its knowledge, that which pertains to the circle of sameness[14] is the knowledge of intelligibles, but that which pertains to the circle of difference is the knowledge of sensibles. Hence, through these the soul elevates herself to the vision of the former, and investigates the nature of the latter. The irrational powers, therefore, are images of these, the orective of the rational appetites, and the gnostic of rational knowledges. Imaginative or phantastic is indeed the image of intelligible, and sensitive of doxastic knowledge. Thus, too, the appetite of the irascible part is an image of re-elevating appetite, and of the desiderative part, of that appetite which produces generation: for this supervenes body, in the same manner as the former embraces generation. And anger despises body, but looks to honour, the good of incorporeal natures. The phantasy being a figured intellection of intelligibles, wills to be the knowledge of certain things; but sense is conversant with the same object as opinion, *viz.* a generated nature."

BOOK V.

544

Page. 319. *The riddle of children about the Eunuch striking the but.*

This, according to the Greek Scholiast on this part, was the riddle of Clearchus, and is as follows: A man and not a man, seeing and yet not seeing, struck and yet did not strike, a bird and not a bird, sitting and not sitting, on a tree and yet not on a tree. That is, a Eunuch blind of one eye struck with a pumice stone the wing of a bat perched on a reed.

Notes

Book I

1. Glauco and Adimantus were the brothers of Plato, whom, as Plutarch justly observes in his Treatise on Brotherly Love, Plato has rendered famous by introducing them into this dialogue.

2. It is necessary to observe that this form of a Republic is thrice related, according to Plato; the first time, in the Piræum, *agonistically*, or with contention; the third time, in the introduction to the Timæus, without persons, *synoptically*; and the second time *narratively*, with the persons and things pertaining to the narration. This second relation was made in the city, to Timæus, Critias, Hermocrates, etc., as we learn from Plato in the Timæus. Proclus, therefore, observes as follows respecting the Piræum, the place of the first conversation, that, as maritime places are necessarily full of a tumultuous and various life, the Piræum was most adapted to a discourse concerning justice, attended with tumult, and in which Socrates, not without sophistical contests, defended justice against the many-headed sophistical life. But the city, the place of the second relation, is accommodated to a life unattended with tumult, and with philosophic tranquillity retiring into itself, and quietly contemplating, in conjunction with those similar to itself, things which it had surveyed with much trouble in a tumultuous place And perhaps, says he, you may say that the Piræum is analogous to the realms of generation, (*i.e.* the sublunary region) but the city to a place pure from generation, and, as Socrates in the Phædo says, to the æthereal region. For generation is full of a bitter and tempestuous life, and of mighty waves under which souls are merged, whence their life is not without tumult, though they may live according to reason. But the æthereal region is the place of souls who are now allotted a pure and blameless period of existence, though they still retain the memory of the tumult in generation, and of the labours which they endured in its fluctuating empire.

3. This festival, according to Proclus, (in Plat. Polit. p. 353.) was the Bendidian, in which Diana was worshipped agreeably to the law of the Thracians. For Bendis, says he, is a Thracian name. He adds, "The theologist of Thrace (Orpheus), among many names of the Moon, refers that of Bendis also to the goddess:

Plutonian, joyful goddess, Bendis strong."

4. This nocturnal solemnity was the lesser Panathenæa, which, as the name implies, was sacred to Minerva. Proclus (in Plat. Polit. p. 353) observes of this goddess and Diana, that they are both daughters of Jupiter, both virgins, and

both light-bearers. The one (Diana) is Phosphor, as benevolently leading into light the unapparent reasons (*i.e.* productive principles) of nature; the other as enkindling intellectual light in the soul—

>His helmet and his shield she gave to blaze
>With fire unweary'd*—

and is removing those dark mists, which, when present, prevent the soul from seeing what is divine, and what is human. Both, therefore, possessing idioms of this kind, it is evident that the one presides over generation, and is the midwife of its productive principles; but the other elevates souls, and imparts intellect and true prudence: and in the celestial regions she exerts a still greater power, supernally perfecting the whole of the lunar order. If these things, then, be true, the Bendidian festival, as well as the place in which it was celebrated, will be adapted to the first conversation, which imitates the soul becoming adorned, but not free from the tumult of generation. But the Panathenæa will be adapted to the second and third narration of a republic, which imitate the soul retiring into herself, and withdrawing her life from things below, to her own intellect, and, instead of adorning things dissimilar, associating with such as are similar to herself, and communicating in intellectual conceptions, and spectacles adapted to happy spectators.

---

* Δαιε οι εκ κορυθος τε και ασπιδος ακαματον πυρ. Iliad. lib. 5, I, 4.

---

5. *i.e.* Inherited. [Ed.]

Introduction to Books 2 and 3

1. Hyparxis signifies the summit of essence; and, in all the divinities except the first God, is *the one* considered as participated by essence. See the Introduction to the Parmenides.

2. The Eleusinian, which Proclus calls the most holy of the mysteries, are likewise always denominated by him τελεται: and Suidas informs us that τελετη signifies a mysterious sacrifice, the *greatest* and *most honourable*. So that Socrates in the above passage clearly indicates that such fables belong to the most sacred of the mysteries.

3. Hence, according to the fable, Saturn was bound by Jupiter, who is the demiurgus or artificer of the universe.

4. The Titans are the ultimate artificers of things.

5. See the notes to the Cratylus.

6. Such fables, also, call forth our unperverted conceptions of divine natures, in which they efficaciously establish us, by untaught sacred disciplines; and, in short, they give perfection to the vital powers of the soul.

7. Αδυνατοις is erroneously printed in the original for αδυτοις.

8. Proclus says this with reference to what took place in the mysteries, as is

evident from the following extract from his MS. Commentary on the first Alcibiades:

Εν ταις ἁγιωτάταις των τελετων προ της του θεου παρουσιας δαιμονων χθονιων τινων συμβολοι προφαινονται, και οψεις εκταραττουσαι τους τελουμενους, και αποσπωσαι των αχραντων αγαθων, και εις την ὑλγν εκπροκαλουμεναι· δια το και ὁι θεοι παρακελευνται μη προτερον εις εκεινους βλεπειν, πριν ταις απο των τελετων φραχθωμεν δυναμεσιν· ου χρη κεινους σε βλεπειν πριν σωμα τελεσθεις, και δια τουτο τα λογια προστιθησιν, ὁτι τας ψυχας θελοντες αει των τελετων ἀπαγουσιν.

i.e. In the most holy of the mysteries, before the God appears, certain terrestrial dæmons present themselves, and lights which disturb those that are to be initiated, tear them away from undefiled goods, and call forth their attention to matter. Hence the Gods exhort us not to look at these, till we are fortified by the powers which the mysteries confer. For thus they speak: It is not proper for you to behold them till your body is initiated. And on this account the oracles (*i.e.* the Chaldæan) add, that such dæmons, alluring souls, seduce them from the mysteries."

Agreeably to this, Proclus, also, in Plat. Theol. p. 7. observes:

Εν ταις των τελετων ἁγιωτάταις φασι τους μυστας, την μεν πρωτην πολυειδεσι και πολυμορφοις των θεων προβεβλημενοις γενεσιν ἁπανταν.

i.e. "In the most holy of the mysteries they say that the mystics at first meet with the multiform and many-shaped genera which are hurled forth before the gods."

9. For ὑπερ , as in the original, read ὑπαρ.

10. *viz. bound* and *infinity*, which are the highest principles after the ineffable cause of all.—See the Philebus, and the Notes to my Translation of Aristotle's Metaphysics.

11. The form of a thing considered according to its causal subsistence, or a subsistence in its cause, is said to be a whole prior to parts.

12. Iliad. lib. 2. ver. 288, etc.

13. See the Phædrus.

14. For five is not only an odd, but also a spheric number: for all its multiplication into itself terminate in five; and therefore end where they began.

15. For six is a perfect number, being equal to the sum of all its parts.

16. That is to say, though Venus is not represented by Homer as actually producing friendship in the adverse Gods, yet this is occultly signified by her being present; for she is the source of all the harmony, friendship, and analogy

in the universe, and of the union of form with matter.

17. Iliad. lib. 24. ver. 527.

18. *viz. bound* and *infinity*.

19. These two-fold coordinations of the Pythagoreans are as follow: Bound, infinity: the odd, the even: the one, multitude: right hand, left hand: the masculine, the feminine: the quiescent, that which is in motion: the straight, the curved: light, darkness: good, evil: the square, the oblong. See my Translation of Aristotle's Metaphysics, book I.

20. For πειθω signifies persuasion, and πιθος is a tub.

21. Iliad. Lib. 24. ver. 534, etc.

22. For ὁ δε ὁμες, in the original, read ὁ δε Ὁμηρος.

23. Δεινη γαρ Κρονιδαο νοου κραντειρα τετυκται.

24. *Pandarus* seems to be derived απο του παντα δραν, that is, as we commonly say of a very depraved character, he was a man *capable of any thing*.

25. Iliad. lib. 4. ver. 86.

26. See the 10th Book.

27. For δημιουργιας, read δημηγοριας.

28. Iliad, lib. 20.

29. Odyss. lib. 17. ver. 485.

30. *viz.* the Chaldean Oracles. See my Collection of these Oracles.

31. Hence also Homer, Iliad. lib. 20. ver. 131. says, χαλεποι δε θεοι φαινεσθαι εναργεις-*i.e.* O'er-powering are the Gods when clearly seen.

32. Iliad. lib. 5.

33. A divine nature must necessarily produce the sensation of weight in the body by which it is received, from its overpowering energy; for body lies like non-entity before such a nature, and fails, and dies away, as it were, under its influence.

34. Iliad. lib. I.

35. Iliad. 21. ver. 285.

36. Heroes are divided into two kinds: those that energize according to practical, and those that energize according to intellectual virtue. Achilles was a hero of the former class, and Hercules of the latter. For an ample account of the characteristics of these two kinds, see my Pausanias, vol. iii. p. 229.

37. The irrational part of the soul is the *image* of the rational, in the same manner as the rational soul is the image of intellect. Body also is the image of the irrational soul, and matter, or the last of things, is the image of body.

38. For αγμων here read ατμων.

39. Instead of reading the latter part of this sentence, and the beginning of the next; as it is erroneously printed in the original, *viz.* φερομενων πορρωτατω. it is necessary to read, as in the translation, φερομενων. Πορρωτατω δε εστι etc.

40. Iliad. 22.

41. Iliad. 18.

42. *i.e.* Jupiter, who is called the *greatest* of the Gods, with reference to the mundane God, of whom he is the demiurgus and father. For, that he is not the first God, is evident from the Cratylus, Timæus and Parmenides of Plato.

43. Δακρυα μεν σεθεν εστι πολυπλημων (lege πολυτλημων) γενος ανδρων.

44. *viz.* the Eleusinian mysteries.

45. *viz.* Rhea, who is the mother of the Gods.

46. Iliad. lib. 1. circa sinem.

47. *viz.* He is the artificer of the whole of a corporeal nature. Proclus also, somewhere in his comment on the Timæus, assigns another reason for the fiction of Vulcan's lameness, *viz.* because he is the fabricator of things last in the progressions of being (for such are bodies), and which are not able to proceed into another order. I prefer this explanation to the former.

48. Instead of και της οικειας ευπαθειας αφισταμενοι, read και της οικειας ευπαθειας ουχ αφισταμενοι.

49. Illiad. lib. I.

50. Odyss. Lib. 10. at the beginning.

51. See these explained in my History of the Platonic Theology, annexed to my Translation of Proclus on Euclid.

52. Iliad. lib. 14.

53. *viz.* the great Syrianus.

54. In the original μεριστην; but it is necessary to read χωριστην, as in our translation.

55. This is a part of one of the Chaldean Oracles, to my collection of which I have already referred the reader.

56. *viz.* Dæmonical powers. The dress therefore of Juno signifies her being invested with powers of this kind.

57. *viz.* The Curetes.

58. *viz.* The dodecahedron, which is bounded by twelve equal and equilateral pentagons, and consists of twenty solid angles, of which the tripods of Vulcan are images; for every angle or the dodecahedron is formed from the junction of three lines.

59. Iliad. lib. 18. ver. 402.

60. Iliad. lib. 1.

61. Iliad. lib. 1.

62. Iliad. lib. 9.

63. Iliad, lib, 22.

64. Iliad. lib, 18.

65. Iliad. lib. 24.

66. Iliad, lib. 2.

67. Iliad. lib. 23.

68. For τον θεον in the original, read των θεων.

Book 2

1. Gyges slew Candaules in the second year of the 16th Olympiad. Vid. Cic. de Offic. lib. 3.

2. Hesiod. Oper. et Di. lib. 1.

3. Hom. Odyss: lib. 19.

4. By inebriation, theological poets signify a deific energy, or an energy superior to that which is intellectual.

5. See the notes to Phædo.

6. Hesiod. Oper. et Di. lib. 1.

7. Hom. Iliad. lib. 9.

8. The word used here by Plato is τελεται: and this word, as we have observed in the introduction to this book, signifies the greatest of the mysteries, or the Eleusinian. As therefore the Orphic hymns now extant are so called, there can be no doubt but that these were used in the Eleusinian mysteries: and this confirms what I have observed in my notes to Pausanias. [See also Taylor's Introduction to his second revised edition of the *Hymns of Orpheus*.—Ed.]

9. Hom. Iliad. lib. 24.

10. Hom. Odyss. lib. 17. ver. 485.

Book 3

1. Hom. Odyss. lib. 11.

2. Hom. Iliad. lib. 22.

3. Hom. Odyss. lib. 17.

4. Hom. Iliad. lib. 22.

5. Hom. Iliad. lib. 27.

6. Hom. Iliad. lib. 24.

7. Hom. Iliad. lib. 11.

8. Hom. Iliad. lib. 1.

9. Hom. Iliad. lib. 4.

10. Hom. Iliad. lib. 4.

11. Hom. Iliad. lib. 1.

12. Hom. Odyss. lib. 12.

13. Hom. Iliad. lib. 6.

14. Hom. Iliad. lib. 3.

15. Hom. Iliad. lib. 22.

16. See the notes at the end of the Sixth Book.

Book 4

1. Odyss. lib. 20. ver. 18.

Book 5

1. Hesiod. Op. et Di. Lib. 1.

Book 6

1. *viz.* An intelligible and intellectual essence.

2. A Diomedæan necessity is a proverbial expression applied to those who do any thing from necessity; and originated from the following history: Diomed and Ulysses, having stolen the Palladium from Ilium, returned by night to their ships. But Ulysses, being ambitious that the glory of the deed might be given to him alone, endeavoured to slay Diomed, who walked before him with the Palladium. Diomed, however, by the light of the moon, beholding the shadow of the sword raised over him, caught hold of Ulysses, bound his hands, ordered him to walk before him, and, striking him on the back with the broad part of his sword, arrived among the Greeks. This note is extracted from the Greek Scholia on Plato, collected from many manuscripts by Ruhnkenius, and published at Lyons 1800. As this work is but just come to my hands, I could not avail myself of it before; but I shall endeavour to supply this deficiency in the additional notes at the end of this volume, and shall select what appears to me to be most important, as notes to this and the subsequent books and dialogues. Unfortunately, these Scholia are mostly grammatical.

3. Heraclitus the Ephesian said that the sun descending to the western sea, and setting in it, was extinguished; and that afterwards, ascending above the earth, arriving at the east, it was again enkindled; and that this took place perpetually. See the Introduction to the Timæus.

4. Socrates by philosophy here means the mathematics; and agreeably to this Plotinus also says, that youth should be taught the mathematical disciplines, in order to become accustomed to an incorporeal nature.

5. This is said ironically. For truth comes spontaneously; once the soul does not resemble an unwritten, but an ever-written tablet; herself, as Proclus well observes, inscribing the characters in herself, of which she derives an eternal plenitude from intellect.

6. *viz.* From the genera of beings more excellent than human nature, such as dæmons and heroes.

7. Socrates says this in consequence of the inability of his auditors to understand the nature of *the good:* for, as it is well observed in the Greek Scholia on this part of the Republic, through the inaptitude of subordinate natures, such as are more excellent are unable to energize. Παρα γαρ των καταδεεστερων ανεπιτηδειοητα τα κρειττονα αδυνατουσιν ενεργειν.

8. When we consider the generation of things illuminated by the sun, we shall find that it is perfectly unbegotten. For, according to the Platonic philosophy, the sun alone of all things in the universe which are connected with a body is without generation, neither receiving any accession nor diminution. But every thing else which it illuminates receives light from a different part of it, through the motion of the solar sphere about its proper centre, which at different times sends different rays in a circle to the celestial and sublunary bodies. The sun however has generation and corruption so far as it is illuminated, just as the moon also receives augmentations and diminutions of light. So far therefore as the sun illuminates, it is unbegotten; and according to this it is assimilated to *the good*, and not so far as it is a body. See more concerning the sun in the Notes to the Cratylus.

9. *The good*, which is here celebrated by Socrates as that which reigns in the intelligible place, is neither the same with that which subsists in our nature, (for we rank in an order far below intelligibles) nor with that form of things good, which is coordinate with the just and the beautiful. For, forms being twofold, some alone distinguishing the *essences* of the things fashioned by form, but others their *perfections*, the genus of essence, same and different, and the form of animal, horse and man, and every thing of this kind, give distinction to essence and subjects; but the form of *the good*, the beautiful and the just, and in like manner the form of virtue, health, strength, and every thing of a similar nature, are perfective of the beings to which they belong: and of some, essence is the leader of every thing, but of others *the good*. For, as Plato says, every thing must necessarily participate of essence; and whatever preserves, gives perfection to, or defends any being must be good. Hence, since these two are leaders, the one of forms which give subsistence to things, and the other of such as are the sources of their perfection; it is necessary that one of these should be subordinate to the other; I mean that *the good* which is allotted a coordination among forms that are the sources of perfection should be subordinate to *essence*, which ranks among causes whence subsistence originates, if *the good* is being and a certain being. For it is either the same with or different from essence, which the Eleatean guest in the Sophista shows to be the genus of being. And if *the good* is the same with essence, an absurdity must ensue: for being and well-being are not the same. But if *the good* is something different from essence, it must necessarily participate of essence, in consequence of that being the genus of all forms. But if genera are more ancient than forms, *the good* which ranks among forms, and is posterior to their genus, will not be *the good* which reigns over in intelligibles; but this must be asserted of that good under which this and every form is arranged which possesses being, and which is the leader of the other genera of being. When therefore Plato says that *the good* reigns over intelligibles, he means

that good which is superior to essence.

But to lead us up to this supreme good, he appears to employ three orders of good as so many steps in this arduous ascent; *viz.* that which is imparticipable and superessential, that which is imparticipable and essential, and that which is essential and participable. On these the last is such as our nature contains; *the good* which ranks among forms is essential; and that which is beyond essence is superessential. Or we may say that *the good* which subsists in us may be considered as a habit, in consequence of its subsisting in a subject; the next to this ranks as essence, and a part of essence, I mean *the good* which ranks among forms; and the last as that which is neither a habit nor a part. When therefore Socrates says, that "to the multitude pleasure seems to be *the good,* and to the more elegant it seems to be prudence," he signifies that good which is resident in our nature, and which, from its being an impression of the ineffable principle of things, may be called the summit or flower of our essence. And when he also says that the idea of *the good* is the greatest discipline, which renders both such things as are just, and other things which employ it, useful and profitable, and that we do not sufficiently know it,— these assertions accord with *the good* which is in us, with that which is in forms, and with that which is understood to be before all things. For the idea of *the good* signifies a participated form, a separate intelligible, and that which has a separate subsistence prior to intelligibles; since the term *idea,* according to Plato, indicates that object of desire which is established prior to all things, *viz.* prior to all things belonging to a certain series. Thus, for instance, *the good* in our nature is prior to every thing else pertaining to the soul; *the good* which ranks among forms is prior to every thing which is the source of essential perfection; and *the good* which reigns in the intelligible world is prior to every series, and to all things.

Again, when Socrates says, "Let us at present dismiss this inquiry what *the good* is, for it appears to me a greater thing than we can arrive at according to our present impulse," it may be inferred, that though he appears to say something concerning *the good* from an image, and to unveil something pertaining to things occult, yet he does not unfold the whole truth concerning it; and this perhaps in consequence of Thrasymachus and Clitopho being present, and not thinking it fit to disclose the most mystical truths to sophists. Hence, on his asserting after wards that *the good* is superessential, he appeared to Glauco to peak ridiculously; and in consequence of Glauco in vain attempting the vision of that which is beyond all things, he again says that he willingly omits many things, and alone unfolds the analogy respecting the sun. But if his hearers had been adapted to such discourses, he would have disclosed to us many and truly theological particulars respecting it; and such as he discloses to us in the Parmenides concerning *the one.*

As we have said, therefore, Plato, transferring the investigation from *the good* which is in us, and concerning which those inquire who say that it is prudence or pleasure, to *the good* itself, and beginning the image respecting the sun, in the first place, he exhorts his hearers to take care that he does not give them an adulterate account of the offspring of the good; calling the sun the offspring, and transferring the term adulterate from the impressions in coin. He also indicates that the mode of teaching by analogy is not safe. For there is danger of introducing sophistry into the demonstration, by considering things beyond what the analogy will admit. Thus, in the present instance, if in consequence of Plato asserting that the sun is analogous to *the good*, so far as the former is the cause of light, as the latter is of truth, some one should consider the sun, no longer as the cause alone of light, but so far as it is moved, and should investigate that which is similar to this motion, in *the good*, he would no longer preserve the proper analogy. For the sun is not analogously assumed, so far as he is a thing caused, but so far as he is a cause alone; since it is impossible to assume any thing which is in all respects similar to *the good*. For every thing posterior to *the good*, by the assumption of something becomes worse than *the good;* one thing by assuming intelligence, as intellect; another by assuming motion, as soul; and another by the assumption of generation, as body. If therefore, in intellects, in souls, and in bodies, you consider that which is first in each, as analogous to *the good*, you must consider it so far only as it is similar to *the good*, viz. so far as it is the leader of its subject series, and is imparticipable with respect to a subordinate nature, and not so far as it is separated from *the good*. For every thing which is assumed analogously to *the good*, must necessarily possess dissimilitude in conjunction with similitude. Analogies however and ratios are not assumed according to the dissimilar, but on the contrary according to the similar.

Again, when in the beginning of this discourse about *the good*, and wishing to determine that some forms are intelligible and others sensible, he makes mention of the beautiful itself and *the good* itself, and, placing these as the forms of many things beautiful an good, he says that sensible forms are seen indeed, but are not the objects of intellect, but that ideas are the object of intellect, and not of the sensible eye,—it is evident that he refers us to ideas, and the universal prior to the many. If therefore Plato had added nothing further, we should not have had any authority from the Republic for conceiving any other good than this, which is the first among forms that give perfection to things; but since he touches on the analogy respecting the sun, sight and light, he in a wonderful manner asserts that all intelligible ideas, the beautiful itself, *the good* itself, the just itself, and not these only, but those of actions also, are illuminated by *the good*. Here therefore he ascends to the first cause of wholes, which he is unable to call by a better name than *the good:* for *the good* is the most venerable of all things, and is that which all things desire; and that which all things desire is the cause of all. Fearful however lest we should apprehend a first of such a kind as that good which is the cause of perfection alone in ideas, he shows in the first place that *the good* is beyond science and truth, in the same manner as the sun is beyond sight and light; and afterwards he evinces that it is the primary cause of intelligibles, and is superessential, in the same manner as the sun is above generation; and thus he shows that *the good itself* is the first cause of the good and the beautiful in forms, and of all intelligible essences.

But that we may not deviate from the doctrine through analogy, he says that the sun is analogous to *the good*, not according to any thing else than his being the cause of light, through which all visible things are seen: I mean, not so far as the sun has a body, and a corporeal place, and is moveable. And again, such a light is analogous to truth, not so far as it possesses interval, or all-various refractions, but so far only as it imparts the power of being seen to things visible, and light to things that see; in the same manner as truth imparts to intelligibles the power of being intellectually apprehended, and to intelligent natures the power of intellectual perception; and visible objects are analogous to intelligibles, not as subsisting in place and being moved, but as visible alone.

These things being premised, it is shown by Socrates that *the good* is beyond truth, in the same manner as the sun is beyond light: and hence it follows that *the good* does not participate of truth. For that which is above truth neither *is truly*, nor can *truly* be any thing else: so that if *the good is*, but *is* not *truly*, it will be that which is not *truly* being. But this is impossible. For, according to Plato, that which is not *truly* being subsists after true being. But *the good* is not true being, since it generates truth; and it must be entirely unreceptive of that which it generates. But all true being necessarily participates of truth. Hence it follows that *the good* is above being. For, if being is *truly* being, but *the good* gives subsistence to truth, which is inseparable from and characterizes being, it must also be above being.

Again, when Socrates says, "You know that the eyes, when they are no longer directed towards objects whose colours are shone upon by the light of day, but by the splendour of the night, grow dim, and appear almost blind, as if they had in them no pure sight. But when they turn to objects which the sun illuminates, then I think they see clearly, and in those very eyes there appears now to be light:" he here makes a division in things visible into colours, light, eyes, and the sun. Afterwards he adduces things analogous to those in the objects of intellect, as follows: "Understand then in the same manner with reference to the soul: when it firmly adheres to that which truth and real being enlighten, then it understands and knows it, and appears to posses intellect: but when it adheres to that which is blended with darkness, which is generated, and which perishes, it is then conversant with opinion, its vision becomes blunted, it wanders from one opinion to another, and resembles one without intellect." Socrates, therefore, assumes being analogous to colour, truth to light, and *the good* to the sun. He also places being after truth, in the same manner as colour after light and the sun. *The good* therefore is beyond being. For he does not say that which *beings* enlighten, but that which *being* enlightens. If therefore *the good* is above being, it will also necessarily be above essence.

Having asserted these things through analogy, he adds what is still greater, that *the good* is the cause of intelligibles, not of their being understood only, but also of their essence, in the same manner as the sun is the cause to things visible, not only of their being seen, but of their generation, nourishment and increase; and, as he is not generation, in like manner *the good* is not essence. It is evident, therefore, that *the good*, being the cause of an intelligible essence, will be in the most eminent degree superessential; for these, as will appear from the Parmenides, are superessential essences, or, in other words, beings absorbed in the superessential. It likewise follows from this analogy that truth also is superessential; for Socrates says that this illuminates all things that are known, in the same manner as the light of the sun irradiates visible objects. Truth indeed appears to be an illumination from the superessential principle of wholes, which both intelligible and intellectual natures participate, and which unites them to themselves, and to each other. Hence it is said to impart the power of being intellectually apprehended to the former, and of intellectual vision to the latter: for these could not be conjoined without a certain common bond. As light therefore illuminates visible and visive natures, but conjoins both through similitude, imparting to both a greater light than they contained before—in the same manner that which is intellective and that which is intelligible, being united by truth, coalesce with each other.

From hence also it will follow that *the good* cannot be known either by opinion or science. That it cannot indeed be known by opinion may be easily proved. For Plato, with great propriety, considers the object of opinion as that which is partly being, and partly non-being. It is also evident that *the good* is not the object of science. For, if every object of science is known from from a cause, that of which there is no cause cannot be scientifically known. And if *the good* is above truth, it will not be so known as intelligibles are known to intellectual natures. It can therefore only be known by a divine projection of the summit of the soul, a projection of that which is better than intellect, and which Plato* calls the ray of the soul. According to Plato, the soul inclining this ray should project herself to *the good* through an ablation of all things posterior to it. For he clearly says that it is necessary to take away the idea of *the good* from all things, and thus to incline towards it the ray of the soul, if we in tend to perceive it, itself by itself. From these thing therefore it is evident, by what kind of knowledge *the good* is known, how it is known, and how it is the last discipline, and what the dialectic method contributes to the vision of it, by leading the intellect of the soul up to it, through a scientific series of ablations.

Again, since Socrates asserts that *the good* is not only beyond essence, but likewise above that which is (επεκεινα του ειναι) it follows that it is not proper to say *the good is;* and hence neither is it proper to say that it is not; for again this assertion *that it is not* is common to other things, to which non-being is adapted. Both therefore must be said, that it is neither being nor non-being; and in consequence of this, it is called by some unknown and ineffable; since every thing is either being or non-being. Nor must we suppose, when Plato calls *the good* known, and the last discipline, and every thing of this kind, that he removes us from an indefinite energy about it, and apprehends it to be known in such a manner as beings: for these are known, and are the objects of scientific knowledge, according to that most accurate mode of science which he defines, and according to which he despises the sciences which originate from hypothesis. For thus he speaks, teaching us his conceptions about these particulars: that other sciences, or which appear to be such, make hypotheses their principles; but dialectic alone being impelled to the principle, takes away hypotheses, till it discovers that which is truly the principle, not as an hypothesis, but truly unhypothetical. But such a principle is *the one,* in which every subsistence of things known terminates. From these things, therefore, it is evident, that calling dialectic the defensive enclosure of things which appear to be sciences, and defining that which is truly science, he says that dialectic, beginning from an unhypothetic principle, considers the nature of every thing. If therefore beholding also the idiom of *the good,* and in what respect it differs from other things, this science speculates from an unhypothetic principle, this perhaps will be a certain science, and a science of *the good,* what it truly is, or is not. But if this is the principle of all thing, and a principle cannot be assumed of a principle, by what contrivance can it be said that there is a certain science of *the good?* For every scientific object is apprehended from an unhypothetic principle; and that which is so apprehended is properly a scientific object: but *the good* is not apprehended from an unhypothetic principle, because it has not any principle whatever. So that, if this is the definition of science, *the good* is by no means an object of scientific knowledge. From hence also it again follows that *the good* is not being, since Plato most clearly asserts that science is of being; but that faith pertains to that which appears and is sensible, the dianoëtic power to dianoëtic objects, assimilation to things assimilated, opinion to sensibles and things assimilated, and intelligence to intelligibles. And this he not only asserts here, but in the Timæus also he says, that "what essence is to generation, that faith is to truth," and attributes arguments which cannot be confuted to beings, but assimilative arguments to generated natures, signifying that science is speculative of true beings. If therefore being is the object of scientific knowledge, but *the good* cannot be scientifically known, *the good* is not being.

Hence we must conclude that *the good* is only to be known by an ablation or all things from its ineffable nature; and this is what Socrates insinuates when in the 7th book he speaks of separating the idea of *the good* from all others, and as in a battle piercing through all arguments. It is not therefore either science, or truth, or being: and if employing these things as principles we are willing to consider the consequences, we shall find that if *the goad* is not being, it is neither same nor different, neither moved nor at rest, neither possesses figure nor number, is neither similar nor dissimilar, is neither equal nor unequal, nor participates of time; all which Parmenides collects in the first hypothesis, and, having collected, adds, that there is neither science nor opinion of *the one*, for it is beyond generation and essence. So that whatever is asserted of *the one*, in the Parmenides of Plato, must also necessarily be asserted of *the good*, from what is here delivered by Plato concerning it; and hence *the good*, according to Plato, is the same with *the one*. We not only therefore have this information from the assertions of Socrates, that *the goad* is not the object of scientific knowledge, but that it may after another manner be known through arguments and ablations.

---

* In the 7th book of this Dialogue, near the end: As man is a microcosm, this ray of his soul will evidently be analogous to truth, or superessential light, in the intelligible worlds will be the summit of the soul, and that which the Platonists very properly call *the one* and the flower of our nature: for it is an illumination from the ineffable principle of all things.

---

10. The Greek Scholiast on the laughter of Glauco observes, that

"this laughter is through transcendency; for *the good* is incomparable with respect to all things. Or this laughter may be considered according to a mundane signification; for the junior and mundane Gods are obscurely signified by it; since every thing corporeal is a jest when compared with intelligibles. But to jest and laugh belong to youth. And

Amidst them laughter unextinguish'd rose

is said concerning the mundane Gods. Glauco therefore being analogous to a mundane person very properly speaks laughing.

Γελοιως δια την υπερβολην· ασυγκριτον γαρ τα'γαθον απλως προς παντα· αλλως το γελοιως, ητοι εγκοσμιως· οἱ γαρ νεοι και εγκοσμιοι Θεοι τουτο (lege τουτῳ) αινιττονται· καιγνιον γαρ το σωματικον παν τοις νοητοις παραβαλλομενον· το δε παιζειν και γελαν των νεων οικειον· και το,

Ασβεστος δ'αρ ενωρτο γελως μακαρεσσι θεοιτι.

Περι των εγκοσμιων ειρηται θεων· ὁ γ᾽ ουν γλαυκων αναλογως εγκοσμιω προσωπω εικοτως γελοιως λεγει.

11. The rational and gnostic powers of the soul receive a triple division: for one of these is opinion, another the dianoëtic power, and another intellect. Opinion therefore is conversant with the universal in sensibles, which also it knows, as that *every* man is a biped, and that *all* colour is the object of sight. It likewise knows the conclusions of the dianoëtic energy; but it does not know them scientifically. For it knows *that* the soul is immortal, but is ignorant *why* it is so, because this is the province of the dianoëtic power. Hence the Eleatean guest in the Sophista very properly defines opinion to be the termination of the dianoëtic power. For the dianoëtic power, having collected by a syllogistic process that the soul is immortal, opinion receiving the conclusion knows this alone *that* it is immortal. But the dianoëtic power is that which passes through as it were a certain way (ὁδον τινα διανυει) by making a transition from propositions to conclusions, from which also it derives its appellation. Thus, for instance, the dianoëtic power investigates whence it is that the soul is immortal. Afterwards, beginning from things most clear, it passes on to the object of investigation, saying that the soul is self-moved; that which is self-moved is also perpetually moved; and this is immortal. The soul therefore is immortal. And this is the employment of the dianoëtic power. But the province of *intellect* is to dart itself as it were to things themselves, by simple projections, like the emission of the visual rays, and by an energy superior to demonstration. And in this respect intellect is similar to the sense of sight, which by simple intuition knows the objects which present themselves to its view. That we actually possess all these gnostic powers, thus distinguished from each other, is evident from our possessing these different kinds of knowledge; for it is impossible that one and the same power could know things demonstratively, and in a manner superior and inferior to demonstration; since diversity of knowledge must arise from a diversity of gnostic energy.

It may also be proper to observe that opinion is the boundary of the rational part of the soul and that the phantasy, or that power which apprehends things invested with figure, is the summit of the irrational part, under which anger like a raging lion, and desire like a many-headed beast, subsist.

12. With respect to the manner in which Plato represents the distribution of all things by the section of a line, it is necessary to observe, that as the progression of all things from *the one* is continued and united, Plato presents us with an image of this continuity in one line, through the similitude and coherence of secondary natures always proceeding from such as are first, no vacuum by its intervention separating them from each other. For, as *the one* produces all things, it is necessary that their procession from him should be

continued: for the continued is allied to *the one*. And the cause of this continuity is the similitude of those sections which are in a consequent to those which are in a precedent order: for similitude is oneness. On this account he assumes one line, but this he cuts into two parts, and these not equal but unequal: the parts are however two. For in the Philebus he exhorts those that speculate things, after *the one*, to consider two things, if they have a subsistence, if not, the number which is allied to the dad. The division therefore of all things into unequal parts, indicates the rank of the divided natures, the inequality according to continuity exhibiting an image of inequality according to hyparxis. But each of these unequal sections he cuts analogous to the first division of the line; this analogy again clearly manifesting the subjection through sameness of secondary from primary natures. For analogy is identity of ratio, and the most beautiful of bonds, as we learn in the Timæus, and is the judgment of Jupiter, as we are informed in the Laws. As therefore the universe was fabricated according to analogy, all things receiving an indissoluble friendship with each other, so all things proceed bound, and in mutual consent through analogy.

But as there are four sections of one line, two of these, which complete its larger section, Plato establishes as the genus of the intelligible, but the other two, which form the lesser division, as the genus of that which is visible. For it was necessary to assign the larger section to the intelligible, as being more excellent, and comprehending the other, but the lesser to that which is visible; for it is comprehended in the intelligible order according to cause. And that which is comprehended is every where less than that which comprehends, whether the comprehension is considered according to essence, or according to power, or according to energy; as is seen in all continued and divided natures.

I only add that Plato in this representation of the series of things, by the sections of a line, follows the Pythagoreans, Brontinus and Archytas; but his explanation is both more elegant and more extended, as the learned reader may be convinced by consulting that part of the Anecdota Græca of Villoison, which contains the Treatise of Iamblichus on the common Mathematical Science.

13. The original here is αλλ’ ουν; but from the version of Ficinus, it appears that we should read αλλ’ ουκ νουν. And the sense indeed requires this emendation.

Book 7

1. Every thing in this cave is analogous to things visible; the men, animals and furniture of every kind in it corresponding to the third, and the shadows in it, and the images appearing in mirrors, to the fourth section in the division

of a line at the end of the preceding book. Things sensible also are imitations of things dianoëtic, or, in other words, of the objects of scientific energy, which form the second section of Plato's line. For the circle and triangle which are described upon paper are imitations of those which geometry considers; and the numbers which are beheld in things visible, of those which the arithmetician contemplates; and so with respect to every thing else. But observe that Plato here does not consider human life so far as it is essence, and is allotted a particular power, but merely with reference to erudition and the want of erudition. For in the ninth book he assimilates our essence to an animal whose nature is mingled from a man and a lion, and a certain many-headed beast. But the present image in the first place shows what human life is without erudition, and what it will be when educated conformably to the above mentioned sections, and acquiring knowledge corresponding to that arrangement. In the next place, when Plato says that we must conceive a road above between the fire and the fettered men, and that the fire from on high illuminates the men bearing utensils, and the fettered men who see nothing but the shadows formed by the fire, it is evident that there is a certain ascent in the cave itself from a more abject to a more elevated life. By this ascent, he signifies the contemplation of dianoëtic objects, (which form the second section of his line,) in the mathematical discipline. For as the shadows in the cave correspond to the shadows of visible objects, and visible objects are the immediate images of dianoëtic forms, or the essential reasons of the soul, it is evident that the objects from which these shadows are formed must correspond to such as are dianoëtic. It is requisite therefore that the dianoëtic power, exercising itself in these, should draw forth from their latent retreats the reasons of these which she contains, and should contemplate these, not in images, but as subsisting in herself in impartible involution; which when she evolves, she produces such a beautiful multitude of mathematical theorems. After these things, he says that "the man who is to be led from the cave will more easily see what the heavens contain, and the heavens themselves, by looking in the night to the light of the stars, and the moon, than by day looking on the sun, and the light of the sun." By this he signifies the contemplation of intelligibles: for the stars and their light are imitations of intelligibles, so far as all of them partake of the form of the sun, in the same manner as intelligibles are characterized by the nature of *the good*. These then such a one must contemplate, that he may understand their essence, and those summits of their nature by which they are deiform processions from the ineffable principle of things. But if as prior to the vision of the sun it is requisite to behold the whole heaven, and all that the heavens contain; in the same manner prior to the vision of *the good*, it is necessary to behold the whole intelligible order and all that it comprehends, we may from hence collect that some things in intelligibles are analogous to the whole starry spheres,* but others to the stars which those spheres comprehend, and others again to the circles in them. Hence too, the spheres themselves, considered as wholes, may be said to be images of those Gods that are celebrated as total;† but the circles of those that are called total, and at the same time partial;‡ and the stars, of those that are properly denominated partial§ Gods.

After the contemplation of these, and after the eye is through these accustomed to the light, as it is requisite in the visible region to see the sun himself in the last place, in like manner, according to Plato, the idea of *the good* must be seen the last in the intelligible region. He likewise adds, in a truly divine manner, that it is scarcely to be seen; for we can only be conjoined with it through the intelligible, in the vestibule of which it is beheld by ascending souls. The intelligible indeed is the first participant of *the good*, and indicates from itself to those that are able to behold it, what that nature is, if it be lawful so to speak, which is the superintelligible cause of the light it contains. For the light in an intelligible essence is more divine than that in intellectual natures, in the same manner as the light in the stars is more divine than that which is in the eyes that behold them. Thus also Socrates, in the Philebus, says, that *the good* is apprehended with difficulty, and is scarcely to be seen, and that it is found with three monads, and these intelligible, arranged in its vestibule, truth, beauty, and symmetry. For these three produce the first being, or being itself, and through these the whole intelligible order is unfolded into light, With great propriety, therefore, does Plato assert, that the idea of *the good* is to be seen the last thing in the intelligible: for the intelligible is the seat of its vision. Hence it is seen in this, as so its first participant, though it is beyond every intelligible. And in the last place Plato exhorts him who knows *the good*, "to collect by reasoning that it is the cause to all of every thing right and beautiful, in the visible place generating light, and its lord the sun, and in the intelligible place being itself the lord of all things, producing intellect and truth." For, if it generates the sun, it must by a much greater priority be the cause of those things which originate from the sun; and if it is the cause of essence to intelligibles, it must be celebrated as in a greater degree the cause of things of which these are the causes.

---

* For an account of these see the Introduction ta the Timæus.

† That is to say, all the Gods denominated intelligible and intellectual. See the Introduction to the Parmenides.

‡ That is to say, the supramundane Gods.

§ These are of a mundane characteristic.

---

2. The Greek Scholia inform us that this is a proverb, said of those who do any thing quickly. It is also the name of a sport. It is likewise applied to those

who rapidly betake themselves to flight, or to those who are easily changed.

3. For a copious account of the dialectic of Plato, which is the same with the metaphysics of Aristotle, see the Introduction and Notes to the Parmenides.

4. Instead of εωσι here, I read σωζουσι.

Book 8

1. The Greek Scholiast on this passage observes, that the ancients apprehended their ancestors were generated from oaks and rocks, because mothers used to place their infants in caverns and the trunks of trees. For men, in times of remote antiquity, were accustomed to have connexion with women near oaks or rocks.

2. A government in which honours subsist with a view to possessions was called by the ancients a Timocracy. It was opposed to a Democracy, because the most wealthy and not the poor were the rulers in this government. Just as an Oligarchy was opposed to an Aristocracy, because in the former not the best, but a few only, and those the worst, governed the city.

3. All the parts of the universe are unable to participate of the providence of divinity in a similar manner, but some of its parts enjoy this eternally, and others temporally; some in a primary and others in a secondary degree. For the universe, being a perfect whole, must have a first, a middle, and a last part. But its first parts, as having the most excellent subsistence, must always exist according to nature; and its last parts must sometimes subsist according to, and sometimes contrary to, nature. Hence the celestial bodies, which are the first parts of the universe, perpetually subsist according to nature, both the whole spheres and the multitude coordinate to these wholes; (see the Introduction to the Timæus) and the only alteration which they experience is a mutation of figure, and variation of light at different periods: but in the sublunary region, while the spheres of the elements remain on account of their subsistence as wholes, always according to nature; the parts of these wholes have sometimes a natural and sometimes an unnatural subsistence: for thus alone can the circle of generation unfold all the variety which it contains.

The different periods in which these mutations happen, are called by Plato, with great propriety, periods of *fertility* and *sterility:* for in these periods a fertility or sterility of men, animals, and plants takes place; so that in fertile periods mankind will be both more numerous, and upon the whole superior in mental and bodily endowments to the men of a barren period. And a similar reasoning must be extended to animals and plants. The so much celebrated heroic age was the result of one of these fertile periods, in which men transcending the herd of mankind both in practical and intellectual virtue abounded on the earth.

4. The Greek Scholiast on this place well observes, that Plato, by that which

is divinely generated, does not mean either the whole world, though the epithet is primarily applicable to this, nor the celestial regions only, nor the sublunary world, but *every thing which is perpetually and circularly moved*, whether in the heavens or under the moon; so far as it is corporeal, calling it *generated;* (for no body is self-subsistent) but so far as it is perpetually moved, *divine:* for it imitates the most divine of things, which possess an ever-vigilant life. But with respect to the perfect number mentioned here by Plato, we must not only direct our attention to a perfect number in vulgar arithmetic, for this is rather numbered than number, tends to perfection, and is never perfect, as being always in generation; but we must survey the cause of this number, which is indeed intellectual, but comprehends the definite boundary of every period of the world.

Θεοιν γεννητον ου τον ὁλον φησι κοσμον, ει και προηγουμενως τουτον, ουτε τον εν ουρανω μονον, ουτε το ὑπο σεληνην, αλλα παν το αεικινητον και περιφερομενον, ειτ᾽ εν ουρανω, ειθ᾽ ὑπο σεληνην· ὡς μεν σωματικον γεννητον καλουμενον· ουδεν γαρ σωμα αυθυποστατον· ὡς δ᾽ αεικινητον, θειον· μιμειται γαρ τα θειοτατων (lege θειοτατα των) οντων αγρυπνον εχοντα ζωην· τον τελειον δ᾽ αριθμον ου μονον χρη νοειν επι δακτυλων τιθεντας· ουτος γαρ εστιν αριθμητον μαλλον, ἢ αριθμος, και τελειουμενον, και ουδεποτε τελειος αει γιγνομενος· αλλα την αιτιαν τουτου νοεραν μεν ουσαν, περιεχουσαν δε τον πεπερασμενον ὁρον της του κοσμου πασης περιοδον.

5. The obscurity of these numbers, which is so great as to have become proverbial among the ancients, is not elucidated in any of those invaluable remains of Grecian philosophy which have survived to the present time. And yet it may be fairly concluded that this mysterious passage was most satisfactorily unfolded by the commentaries of such men as Iamblichus, Syrianus and Proclus, on this part of the Republic, though they have unfortunately perished in the wreck of ages. The following attempt, however, may perhaps show that it is not impossible to penetrate this mystery, though deprived of such mighty aid, since it is only to be solved by the assistance of Mathesis, who at all times willingly acts ministrant to Inspiration.

In the first place then, let us consider what Plato means by augmentations surpassing and surpassed; things assimilating and dissimilating, increasing and decreasing, correspondent and effable.

Augmentations surpassing, are ratios of greater inequality, *viz.* when the greater is compared to the lesser, and are multiples,* superparticulars, superpartients, multiple-superparticulars and multiple-superpartients. But augmentations surpassed are, ratios of lesser in equality, *viz.* when the lesser is compared with the greater quantity, as for instance, submultiples, subsuperparticulars, subsuperpartients, and those which are composed from these three. Those numbers are called by Plato *assimilating* and *dissimilating*, which are denominated by arithmeticians *similar* † and *dissimilar:* but he calls those *increasing* and *decreasing*, which they denominate *abounding*[‡] and *diminished*, or *more than perfect* and *imperfect*. Things correspondent and effable, are boundaries which correspond in ratio with each other, and can be expressed in numbers either integral or fractional, such as are these four terms or boundaries, 27, 18, 12, 8, which are in sesquialter and subsesquialter ratios; since these mutually correspond in ratio, and are effable. For effable quantities are those which can be expressed in whole numbers, or fractions; and, in like manner, ineffable quantities are such as cannot be expressed in either of these, and are called by modern mathematicians surds.

In the next place, let us consider what we are to understand by *the sesquitertian progeny when conjoined with the pentad and thrice increased, affording two harmonies*. By the *sesquitertian progeny* then Plato means the number 95: for this number is composed from the addition of the squares of the numbers 4 and 3, which form the first sesquitertian ratio, (*viz.* 25) and the number 70, which is composed from 40 and 30, and therefore consists of two numbers in a sesquitertian ratio. Hence, as 95 is composed from 25 and 70, it may with great propriety be called a sesquitertian progeny. This number conjoined with 5 and thrice increased produces ten thousand and a million: for 100 x 100 = 10000, and 10000 x 100 = 1000000. But it must here be observed that these two numbers, as will shortly be seen, appear to be considered by Plato as analogous to two parallelopipedons, the former, *viz.* ten thousand, being formed from 10 x 10 x 100, and the latter from 1000 x 10 x 100. These two numbers are called by Plato two harmonies, for the following reason: Simplicius, in his Commentary on Aristotle's books De Cœlo, informs us that a cube was denominated by the Pythagoreans *harmony;* because it consists of 12 bounding lines, 8 angles, and 6 sides; and 12, 8, 6, are in harmonic proportion: for the difference between 12 and 8 is to the difference between 8 and 6, *i.e.* 4 is to 2 as the first term to the third, *i.e.* as 12 to 6, which, as is well known, is the law of harmonic proportion. As a parallelopipedon therefore has the same number of sides, angles, and bounding lines as a cube, the reason is obvious why the numbers 10000 and 1000000 are called by Plato harmonies. Hence also it is evident why he says that "the other of these harmonies, *viz.* a million, is of equal length indeed, but more oblong:" for, if we call 100 the breadth and 10 the depth both of ten thousand and a million, it is evident that the latter number, when considered as produced by 1000 x 10 x 100, will be analogous to a more oblong parallelopipedons than the former.

Again, when he says that "the number 1000000 consists of a hundred numbers from effable diameters of pentads, each being deficient by unity, and from two that are ineffable, and from a hundred cubes of the triad," his meaning is as follows: The number 1000000 consists of a hundred numbers, *i.e.* of a hundred such numbers as 10000, each of which is composed from effable diameters of pentads, etc. But in order to understand the truth of this assertion, it is necessary to observe that there are certain numbers which are called by arithmeticians effable diameters, these also are twofold; for some are the diameters of even squares, and others of odd squares. And the diameters of effable even squares, when multiplied into themselves, produce square numbers double of the squares of which they are the diameters, with an excess of unity: Thus, for instance, the number 3 multiplied into itself produces 9, which is double of the square number 4, with an excess of unity; and therefore 3 will be the diameter of the even square 4. But the diameters of effable odd square numbers are in power double of the squares of which they are the diameters, by a deficiency of unity. Thus, the number 7 multiplied into itself produces 49, which is double of the odd square number 25 by a deficiency of unity. This being premised, it follows that the number 10000 will consist of a certain number of heptads; for 7 is the effable diameter of the square number 25: and from what follows it will be found that this number is 1386.

But the number 10000 not only consists of 1386 heptads, but Plato also adds, "from two numbers that are ineffable,"[§] *viz.* from two numbers the roots of which cannot be exactly obtained, nor expressed either in whole numbers or fractions, such as the roots of the numbers 2 and 3. The numbers 15 and 13 are also of this kind; and, as we shall see, appear to be the numbers signified by Plato. In the last place he adds, "and from a hundred cubes of the triad," *viz.* from the number 270; for this is equal to a hundred times 27, the cube of 3. The numbers therefore that form 10000 are as below:

$$
\begin{array}{r}
1386 \\
7 \\
\hline
9702 \\
15 \\
13 \\
270 \\
\hline
10000
\end{array}
$$

viz. 1386 heptads, two ineffable numbers 15 and 13, and a hundred times the cube of 3, *i.e.* 270: and the whole geometric number is a million.

One Massey, who published a Greek and Latin edition of the Republic, at Cambridge, in the year 1713 observes respecting this most obscure passage, that

> "what Plato distinctly means by it, he neither knows nor cares; since it appears to him that what affords so much difficulty has but little weight."
>
> "Quid in hoc loco distincte velit Plato profecto nescio, nec curo. Quod enim tantum difficultatis præbet minimum ponderis habere suspicor."

This is in the true spirit of a verbal critic: and the reason which he assigns for this carelessness is admirable; since on the same account the highest parts of the mathematics ought to be rejected.

---

* Multiplex ratio is when a greater quantity contains a lesser many times. Superparticular ratio is when the greater contains the lesser quantity once, and some part of it besides; and superpartient ratio, is when the greater contains the lesser quantity once, and certain parts of it likewise. Again, multiple superparticular ratio is when the greater contains the lesser many times and some part of it besides; and multiple superpartient ratio is when the greater contains the lesser many times, and also some of its parts.

† Similar numbers are those whose sides are proportional, *i.e.* which have the same ratio; but dissimilar numbers those whose side are not proportional.

‡ As perfect numbers are these which are equal to their parts collected into one, such as 6 and 28. (for the parts of the former are 1 , 2, 3, which are equal to 6, and the parts of the latter are 14, 7, 4, 2, 1, the aggregate of which is 28) so a diminished number is that which is greater than the sum of its parts, as 8, whose parts are 4, 2, 1, the aggregate of which is 7; and an abounding number is that which is exceeded by the sum of its parts, as 12, whose parts are 6, 4, 3, 2, 1, the sum of which is 16.

§ As every number may be measured by unity, no number is properly speaking ineffable; but the truly ineffable belongs to continued quantity.

---

6. The tiara, says the Greek Scholiast on this place, is that which is called *kurbosia*. It is an ornament for the head, which the Persian kings alone wore in an upright, but the commanders of the army in an inclined position. Some also call it *kilaris*, as Theophrastus in his treatise concerning the kingdom old Cyprians.

7. *viz.* wealth.

8. *viz.* as the Greek Scholiast well observes, not persuading himself, nor giving an orderly motion to the parts of his soul, and studying virtue on account of that which is more excellent.

9. By public spectacles here, Plato means solemn festivals which, as the Greek Scholiast on this place informs us, were called *spectacles* from the concourse of those that came to *behold* the celebration of them. For the transactions on these occasions were entirely different from those at any other period of life.

10. By the Lotophagi we must understand, says the Greek Scholiast, that false and arrogant persons and opinions are allegorically signified.

11. This, says the Greek Scholiast, is said of Pisistratus, who, insidiously endeavouring to tyrannize over the citizens, gave himself many and dangerous wounds, and then presented himself to the Greeks as if he had been thus wounded by his enemies. He also requested guards for his body, and received three hundred spearmen from the city; which introducing into his house, and rendering subservient to his purpose, be tyrannized over the Athenians.

12. This, says the Greek Scholiast, is from the Ajax of Sophocles, but here it is said to be an iambic of Euripides. He adds, there is nothing wonderful in poets according with each other. This iambic is in the Antigone of Euripides.

Book 9

1. *viz.* the *love* of evil, when it fashions evil images in the phantasy. Schol. Græc. p. 189.

2. *viz.* evil desires, acting as life-guards to love, vanquish the good opinions which such men formerly possessed. Idem.

3. The reasoning power of the soul of a tyrant, says the Greek Scholiast, p. 190, being vanquished by anger and desire, the soul does not accomplish that which it wishes; but not acting according to its better part, it is said, as speaking of the whole soul, to do what it wishes in the smallest degree: for the whole soul does not then act.

4. The following numbers are employed by Plato in this place. He considers the *Royal* character as analogous to unity, the Oligarchic to the number 3, and the Tyrannic to the number 9. As 3 therefore is triple of unity, the Oligarchic is the third from the Royal character; and in a similar manner the Tyrant is distant from the Oligarchic by the triple in number; for 9 is the triple of 3, just as 3 is the triple of 1. But 9 is a plane number, the length of which is 3, and also its breadth. And a tyrannic, says Plato, is the last image of a royal life. He also calls 3 a *power*, because unity being multiplied by it, and itself by itself, and 9 by it, there will be produced 3, 9, 27. But he calls the third augment 27, arising from the multiplication of the power 3, and producing depth or a solid number. Lastly, 27 multiplied into itself produces 729, which may be considered as a perfect multiplication, this number being the 6th power of 3; and 6 as is well known is a perfect number. Hence, as the King is analogous to 1, he is said, by Plato, to be 729 times distant from the Tyrant.

5. By this many-headed beast, *desire* is signified.

6. The lion signifies *anger,* and the figure of a man *reason;* for the whole soul is divided into reason, anger, and desire.

Book 10

1. The following admirable account of poetry, from the Explanation of the more difficult questions in the Republic, by Proclus, will I doubt not be highly acceptable to the reader, as it both contains a most accurate and scientific division of poetry, and perfectly reconciles the prince of philosophers with the first of poets.

"There are three lives in the soul, of which the best and most perfect is that according to which it is conjoined with the Gods, and lives a life most allied, and through the highest similitude united to them; no longer subsisting from itself but from them, running under its own intellect, exciting the ineffable impression of *the one* which it contains, and connecting like with like, its own light with that of the Gods, and that which is most uniform in its own essence and life, with *the one* which is above all essence and life. That which is second to this in dignity and power, has a middle arrangement in the middle of the soul, according to which indeed it is converted to itself, descending from a divinely inspired life; and placing intellect and science as the principles of its energy, it evolves the multitude of its reasons, surveys the all-various mutations of forms, collects into sameness intellect, and that which is the object of intellect, and expresses in images an intellectual and intelligible essence. The third life of the soul is that which accords with its inferior powers, and energizes together with them, employing phantasies and irrational senses, and being entirely filled with things of a subordinate nature.

"As there are therefore these three forms of life in souls, the poetic division also supernally proceeds together with the multiform lives of the soul, and is diversified into first, middle, and last genera of energy. For, of poetry also, one kind has the highest subsistence, is full of divine goods, and establishes the soul in the causes themselves of things, according to a certain ineffable union, leading that which is filled, into sameness with its replenishing source; the former immaterially subjecting itself to illumination, but the latter being incited to a communication of light; thus according to the Oracle 'perfecting works, by mingling the rivers of incorruptible fire.' It also produces one divine bond and a unifying mixture of that which is participated and the participant, establishing the whole of that which is subordinate in that which is more excellent, and preparing that which is more divine alone to energize, the inferior nature being withdrawn, and concealing its own idiom in that which is superior. This then, in short, is a mania better than temperance, and is distinguished by a divine characteristic. And as every different kind of poetry subsists according to a different hyparxis, or summit of divine essence, so this fills the soul energizing from divine inspiration, with symmetry; and hence it adorns it last energies with measures and rhythms. As therefore we say that prophetic fury subsists according to truth, and the amatory according to beauty, in like manner we say, that the poetic mania is defined according to divine symmetry.

"The second kind of poetry which is subordinate to this first and divinely inspired species, and which has a middle subsistence in the soul, is allotted its essence, according to a scientific and intellectual habit. Hence it knows the essence of things, and loves to contemplate beautiful works and reasonings, and leads forth every thing into a measured and rhythmical interpretation. For you will find many progeny of good poets to be of this kind, emulous of those that are truly wise, full of admonition, the best counsels, and intellectual symmetry. It likewise extends the communication of prudence and every other virtue to those of a naturally good disposition, and affords a reminiscence of the periods of the soul, of its eternal reasons, and various powers.

"The third species of poetry subsequent to these, is mingled with opinions and phantasies, receives its completion through imitation, and is said to be, and is nothing else than imitative poetry. At one time, it alone uses assimilation, and at another time defends apparent and not real assimilation. It considerably raises very moderate passions, astonishes the hearers; together with appropriate appellations and words, mutations of harmonies and varieties of rhythms, changes the dispositions of souls; and indicates the nature of things not such as they are, but such as they appear to the many; being a certain adumbration, and not an accurate knowledge of things. It also establishes as its end the delight of the hearers; and particularly looks to the passive part of the soul, which is naturally adapted to rejoice and be afflicted. But of this species of poetry, as we have said, one division is *assimilative*, which is extended to rectitude of imitation, but the other is *phantastic*, and affords apparent imitation alone.

"Such then in short are the genera of poetry. It now remains to show that these are also mentioned by Plato, and to relate such particulars as are conformable to his dogmas respecting each. And in the first place we shall discuss those wonderful conceptions respecting divine poetry which may be collected by him who does not negligently peruse his writings. For, these things being previously determined, it will I think be easy to assign apt reasons respecting the subsequent species. In the Phædrus, then, he denominates this divine poetry, a possession from the Muses, and a mania, and says, that it is supernally imparted to a tender and solitary soul; but that its employment is to excite and inspire with Bacchic fury, according to odes, and the rest of poetry, and its end, to instruct posterity in celebrating the infinite transactions of the ancients. From these words, it is perfectly evident that he calls the original and first-operating cause of poetry, the gift of the Muses. For, as they fill all the other fabrications of the father of the universe, both the apparent and unapparent, with harmony and rhythmical motion, in like manner in the souls which are possessed by them they produce a vestige of divine symmetry which illuminates divinely inspired poetry. But since the whole energy of the illuminating power is in divine advents, and that which is illuminated gives itself up to the motions proceeding from thence, and, abandoning its own habits, spreads itself under the energies of that which is divine and uniform; on this account, I think, he denominates such an illumination a *possession* and *mania*. He calls it a *possession,* because the whole illuminated soul gives itself up to the present effect of illuminating deity; and a *mania,* because such a soul abandons its own proper energies for the idioms of the illuminating powers.

"In the next place, he describes the habit of the soul possessed by the Muses; and says it ought to be *tender* and *solitary*. For a soul hard and resisting, and disobedient to divine illumination, is disposed contrary to the energy of divinely inspired possession; since it thus rather subsists from itself than from that which illuminates, and is incapable of being properly impressed with its gifts. But a soul which is possessed by other all-various opinions, and is filled with reasonings foreign from a divine nature, obscures divine inspiration, mingling with the motions thence derived its own lives and energies. It is requisite therefore that the soul which is to be possessed by the Muses should be tender and solitary, that it may be properly passive to, and perfectly sympathize with, divinity, and that it may be impassive, unreceptive, and unmingled with respect to other things.

"In the third place, therefore, he adds the common employment of such an aptitude, and of possession and mania from the Muses. For to excite and inspire with Bacchic fury, is the province both of that which illuminates and that which is illuminated, and which gives completion to the same thing; the former moving supernally, and the latter spreading itself under the moving cause. Excitation is indeed a resurrection and unperverted energy of the soul, and a conversion to divinity from a lapse into generation. But Bacchic fury is a divinely inspired motion, and an unwearied dance, as it were, toward a divine nature, giving perfection to the possessed. But again, both these are requisite, that the possessed may not incline to that which is worse, but may be easily moved to a more excellent nature.

"In the fourth place he adds, that the end of this divine poetry is lo instruct posterity in celebrating the infinite deeds of the ancients. Hence, he evidently testifies that human affairs become more perfect and splendid when they are delivered from a divine mouth, and that true erudition is produced in the auditors of such poetry. Not that it is adapted to juvenile tuition, but pertains to those that are already perfect in politic discipline, and require a more mystic tradition respecting divine concerns. Such poetry, therefore, instructs the hearers more than any other, when it is divine, and when its divine nature becomes manifest to its auditors. Hence Plato very properly prefers this poetry which subsists from the Muses in tender and solitary souls, to every other human art. 'For the poet,' says he, 'who approaches to the poetic gates without such a mania, will be imperfect, and his poetry, so far as it is dictated by prudence, will vanish before that which is the progeny of fury.' In this manner, therefore, does Socrates in the Phædrus instruct us in the peculiarities of divine poetry, which differs both from divine prophecy, and the telestic art, and refer its first unfolding into light, to the Gods.

"With these things also, what he says in the Io accords, when he is discoursing with the rhapsodist about this species of poetry; for here he most clearly evinces that the poetry of Homer is divine, and, to others that are conversant with it, is the cause of enthusiastic energy. For when the rhapsodist says, that he can speak copiously on the poems of Homer, but by no means on the writings of other poets, Socrates assigning the reason of this says, 'It is not from art, that you speak well concerning Homer, but because you are moved by a divine power.' And that this is true is indeed perfectly evident. For those who do any thing by art, are able to produce the same effect in all similars; but those that operate by a certain divine power about any thing which subsists with symmetry, can no longer thus operate with respect to other things which necessarily have the same power. Whence then a power of this kind is derived to the rhapsodist, which particularly connects him with Homer, but no longer with other poets, Socrates afterwards teaches us, using the stone which is vulgarly called Herculæan, as a most perspicuous example of the most perfect possession from the Muses. 'This stone then,' says he, 'not only draws to itself iron rings, but inserts in them a power attractive of things similar, so as to enable them to draw other rings, and form a chain of rings, or pieces of iron, depending one from another.'

   "Let us in the next place hear what Socrates adds similar to these things, respecting divine poetry. 'Thus then,' says he, 'the Muse makes men divine; and from these men thus inspired, others catching the sacred power form a chain of divine enthusiasts.' Here, in the first place, he speaks of the divine cause in the singular number, calling it the Muse, and not, as in the Phædrus, a possession from the Muses, and a mania pertaining to their whole multitude, that he may refer all the number of those that are moved enthusiastically to one monad, as it were, the primary principle of poetry. For poetry subsists uniformly and occultly in the first mover; but secondarily, and in a revolved manner, in poets moved by that monad; and lastly, and in a ministrant degree, in the rhapsodists, who are led back to this cause through poets as the media. In the next place, by extending divine inspiration supernally, as far as to the last mixtures, he evidently, at the same time, celebrates the fecundity of the first moving principle, and most clearly evinces the participation of the first participants. For that poets should be able to excite others by their poems to a divinely inspired energy, indicates that there is a most conspicuous preference in them of a divine nature. Consequent to these things, therefore, he also adds what follows respecting the possession of poets. 'The best epic poets,' says he, 'and all such as excel in composing any kind of verses to be recited, frame not those their admirable poems from the rules of art, but, possessed by the Muse, they write from divine inspiration. Nor is it otherwise with the best lyric poets, and all other fine writers of verses to be sung.' and again, afterwards, he says, 'For a poet is a thing light and volatile, and sacred, nor is he able to write poetry till he becomes divine, and has no longer the command of his intellect.'

And lastly, he adds: 'Hence it is that the poets indeed say many fine things, whatever their subject be, just as you do concerning Homer; but, not doing it through any rules of art, each of them is able to succeed from a divine destiny in that species of poetry only to which he is impelled by the Muse.'

"In all these citations, therefore, Plato evidently establishes divine poetry in a divine cause, which he calls a Muse; in this emulating Homer, who at one time looks to the multitude, and at another to the union of the series of the Muses; as when he says, 'O Muses, sing,' and 'Sing me the man, O Muse.' In the middle of this principle of enthusiastic motions, and of the last echoes* of inspiration, beheld in rhapsodists according to sympathy, Plato establishes poetic mania, moving and being moved, supernally filled, and transferring to others the illumination which originates from thence, and which imparts one conjunction to the last participants with the participated monad.

"With these things also we may coharmonize what is said by the Athenian guest in the third book of the Laws concerning poetry, and what Timæus says respecting poets. For the former says, that 'the poetic genus is divinely inspired,' that 'it composes sacred hymns,' and, 'with certain Graces and Muses, relates many things that have been truly transacted'; and the latter exhorts us to follow poets inspired by Phœbus, as 'being the sons of Gods, and knowing the concerns of their progenitors, though their assertions are not probable, and are unaccompanied with demonstrations.' From all which it is easy to understand what the opinion of Plato was concerning divine poetry, and the poets characterized according to it; and that these are especially messengers of divine names, and are in an eminent manner acquainted with the affairs of their fathers. When, therefore, he takes notice of mythical fictions, and corrects the more serious part of the writings of poets, such as those respecting bonds, castrations, loves, venereal connections, tears and laughter, we must say that he also especially testifies that these things are properly introduced, according to the theory, which is concealed in these symbols, as under veils. For he who thinks that poets are particularly worthy of belief in affairs respecting the Gods, though they speak without demonstration from divine information, must certainly admire divine fables,† through which they deliver the truth concerning divine natures. And he who calls the poetic genus divine, cannot also ascribe to it an impious and gigantic opinion respecting divine concerns. He likewise who evinces that the assertions of poets are attended with certain Graces and Muses, must entirely consider an inelegant, unharmonious, and ungraceful phantasy, as very remote from the theory of divine poets. When therefore in his Republic he establishes by law, that poetry, and the indication through fables, are not adapted to the ears of youth, he is very far from despising poetry itself, but removes the juvenile habit, as unexercised in the hearing of such things, from fiction of this kind.

For, as he says in the Second Alcibiades, 'the whole of poetry is naturally enigmatical, and is not obvious to the understanding of every one.' And hence, in the Republic, he clearly says, that 'a youth is not able to distinguish what is allegory, and what is not.' We must say, therefore, that he entirely admits inspired poetry, which he calls divine, and thinks it proper that those by whom it is possessed should be venerated in silence. And thus much concerning the first kind of poetry, which subsists, from a divine origin, in tender and solitary souls.

"In the next place, let us contemplate that species of poetry, which has a scientific knowledge of things, and which energizes according to intellect and prudence; which unfolds to men many names concerning an incorporeal nature, and leads forth into light many probable dogmas respecting a corporeal subsistence; investigates the most beautiful symmetry in manners, and the disposition contrary to this; and adorns all these with proper measures and rhythms. The Athenian guest says, that the poetry of Theognis is of this kind, which he praises beyond that of Tyrtæus, because Theognis is a teacher of the whole of virtue, and which extends to the whole political life. For the one admits a fidelity which receives its completion from all the virtues, expels from politics that most true vice sedition, and leads into consent the lives of those that are persuaded. But the other praises the habit of fortitude by itself alone, and exhorts to this those that neglect the other virtues. It will however be better to hear the words themselves of Plato:[‡] 'We have, too, the poet Theognis a witness in our favour, who was a citizen of the Megarensians in Sicily. For he says,

Who faithful in insane sedition keeps,
With silver and with ruddy gold may vie.

We say therefore that such a one will conduct himself in the most difficult war, in a manner nearly as much superior to the other, as justice, temperance, and prudence, when conjoined with fortitude, are superior to fortitude alone. For no one can be found faithful and found in seditions without the whole of virtue.' Here, therefore, he admits Theognis as partaking of political science, and all the virtues.

"But in the Second Alcibiades, defining the most right and safe mode of prayer, he refers it to a certain wise poet: 'To me,' says he, 'Alcibiades, it seems probable that some wise man or other, happening to be connected with certain persons void of understanding, and observing them to pursue and pray for things which it would be better for them still to be without, but which appeared to them good, composed for their use a common prayer; the words of which are nearly these: King Jupiter, grant us what is good, be it or not the subject of our prayers, and avert from us what is evil, though we should pray for it.' For the scientific man alone knows how to distinguish the separation of good and evil, and a converse with a divine nature adapted to the middle habits of men. And on this account Socrates calls the poet that composed this prayer a wise man, as forming a judgment of the natures of those that prayed, neither through divine inspiration, nor right opinion, but through science alone, as regarding their habits, and preserving that which becomes the beneficent powers of the Gods. For, to convert all of them through prayer to the one royal providence of Jupiter, to suspend the subsistence of good from the power of divinity, to obliterate the generation of true evils through the benevolence of a more excellent nature, and, in short, to assert that these things are unknown to thole that pray, but are separated by divinity according to proper boundaries, is the work of wisdom and science, and not of any thing casual. Very properly therefore do we say that such poetry is wise and scientific. For the poetry which is able to assign right opinions to middle habits, must itself subsist according to perfect science.

"In the third place, therefore, let us speak concerning imitative poetry, which, we have already said, at one time assimilates things, and at another expresses them according to appearance.—The Athenian guest clearly delivers to us the assimilative part of this poetry; but Socrates, in the Republic, describes its phantastic part: and how these differ from each other, I mean the assimilative and phantastic species of imitation; the Eleatean guest sufficiently informs us: 'For I appear,' says he, 'to perceive two species of imitation, one, the conjectural or assimilative art, which then especially takes place when some one gives birth to imitation by imparting to every particular such things as are fit, in length, breadth, and depth, according to the symmetries of its exemplar, and besides these things colours also.—THEÆ. Do not all imitators endeavour to effect this?—GUEST. Not those who perform or paint any great work. For, if they were to impart to the the true symmetry of things beautiful, you know that the parts above would appear smaller, and those below larger than is fit; through the one being seen by us afar off, and the other near.—THEÆ. Entirely so. Artists therefore, bidding farewell to truth, do not produce in images truly beautiful symmetries, but those which appear to be so.' Very properly therefore, I think, does the Eleatean guest at the end of the dialogue, wishing to bind the sophist by the definitive method, establish one part of the art effective of images to be assimilative, and the other phantastic; the one fabricating the image such as is the exemplar; the other preparing that which it produces to appear like that which it imitates. However, of assimilative poetry the Athenian guest speaks separately in the second book of the Laws, where he treats of music which does not make pleasure its end, but a true and similar imitation of its exemplar, to which place we refer the reader.

"But Socrates speaking in this book of phantastic poetry, and having shown that a poet of this kind is the third from truth, and imitative, compares such poetry to a picture, which represents not the works of nature but of artificers, and these not such as they are, but such as they appear. Hence, he clearly evinces that the phantastic species of poetry regards pleasure alone, and the delight of those that hear it. For, of imitative poetry, the phantastic falls short of the assimilative, so far as the latter regards rectitude of imitation, but the former the pleasure produced in the multitude from the energies of the phantasy. Such then are the genera of poetry which are thought worthy of distinction by Plato; one, as better than science, an other as scientific, a third as conversant with, and a fourth as falling off from, right opinion.

"These things then being determined, let us return to the poetry of Homer, and contemplate resplendent in it every poetic habit, and particularly those which regard rectitude and beauty. For when he energizes enthusiastically, is possessed by the Muses, and narrates mystic conceptions about the Gods themselves, then he energizes according to the first and divinely inspired species of poetry. But when he relates the life of the soul, the diversities in its nature and such political concerns as pertain to it, then he especially speaks scientifically. Again, when he presents us with forms of imitation adapted to things and persons themselves, then he employs assimilation imitation. But when he directs his attention to that which appears to the multitude, and not to the truth of things, and thus seduces the souls of his hearers, then he is a poet according to the phantastic species. To illustrate what I mean, that I may begin from the last imitation of the poet, he sometimes describes the rising and setting of the sun, not as each of these is, nor as each is effected, nor imitating this in his verses, but as it appears to us through distance. This then, and every thing of this kind may be called the phantastic part of his poetry. But when he imitates heroes warring, or consulting, or speaking according to the forms of life, same as prudent, others as brave, and others as ambitious, then I should say that this is the work of assimilative poetry. Again, when in consequence of knowing either the diversity of subsistence in the parts of the soul, he unfolds and teaches it, or the difference between the image and the soul by which it is used, or the order of the elements in the universe, *viz.* of earth, water, æther, heaven, or any thing else of this kind, then I should confidently assert that this originated from the scientific power of poetry. And after all these, when he teaches us concerning the demiurgic monad, and the triple distribution of wholes, or concerning the bonds of Vulcan, or the connection of the paternal intellection of Jupiter with the prolific divinity of Juno, then I should say that he is clearly enthusiastic, and that such like fables are devised by him, in consequence of his being possessed by the Muses. But Homer himself also manifests in the bard Demodocus, an energy originating from the Gods, when Ulysses says of his song, that he began it impelled by a God, that he was divinely inspired, and that the Muse loved him, or the God that is the leader of the Muses:

> The Muse, Jove's daughter, or Apollo, taught
> Thee aptly thus the fate of Greece to sing,
> And all the Grecians, hardy deeds and toils.[§]

And that Homer by Demodocus intended after a manner to represent himself, and introduced him as a pattern of his own calamities, is an opinion sufficiently celebrated. And the verses,

> With clouds of darkness quench'd his visual ray,
> But gave him skill to raise the lofty lay,

appear directly to refer to the fabled blindness of Homer. He therefore clearly contends, that Demodocus says what he does say from divine inspiration. But it is well that we have mentioned Demodocus, and his divinely inspired song. For it appears to me that the musicians who are thought worthy of being mentioned by Homer, unfold the above mentioned genera of poetry. For Demodocus, as we have said, was divinely inspired, both in narrating divine and human concerns, and is said to have suspended his music from divinity. But Phemius, the Ithacensian bard, is principally characterized according to a mere knowledge of divine and human affairs. For Penelope says to him,

> Alluring arts thou know'st, and what of old
> Of Gods and Heroes sacred bards have told.[¶]

The third is the lyrist of Clytemnestra, who was as it seems an imitative poet, employed right opinion, and extended the melodies of temperance to that female. Hence, as long as he remained with her, she perpetrated no unholy deed, in consequence of her irrational life being charmed to temperance by disciplinative song. The fourth musician may be placed as analogous to the phantastic species of poetry; and this is that Thamyris with whose song the Muses being indignant, are said to have caused it to cease. For he was conversant with a music much more diversified and sensible, and calculated to please the vulgar. Hence he is said to have contended with the Muses, as preferring a more various music to that which is more simple and more adapted to those divinities, and as falling from the benevolence of the Goddesses. For the anger of the Muses does not refer any passion to them, but indicates the inaptitude of Thamyris to their participation. This then is the song which is most remote from truth, which calls forth the passions of the soul, and is phantastic, and neither possesses with respect to imitation, right opinion, or science. We may therefore behold all the kinds of poetry in Homer, but particularly the enthusiastic, according to which, we have said, he is principally characterized. Nor are we singular in this opinion; but, as we have before observed, Plato himself, in many places, calls him a divine poet, the most divine of poets, and in the highest degree worthy of imitation. But the imitative and at the same time phantastic poetry has a most obscure subsistence in Homer; since he never uses it but for the purpose of procuring credibility from the vulgar, and when it is perfectly unavoidable. As therefore, if a man entering into a well regulated city, and beholding intoxication there employed for a certain useful purpose, should neither imitate the prudence in the city, nor its whole order, but intoxication itself alone,—as in this case the city is not to be blamed as the cause of his conduct, but the peculiar imbecility of his judgment; in like manner, I think, tragic poets, being emulous of the last species of Homeric poetry, should refer the principle of their error not to Homer, but to their own impotency. Homer therefore may be called the leader of tragedy, so far as tragic poets emulate him in other respects, and distribute the different parts of his poetry; imitating *phantastically* what he asserts assimilatively, and adapting to the care of the vulgar what he composes scientifically. Homer, however, is not only the teacher of tragedy (for he is this according to the last species of his poetry), but likewise of the whole of that which is imitative in Plato, and of the whole theory of that philosopher."

Proclus concludes his apology for Homer with observing as follows: "The reason," says he, "as it appears to me, that impelled Plato to write with such severity against Homer, and the imitative species of poetry, was the corruption of the times in which he lived: for philosophy was then despised, being accused by some as useless, and by others entirely condemned. On the contrary, poetry was then held in immoderate admiration; its imitative power was the subject of emulation; it was considered as adequate alone to disciplinative purposes; and poets, because. they imitated every thing, persuaded themselves that they knew all things, as is evident from what Socrates says in this dialogue. Hence Plato, indignant at the prevalence of such an opinion, shows that the poetic and imitative genus wanders far from the truth, which philosophy, the saviour of souls, imparts. For, from the same benevolent wish through which he accuses the sophists and popular orators, as unable to contribute any thing to virtue, he also blames the poets, and particularly the composers of tragedy, and such imitators as devise that which may charm their hearers, and not that which may promote virtue; and who enchant, but do not instruct, the multitude. But he considers Homer as deserving a similar reprehension, because he is the leader of this species of poetry, and affords to tragedians the feeds of imitation. For thus it was requisite to recall the men of his age from astonishment respecting poetry, through an immoderate attachment to which, they neglected true discipline. With a view therefore to the instruction of the multitude, to correct an absurd phantasy, and exhort to a philosophic life, he reprobates the tragedians, who were then called public preceptors, as directing their attention to nothing sane; and, at the same time, remits his reverence for Homer, and, ranking him in the same class with tragic poets, blames him as an imitator.

"Nor is it wonderful, that the same poet should be called by him, both divine, and the third from the truth. For, so far as he is possessed by the Muses, he is divine; but, so far as he is an imitator, he is the third from the truth."

* For απογηματων in the original read απηχηματων.

† Instead of reading τοις εν τοις μυθοις after θαυμασεται, I read τους ενθεους μυθους.

‡ See the 1st book of the Laws. § Odyss. lib. viii. Ver. 488. ¶ Odyss. lib. i.

2. We must not suppose that Plato, in speaking of the idea of a bed and table, mean to signify that there is an idea of each of these in the intellect of the demiurgus of the universe; or, in short, that there are ideas of things artificial; but he calls by the name of idea, the reason or productive principle which subsists in the dianoëtic power of the artificer: and this reason, ha says, is the offspring of deity, because he is of opinion, that this very artificial principle itself is imparted to souls from divinity. Proclus, on the Parmenides, well observes, that an argument of the truth of this may be derived from hence, — that Plato calls a poet the third from, or with respect to, the truth, placing him analogous to a painter, who does not make a bed, but the image of it. The form of bed, therefore, in the dianoëtic part of the artificer, ranks as first with respect to truth; the bed which he makes as second; and that which is painted as the third. But if there was an idea of bed in the intellect of divinity, the painter would be the fourth and not the third from the truth.

3. According to the Greek Scholiast on this place, Creophilus was an epic poet of Chios. Some relate of him that Homer married his daughter, and that Homer dwelling in his house, he had from him the poem of the Iliad. His name, to which Socrates alludes, signifies a lover of flesh.

4. According to the Greek Scholiast, Glaucus is said to have been the son of Sisyphus and Merope, and to have become a marine dæmon. For, meeting with an immortal fountain, and descending into it, he became immortal. Not being able however to point out this fountain to certain persons, he threw himself into the sea; and once every year coursed round all shores and islands in conjunction with whales.

5. The helmet of Pluto is said to be an immortal and invisible cloud, with which the Gods are invested when they wish not to be known to each other. And it is applied as a proverb to those that do any thing secretly.—Schol. Græc. in Plat. p. 197.

6. That is to say, one of these through aptitude will receive the illuminations of divinity, and the other through inaptitude will subject himself to the power of avenging dæmons.

7. In the manuscript Commentary of Proclus on this book of the Republic,

five examples are given of persons that have revived after they have been for many days dead. That part of the Commentary containing these examples is preserved by Alexander Morus, in his "Notæ ad quædam Loca Novi Fœderis," which, as the book is scarce, I shall present to the public, for the sake both of the learned and unlearned English reader.

Proclus then, after having observed that some in his time have been seen sitting or standing on the sepulchres in which they had been buried, which, says he, is also related by the ancients of Aristeas, Hermodorus, and Epimenides, subjoins the following example, taken from the History of Clearchus, the disciple of Aristotle:

"Cleonymus, the Athenian, who was a man fond of hearing philosophic discourses, on the death of one of his associates, becoming very sorrowful, and giving himself up to despair, apparently died, and was laid out according to custom. His mother, as she was folding him in her embraces, taking off his garment, and kissing him, perceived in him a gentle breathing, and, being extremely joyful on the occasion, delayed his burial. Cleonymus in a short time after was restored to life, and told all that he saw and heard when he was in a separate state. He said that his soul appeared, as if liberated from certain bonds, to soar from its body, and that, having ascended above the earth, he saw in it places all-various, both for their figure and colour, and streams of rivers unknown to men. And that at last he came to a certain region sacred to Vesta, which was under the direction of dœmoniacal powers in indescribable female forms."

Κλεωνυμος ὁ Αθηναιος, φολήκοος ενηρ των εν φιλοσοφιᾳ λογων, εταιρου τινος αντῳ τελευτησαντος, περιελης γενομενος και αθυμησας, ελιποψυχησεν τε, και τεθναναι δοξας, τριτης ἡμερας ουσης, κατα τον νομον προυτεθη· περιβαλλουσα δ' αυτον ἡ μητηρ, και πανυστατον ασπαζομενη του προσωπου θοιματιον αφελουσα, και καταφιλουσα τον νεκρον, ησθετο βραχειας αναπνοης αυτῳ τινος εγκειμενης. Περιχαρη δ' αυτην γενομενην επισχειν τον ταφην· τον δε Κλεωνυμον αναφεροντα κατα μικρον εγερθηναι, και ειπειν οσα τε επειδη χωρις ην και οια του σωματος ιδοι και ακουσειεν. Την μεν ουν αυτου ψυχην φαναι παρα τον θανατον οιον εκ δεσμων δοξαι τινων αφειμενην, του σωματος παραθεντος μετεωρον αρθηναι, και αρθεισαν ὑπερ γης ιδειν τοπους εν αυτη παντοδαπους, και τοις σχημασι, και τοις χρωμασι, και ῥευματα ποταμων απροσαπτα ανθρωποις· και τελος αφικεσθαι εις τινα χωρον ιερον της Εστιας, ὁν περιεπειν δαιμονιων δυναμεις εν γυναικειων μορφαις απεριηγητοις.

The second example is from the historian Naumachius, "who flourished (says Proclus) in the time of our ancestors, and is of one Polycritus, who was an illustrious and principal man among the Ætolians. This Polycritus died, and returned to life in the ninth month after his death; came to the general assembly of the Ætolians, and joined with them in their consultations about what measures were best to be adopted. Hiero the Ephesian, and other historians, testify the truth of this, in that account of transactions which they sent to king Antigonus, and their other absent friends."

Τον επιφανεστατον Αιτωλων και Αιτωλαρχιας τυχοντα, και αποθανειν, και αναβιωσαι μηνι μεν μετα τον θανατον εννατω, και αφικεσθαι εις εκκλησιαν κοινην των Αιτωλων, και συμβουλευσαι τα αριστα περι ὡν εβουλευοντο· και τουτου ειναι μαρτυρας Ἱερωνα τον Εφεσιον, και αλλους ἱστορικους, Αντιγονω τε τω βασιλει, και αλλοις ἑαυτων φιλοις απουσι τα συμβαντα γραψαντα.

The third is as follows:

"In Nicopolis also (says Proclus), not long since, the same thing happened to one Eurynous. This man, who was buried before the city, revived fifteen days after, and said that he saw and heard many wonderful things under the earth, which he was ordered not to relate. He lived some time after this, and his conduct was more just after his revival than before."

Και ου τουτου μονον, αλλα και εν τη Νικοπελει, των ου προ πολλου γεγοντων, Ευρυνουν το ονομα ταυτον παθειν, και ταφεντα προ της πολεως ὑπο των προσηκοντων, αναβιωσαι μετα πεντε και δεκατην ἡμεραν της ταφης, και λεγειν ὁτι πολλα μεν ιδοι και ακουσειεν ὑπο γης θαυμαστα· κελευθηναι δε παντα αρρητα φυλαττειν, και επιβιωναι χρονον ουκ ολιγον, και οφθηναι δικαιοτερον μετα την αναβιωσιν ἠ προτερον.

The fourth is of Rufus, a priest of the Thessalonians, who lived near the time of the historian Naumachius. This man was restored to life the third day after his death, for the purpose of performing certain sacred ceremonies, which he had promised to perform, and, having fulfilled his promise, again died.

Χθες, ὡς φησι, γεγονοτα Ρουφον, τον εκ Φιλιππων των εκ Μακεδονια, της δε εν Θεσσαλονικη μεγιστης αρχιερωσυνης αξιωθεντα· τουτον γαρ αποθανοντα τριταιον αναβιωναι, και αναβιωντα ειπειν ὁτι ὑπο των χθονιων ὑπεπεμφθη θεων, ινα τας θεας επιτελεση τω δημω ας ὑπισχομενος ετυγχανε, και μεχρς της εκεινων συμπληρωσεως επιβιωντα αυθις αποθανειν.

The fifth and last is of one Philonæa, who lived under the reign of Philip. "She was the daughter (says Proclus) of Demostratus and Charite, who lived in Amphipolis, and died soon after her marriage to one Craterus. She revived, however, in the sixth month after her death, and, through her love of a youth named Machates, who came to Demostratus from his own country Pelle, had connection with him privately for many nights successively. This amour, however, being at length detected, she again died; previous to which she declared, that she acted in this manner according to the will of terrestrial dæmons. Her dead body was seen by every one, lying in her father's house; and on digging the place, which prior to this had contained her body, it was seen to be empty, by those of her kindred who came thither, through unbelief of what had happened to her. The truth of this relation is testified both by the epistles of Hipparchus and those of Arridæus, to Philip, in which they give an account of the affairs of Amphipolis."

Και τον κολοφωνα τουτου υπαρχειν Φιλοναιον κατα τους Φιλιππου Βασιλευσαντος χροιους· ειναι δε αυτην θυγατερα Δημοστρατου και Χαριτους των Αμφιπολιτων νεογαμον τελευτησασαν, εγεγαμητο δε Κρατερω· ταυτην δε εκτω μηνι μετα τον θανατον αναβιωναι, και τω νεανισκω Μαχατη, παρα τον Δημοστρατον αφικομενω εκ Πελλης της πατριδος, λαθρα συνειναι δια τον προς αθτον ερωτα πολλας εφεξες νυκτας· και φωραθεισαν αυθις αποθανειν, προειπουσαν κατα βουλησιν των επιχθονεων δαιμονων αυτη ταυτα πεπραχθαι, και ορασθαι πασι νεκραν εν τη πατρωα προκειμενην οικια, και τον προτερον δεξαμενον αυτης το σωμα τοπον ανορυχθεντα κενον οφθηναι τοις οικειοις επ' αυτην ελθουσι δια την απιστιαν των γεγονοτων· και ταυτα δηλουν επιστολας τας μεν παρ' Ιππαρχου, τας δε παρ' Αρριδαιου γραφεισας, τους τα πραγματα της αμφιπολεως εγκεχειρισμενους προς Φιλιππον.

Proclus then with his usual sagacity observes, concerning the cause of this phenomenon, as follows: "Many other of the ancients have collected a history of those that have apparently died, and afterwards revived; and among these are, the natural philosopher Democritus, in his writings concerning Hades, and that wonderful Conotes, the familiar of Plato. * * * For the death was not, as it seemed, an entire desertion of the whole life of the body, but a cessation, caused by some blow, or perhaps a wound. But the bonds of the soul yet remained rooted about the marrow, and the heart contained in its profundity the empyreuma of life; and this remaining, it again acquired the life which had been extinguished, becoming adapted to animation."

Την μεν περι των αποθανειν δοξαντων, επειτα αναβιοθντων, ιστοριαν αλλοι τε πολλοι των παλαιων ηθροισαν, και Δημοκριτος ὁ φυσικος εν τοις περι του ἁ'δου γραμμασι, και τον θαυμαστον εκεινον Κονωτην, του Πλατωνος εταιρον, * * *† ουδε γαρ ὁ θανατος ην αποσαλευσις, ὡς εοικε, της συμπασης ζωης του σωματος, αλλ' υπο μεν πληγης τινος, ισως του τραυματος, παρειτο· της δε ψυχης ὁι περι τον μυελον εμενον εστι δεσμοι κατερριζωμενη, και ἡ καρδια το εμπυρευμα της ζωης ειχεν εγκειμενον τω βαθει· και, τουτου μενοντος, αυθις ανεκτησατο την απεσβηκυιαν ζωην επιτηδειαν προς την ψυχωσιν γενομενην.

Lastly, Proclus adds: "That it is possible for the soul to depart from, and enter into the body, is evident from him, who, according to Clearchus, used a soul-attracting wand, on a sleeping lad, and who persuaded the dæmoniacal Aristotle, as Clearchus relates in his Treatise on Sleep, that the soul may be separated from the body, and that it enters into the body, and uses it as a lodging. For, striking the lad with the wand, he drew out, and as it were led his soul, for the purpose of evincing that the body was immoveable when the soul was at a distance from it, and that it was preserved uninjured. The soul being again led into the body, by means of the wand, after its entrance related every particular. From this circumstance, therefore, both other spectators, and Aristotle, were persuaded that the soul is separate from the body."

Οτι δε και εξιεναι την ψυχην, και εισιεναι δυνατον εις το σωμα, δηλοι και ὁ παρα τῳ Κλεαρχῳ τῇ ψυχιουλκῳ ραβδῳ χρησαμενος επι του μειρακιου του καθευδοντος, και πεισας τον δαιμονιον Αριστοτελη, καθαπερ ὁ Κλεαρχος, εν τοις περι ὑπνου φησι πε ι της ψυχης, ὡς αναχωριζεται του σωματος, και ὡς εισεισιν εις το σωμα, και ὡς χρηται αυτῳ οιον καταγωγιῳ· τῇ γαρ ραβδῳ πληξας τον παιδα, την ψυχην εξελκυσειεν, και οιον αγων, οτ' αυτης πορρω του σωματος, ακινητον ενεδειξε το σωμα, και αβλαβη σωζομενον.—Αυτης αγομενην παλιν της ραβδου μετα την εσοδον απαγγελειν εκαστα· τοιγαρ ουν, εκ τουτου πιστευσαι τους τε αλλους της τοιαυτης ἱστοριας θεατας, και τον Αριστοτελη χωριστην ειναι του σωματος την ψυχην.

† There is an unfortunate chasm here in the manuscript, of two or three lines.

8. By these, dæmons of a punishing characteristic are signified.

9. By the eight whirls, we must understand the eight starry spheres, *viz.*, the sphere of the fixed stars, and the spheres of the seven planets.

10. In order to understand what is here delivered by Plato respecting the Fates, it is necessary to observe that there is an order of Gods immediately above those of a mundane characteristic, which was denominated by ancient theologists liberated, and supercelestial. The peculiarity of this order is represented to us by Plato, in what he now says concerning the Fates.

"In this place, therefore," says Proclus, "Plato instructing us in the order of the universe, which supernally pervades through the whole of mundane natures, from the inerratic sphere, and in that order which governs human life, at different times proposing elections of different lives, and varying the measure of justice adapted to them, he refers the primary cause of this order to a monad and triad exempt from mundane wholes. And to the monad he ascribes an inspective government, extending its dominion at the same time to all heaven, and represents it as being impartibly present with all things, as governing all things indivisibly, and according to one energy, and as moving wholes with its most subordinate powers. But to the triad he assigns a progression from the monad, an energy proceeding into the universe, and a divisible fabrication. For that which is simple and united in the exempt providence of the monad is produced into multitude, through the secondary inspection of the triad.

"The one cause, therefore, (*i.e.* the monad) possesses more authority than the triadic multitude. For all the variety of powers in the world, the infinity of motions, and the multiform difference of reasons, is convolved by the triad of the Fates; and this triad is again extended to one monad prior to the three, which Socrates calls necessity, not as governing wholes by violence, nor as obliterating the self-motive nature of our life, nor as deprived of intellect and the most excellent knowledge, but as comprehending all things intellectually, and introducing bound to things indefinite, and order to things disordered. It is likewise so called by Socrates, as causing all things to be obedient to its government, and extending them to the good, as subjecting them to demiurgic laws, and guarding all things within the world, and as circularly comprehending every thing in the universe, and leaving nothing void of the justice which pertains to it, nor suffering it to escape the divine law.

"With respect to the order in which the Fates are arranged, it appears from Plato in the Laws, that the first is Lachesis, the second Clotho, and the third Atropos. And here it must be diligently observed, that Socrates uses the parts of time as symbols of comprehension according to cause. For that which *was,* was once future and the present, and that which now *is,* was once future; but the future is not yet the past, but has the whole of its essence in becoming the future. These three causes, therefore, or the three Fates, are analogous to these three portions of time: and of these, the most perfect, and which comprehends the others, is that which sings the past; for the past, having once been both the present and the future, may be considered as comprehending these. The next to this in perfection is the *present*, which partly comprehends, and is partly comprehended; for it comprehends the future, and is comprehended in the past. But the third is the future, which is comprehended both in the past and the present; the latter unfolding, and the former bounding, its progression. Hence Lachesis is the primary cause, comprehending in herself the others; and Clotho is allotted a superior, but Atropos an inferior order. And on this account Lachesis moves with both her hands, as in a greater and more total degree, giving completion to the more partial energies of the other two. But Clotho turns the spindle with her right hand, and Atropos with her left, so far as the former precede with respect to energy, but the latter follows, and, in conjunction with the former, governs all things. For in mortal animals the right hand is the principle of motion; and in the wholes of the universe the motion to the right hand comprehends that to the left.

"Observe too, that as it was before said that the whole spindle is turned on the knees of Necessity, so the fable suspends the providence about partial souls from the knees of Lachesis, who, with her hands, as with her more elevated powers, perpetually moves the universe, but possesses with subjection in her knees the causes of the periods of souls.

"In the next place, let us consider the symbols with which the fable celebrates their dominion. Their walking then in the celestial circles signifies their exempt and separate government. But their being seated on thrones, and not in the circles themselves, like the Sirens, indicates that the receptacles which are first illuminated by them are established above the celestial orbs. For a throne is the vehicle and receptacle of those that are seated on it: and this perspicuously signifies that these divinities are proximately placed above the mundane Gods. Their being seated at equal distances manifests their orderly separation, their subjection proceeding according to analogy, and their distribution supernally derived from their mother: for that which is orderly in progression, and according to dignity in energies, is thence imparted to the Fates. The crowns on their heads indicate the purity* of their intellectual summits. Their white garments signify that the essences which participate of these divinities are intellectual, luciform, and full of divine splendour. And as it is said that one of these sings the past, the second the present, and the third the future, this indicates that all their externally proceeding energies are elegant, intellectual, and full of harmony.

"Lastly, the Sirens signify the divine souls of the celestial spheres, who incline all things through harmonic motion to their ruling Gods. The song of these, and the well-measured motion of the heavens, are perfected by the Fates, who call forth the fabricative energy of Necessity into the universe through intellectual hymns, and convert all things to themselves through the harmonious and elegant motion of wholes."

* For crowns are of gold; and gold, from its incorruptibility, and never admitting rust, is an image of intellectual and divine purity.

11. The soul of a man never becomes the soul of a brute, though it may be bound to it, and as it were carried in it by way of punishment. Hence Plato says, that the soul of Thersites *assumed* the ape; signifying that it entered into the body of an ape when it was animated, and not before.

12. See the note concerning dæmons at the beginning of the First Alcibiades.

13. By *Lethe* we must understand the whole of a visible nature, or, in other words, the realms of generation, which contain, according to Empedocles, oblivion and the meadow of Ate; and, according to the Chaldæan Oracles, the light-hating world, and the winding streams, under which many are drawn. By *the dreadful heat and scorching*, Plato appears to signify the sphere of fire, through which descending souls pass. And as, through an anxious attention to mortal concerns, things eternal are neglected, hence he says that souls descending into the plain of Lethe encamp beside the river Amelete, *i.e.* through a connection with body they pass into extreme negligence; and there fall asleep; signifying by this their being merged in a corporeal nature, no longer possessing vigilant energies, and being alone conversant with things analogous to the delusions of dreams. But when he says that no vessel contains the water of Amelete, this signifies that nothing can restrain the ever-flowing nature of body. This, however, it must be observed, is the condition of the soul while connected with a gross aërial body, and before its perfect descent to the earth: for the descent from celestial bodies to such as are terrene is effected

through an aërial body. Souls therefore being laid asleep in this body, at midnight fall to the earth; *i.e.* when they enter into a terrene body they become involved in profound night.

Additional Notes to The Republic

1. See the Timæus and Atlanticus.

2. A man *unknown,* Author of a work called The Pursuits of Literature.

3. For an account of the virtues superior to the political, see the Phædo, Theætetus, and Phædrus.

4. The harmony diapason includes all tones, and is the some as what is called in modern music an octave or eighth. It is also a duple proportion, or that of 4 to 2.

5. This is an interval which is called in modern music a perfect fourth, and is a sesquitertian proportion, or that of 4 to 3.

6. This is the second of the concord, and is now called a perfect fifth. It is also a sesquialter proportion, or that of 3 to 2.

7. *viz.* Anger and desire, as being irrational parts, are both of them, according to Plato in the Timæus, the offspring of the junior Gods, but the rational part is alone the offspring of the one demiurgus of all things.

8. An oak may be said to be an image of the lowest nature, or natural life, from the great imbecility of this life, which is evident in the flow growth of the oak.

9. If Priestley, Hartley, and other modern metaphysical writers, had but known that the undisciplined are governed by the corporeal temperament, and that men of true science govern those temperaments, they certainly would not have poisoned the minds of the unscientific with such pernicious and puerile conceptions about necessity.

10. Proclus here means the dianoëtic power of the soul, of which intellect is the summit.

11. This is shown in the Timæus, where it is proved that the three elements, fire, air, and water, are the connecting media of the two contrary extremes, heaven and earth.

12. It is placed under reason, to which it is subservient in exciting its energies; and it is also placed under anger and desire, to the motions of which it is subservient, so far as these motions subsist in conjunction with sense.

13. See the Timæus.

14. That part of the soul which energizes dianoëtically and scientifically is called by Plato, in the Timæus, *the circle of sameness;* and that which energizes according to opinion, *the circle of difference.*

Made in the USA
Coppell, TX
25 August 2023

20780112R00243